Written Work

THE MIDDLE AGES SERIES

Ruth Mazo Karras, General Editor
Edward Peters, Founding Editor

A complete list of books in the series
is available from the publisher.

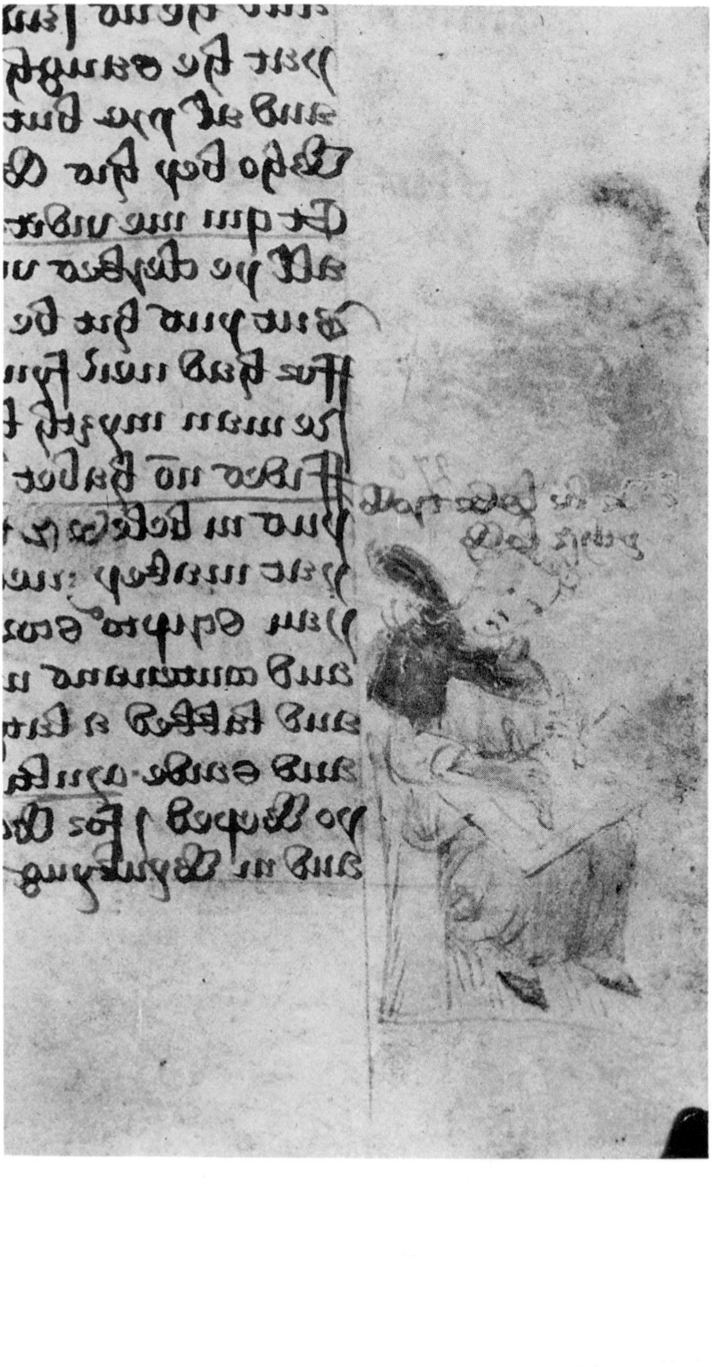

Written Work

Langland, Labor, and Authorship

Steven Justice and
Kathryn Kerby-Fulton

University of Pennsylvania Press

Philadelphia

10 9 8 7 6 5 4 3 2 1

Published by
University of Pennsylvania Press
Philadelphia, Pennsylvania 19104-4090

Library of Congress Cataloging-in-Publication Data
Written work : Langland, labor, and authorship / edited by Steven
Justice and Kathryn Kerby-Fulton.
    p.   cm. — (The Middle Ages series)
Includes bibliographical references and index.
ISBN 0-8122-3396-4 (alk. paper)
    1. Langland, William, 1330?–1400?   Piers the Plowman.
2. Christian poetry, English (Middle) — History and criticism.
3. Langland, William, 1330?–1400? — Authorship.   4. Civilization,
Medieval — 14th century.   5. London (England) — In literature.
6. Mendicant orders — England.   7. Persona (Literature)   8. Self in
literature.   9. Autobiography.   I. Justice, Steven, 1957–
II. Kerby-Fulton, Kathryn.   III. Series.
PR2015.W75   1997
821'.1—dc21
                                                                      97-2224
                                                                      CIP

Frontispiece: Will writing, MS. Douce 104, fol. 52v, the Bodleian Library, Oxford.

Contents

We have dedicated the book to our fathers.
They died in the same year; neither lived to see
his first child's first book.

Acknowledgments

Among those to whom the editors owe a debt of gratitude, the authors hold pride of place, especially for their patience during the several years that this volume was in preparation and for their timely cooperation during its last stages. Penn Szittya, one of the readers for the Press, gave meticulous readings of the individual essays and of the book as a whole; his suggestions were crucial in shaping the final form of the book, and his enthusiasm in sustaining our sense of its importance. Special gratitude is due to Jerry Singerman and the University of Pennsylvania Press, who have given good counsel and trenchant exhortation; this editor, and this press, have remained committed to the publication of scholarship in a decade that has seen the difficulties of academic publishing drive one university press after another from the presentation of scholarship.

We would also like to acknowledge the devoted and painstaking help of two graduate research assistants, Linda Olson, who did the initial copyediting for us, and Deborah Moore, who did the indexing (both underpaid, both overworked and both endlessly cheerful). At the Press we'd especially like to mention Carol Gaines, Ellen Fiskett, Alison Anderson, and, again, Jerry Singerman, all of whom bore with the special difficulties our volume presented with patience and professionalism.

We would like to thank the Vicar, Ruth Wigram, and the Church Wardens of St. Agatha's, Easby, in Yorkshire, for their courteous permission to reproduce the wall-painting that appears on the cover. We are also grateful to the Bodleian Library, Oxford, for permission to reproduce the image from MS Douce 104, and to the Keeper of Western Manuscripts for kindly reducing the fee for doing so.

Our spouses—Gordon Fulton and Jill N. Levin—have not stinted, in the midst of their own academic careers, to give aid and comfort in ours. Thanks are due, most especially, to Gordon Fulton for his generosity and wisdom during the two most difficult periods in this volume's history.

Introduction: Authorial Work and Literary Ideology

Steven Justice

"Everything that Skeat says about *Piers Plowman* is worth attending to," begins Derek Pearsall's essay in this volume, and our motive curiosity is one to which Skeat gave voice. *Piers Plowman* "is a true autobiography in the highest sense of the word," he said in his A-text edition.[1] All the essays here presented take as a point of departure or of conclusion the single C version passage in which Langland seems explicitly to offer autobiographical detail. (Derek Pearsall's revised edition of these lines, with facing modern rendering, appears immediately after this introduction.) None of the contributors, I think, would subscribe to Skeat's assertion—his language of description is not easily available to any living generation of critics—but each of them finds in this moment of apparent self-portraiture an opening, intended or otherwise, into the character of vernacular authorship in Ricardian England.

And the paths taken through this opening to one or another version of "William Langland" do something to explain the peculiar status of Langland's life-work even among literary historians, its status as one of those works (*Clarissa* also comes to mind) that everyone knows of and few know—works whose historical importance can neither be denied nor be very convincingly articulated by inherited protocols of literary interpretation. Here too Skeat is crucial, in identifying as a textual problem what would became (a little prematurely, I'll suggest) a conceptual one; for what he most famously said about *Piers Plowman* is that Langland wrote it three times. Langland seems to have refused to create a poem separable from his continuing labor of authorship. This refusal perhaps explains something of the poem's power: Anne Middleton suggests, in the essay concluding this

volume, that Langland imagined and presented his writing as *work* analogous to agricultural labor, a notion that would seem to imply that the text
not merely is the result of, but is in some sense constituted by, the history
of the poet's activity. But if Langland's refusal to separate himself from
his poem is one source of its riddling attraction, it may also be a source
of the ambivalence that has marked the writing about and teaching of the
poem in medieval literary history. At least it is hard otherwise to explain
how, in the first decade of the century, John M. Manly's "lost leaf" argument—that "Langland" wrote only the A version, which some alien hand
bungled into B—could have hijacked its study, not only for the forty years
or so that the authorship controversy it initiated was current, but nearly to
the present day. The attraction of Manly's proposal was so far in excess of
its slender evidential basis that it must be explicable otherwise, must have
been mortgaged to the ideology that underwrote the development of literary study as an academic discipline distinct from the philological labors
of Victorian and Edwardian predecessors.[2]

I do not think that it's tendentious to say that Manly wanted to rescue the poem from the poet, to banish Langland's meddling insistence that
his "work" is not a completed *opus* but self-perpetuating *labor*. The essay
in which Manly announced his "discovery" of the "lost leaf" begins with a
weird little memoir recounting how ("Summer before last") he had reread
Piers "in the enforced leisure of a long convalescence"—read it in effect "for
the first time," read each of the versions entire ("fortunately," he did not
have Skeat's parallel-text edition). "Before the reading was completed, I
found myself obliged to question very seriously the current view in regard
to the relations of the three versions."[3] The fresh and generous clarity of
convalescence—allowing him for once to read the book *through* (as Johnson would have said) and thereby (as Johnson's crack implied) to read as a
kind of honorary amateur—has moved out the clutter of scholarship and
let him finally experience what was really there, free of the prejudices of
scholarship; and what was there was *a* poem, not three poems, not Langland's continued process of revision.

The vision achieved in Manly's story represents, in a comparatively
unarticulated form, the impulses that shaped modernist literary criticism,
impulses seen in I. A. Richards's vision of poetry as psychological and
ethical refinement, in Eliot's understanding of "individual talent" as ca-
talysis reformulating tradition, in Cleanth Brooks's construction of irony
as a species of moral ecstasy. The Leavises are too obvious to mention;

Frye's criticism, in which literature embodies humankind's continuously self-elaborated *Bildung*, might be called the late systematic theology of this literary modernist vision. In fact, the conclusion to Frye's classic essay on the *Faerie Queene* mirrors and explains the oddly aggressive and disenfranchising attitude toward the author that drove Manly's argument half a century earlier: "At the end of the sixth book the magician in Spenser had completed half of his gigantic design, and was ready to start on the other half. But the poet in Spenser was satisfied: he had done his work, and his vision was complete."[4] Spenser "the poet" is different from Spenser "the magician" (the latter itself an odd locution: how is Spenser the magician related to the Spenser who left for Ireland?)—an ideal and ideally literary Spenser who refuses to intrude on and to compromise, as the other Spenser offered to do, the unity and fullness of the *Faerie Queene*, a unity that Frye's argument evidently requires. To put it another way, the supposition that there is in Spenser "a poet" who operates in independence from the historical Spenser's conscious or unconscious intentions banishes contingency from the poem, abolishes the possibility that the student of the *Faerie Queene* might be left with something *inparfit* or imperfect.

Of course Frye ("the critic in" Frye) would have to object: he was making a point about the autonomous logic of literary form; he was not urging acceptance of a biographical fact. But that is the point. The power of modernist formalism as a conceptual tool derived from the audacity with which it pulled writing free from contingency, and when it seemed to speak biographically it often made biography the metaphorical expression of literary form. The curious upshot was its inability to speak of authorial agency in a manner that could be assimilated to any ordinary understanding of agency. Manly and those who immediately followed him did not have this conceptual tool, and so tried to express in plain biographical terms some such desire for the work's autonomy from its maker. The translation of these factual concerns into the aesthetic language of academic criticism was one of the accomplishments of E. Talbot Donaldson's great 1949 book on Langland's C version. Though he framed his contribution as a kind of contribution to the authorship question, his real battle concerned not authorship but aesthetic quality; as he observed, the controversy had dwindled (or escalated) into an axiological contest between the versions.[5] The authorial version of the poem was the best version: why would Langland spoil his work? But the logic of this argument made it detachable from that originating controversy: why couldn't Langland spoil his work (the 1850 *Prelude* was mentioned in this connection)? Aesthetic criteria could not solve the authorship question, but it could do something just as good: locate the real *Piers*, meaning (this time) not the one *Piers* Langland had truly made, but the one *Piers* he had made best.

Donaldson's approach to *Piers* participated, brilliantly, in the best literary thought of its time, and institutionalized itself by sheer force of intelligence. But the general terms of his understanding were more than institutionalized—were nearly legislated—in the Athlone edition that we, like all Langland scholars, cite in this volume, and especially the edition of B. In the editors' refusal to privilege any text, even, provisionally, a copy-text, as a "better" or "closer" manuscript in the shape and direction of their emendation, and in their determination that metrical imperfection must signal scribal imperfection, this edition orients its choice of lections toward an author who exists only as the guarantor of moment-by-moment, word-by-word aesthetic perfection. The editors describe their edition as "a theoretical structure, a complex hypothesis designed to account for a body of phenomena in the light of knowledge about the circumstances which generated them," and they go on to explain that an edition working with such "knowledge" is "governed by a presumption of the quality of Langland's art and by established information about the effects of manuscript copying on the language, form, and meaning of texts."[6] "Quality" here is an important equivocation, at once descriptive (what Langland's art is like) and evaluative (how good it is). For a little later, they defend against the possible criticism that they have "improved" Langland's text by appealing to "the fact that the excellence of Langland's poem, having survived the axiomatic deterioration of scribal transmission, must once have been even greater than the received copies now present it to be."[7] In critics so severely logical as these, the logical difficulties in these lines (which could as easily justify, for example, the poetic improvements worked by the redactor of the Hofni and Phineas lines in the Ilchester MS prologue)[8] might indicate some important blindness. In fact, Kane and Donaldson's procedure renders Langland's text according to the intellectual and pedagogical habits of Anglo-American formalism. Their logic is summed up in that most celebrated of new critical pronouncements, one I've had occasion to discuss recently in another context, that of Wimsatt and Beardsley answering "the intentional fallacy": "How is [the critic] to find out what the poet tried to do? If the poet succeeded in doing it, the poem itself shows what he was trying to do."[9] As anyone trained under this new critical regime of interpretation can say, you can *always* show that the poet "succeeded in doing it"; even the most apparently ill-fitting or ill-judged element in a work can be shown to enjoy a plenary and (yes) "organic" unity with all the other elements. Kane and Donaldson acknowledge that their procedure is circular; what is interesting is how exactly the logic of the circularity they describe measures against that of Wimsatt and Beardsley, who, without quite saying so, are discriminating between poems that would need some sort of external datum to guide their interpretations (ones that, as poems, do not "succeed" in communicating the author's purpose—and that hardly therefore merit study as poems) and those successful poems that, by their success, render themselves independent of the contingencies of their authors' lives. Kane and Donaldson simply invert this logic of reading: they *presume* Langland's aesthetic "success," presume either that Langland cared for no other concern or that no other care mattered for the poem. This presumption occasionally leads them to reject the plain sense of textual evidence in order to preserve the poem's integrity against the accidents of its author's life, so that of "William Langland" little remains but a warrant of stylistic perfection and classical regularity.[10]

Take B 15.504–69, where the text has been, according to the Athlone editors, disarranged.[11] Anima (the last of Will's interlocutors before his renewed vision of Piers Plowman and the vision of the Passion that follows) surveys the state of the church, especially of those charged with extending its salvation by preaching and example, and lays the blame for unbelief at the feet of those prelates and preachers who have lived in ease and wealth in despite of their vocations. Scattered among Kane and Donaldson's app. crit. for these pages are the following:

504–10, 529–32 *copied after lines* 533–69 (*which* RF *omit*)WHmCrGYOC2C BLM: *see above,* pp. 176–9.

511–28 RF; *lines om* WHmCrGYOC2CbLM; *here in the spelling of* W.

533–69 *lines om* RF; *copied after line* 503 *and followed by lines* 504–10, 529–32 WHmCrGYOC2CBLM.

As the first of these entries notes, there is a discussion of this section in the editors' introduction, where it is explained that the common ancestor of both manuscript families disarranged the text, swapping the positions of 529–32 and 533–69. Then, independently and through scribal error, lines 511–28 were ommitted from the W tradition and lines 533–69 from the RF tradition. What they do not note there is the perfect fit between the two MS traditions. The two traditions give precisely different passages: between what Kane and Donaldson number as lines 503 and 570, the two manuscript traditions render the text as follows:

RF	W
not in RF	533–69
504–10	504–10
511–28	*not in W*
529–32	529–32
570–	570–

Of course what this shows is that there are two distinct versions of the passage between these MSS. The sheer exactness of the fit *could* be accounted for by their narrative of contingent mistakes by the different scribes, but it is not clear on what basis we are asked to believe that it *is* thus accounted for. The W tradition in particular has something to be said for it. What the Athlone edition (following the RF tradition) presents as its lines 526–30—which contrast today's shirking bishops with Thomas, the apostle and martyr—is a syntactical mess:

Holy chirche is honored heiȝliche þoruȝ his deying;
He is a forbisene to alle bisshopes and a briȝt myrour,
And souereynliche to swiche þat of surrye bereþ þe name,
[And nauȝt to] huppe aboute in Engelond to halwe mennes Auteres
And crepe [in] amonges curatours, confessen ageyn þe lawe.

Now there would seem to be no question but that Langland wrote these lines as Kane and Donaldson print them. The question is whether he wrote them only in that way. For the awkward "And nauȝt to"—which lacks a first term for the implied grammatical parallelism—occurs just at the splice where RF includes lines that are not present in W. Reconstructing W from the *app. crit.*, one gets the following for lines 506–9 and their jointure with 529:

Thus in a feiþ leue þat folk, and in a fals mene,
And þat is rouþ for riȝtful men þat in þe Reawme wonyen,
And a peril to þe pope and prelates þat he makeþ
That bere bisshopes names of Bethleem and Babiloigne
That huppe aboute in Engelond to halwe mennes Auteres
And crepe [in] amonges curatours, confessen ageyn þe lawe.

Since the whole passage has concerned the "bisshopes . . . of Bethleem and Babiloigne" who "huppe aboute in Engelond" rather than occupying their sees, the connection in this attested version of the lines supplements a grammatical parallelism with continuity of sense.

My solution to the bad jointure in RF is of course speculative and circumstantial, like the solution in the Athlone edition, and it does no more than show the likelihood that this passage came from Langland's pen with line 510 (in the Kane–Donaldson numbering) joined to line 529. But the tabulation I have offered above suggests further problems. The RF tradition shows what appears to be a continuous passage, following the line numbering that Kane and Donaldson offer, lacking only lines 533–69 where W has them and including lines 511–28 where W does not. Since I have proposed a reading of the manuscript evidence tending to suggest that one tradition preserves a clearly authorial connection where another has at best a patchwork integrity, a conclusion might be that the fault lies with the RF tradition. But this will not do either: that the lines unique to RF are authorial has never been doubted. The real puzzle about this passage, in other words, is why Langland seems to have written it twice, culminating both times in line 529.

The question implies one possible answer. Langland wrote separate and alternative passages, one perhaps meant to supplant the other, either permanently or in some circumstances. If the evidence I have cited so far hardly proves this, it at least permits it; and another aspect of the passage renders it likely. For if we look not at the form but at the matter of the text exclusive to each of the manuscript traditions, the two forms bespeak different rhetorical positions. Lines 533–69, exclusive to W, would have some claim on our attention even without the textual difficulties of Passus 15, because they are the most imposing advocacy of disendowment offered in any version of *Piers*. Indeed the passage is unique among Langland's considerations of clerical wealth and its possible reform, because it is not a prophecy of disendowment but an exhortation to it:

Takeþ hire landes, ye lordes, and leteþ hem lyue by dymes.
If possession be poison and inparfite hem make
[Charite] were to deschargen hem for holy chirches sake,
And purgen hem of poison er moore peril falle. (15.564–67)

Here alone in *Piers Plowman* Langland uses the imperative rather than the future indicative to imagine the prelacy reduced forcibly to poverty; ordinarily his characters speak of disendowment evasively, returning back to its roots in prophecy so as, perhaps, to avoid being heard to advocate it as policy. Here alone he allows one of his mouthpieces—Anima, in fact, whom few annotators have been able to mistrust—to occupy that more dangerous ground.

And here we have what looks mightily like two different, two *authorial* textual traditions.[12] If we allow for argument this possibility, we still are not asserting any particular story about the relations of the two. Langland, one might say, wrote the assertive disendowment passage and then—learning of Wyclif's proposals, maybe, or just thinking better of his own—revised his opinions or at least their expression.[13] Or maybe he thought those things too dangerous to say to the whole world. Or maybe he wrote the more diffident version first and then attached himself to more radical possibilities. Or maybe he wrote the more radical version first and then recoiled from his own radicalism. Or maybe he wrote the different versions for circulation among different audiences, a more audacious one for patrons or intimates, a bowdlerized one for public release.

Kane and Donaldson cannot admit any of these possibilities, because the alternate passages are sorted between the two manuscript families of the B version: so if the readings there are allowed as alternate authorial versions, then the logic that the editors have applied to the discrimination of readings differing between those two traditions would have to be in every case reconsidered, for the B version would then have to be acknowledged to comprise two subordinate versions; the possibility would then have to be entertained that readings rejected as scribal on the strength of readings from the other manuscript families would have to be reargued. So the Athlone editors could not allow any connection between the odd state of these lines from B 15 on the one hand and the explosive character of the matter in the W version on the other; certainly they cannot allow the latter to be urged as an explanation of the former. And yet no ordinary understanding of action and motive would account this portrait of an author's concerns either improbable or disreputable. The Athlone editors must of course suppose an author for the poem edited; but they must rescue the poem from the possibility of his authorship being anything more than (so to speak) an agent pronoun. And the particular oddity of the situation in the passage here discussed is that to do so they must simply ignore what the author cares to be saying.

As I said, even if one allows the existence of these two versions of B 15 as probable, one does not thereby decide the sequence or context of this "internal" revision, nor does one thereby establish the status of the RF and W traditions as separate internal versions of the B-text; one has in fact raised, not answered, those questions. But one has done more than that: one has also specified a notion of what would count in the provision of an answer, and therefore, and further, a notion of how authorship happens in the world—a notion, for that matter, *that* authorship happens in the world.

A further question issues from these considerations, and I might use the same lines to pose it. The C version of the passage I have been discussing includes all the lines. That is (to use Kane and Donaldson's explanation), Langland has retained the lines as originally disordered, or (to use mine) he has conflated into a single passage the separate versions represented in the W and RF traditions. How do we assess this? The attitude I've adopted in this introduction is one in which one derives information from the fractured evidence of textual difference; this would seem to imply that the portrait of Langland available to this sort of inference is a portrait he never thought of drawing; if he wrote two versions of the passage for (say) two different audiences, then (it would seem to follow) he at no point anticipated a reader who would be able to discover that fact. But in her essay below, Kathryn Kerby-Fulton suggests that the problem of "the C-reviser's B," as Kane and Donaldson put it—the problem that, in revising the text for the last time, Langland used a B version with the archetypal errors preserved in all extant B-manuscripts—might be explained, not as an accident that befell the poet (loss of his foul or fair papers, for example, or poverty), but as the deliberate choice of a poet writing for an audience that already knew his work, and choosing therefore to correct it from the faulty one generally in distribution.[14] The suggestion has profound implications, for it suggests that Langland might consciously have shaped the textual tradition of the poem in response to its public acceptance, and that (therefore) such a "portrait" as I have been speaking of might be self-drawn, and therefore manipulated.

In the essays that follow, "Langland" is sometimes a presumptive biographical self inferred from his poetry and its circumstances, sometimes the constructed persona. This is at it should be: the biographical person constructed the persona, the construction of a persona itself feeds inference about the man who constructed it. If the Langland who emerges from these pages seems shadowy, at least a shadow reassures us that we have to do with a body solid enough to block light. And the shadow falls sometimes across real people (like Kerby-Fulton's scribes) and on solid walls (like those of Pearsall's London). Hanna's essay, "Will's Work," is an appropriate beginning for the volume, since he enacts in it the ragged logic of discursive inquiry. Though he insists at the beginning that his discussion of eremiticism is about the discourse rather than any demographically renderable instance of the practice, and though the eremiticism practiced by Will—that "covert learned man in drag"—turns out to be an appropriation of several eremitic *topoi* patched together in the maintenance of a masculine and speculative learnedness, the riddle posed by the eccentric character of its delineation presses toward an answer that is not a concept but simply the situation of the author: patronage—the poet's need for it and his need to maintain his independence of it.

In fact, the essays in this volume have the cumulative effect of showing how promising and urgent some questions about Langland are, and patronage is perhaps the most important of them. If it has seemed difficult to imagine Langland having a patron, Kathryn Kerby-Fulton says in "Langland and the Bibliographic Ego," a little information makes it "harder to imagine him *not* having a patron," and her virtuoso survey of the traditions of authorial self-assertion and self-identification—which tracks clues all over Europe, from the twelfth through the fifteenth century—*and* of the particular conditions of publication and circulation in late medieval London point to a place no one has put Langland: around the Privy-Seal office, around Chancery Lane, around Hoccleve and Usk, around the Ellesmere Scribe B—precisely, it turns out, where Anne Middleton's essay later in this volume would have to expect him to be. The strange and difficult facts that have seemed to emerge from the surviving evidence find, in this nearest context to Langland's making, possibilities for new and more interesting answers; we have all accepted since Kane and Donaldson that the C-reviser worked from a faulty B-manuscript, for example, and Kerby-Fulton suggests that this may have been the choice of a man whose purpose in the revision had less to do with restoring the integrity of his text than with asserting control over the (faulty) version that was already in circulation, first (presumably) among members of a coterie, and then to a larger, unknown public. Even the apparently narrowest of Langland's ecclesiastical concerns seem to place him near centers of power where these concerns are the issues of the moment.

Lawrence M. Clopper's essay, "Langland's Persona: An Anatomy of the Mendicant Orders," addresses one of those issues: the friars' "rule and life" (as Francis had put it) and the various pressures for their reform. Clopper makes again and from a new angle the important point that he has been arguing for some years now: that "antifraternalism," especially the sort that Langland employs, is an overwhelmingly fraternal production—reformist polemic from within the orders rather than attacks from without. That John XXII's bloody silencing of Franciscan opinions on Christ's poverty had not resolved the issue even at the highest reaches of the order in England was shown in 1373, by the ease and confidence with which the very Provincial Minister of the Franciscans could use arguments associated with the condemned positions in a debate before the king's council.[15] These were live issues, understood and debated in detail and with precision, and Clopper's Langland is engaged directly and polemically in them.

Derek Pearsall's essay suggests how a deliberate and conscious return to procedures deemed old-fashioned (a judgment that, as Adorno said, signals chiefly bad conscience about possibilities abandoned before their fruition) can produce something original and timely. For this appreciation of "Langland's London" structures itself after, and evokes place with the force of, nineteenth-century antiquarianism. But this virtuoso evocation of the city and its poet produces something other and more interesting than a mythically seamless fit between subject and landscape that the more nostalgic versions of antiquarianism tend to offer. It produces, in fact, precisely the opposite: the degree to which London remained (in Pearsall's words) "the problem Langland never solved," a place whose economic organization Langland needs as the illness that his prescription will solve and avoids as the demonstration of his prescription's irrelevance. This essay contributes something to the understanding of economic phenomenology in the fourteenth century; while in recent years it has been fashionable and hardly incorrect to say that the countryside was the place of fullest capitalist enterprise, Pearsall shows that, for Langland at least, the countryside could still be absorbed back into nostalgias of political and social organization in ways that the city simply could not.

With Anne Middleton's "Acts of Vagrancy," the volume returns to the topic of labor—Will's and others'—with which it began, and in fact to nearly all the problems of authorial identity and literary publication that the other essays have raised. Middleton argues not merely that the interrogation of Will by Reason in C 5 is modeled after prosecution under the Statute of Laborers—a point that has been made before—but that it is modeled specifically after the particular version of that Statute promulgated during the Cambridge Parliament of 1388. No merely regulatory fantasy, as the earlier statute had been, this impossibly ambitious act was an instance of what Middleton calls "visionary legislation" and an index of ideologies in meltdown. The essay makes a series of empirical claims about the statute and about the chronology of Langland's writings as well as using these claims to investigate the poem's relation to history: its own and its author's as well as its society's.

Notes

1. Walter W. Skeat, *Langland's Vision of Piers Plowman: The Vernon Text; or Text A*, EETS o.s. 28 (London, 1867), xxxviii.

2. This history has often been written about in recent years; Lee Patterson, *Negotiating the Past: The Historical Understanding of Medieval Literature* (Madison: University of Wisconsin Press, 1987) specifically concerns the discipline of medieval studies, and is far the best in any case.

3. John M. Manly, "The Lost Leaf of 'Piers the Plowman'," *Modern Philology* 3 (1906): 359–66.

4. Northrop Frye, "The Structure of Imagery in *The Faerie Queene*," in *Fables of Identity: Studies in Poetic Mythology* (New York: Harcourt Brace Jovanovich, 1963), 69–87.

5. As Donaldson notes in his witty survey of the authorship controversy; E. Talbot Donaldson, *Piers Plowman: The C-Text and Its Poet* (New Haven, Conn.: Yale University Press, 1949), 9–14.

6. George Kane and E. T. Donaldson, eds., *Piers Plowman: The B Version* (London: Athlone Press, 1975), 212.

7. Ibid., 213.

8. See Derek Pearsall, "The 'Ilchester' Manuscript of *Piers Plowman*," *Neuphilologische Mitteilungen* 82 (1981): 181–92.

9. W. K. Wimsatt and Monroe K. Beardsley, "The Intentional Fallacy," in *The Verbal Icon: Studies in the Meaning of Poetry* (Lexington: University Press of Kentucky, 1954), 4.

10. The fine description of Kane and Donaldson's "classical" aesthetic I take from Anne Middleton, "Life in the Margins, or, What's an Annotator to do?" *Library Chronicle of the University of Texas at Austin* 20 (1990): 180.

11. Kane and Donaldson, *Piers Plowman: The B Version*, 176–79.

12. Only as I write this do I discover that Ralph Hanna has just published a similar argument, on quite different grounds; Ralph Hanna III, "On the Versions of *Piers Plowman*," in *Pursuing History: Middle English Manuscripts and Their Texts* (Stanford, Calif.: Stanford University Press, 1996), 203–43.

13. This is not unlike a suggestion that I overconfidently asserted; Steven Justice, *Writing and Rebellion: England in 1381* (Berkeley and Los Angeles: University of California Press, 1994).

14. I have argued that Langland, writing C, was imagining an audience that knew B; ibid.

15. Jeremy I. Catto, "An Alleged Great Council of 1374," *English Historical Review* 82 (1967): 764–71.

Passus 5.1–104:
Will's "Apologia pro vita sua"

Edited and translated by Derek Pearsall

Text

Thus I awakede, woet God, whan I wonede in Cornehull,
Kytte and I in a cote, yclothed as a lollare,
And lytel ylet by, leveth me for sothe,
Amonges lollares of Londone and lewede ermytes,
For I made of tho men as resoun me tauhte.   5
    For as I cam by Consience with Resoun I mette
In an hot hervest whenne I hadde myn hele
And lymes to labory with and lovede wel fare
And no dede to do but to drynke and to slepe.

In hele and in inwitt oen me apposede;   10
Romynge in remembraunce, thus Resoun me aratede.
    "Can thow serven," he sayde, "or syngen in a churche,
Or koke for my cokeres or to the cart piche,
Mowen or mywen or make bond to sheves,

Repe or been a rype-reve and aryse erly,   15
Or have an horn and be hayward and lygge theroute nyhtes
And kepe my corn in my croft fro pykares and theves?
Or shap shon or cloth, or shep and kyne kepe,
Heggen or harwen, or swyn or gees dryve,
Or eny other kynes craft that to the comune nedeth,   20
That thou betere therby that byleve the fynden?"
    "Sertes," I sayde, "and so me god helpe,
I am to wayke to worche with sykel or with sythe
And to long, lef me, lowe to stoupe,
To wurche as a werkeman eny while to duyren."   25
    "Thenne hastow londes to lyve by," quod Resoun, "or lynage ryche
That fynde the thy fode? For an ydel man thow semest,
A spendour that spene mot or a spille-tyme,
Or beggest thy bylyve aboute at men hacches

Or faytest uppon Frydayes or feste-dayes in churches,   30
The whiche is lollarne lyf, that lytel is preysed
There ryhtfulnesse rewardeth ryht as men deserveth.
    Reddet unicuique iuxta opera sua.
Or thow art broke, so may be, in body or in membre
Or ymaymed thorw som myshap, whereby thow myhte be excused?"

Translation

So I awoke, God knows, when I lived in Cornhill,
Kitty and I in a little cottage, dressed like some idle layabout,
And not in high favor, believe me truly,
Among the drifters of London and lay "hermits" (so-called),
For I wrote about those people what reason taught me to say.   5
   For as I was passing by Conscience I met with Reason
One hot harvest-time when I was in good health
And had limbs to work with and enjoyed living well
And had nothing to do but drink and sleep.
In this state of health and sound possession of my faculties, someone
     questioned me;   10
As I wandered about lost in reminiscence, Reason berated me thus:
   "Can you serve at mass," he said, "or sing in church,
Or pile hay for my haycock-makers or pitch it into the cart,
Mow or stack the mown swathes or make the straw binding for the
     sheaves,
Reap or be a head-reaper and get up early,   15
Or have a horn and be the hedge-ward and lie out at night
And keep my corn in my field from pilferers and thieves?
Or make shoes or cloth, or keep sheep and cattle,
Make hedges or harrow the land, or drive pigs and geese,
Or do any other kind of job that is needful to the community,   20
Whereby you might improve the life of those who provide for you?"
   "Indeed," I said, "as God be my helper,
I am too weak to work with a sickle or a scythe
And too tall, believe me, to stoop down low
Or to survive for any length of time working as a labourer."   25
   "Then have you got income from land," said Reason, "or rich relations
That provide you with a living? For you seem to be an idle man,
A spendthrift that can't resist spending or a time-waster,
Or else maybe you are one of those that beg for food around at people's
     back-doors
Or operate as a beggar on Fridays or church fast-days,   30
Which is the kind of life that idlers lead, and that gains little credit
Where men are rightfully rewarded as they deserve.
   He will repay every man according to what he has done (Matt. 16.27).
Or perhaps you are crippled, maybe, in body or limb,
Or maimed through some accident, and that's your excuse?"

"When I yong was, many yer hennes,   35
My fader and my frendes foende me to scole,
Tyl I wyste witterly what holy writ menede
And what is beste for the body, as the boek telleth,
And sykerost for the soule, by so I wol contenue.
And foend I nere, in fayth, seth my frendes deyede,   40
Lyf that me lykede but in this longe clothes.
And yf I be labour sholde lyven and lyflode deserven,
That laboure that I lerned beste therwith lyven I sholde.
    In eadem vocacione in qua vocati estis.
And so I leve yn London and opelond bothe;
The lomes that I labore with and lyflode deserve   45
Is *pater-noster* and my prymer, *placebo* and *dirige*,
And my sauter som tyme and my sevene psalmes.
This I segge for here soules of suche as me helpeth,
And tho that fynden me my fode fouchen-saf, I trowe,

To be welcome when I come, other-while in a monthe,   50
Now with hym, now with here; on this wyse I begge
Withoute bagge or botel but my wombe one.
    And also moreover me thynketh, syre Resoun,
Me sholde constrayne no clerc to no knaves werkes,
For by the lawe of *Levyticy* that oure lord ordeynede,   55
Clerkes ycrouned, or kynde understondynge,
Sholde nother swynke ne swete ne swerien at enquestes
Ne fyhte in no faumewarde ne his foe greve.
    Non reddas malum pro malo.
For hit ben eyres of hevene, alle that ben ycrouned,

And in quoer and in kyrkes Cristes mynistres.   60
    Dominus pars hereditatis mee.
    Et alibi: Clemencia non constringit.
Hit bycometh for clerkes Crist for to serve
And knaves uncrounede to carte and to worche.
For sholde no clerke be crouned but yf he come were
Of frankeleynes and fre men and of folke ywedded.
Bondemen and bastardus and beggares children,   6
Thyse bylongeth to labory, and lordes kyn to serve
God and good men, as here degre asketh,

"When I was young, many years ago, 35
My father and my relatives provided for my schooling,
Until I knew truly what was the meaning of the scriptures
And what is best for the body, as the Bible tells,
And safest for the soul—provided I persevere in well-doing.
And I never found, indeed, since my relatives died, 40
Any life that suited me except in these long clerical robes.
And if I must live and earn my living by my labor,
Then I should do so by doing the job that I have learned best.
   In that state to which you are called (remain) (1 Cor. 7.20).
And so I live in London and also sometimes up-country;
The tools that I work with and earn my living by 45
Are the "our Father" and my prayer-book, with the familiar phrases "I
     shall be pleasing" and "Lead me," of the Office of the Dead,
And sometimes my psalter and my seven penitential psalms.
These I say for the souls of such as give me help,
And those that provide me with my food guarantee, I am sure,
That I am welcome when I turn up, from time to time in the month, 50
Now with him, now with her; in this way I beg
Without any bag or bottle to carry things away but just my stomach.
   "And also, moreover, it seems to me, Sir Reason,
That clerics should not be made to do the work of low-born men,
For by the law of Leviticus that our Lord ordained, 55
Tonsured clerics, as seems only reasonable,
Should not toil nor sweat nor have to give evidence on oath in courts
     of law
Nor fight in the vanguard of an army nor harm any enemy.
   Do not render evil for evil (1 Thess. 5.15).
For all that bear the tonsure are the inheritors of heaven,
And Christ's own ministers in choir and in church. 60
   The Lord is the portion of my inheritance (Ps. 15.5).
   And elsewhere: The quality of mercy is not strained.
It is appropriate for clerics to serve Christ
And for untonsured workmen to drive carts and to labor.
For no cleric should be tonsured unless he come
Of freehold landowners and freeman and of wedded folk.
Bondmen and bastards and beggars' children 65
It befits these to labor, and for the relatives of high-born men to serve
God and good men, as their rank requires,

Somme to synge masses or sitten and wryten,
Redon and resceyven that resoun ouhte to spene.
   Ac sythe bondemen barnes haen be mad bisshopes   7c
And barnes bastardus haen be erchedekenes
And soutares and here sones for sulver han be knyhtes
And lordes sones here laboreres and leyde here rentes to wedde,
For the ryhte of this reume ryden ayeyn oure enemyes

In confort of the comune and the kynges worschipe,   75
And monkes and moniales, that mendenantes sholde fynde,
Imade her kyn knyhtes and knyhtes-fees ypurchased,
Popes and patrones pore gentel blood refused
And taken Symondes sones seyntwarie to kepe,

Lyf-holynesse and love hath be longe hennes,   8c
And wol, til hit be wered out, or otherwyse ychaunged.
   Forthy rebuke me ryhte nauhte, Resoun, I yow praye,
For in my consience I knowe what Crist wolde I wrouhte.
Preyeres of a parfit man and penaunce discret

Is the levest labour that oure lord pleseth.   85
Non de solo," I sayde, "for sothe *vivit homo*,
Nec in pane et in pabulo, the pater-noster witnesseth;
Fiat voluntas dei—that fynt us alle thynges."
   Quod Consience, "By Crist, I can nat se this lyeth;
Ac it semeth no sad parfitnesse in citees to begge,   9c
But he be obediencer to prior or to mynstre."
   "That is soth," I saide, "and so I beknowe—
That I have ytynt tyme and tyme myspened;
Ac yut, I hope, as he that ofte hath ychaffared

And ay loste and loste, and at the laste hym happed   9.
A bouhte suche a bargayn he was the bet evere,
And sette al his los at a leef at the laste ende,
Suche a wynnyng hym warth thorw wordes of grace.
      Simile est regnum celorum thesauro abscondito in agro.
      Mulier que inuenit dragmam, etc.

Some to sing masses or to sit at a desk and write,
Advise and make accounting of what is reasonable should be spent.
But since bondmen's children have been made bishops   70
And bastard children have been made archdeacons
And shoemakers and their sons have bought themselves knighthoods
And lords' sons have been made their servants and had to mortgage their
          estates
In order to ride out in the realm's just wars against our enemies
For the good of the community and the honor of the king,   75
And monks and nuns, who should be providing for beggars,
Have got their relatives made knights and bought them the estates
          appropriate to their status,
(And) popes and patrons of livings have turned down applicants of gentle
          birth who are poor
And appointed the sons of Simony to the guardianship of the
          sanctuary—
Holiness of life and love have long been a remote idea,   80
And will remain so, until these customs die out, or are changed in
          other ways.
     "Therefore do not by any means rebuke me, Reason, I pray you,
For in my conscience I know what Christ would have me do.
The prayers of a perfect man and a properly discerning penance
Are the work that is dearest and most pleasing to our Lord.   85
"*Not alone,*" I said, "in truth *lives man
By bread and food,*" as the "Our Father" bears witness;
"*God's will be done*"—that provides us with all things."
     Conscience said, "By Christ, I cannot see that this is at all to the point;
And it seems no steadfast life of perfection to go about begging in cities   90
Unless one is licensed to beg by some priory or monastery."
     "That is true," I said, "and indeed I acknowledge
That I have wasted and frittered away time,
But yet I hope, like one who has often been engaged in making
          business deals
And always lost and lost again, and at the last it happened   95
That he made such a bargain he was the better off ever after,
And set all his losses at nothing in the end,
Such a profit came to him through the destined purposes of grace.
     The kingdom of heaven is like a treasure hidden in a field (Matt. 13.44).
     The woman that found a silver coin . . . (Luke 15.10).

So hope I to have of hym that is almyghty
A gobet of his grace, and bigynne a tyme
That alle tymes of my tyme to profit shal turne."
　　"I rede the," quod Resoun tho, "rape the to bigynne
The lyf that is louable and leele to thy soule"—
"Ye, and contynue," quod Consience; and to the kyrke I wente.

So I hope to have of the almighty
A portion of his grace, and begin a time 100
That will turn to profit all the moments of my life."
    "I advise you," said Reason then, "to set about quickly to begin
The life that is praiseworthy and truly in accord with the soul."
"Yes, and persevere in it!" said Conscience; and off I went to church.

I

Will's Work[1]

Ralph Hanna III

MOST RECENT DISCUSSIONS OF *Piers Plowman* have found the dreamer-poet and his status one of the most problematic features of the poem. What should one make of his whole enterprise, one which every character who addresses the issue tells him is in some measure misconceived?[2] And if this is the case, what is Will supposed to be doing anyhow? More bluntly, just what should constitute Will's work, his vocation?

The most explicit answers to these questions necessarily center around the C version and the dreamer's extended self-defense (or autobiography or *apologia*; 5.1–108).[3] And in such discussions, E. Talbot Donaldson's treatment still holds pride of place.[4] Donaldson, who interprets the passage as if fully autobiographical, follows Skeat's note to 5.2 and takes "Kytte" to be Will's wife and, thus, Will himself as some variety of failed priest. He then (206–8) analyzes the priestly dreamer's relation to *ordo*. In his lengthy discussion, for the most part based on William Lyndwood's *Provinciale*, he identifies Langland's dreamer as an acolyte. Upon his marriage, Donaldson says (206–7), Will would have entered a quite anomalous status. He could not have advanced beyond his current rank and would have been unable to serve at the altar, and thus incapable of fulfilling a truly clerical function and resembling a layperson (hence the embarrassment of Reason's opening question in 5.12). But so long as he retained his tonsure (which he apparently has done; see 5.56) and wore appropriate clerical clothing (see 5.41), he would have retained his *privilegium clericale*. And Donaldson (208–19) pursues his autobiographical argument by urging that Langland was "an itinerant handy man" who dealt in intercessory prayer of a particularly commonplace sort; this would have been one of the few jobs open to him as "a married clerk without benefice" (208).

I don't think that my argument will change many of the "facts" of Will's case. But I do think it possible to be considerably more precise about the dreamer's vocation (and thus, presumptively, his aspirations) than Donaldson. And I think these arguments demonstrate that the "autobiography" of C 5 is integrated with all the major revisions which transformed the second vision of B into the C version and that these revisions—three extensive added passages and the advancement of Deadly Sins materials from B passus 13—are designed to address "vocation" quite directly and doubly. Not only does Langland represent himself within his poem as a member of a specific vocational group, hermits,[5] but he chooses that social designation precisely to adumbrate a particular variety of poetic career.

In presenting this argument, I adopt a bifid strategem. I first present a series of institutional topics, issues concerning the life of hermits which were matters of some contention from the twelfth century until the sixteenth. These I align with relevant aspects of Will's self-description in C 5 (with glances at their reappearance and their antitypes in other parts of the poem). I then, in the second portion of the paper, pass on to consider these institutional topics in the light of revision to the C-text "Visio" generally, to demonstrate that the revisions, with increasing precision, describe—for the C-text at least—a particular variety of poet who conceives himself as responsible for a particular variety of poetry. I thus hope to pass beyond Donaldson's formulation of the problem, to see Will's work, not just as a reflection of some specifically biographical given, but as a discursive function which motivates large portions of the poem *Piers Plowman*.

A few introductory caveats about what I understand myself to be doing here. First, I should not be construed as making any particular claims about any specifiable history external to *Piers* itself: I have no idea whether there was, demographically, a large number of wandering hermits in late fourteenth-century England, nor whether they caused social problems,[6] nor whether Langland in fact was one such. I am dealing simply with a discursive formulation, quite attenuated in quantity and very little of it written by practitioners,[7] about a particular group of religious figures.

This raises a second issue. The placement of the discourses from which I draw my material needs to be acknowledged at the outset as fundamentally "prescriptive" and "disciplinary" in its nature. My sources are heavily skewed toward rules, orders, works of private instruction (often explicitly letters), and legal records.[8] These contexts, with their insistence on proprieties easily violated, do not predictably allow one to achieve anything like what some would consider a "rounded historical view" of the topics I will discuss.

Finally, although the evidence shows that Langland's thought about the vocation "hermit" has been deeply constituted by such materials and their regulative emphases, I implicitly argue, in the second half of this paper, Langland's relative discursive freedom. As poet, he does not merely ventriloquize a preexisting discursive totality but remains capable precisely of discursive intervention, of adopting those received forms which simultaneously shape him. This activity—indeed, it is the activity of the entire poetic effort, what makes *Piers Plowman* read, as Bloomfield says, like "a commentary on an unknown text"[9]—occurs, at the minimum, because of Langland's openness to a wide variety of disparate discourses and by the consequent possibility of motivated *bricolage*. The poem functions precisely because of the unpredictable confluence and dissonance of separate discursive realms, relationships of which Langland is cognizant and which he manipulates to idiosyncratic advantage.[10]

I. Some Institutional Considerations

When Reason addresses Will, he first asks him whether he can claim any clerical privilege: "Can thow seruen . . . or syngen in a churche?" (5.12). Were Will able to answer positively, he would apparently avoid the barrage of subsequent questions—all directed to his aptitude for agricultural labor (and assuming the requirements of English statute law). His silence, I take it, indicates that Will cannot perform any such function—not even, in spite of the grammar-school training of which he is later so proud, perform as a chorister.[11] He certainly, whatever his subsequent claims to offer prayers for others, cannot be a chantry-man, for that (overpopulated) profession requires precisely a capacity which he lacks—to "serue," to say a mass.[12] Both the question and Will's nonresponse imply that his status is considerably less regular than Reason's sense of what may comprise "clerical orders."

Imagining Will as a hermit, however, addresses quite directly this initially posed issue of unregulated status. For the supervision and obedience of hermits constitute a central topic about the state, one which animates a variety of issues I will discuss. Moreover, the dreamer's interrogation by Conscience and Reason itself enacts problems associated with the regulation of one's life, and his apparent lack of regulation creates constant difficulties for Will as he attempts to respond to his accusers.

The problem of the unsupervised hermit inheres in the first canonical description of the status, Benedict, *Regula* 1:

It is clear that there are four kinds of monks. The first type, the monastic, are called cenobites and carry on their spiritual warfare under a rule or an abbot. The second type is comprised of ancorites, that is hermits. They—not in the heat of a recent conversion, but only after the daily testing of monastic life—now instructed have already learned to battle against the devil with the aid of many fellows, and are now well formed in virtue in the battle lines shared with their brothers for the solitary warfare of the desert. There, safe without the aid of any other person, they, enjoying God's support, avail in their battle, using their own members alone against the vices of the flesh and of their thoughts.[13]

Benedict sets the hermit off from the monk-cenobite: he is beyond the scope of The Rule because his life is noncommunal; moreover, he might potentially be confused with Benedict's third and fourth varieties of monks, criminal *sarabaitae* and *gyrovagi*.[14] But unlike these dissolute figures, hermits have distinguished models for their behavior, all isolates who seek the desert for spiritual purposes: the Israelites, the prophets (especially Elijah), John the Baptist, Jesus in his wilderness withdrawal (Matt. 4). Like his biblical progenitors, the hermit engages in spiritual battle against temptation in the interests of self-purgation. This is an act of perfection, a forsaking of the things of this world.[15]

But equally clearly, hermits vis à vis monks express a lack. Monks battle in a brotherly front line ("fraterna acies"), says Benedict, whereas hermits exist without the aid of any other person ("sine consolatione alterius"). But this loneliness does not simply represent a battle of greater difficulty, one unsupported: because the Benedictine Rule guides a community, a hermit stands outside it, unregularized. And in so doing, he necessarily fails to live one third of the rule—the command of obedience. In his singularity, the hermit is his own "master," beyond regulation or rule, dependent only on his own will.

"Official" hermit documents display a telling restiveness about this issue. They simultaneously adopt modes both prescriptive and defensive/apologetic. Thus Oxon. Reg.,[16] although certainly instructing hermits in requisite duties, at its head acknowledges its less than official standing: "the state of hermits lacks any canonical rule" ("status heremitarum regula car[e]t canonica"). And surviving episcopal *ordo*s show similarly equivocal stances. Rawlinson (fol. 5), for example, has hermits make a vow predicated upon a "promise of perpetual chastity following the rule of the blessed John Doe" ("propositum castitatis perpetue iuxta regulam beati .N."), indicating that individual hermits might in fact name a patron ad lib., creating some highly personalized "order." This text also prefaces an extensive series of "observancie" (fol. 8ᵛ) with the apology that a hermit "should scarcely be restricted under some specific rule" ("sub aliqua certa regula minime debet coartari").[17]

Extra-eremitic authority, considerably less ambivalent, often adopts a far more critical view of nonobedience. Anti-eremitic statements focus upon Eccles. 4:10, "Woe to him who is alone" ("Vae soli"). The verse, a standard rebuke since Basil's rule in the 350s, identifies the hermit as not simply an isolate but as the "uncorrectible man who has no teacher" to restrain him.[18] For the precise danger of hermit professions, within this negative view of solitude, rests in untrammeled W/will. Thus, when the Cistercians of Barnoldswick (W. Yks.) went looking for a new site in 1153, their abbot convinced an eremitic group at Kirkstall to surrender their location to the house—and to convert to the cenobitic life:

He then began to warn the brothers in a mild way about their salvation and the advancement of their souls, proposing to them the dangers of following one's own will, the fewness of companions, the perilous state of being students without a master, laymen without a priest, urging them to follow the greater and better form of the religious life.[19]

Similarly, Bernard of Clairvaux, in a brief letter known only from English sources, discredits hermits by arguing that a solitary "so long as he is subject to no one, always does what his own desires teach him, and thus does not earn the merits of the splendid virtue of obedience" ("dum nulli subiectus est, suas semper facit voluntates, praeclarae huius oboedientiae merita non debentur").[20] Such a discourse should recall the negative aspects of Will's presentation of hermits, efforts to distinguish his state from that of others: for example, in the later diatribe (9.213–39) against "lollarne lyf," he argues that this state—but not his own—exists outside obedience, outside rule.[21]

Will's ability to denounce others for behaviors strikingly like his own should suggest that eremitic obedience forms a discursively contentious issue, a case of blurry party advocacy. For absence of obedience may be construed, not as spiritual danger, but precisely as the pursuit of deeper and greater perfection. This possibility, of course, Benedict notes: the hermit retreats "not in the heat of a recent conversion" ("non conversationis fervore novicio"), and the state is only appropriate for one already proven in communal discipline. This expectation that a personal sanctity beyond the norm must precede the withdrawal to the *eremus* forms the usual line of late medieval argument in defense of the status.[22] But whatever the ancient practice, such an expectation becomes inherently problematic in the different context of post-twelfth-century eremiticism, where laymen may assume the life ad lib. from a sense of devotion.

In this context, nonregulation may be conceived as a virtue in terms at the least ebullient, if not downright strident. Rolle, for example, formulates the issue bluntly (if in customarily defensive terms, rather like Will's unargued claim that he is "a parfit man" at 5.84):

He þat þis ioy has & in þis lyfe þus is gladdynd, of þe holy goste he is inspiryd, he may not erre; whateuer he do, leefful it is. No man dedely so gude counsayle to hym may gyfe als þat is þat he in hymself has of god vndedly. Odyr treuly if þa to hym wald gif counsale, withouten doute þai sall erre, for þa ha not knawen hym: he treuly sall nott erre, & if he wald to þer skyllis gif assent, of gode he sal not be suffyrd, þat to hys will constrenys hym þat it he pass not.[23]

And Rolle deliberately redefines that verse which was a constant slur against the eremitic life, "Vae soli": "Odyr wars erre þat solitary lyffe to repreue & sclaunder cessys not, sayand *Ve soli*, þat is to say 'wo be to man allone!' not expownyng 'allone' þat 'withoute gode,' bot 'withoute a fela.' He treuly is allone with whome god is not."[24] A similar rejection of regulation characterizes all English hermit rules; these direct the hermit not to establish his obedience to constituted church authority:

A hermit should show obedience to God alone, because God is his abbot, prior, and provost of the cloister of his heart. Nevertheless he should inform the bishop in whose diocese he lives or the patron of his place, if he should be a prelate or a priest of good discretion, about his mode of living.[25]

Although for the author of these rules "informing" or "notification" includes the possibility of being given good, if extra-regular, advice (which should be accepted), it remains a notion considerably less binding than pledged obedience to a superior.

Indeed, eremitic discourse can express an intense hostility to monastic conceptions of regulation. Rainald the hermit lashes out at the monastic rule as a coerced obedience, thus altogether lacking in merit, and Rolle refers with contempt to monastics as "obedienciarii," as if that docility were their only virtue.[26] Contemplation, whether "obedient" or not, Rolle always argues, constitutes the highest step, the most perfect and developed, of the Christian life. In such a claim, he follows such traditional theorists of the hermit life as Peter Damian.[27]

A final, and somewhat more moderate, defense of the eremitic life is distinctively twelfth century, although, as we will see, of considerable appeal to Langland. In this line of argument, the hermit requires no formal rule, for it appears ready-written in the gospels. His state represents the only true living out of the apostolic life: "it is nothing else except the life of the apostles and disciples of Christ fully informed by the precepts of the gospels" ("nihil aliud esse quam apostolorum discipulorumque Christi vitam evangelicis praeceptionibus plene informatam").[28] Touches of such a view occur in Oxon. Reg., with its counsel of gospel perfection:[29] like Rainald, that author presupposes that apostolic nonpossession (not a property of established monastic institutions) constitutes the single center which orders the hermit's life—even in the absence of formal regulation.[30]

Such issues surface explicitly near the end of Will's defense, at the moment when he claims to be a perfect man (5.84) and Conscience responds: "Ac it semeth no sad parfitnesse in citees to begge, / But he be obediencer to prior or to mynistre" (5.90–91). With perhaps typical idealism, Conscience reads the dreamer's claims quite literally. For him, the issue then becomes, not the claim of perfection per se, but a "sad" (stable, regulated) life of that sort (cf. further 5.102–4). Following good monastic precedents, Conscience associates this, not with the individual will to be perfect (which Will claims to personify), but with a stable social status, overseen by someone in an official capacity.

In the reference to an "obediencer" (5.91) Conscience invokes the discourse of English statute law (one of those discursive confluences to which I have alluded). He is citing the one statutory license for beggars—which would absolve Will of that "faitoury" for which Reason has attacked him (5.29–31). Even if Will resembles a "lollare," he still potentially has a licit claim to beg, for the 1388 Statutes extend this privilege to "people of religion and approved hermits having testimonial letters from their ordinaries" ("gentz de religion et heremytes approvez eiantz lettres tesmoniales des ordinairs").[31] Such supervisory figures would include the "prior or mynistre" (for the latter, see MED ministre n., sense 2b, usually used of Franciscan provincial officials) mentioned here. Since Will certainly has no such testimonial letter to show,[32] his state is clearly less regulated, more "lollare-like" than Conscience imagines—although he has already offered the preemptive defense (5.76) that his status may reflect precisely a failure by such supervising regular clergy to aid deserving beggars like himself.

This particular discursive topic—whether the hermit has some form of regulation or simply represents unbridled Will, self-indulgence—displays features which become repetitious as we examine further examples of the institutional discourse of eremiticism. On the one hand, such discourse is not uniform but plural. It is marked by considerable variousness of approach, at least in part the result of historicizable accretion, in which ancient formulations coexist and enter contention with modern innovations. The very meaning of being (or not being) unregularized leaves considerable freedom for maneuver. And, in some measure, Langland in C 5 dramatizes precisely this local and intradiscursive collision, the possibility that an apparently defensible habit of life can be thoroughly indefensible, a source of—and not just a subject for—hostile inquiry.

Moreover, Will's defense—that he is different than he appears to be, "yclothed as a lollare" (5.2) yet not one—engages him in a second problematic. Although, like Rolle, Will can offer a defense against prying strictures which convinces himself at least, this will not defend his life. Even as he enunciates the certainty of his "conscience" (5.83), he does not necessarily distinguish himself from "bad practice" or defend himself from potential charges of being a bad practitioner. The contentiousness of the discourse to which he appeals precludes such absolutism: the actual nature of practice itself cannot be clear-cut, and claims must, like Rolle's remain ill-defended and contention-ridden *ipse dixis* offered from self-interest alone. Hence the stridency that typifies Will's efforts at asserting difference from his similars such as 9.213–39, to which I have referred above. And obviously, the collision with such extra-eremitic discourses as that of labor regulation problematizes such claims even further.

Moreover, eremitic practices, perhaps especially in England, become further compromised through the very effort at giving them something like a canonical form. If the hermit exists, *prima facie*, outside monastic rule, he will lack that standardized direction provided by Benedict's traditional masculine model. The basis for his regulation must come from outside such accepted clerical discourse, and it will thus always be susceptible to querulous readings generated within that discourse. But in England, this difficulty is doubled, because such a discursive gap is filled precisely by appropriation from an overtly feminized context, from regulations for female recluses, figures basically lay whose inclaustration, like a hermit's vow, expresses simply a will to a religious life. The English eremitic rules all descend from such instructions,[33] and they consequently define a religious figure other than the conventional model of learned masculine clericism—a hybrid feminized cleric.

The female pursuit—lay aspiration to an ordered or sanctioned religious life outside "order"—simultaneously shapes and qualifies male eremitic practice. While women provide models for regulation, these very
models by their origin and nature virtually invite critique and a consequent
defensiveness on the part of their adherents—men do not "properly" be-
have this way. It is thus far from accidental that Will's situation should
recall, beyond Rolle, another prominent Middle English religious figure,
Margery Kempe. Like Kempe, Will aspires to an organized life in which
issues of vocation, its meaning, and its regulation constantly are in play;
like her, he seeks textualized (and thus male-legible, learned) models which
might found and simultaneously defend his ambiguous status.[34]

Fundamental to the problem of due obedience is the issue of hermit
wandering. When Benedict defines the hermit, he places him in juxtaposition with the *gyrovagus*;[35] he thereby distinguishes the states and implies that hermits may be identified by stability of residence, literally in
the *eremus* "the desert" from which their name is derived. For Benedict,
the desire to roam thus inherently exemplifies eremitical failure, identifies a will which needs direction (cf. Prol. 30).[36] Langland's evocation of
this topic, of course, testifies to another confluence of discourses, since
fourteenth-century labor regulation criminalizes wandering as vagrancy—
laziness, self-indulgence, and lack of social contribution.[37] The full ramifications of this issue I will take up shortly in considering hermit labor.

For the present, one should note that, like the very issue of regulation,
wandering (as Langland receives it and as aspects of his poem indicate)
again forms a contentious issue within eremitic discourse. The Benedictine
formulation certainly underwrites portions of Langland's presentation, for
example, his appeal to a model antique eremiticism, shut off within the
forest, the cave, or the isolated chapel (9.187–202, 17.6–36). But equally, in
the later Middle Ages (from the eleventh century), a different model of the
hermit developed, in this case that of an individual with potential social
involvements, available to other Christians for a variety of purposes.[38] Implicitly, the revision of Camb. Reg. to create Oxon. Reg. distinguishes
these alternative ways of life: the older work envisions a life of isolated
contemplation (cf. the lengthy attack on wandering ["vagatio"] at 300–
302, where the author labels such wanderers "girovagi vel sarabaite"). But
the later adaptation applauds an actively involved and wandering life—engaged in conversion, preaching, even overseas pilgrimage (313, 315–16, 315,
respectively).[39]

Yet the distinction between active and contemplative neither exhausts nor entirely explains possible permutations of this topic. Rolle can debunk "rynnars aboute, that ar sclaunderes of hermyts,"[40] a language which resonates with Langland's reference to "londleperis heremytes" (B 15.213; cf. Methley's use of "landleper," 116). Yet simultaneously, Rolle, in a typically defensive mode, must acknowledge his own "instability," that his *eremus* is mobile or vagrant.[41] His compromise(d) position relies on claims of future good intent: he may, at any particular moment, have performed the actual act of "rynnand aboute" (*discurrendi*), but he should not be judged by its ostensible nature, for he in fact seeks a place of contemplative rest in which to settle (*sedere*): "Wont I was forsoth, rest to seke, þof all I wentt fro place to place."[42]

Similarly, Margery Kempe's career vacillates between contemplative activity and wandering. Indeed the latter virtually shapes her book/life as a pilgrimage and one which persistently exposes her to hostile notice. This Kempe indeed courts (rather than seeking to evade it, as does Will), for her alternating contemplative moments, her conversations with divinity, instruct her that her troubles are matters of merit, tribulations borne for God's sake. But such hostile notice can never penetrate to the heart of Kempe's good intent, her divine communications: her activities only achieve verifiable warrant through discursive procedures, most notably by textualized gestures—the invocation of writings which are already deemed "holy" and which exhibit behaviors like those her tormentors query most sharply.

Such appeals to (an invisible) intent which licenses a behavior overtly questionable certainly should remind one of Will's final appeal to his interlocutors (5.92–101). Although engaged in actions admittedly criminous (cf. "so y beknowe," 92) and, at the very least, susceptible to negative readings ("chaffare," however much cast in the spirit of Matt. 13, remains a bit too closely implicated in the raw financialism of begging),[43] the dreamer claims ultimately to be pursuing an end—God's grace—appropriate to his way of life. But the acknowledgment equally, like Rolle's, undermines any plausible distinction from other wanderers, who might present similarly compelling claims of good intent.

A hermit's purpose, *propositum*, his expressed deep purpose for adopting his state, offers the most visible and formal sign of his good intent. And the normal representations of such a "purpose" indicate why eremitic discourse has not previously been associated with C 5. As Donaldson shows, Will's married status would have been debilitating for any clerical aspirations; but it would appear even more thoroughly to debar Will's licit claim to be a hermit. Even given the explicit opposition to any formal vow whatsoever (and thus that the evidence of formal professions will far from exhaust the number of possible practitioners, self-proclaimed followers of the state like Will), most formal evidence speaks unequivocally against Will's marriage as licit eremitic behavior. Virtually all available descriptions of hermit vows depict an unmarried candidate (*non coniugatus*) and his *propositum castitatis*.[44] But one can respond to Will's cohabitation with "Kytte" (5.2) in two ways—one internal to *Piers Plowman*, one a function of less formalized hermit representations in the period.

First, it does not seem to me by any means certain that one is to believe Kit to be Will's wife. Such a reading generally has relied on 20.472 (carried over from B 18.426), where the name recurs. But here, given Will's association with "lewede ermytes," Kit may be simply his concubine, one of those "Walsingham wenches" Langland has already described (Prol. 52). Again, Will's effort at constructing an eremitical status distinct from others would seem to erode.

Further, it is uncertain that, in either case, one deals with a specific female with biographical status. The name Kit, just like that of Will's daughter Calot (20.472), identifies the figure as a "type-female." The derived common noun "a Kitte" (7.304) may or may not mean "wife." And Mustanoja provides telling examples of pet names for "Katherine" to define stock feminine "abuses." He thus cites *N-Town Plays* 123/15 and 17 respectively for "Kate kell" (Katherine with her hairnet?) and "Kytt cakelere" (Kitty, who won't—like all women—keep her mouth shut).[45] Rather than a discernible person, Will's wife, Kytte may represent only a type—female companionship, with all those irritations misogynists (Will included)[46] comment upon. Thus, although one certainly doubts Will's chastity (since he appears totally self-created in his status, he cannot be accused of infidelity to a formal *votum castitatis*), the passage does not necessarily have the force Donaldson and others have ascribed to it.

Evidence external to the poem offers alternate explanations. For, as will now appear typical, sporadic evidence indicates that neither rules nor episcopal *ordo*s provide any universal modeling for the possible range of either hermit theory or practice, that this is again a contested piece of representation. In fact, references to married hermits certainly occur; Clay, for example, cites three quite unambiguous examples.[47] In the most relevant of these, one Adam Cressevill married after profession and was held to the vow (*votum*) of his marriage, since, Archbishop Arundel said, taking the hermit's habit was no profession of religion. For Arundel, whom few would imagine anything but a stickler, the hermit's vow exercised a lesser coercion than did the vow of matrimony.

But equally, wedlock and cohabitation may be thoroughly "regular." In 1479, Richard (or Henry) Andrew and Alice his wife made simultaneous vows of chastity, Richard's explicitly as a hermit,[48] but with no indication of separation or change of domicile: cohabitation in this instance appears intended to be chaste. Kempe's life again offers relevant information, for not only did she coerce from her husband John a vow of chastity while they still cohabited, but late in John's life, when, like the incapacitated Will (22.193–98), he had ceased to be sexually dangerous, she resumed cohabitation with him to act as his nurse.[49]

In the Middle Ages, hermits publicly express their *propositum*, their intent to adopt this state, in order to receive a habit, a visibly overt sign of intent.[50] And Will's clothes both identify him professionally and consequently create trouble for him in C 5. At least part of his defense involves constructing for himself a status as a privileged species in unappealing eremitical garb. Indeed, to this point Will has been largely defined by his clothing—which is self-created and self-assumed (Prol. 3–4), as that in many hermit depictions.[51] Rolle's unsupervised dismemberment and reconstitution into a habit of his sister's clothes (another overt appropriation of the feminine) provides the most notorious English parallel—one which we know of, ironically enough, from a text written as part of a campaign for the hermit's beatification, for the highest validation possible of his status. And Kempe similarly creates for herself a habit socially incongruous: her white gown and the ring marrying her to Jesus mark her as a holy person, "a consecrated virgin"—but while she still lives with her husband and only after a lengthy succession of children.[52]

Similarly, Will's garments gesture ambivalently toward beatitude, divine service, and criminality, "vnholy werkes." With whom do his sheeplike coverings align him? Is he to be judged by the apostolic pretensions he will later claim—"I send you forth as lambs among wolves" (Luke 10:3)? Or is he no different from his look-alikes, "lollares and lewede ermytes," "who come to you in the clothing of sheep, but inwardly are ravening wolves" (Matt. 7:15)?[53]

Descriptions of hermit dress occur fairly frequently. In these, theorists emphasize two features of the habit: some harsh external clothing, with proscription of linen; harsh footwear, if any at all: "A hermit should not wear linen or soft clothes next to his flesh, nor should he wear socks, but lowly sandals" ("Non utantur prope carnem lineis vel mollibus ves-

timentis, ne utatur caligis, sed sotularibus humilibus." Camb. Reg., 306).
Oxon. Reg. establishes even more specifically uncomfortable garb: outer
garments should be "made of humble wool" ("laneis et humilibus"); a
hairshirt is certainly appropriate (314),[54] and if feasible, the hermit should
go barefoot (315).[55]

Such antisumptuary prescriptions correspond, of course, to several of
Will's self-descriptions. For example, his initial description of the habit,
"as y a shep were," may, among other things, wittily indicate that he in fact
wears sheep-garb, dresses entirely in woolens, as a hermit ought. Similarly,
"Wollewaerd and watschoed" (20.1) depicts him in the same garments but
following the prescription of barefoot travel ("shod in the wet I picked up
from the ground"; cf. the "lunatyk lollares" of 9.121). And on other occasions, he wears the woolen cloth "russet" (10.1; cf. A 8.43, the imitation
at *Piers the Plowman's Creed* 719–21 and Charity in this garb at 16.298–99,
342–44). And his alter ego Rechelesnesse appears in an appropriately non-
solicitous hermit outfit, "ragged clothes" (11.196).

On the other hand, in C 5, Will clearly is dressed otherwise, in "longe
clothes" (41). In garbing himself thus, he shares the costume, as he says,
of "lollares and lewede ermytes"; we should imagine his clothes as those
"copes" which so often in the poem signify indulgent self-made status
(Prol. 54–55). These garments are apparently what Wood-Leigh describes
as *supertunicae*—manufacturing one required a full four yards of cloth.
(Note 8.185, where the hermits who wear them must cut them down in
order to work.) Wood-Leigh quotes the complaint of one fourteenth-
century clerk in Lincoln diocese; significantly, this man objects to such a
habit because of those very pretentions which may render it attractive to
Will: "since long, closed supertunics do not primarily accord with the acts
of simple priests, but of doctors and men designated as outstanding in
social rank. . . ."[56]

Perhaps typically, Will's use might again be distinguishable from his
look-alikes through a different eremitic discursive formulation. For in refusing the normal woolen habit, "lewede ermytes" fail to preserve their
separate privileged status: "The hermit should beware, lest he have a habit
which accords in all things with that of any other order of religious, lest
he should give such religious the opportunity to slander him" ("Cavere
etiam debet heremita, ne habeat habitum ullius religionis in omnibus con-
formem, ne detur religiosis occasio malignandi in eum").[57] Within the *Piers
Plowman* descriptions, such long cloaks appear as outfits appropriate to
friars, or at least identifiable as part of the normal, if ill-got, garb of modern

members of those orders (cf. Prol. 59 *et alibi*, e.g., 6.288). Wood-Leigh's Lincoln clerk goes on to complain that these mark their wearers as "pharisees distinguished from other secular chaplains" ("pharisei ab aliis capellanis secularibus distincti"), a play on the usual medieval etymology of the noun "Pharisee." And Will characterizes "lewede ermytes" later in the "Visio" (9.208, 247–50) by their illicit acquisition of habits which allow them to present themselves as having a privileged status, as being pseudo-friars.[58]

The attack on an activity which appears similar to his own should recall Rolle's discursive habits—slandering some as "rynnars aboute" while claiming sanctification for his own change of locale. And the analogy is worth pressing, for, so far as I can see, Will's atypical habit does mark the one unequivocal distinction between him and his colleagues—and the one which means the most to him. Will insists that he is learned, thus entitled to look different from the normal scruffy hermit; other hermits who wear similar garb don't deserve it and are engaged only in pretense and in clear violation of rule, because they are "lewede."[59] This terminology is not produced (for a change) by Will's search for an appropriately pejorative epithet, but relies upon a specific legalism derived from hermit discourse. And the appellation may be connected with the Lincoln clerk's complaint about special outfits for those with special offices, since the normal discursive context of the phrase "lewede ermyte" concerns the liturgical offices appropriate to practitioners of different educational backgrounds.[60]

Since a hermit enters a status fundamentally unregulated, this is a profession of desire in which anyone, but most normally laymen, can participate. Thus, Will vehemently attacks on a class basis both peasants who seek clerical titles (5.61–73) and those who attempt to pass themselves off as hermits (9.194–211). In contrast, Will's own "fader" and "frendes" (5.37) had enough money to set him to school. And those "lower class" individuals who assimilate themselves to hermit status may be branded interlopers precisely because they lack Will's "lettrure" (cf. 9.195, 198, in both uses closely associated with "lynage"). Will is not "lewed," but has an education, although he is puzzlingly vague about its extent (at least advanced grammar school training where he learned to read Latin scripture; cf. 5.37).

Given the represented professional demographics I've outlined, hermit materials do not always place great stock in the distinction between lay and cleric. Indeed the whole point of the profession (and one of its difficulties, as Arundel knew) is precisely this ambivalence. Thus discussions frequently replace the lay/cleric distinction with a more fundamental one, originally (but by the fourteenth century no longer) parallel, *literatus/non literatus.* And the documents routinely present this distinction as organizing the hermit's liturgical observations; in the Clay *ordo* (201–2), after making certain that the hermit can say (!) his Pater, Ave, and Creed:

The bishop should give him the charge that for whatever canonical hour of the day established by the church he should say a stipulated number of prayers devoutly asking for the salvation of his own soul and those of all his benefactors, to wit first for vespers twenty Pater nosters with as many Ave Marias, for compline thirteen Pater nosters with the same number of Aves.[61]

Hermits "non literatus," those Langland defines by the word "lewed," are severely restricted in their offices and recite only the most basic prayers in lieu of the canonical hours. But *literati* have more extensive duties; the Clay *ordo* continues:

If, however, he is lettered, so that he knows how to say the hours of the blessed virgin Mary with the seven psalms and the litany and "Placebo" and "Dirige" for the dead, along with whatever of these hours he should say three Pater nosters with the Ave Maria and once a day, leaving aside these others, half a nocturn of the Psalter.[62]

These offices for literates correspond exactly to Will's "lomes." (The locution echoes his distinction in B 12 between "work" at the Psalter and "play" at poetry.)[63] At least in part Will seems to be appealing here directly to the character Conscience, recalling his visionary prediction at 3.464–65, where he defines the prayers which comprise Will's "lomes" as the appropriate duties of perfect, messianic-age priests. Such a memory underwrites Will's later claim to perfection (5.84), itself in part an appeal to the Conscience who spoke these lines to defend him as fulfilling an ideal status.

Will describes his "tools," his occupations:

> The lomes þat y labore with and lyflode deserue
> Is *pater-noster* and my prymer, *placebo* and *dirige,*
> And my sauter some tyme and my seuene psalmes. (5.45–47)

As Donaldson comments, these are texts "not one of which but could be performed by any literate person whatsoever."[64] But as the citation from Clay above indicates, they are specifically observances assigned literate hermits. The primer, the Book of Hours, is Will's source for the Hours of the Virgin, litany, and Office of the Dead (*placebo; dirige* is the opening of the matins of the office). But this volume also includes a wide variety of psalms—the seven penitentials, as well as the graduals and the psalm of commendation. And as the regulations indicate, even literate hermits are expected, in addition to daily recitation of the canonical hours, the hours of the Virgin from the primer, and a substantial chunk of the Psalter, to repeat interspersed Pater Nosters.[65] Such an identification with letters in some sense "re-genders" Will, reassociates him with acceptable male clerical pursuits from which less fortunate hermits are debarred.

Finally, a complex of institutional issues concerning hermit occupations and (not so coincidentally) support needs to be considered together. At least in part, these issues reflect an extraordinarily variegated and not altogether clearly integrated rota of duties which hermits may fulfill. The *ordo*s agree in describing a life apportioned among "wakes, fastings, labors, prayers, works of mercy" ("vigiliis, ieiuniis, laboribus, precibus, misericordie operibus").[66] Prayer, Will's literate liturgy, and wakes (presumably those late night hours when the hermit may, if inclined, perform most of his contemplative activity)[67] would seem, especially on the basis of the institutional materials already surveyed, to form nonproblematic spiritual exercises. But in what relation should they stand to the more clearly physical portions of the regimen, "labor" and "opera"?[68] Second, what sort of dietary restrictions does the term "ieiunia" include? These two questions produce a third series of concerns: if labor is only optional, or if it is insufficient to meet a hermit's needs, how is he to gain his living? May begging, the active solicitation of alms, although unmentioned in the *ordo*s, form part of a hermit's vocation? If it does, how is it to be regulated, both in terms of the relation between "cell time" and extramural "vagrancy" and in terms of possible limitations on the hermit's solicitations? Finally, may a hermit pursue his sustenance in this way through some regular benefactor? Can he have, as it were, a patron?

As I argue in my article " 'Meddling,' " virtually all hermit representations urge manual labor of some variety as a necessity of the state.[69] Camb. Reg. particularly emphasizes such a view (even within a basically contemplative regimen): working is "more perfect" than not doing so. Moreover, the rules draw upon the same biblical injunctions as Langland does in stating this requirement: 2 Thes. 3:10 (cf. the English of 8.140–42, 9.155–58, A 7.125) appears in both. Indeed, the author of Camb. Reg. cites the Gloss to prove that this verse should not be interpreted as referring to spiritual works, and he appends Jerome's traditional list of those manual labors appropriate to hermits (from Ep. 125.11). Oxon. Reg. links the verse with another of Langland's favorites, Ps. 127:2 (see 8.261a).[70]

The episcopal *ordo*s identify two alternative forms of appropriate eremitical work: "The hermit should labor with his hands . . . so as to acquire food but also to build or repair roads and bridges" ("laboret manibus . . . circa uictualia adquirenda at uias et pontes construendos seu reparandos").[71] Minimally, the hermit should grow his own food in a garden attached to his cell (cf. Malory's description at 945/23–26). Alternatively, he should serve the community through one or another out-of-doors job, of which bridge and road work are taken as most normal, since they allow a withdrawn rural cell near the site of pious labor.[72] As Etienne Delaruelle notes, the injunctions for hermits provide "un chapitre de la rehabilitation du travail manuel."[73]

Rather obviously, such an insistence on manual tasks interfaces very neatly with fourteenth-century English labor legislation. And Langland's hermits, of course, routinely violate legislative, in addition to "ordinal," expectations: they "lothe were to swynke," and take up the profession only "her ese to haue" (Prol. 53, 55).[74] Will's distaste even spills over onto contemporary practitioners of the most normally recommended extracellular eremitic labor, road hermits, "ermytes þat inhabiten by the heye weye" (9.188). As Will sees it, they only inhabit—and don't work: roadside hermitages allow a new ostentatiousness, and hermits, whatever their claims for public labor, only hang out there so as to be present to any potential tipper.

Yet Will doesn't note (except when his own behavior comes in question) an alternate theorization of hermit duties, which potentially exonerates such inaction. For within this discourse, there is no universal requirement that a hermit labor. In contrast to the extensive rota of duties I have already cited, one might compare the narrower, more exclusively contemplative lists, usually the triad "prayer, meditation, reading" ("oracio, meditacio, leccio"). And Rolle, of course, rejects work altogether; his hermit should be engaged in higher occupations, which render work intrusive:

But bodily exertion avails little where the mind, drawn away from heavenly thoughts, does not fear to run about in fantasies about failing worldly things and the taste allows the eye of the heart to wander away from an intention of spiritual joy.[75]

Will, of course, also rejects the widely held view that labor makes a perfect hermit (cf. 5.22–25), either in favor of something like Rolle's holy thoughts (even though their form makes them appear just as apt to be Rolle's worldly *fantasmata*) or of the claim to a higher work (literate prayer).

Of course, the attention which any hermit might devote to laboring in the interests of subsistence will be a direct function of his understanding of the *ordos'* requirements of "ieiunia." Diet forms one aspect of the life under fairly strict control, both in terms of quality of food and in terms of prohibitions against eating at will. Oxon. Reg. lays out what appear reasonably standard regulations for fasting, essentially three meatless (Additional denies the use of "white meat," dairy products and eggs, as well) days a week, with protracted seasonal fasts (e.g., at Lent). Although more lenient, perhaps to include a "lewed" lay clientele, the *ordos* prescribe dietary abstention on the same model of three days per week.[76]

And, of course, when he eats, a hermit shouldn't eat well. His poor fare is virtually a comic stock in a variety of Middle English contexts. Most soberly, Robert of Knaresborough eats bread made with ashes, so that he can live out Ps. 101:10; much of the comedy of "Kyng and Hermyt," popularized in Scott's *Ivanhoe*, concerns the expectation of strait rations in the cell.[77] And in another coalescence of disparate discourses, when the wilderness, once the exclusive habitat of hermits, becomes the locale of *aventure*—a place of chivalric, rather than simply spiritual, battle—the confrontation between abstemious and necessarily athletic diets becomes virtually a commonplace.[78] Of course, Will's construction of false hermits relies (9.145–51, 253–54) on their partiality for such active diets—although once again, how such appetites might be distinguished from Will's visits to great houses (5.49–51) remains unclear.[79]

Begging for whatever modicum one eats remains problematic in hermit discourse, for two reasons. It removes the hermit from his cell (thus, Oxon. Reg., 315, suggests having a "famulus" to do it), disrupts (as Rolle sees) eremitical devotions, even if it manages not to turn one into a vagrant; and it involves handling what might be construed as worldly property, a violation of vows of poverty.[80] But two circumstances seem to allow begging. On the one hand, Will pleads that he is physically incapable of performing the agricultural tasks which would feed him (5.22–25, but cf. the shameless "lollare," 9.215–16, also physically debilitated, if only in metaphor): although Camb. Reg. (302) would not count him among the "perfecti," it would excuse him from labor since "his weakness does not permit him to work" ("teneritudo non permittit") and thus implicitly would allow him to seek provision in other ways. Moreover, a hermit who invests his efforts in occupations which do not automatically generate sustenance or provide direct remuneration, e.g., "public works" or preaching or—Will's special metier—intercessory prayer, would clearly also merit support.

But if a hermit might beg, his activities should be limited—should provide a way, for example, to distinguish Will from that "faitoury" of which Reason accuses him (5.29–32a). Implicitly, begging should be limited through the claims of fasting, but in fact those devotionally restricted meals are quite often expressly limited to "in-cell" time (cf. Oxon. Reg., 316). Thus the rules place other controls on the hermit as a loosed beggar. Oxon. Reg. (and its derivatives) offers the most carefully wrought prescriptions, down to comments (315) on the ethics of solicitation (don't be either a pushy bum or a flatterer).[81] From Camb. Reg., Oxon. Reg. develops a system based on the apostolic charge of nonsolicitude, to take nothing in excess of the day's needs (Matt. 6:34). Hermits who dwell in towns are to beg for their day's sustenance only, and to distribute any excess received to the poor before nightfall; in rural areas, the hermit, presumed to require a fair circuit to gain his food, can have at one time only what will sustain him for the following week.[82] These limits underwrite Will's indignant responses to questions about his diet and the extent to which he begs (5.52, 86–88). He operates in accord not only with Oxon. Reg. but also the apostolic command at Luke 9:3 (cited, with reference to "lunatyk lollares" at 9.120a): to have "bagge or botel" implies extra-regular hoarding, the gluttony of seeking more than one needs. And Will hopes, when he alludes to the arch-hermit Jesus (Matt. 4:4), to demonstrate that he lives outside the food chain which dominates statute considerations, that his tester/tormentor Reason will "begone" (Matt. 4:10). In contrast, Will constructs his damnable enemies, the "lewede ermytes" who parody his holy state (9.139–61) by insisting on their failure to observe such limits. In fact, such depictions of evil hermits who seek excessive food and thereby desert any due order compactly indicate their status as *gyrovagi*, rather than *heremite*: Benedict, of course, defines the former as "serving the allurements of gluttony" ("gule illecebris servientes").[83]

A quasi-institutionalized form of begging, the hermit's recourse to a regular patron, appears with some frequency in hermit depictions, although not unproblematically. A hermit can, as Will claims he does, function as a kind of household servant, a domestic spiritual advisor who receives his keep in return for his services. Rolle's Office describes his early career as such a servant to the Daltons of Pickering and also suggests some potential difficulties:

However, at the dinner Rolle was so perfect in preserving his silence that not a single word proceeded from his mouth. When, however, he had eaten enough, he arose, before the table was withdrawn, and disposed himself to depart. But the knight who had called him said to him that this wasn't how things were done, and thus forced him to sit down again. But when dinner was finished, he again wanted to depart, but the knight detained him, asking to have a private chat with him.[84]

Similarly, Methley counsels his addressee Hugh the hermit that, even though the "gentils" who want his services have a power over him which might coerce obedience ("whom thou dare not displeas"), his proper place is his cell. "Tel them . . . that but in the tyme of very great nede, as in the tyme of dethe . . . thou mayst not let thy deuocion" (116).[85] Prayers will serve benefactors just as well if made in one's cell; but the hermit's spiritual instruction and consolation cannot be continuously tapped at the discretion of a lay patron.

Household patronage of hermits thus might be construed as particularly problematic, perhaps more so than simply begging in the street. It disrupts devotion, but it also implicitly compromises the strongest avowals of hermit obedience: if the hermit has God as "the abbot of the cloister of his heart" ("abbas claustri cordis sui"), and can be construed as licensed because of it, what licit relationship can he possibly have with a worldly master? Thus, both Camb. Reg. and Oxon. Reg. categorically state that the hermit should not even "notify" the patron of his cell about his life, if that patron is a layperson. And patronage may inherently signify a disrupted regimen in any case: Methley takes up this topic in a chapter otherwise completely given over to vagrancy (cf. "Be no home-rynner forto see mervels"); and Rolle on several occasions defends himself against charges that he has frequented great houses only out of a taste for too delicate a living or for rich food and against other charges that his changes of patrons should be attributed to their efforts to reduce him to an appropriately straiter rule.[86] Of course, precisely such quasi-regulated household patronage forms, as Will explains it, his life (5.48–52): while his acts are more august than the back-door "faitoury" with which Reason charges him (5.29)—Will claims to be a "welcome" guest—the relation of such patronized welcome to rule remains, like much of the discourse on which Will draws and the life he constructs out of it, problematic.

Yet perhaps, in this explanation of his literate offices and of the rewards his patronized prayers merit, Will makes his strongest vocational claims. Like Rolle, he remains constantly aware of his ambivalent status, and he defends himself by a logic—my work is prayer—analogous to Rolle's claim for his contemplation.[87] But Will ultimately appeals past these visible difficulties of status to the highest rule he can conceive. Like Rainald (and other twelfth-century hermits, as noted), Will turns for his warrant, not to human rules, but to the biblical *originalia*. He constructs a self-description within the limits of gospel "rule" and asserts his accountability to a higher regulatory system than the statute under which he is being interrogated.

Most trenchantly perhaps in 5.52, with its echo of Luke 9:3, Will's self-descriptions echo Jesus' instructions to his apostles and disciples (Luke 9, 10), and Will obviously attempts to present his life as regulated by and formed upon the words of Scripture. As a literate hermit, he is a hired prayer "for the salvation of his own soul and those of all his benefactors ("pro salute anime sue et omnium benefactorum suorum," Clay, 202), with interests in God's kingdom comparable to those of his apostolic forbearers. Further, he is paid for this effort in food and follows a regular rotation of visits among his employers; his behavior thus accords with Jesus' injunction, "eat such things as are set before you" (Luke 10:8).[88] Although he appears to ignore injunctions against wandering house to house in Luke 10:5–7, he perhaps intends his insistence upon following a fixed rotation (cf. "oþerwhile in a monthe" 5.50) to signify his adherence to the gospel spirit, rather than unrestrained opportunism. He thus acquires a "measurable hire" (part of Luke 10:7 he chooses to observe) from his patrons in return for his prayers. Perhaps particularly important, given Will's aggressive turn on Reason (5.53 ff.), is Jesus' command, "salute no man by the way" (Luke 10:4; cf. B 15.3–10, partly retained in the description of "lunatyk lollares" at 9.123–24); in this behavior, he is perhaps especially reminiscent of Margery Kempe, no respecter of persons either (see note 101 below). Thus, although Will, among other debilities, wears the habit of a "lollare," he claims to be truly apostolic, since he does not carry a "lollere"'s equipment and takes no more than his day's food.

Thus, much specific detail in C 5—both Will's positive self-definition as well as his vehement anti-eremiticism, most trenchantly expressed elsewhere—becomes more comprehensible if one reconceives his vocation, his work. Most especially in his emphasis upon his literacy and those liturgical acts it allows him (but not other hermits) to perform, but also in a variety of other details—his usual costume in the poem, his wandering pursuit of patronage, his possession of a consort (if not wife)—his self-description evokes the represented practice of medieval hermits. And, perhaps most tellingly in his profession of a good intent his acts do not overtly communicate, his pursuits remind one of his outstanding mid-century pre-

cursor, Richard Rolle. Like Rolle, Will creates for himself an unregulated
eremitic regimen, one entirely personalized (and attacking, on just such
a personalized basis, the activity of others). But where Rolle "regulates"
himself through a claim to an indwelling divine presence which sanctions
anything—a claim his contemporaries found every bit as problematic as
Reason and Conscience find Will[89]—Will enunciates an equally shaky authority, the biblical text. He imitates, in his search for Truth, Truth's text,
the gospel, and discovers in it a model for his behavior.

II. Hermit, Apostle, and Minstrel

Will's self-depiction draws on hermit discourse and continuously emphasizes a range of problematic alternatives inherent in what is a thoroughly
problematic state—one which in some dubious measure regulates will, but
which in all its regulation is subject to idiosyncratic and contentious expressions of will. Yet this "professional," if nonprofessionalized, state is
paralleled in Will's depiction by a(n a)vocation at least equally nonprofes-
sional, nonregulated, and consequently problematized. For the *apologia* of
C 5 introduces the inquisition of the dreamer's professionalism precisely
through identifying him as a poet of dubious status. He claims to write
satire about other, false hermits under the guidance of Reason (5.5) and at
least to wander through Conscience (as if it were a dead-end off Cornhill,
5.6). Thus, he argues, his poetry in fact performs a social service like his
tormentors' own: in attacking "lewede ermytes," Will avers, he poeticizes
the demands of statute law. Yet neither Reason nor Conscience, once they
begin to interrogate him, appears at all moved by the claims for the poetry
—indeed, neither bothers to address that performance: its nature and its
quality of explanation remain secondary to the dreamer's personal irregularities, those features of his life which, as is typical within eremitic discourse, would expose him to the same strictures he would place on others.

   Thus Will's status preempts his poetic claims, and the value of his
"makings" may only be construed logically as a corollary of, a pendant to,
the value to be attached to his mode of living. If *Piers Plowman* reflects
a personal longing to understand salvation in some experiential fashion,
what animates the person engaged in this pursuit? From what perspective
can he claim, as an individual, any warrant or license for his desire to avoid
all "normal" forms of work to pursue Truth and, then, to write his quest?
And what quality of life might lead him to believe that he can efficaciously

achieve certainty in the pursuit of topics over which greater (and better equipped) minds have fretted for centuries (recall Ymaginatif's "þer are bokes ynowe," B 12.17)? At least one way Will always approaches the question, a way which forms a major theme of the C text's second vision, is to accommodate his quasi-regulated life-style to that of a status which apparently confers upon its holder some license—broadly, the hermit conceived as apostolic man. And the progressive qualification and redefinition of this status animates the major expansions of the C "Visio"—not simply the interrogation which I have aligned with hermit practice, but also the two major additions in the pardon passus (9.70–158, 187–281) and the point at which I begin my discussion, the advancement of Sloth materials from B passus 13 into C 7.

Langland's initial stimulus in moving this material (7.70–119a) into the "Visio" may have been the narrative economy which draws together the B version's two extensive discussions of the Deadly Sins. But the material from B 13 ranges rather far from Sloth per se. Lines 82 ff., not only through their intrusion of the "authorial voice," dissipate the actual sense of a confessional scene: they form a new initiative, a more powerfully integrated way of addressing persistent concerns than Langland has achieved in the B-version.[90]

In all versions of the poem, Will is early on conceived as some variety of poet, perhaps most explicitly at A 1.137–38, where Holychurch associates him with a harp (the old accompaniment to minstrel entertainment)[91] and presenting "ȝeddynges" at meals. Less grandiosely and specifically, in 1.134 (a line common to all versions) she addresses him as potentially an instructor of the "lewed" (and explicitly not of the "lettred")—one might surmise an author of commonplace instructional poetry. And issues relevant to such a poetic stance—the abuse of learning and the concommitant failures of aristocratic entertainments at table—occupy Langland at great length in the AB "Vita," for example at B 9.98–104, 10.31–58, and 93–139— all passages severely truncated or absent in the C version.

In his last revision, Langland reconceives the issue of poetry and entertainment and accords it a central place in his "Visio," not his "Vita." The dreamer Will is concretely identified at 5.3–5 as a young poet—the author of social satire, perhaps works lying behind or incorporated within the limited A version.[92] And in seeking his subsistence (5.48–51), Will tries to live out Scripture as poor apostolic wandering: he prays for those who feed him and, perhaps, following the association in earlier versions of poetry with dinners, offers at table, like Margery Kempe, some variety of "holy con-

versation."[93] The Sloth passage, 7.82–119a, thus forms an important ful-
crum in a developing C version argument. It yokes the patronized hermit
as visitor in a great house, apostolic regulation, and a licit poetic ("god's
minstrelsy"), and it presages further refinements in the two great additions
of passus 9.

Looking back toward passus 5, in the advanced Sloth materials, Langland still presents a young poet.[94] But here, his self-definition relies heavily
upon his poetic roots in the alliterative tradition: if Rolle provides Will
with one mid-century precursor stance, a self-fractured and contentious
eremitic discourse, the contemporary alliterative satire of *Winner and
Waster* provides a second. Will's opening lines here (7.82–97) define a corrupt modern minstrelsy; the remainder develops a new apostolic form
which will confer upon Langland's poetry, God's minstrelsy, an important
social power implicitly denied it by Reason and Conscience. As Thorlac
Turville-Petre has recently noted, Langland certainly learned this theme
from his precursor's prologue.[95]

The speaker of *Winner and Waster*, a "westren wy" (line 7), personi-
fies the old learned man who narrates most Middle English alliterative
poetry. But Langland's Will in some sense is his antitype: not only is he
youthful, but his father (an adherent of the Western Marcher Despensers)
has done what the poet of *Winner* claims no western man should—sent his
son off to London, where he will fall and fail in a treacherous world (lines
7–9).[96] *Winner*'s London contains such delights as the taverns of Cheap
(472 ff., esp. 477–78), that locale where Will becomes indistinguishable
from "lollares" and involved in dissolute poetic acts (cf. 9.98, 188–89, 194;
and the sneaky echoic self-reference of 6.368, unique to C). He looks like
the sort of entertainer *Winner* contemns as "a childe appon chere withowt-
tyn chyn-wedes" (line 24), someone who can't form a decent alliterative
long-line (line 25) but only "iangle and iapes telle" (line 26). In contrast,
the alliterative ancient who speaks the earlier poem applauds, not simply
performance, but the wise man who respects Truth, who can "ma[k]e it
hymseluen" (line 28), and who can speak what he has made.

But in a more positive vein, Will at least aspires to the goals of *Winner*.
And he shares some of that poet's complaints. For as Turville-Petre shows,
the worlds Langland and the *Winner* poet face are remarkably similar—
filled with a verbal treachery (cf. "wytt and wyles," "wyse wordes and slee,"
lines 5–6) which masks serious social disruption and which renders Truth
difficult to achieve. At least within the scope of my argument, one form
such deceptive language might take would reflect discursive contentious-

ness, the effort to constitute problematic behaviors within a justifying, if not thoroughly overdetermined language.[97] For the older poet, this disruption depends upon the decline of poetic patronage (see lines 19–20); the central site of alliterative poetry, the great feast which both organizes and expresses social cohesion, has lost its function.[98] Lords no longer entertain as they once did, no longer respect and support those who purvey wisdom; true poets are exiled and get no hearing. In the discussion of "goddes munstrals," Langland strives for his own partial resolution to that problem: he develops his conception of a legitimate poetic status and of an appropriate poetic presentation.

At 7.104–9, Langland presents three positive poetic types, "The pore, a lered man, a blynd man . . . or a bedredene womman." These replace the three evil modern "minstrels" already described, "foel sages, flateres and lyares" (7.83). In a broad sense, Will derives his distinction from Luke 14:12–24 (the parable of the feast).[99] Jesus enjoins his hearers not to call upon uncaring intimates but "the poor and weak and blind and lame" ("pauperes ac debiles ac caecos et claudos," 14:21, cf. 14:13), and Will, the apostolic hermit who is no stranger to the houses of the great, takes this direct evangelical command as a model which sanctions his visits.

Will's gospel reading is, of course, peculiar and self-serving. While retaining the biblical *pauper*, he collapses the final three figures of Luke 14:21 into alternative forms of a single minstrel type in 7.108 and adds a figure more distinctively minstrel-like (7.105–7).[100] But of course, this exegesis represents an amusing form of self-interest and special pleading: an actual (if would-be) minstrel ends up among the metaphorical ones (and, in turn, confers on them their metaphoric status as entertainers) because those have a legitimate public status as sanctioned poor persons. And in joining himself to them (and them to him) Will offers a way of licensing his behavior. Predictably, he seeks someone to resemble, to assimilate himself to.

Langland's interpretation of Luke 14:21, while it shares much of their spirit, is thus at some remove from more contested public uses of the verse, inspired by Fitzralph.[101] These readings interpret the word "pauperes" as defined by the three terms which follow it. The verse thus distinguishes the worthy poor from other indigents: the worthy poor are those "pauperes *et* debiles (etc.)"—not just poor but infirm as well. To some extent, Will's use displays less interest in slandering imperfectly poor mendicants (Fitzralph's goal) than in constructing the *pauper literatus heremita* as an evangelically protected species.

The "lered man" (7.105–7), who presumably shares the indigence of his two companions, rather obviously speaks to Langland's various concerns about the legitimacy of his own activity. On the one hand, this figure certainly derives from the one introvertible value Will the hermit enacts — his literacy, his ability not simply to offer the full range of eremitical prayer but also to know "what holy writ mene[þ]" (5.37). Langland is, after all, the only contemporary who fiddles up "of god friday þe geste" (7.107, not just in passus 20 but at 1.162–70 and 7.130–36), if one understands by the generic term *geste* "alliterative poem" (a sense suggested by Chaucer's uses at *Canterbury Tales* VII.933, X.43).[102] But even if that sense is not here primary, "gesta" implies an instructive historical narrative (a genre well paralleled within alliterative tradition) far removed from the vacuities of "bad" minstrels. This serious performance, in which the biblically modeled hermit enunciates the Truth of the text he embodies, contrasts with the terms "tales" 7.91 and "lay" 116. And the implication that Langland would provide holy speech while simultaneously earning for himself sustenance obviously is predicated upon the professional endeavors described at 5.45–52.

Even while he suppresses from this discussion any of those eremitic doubts about patronage which we have examined above, Will creates an apostolic function both for his way of life and for his poetry. Although "withoute flaterynge" directly contrasts with 7.90–91, it equally suggests that the minstrel will enjoin upon his rich host harsh gospel precept as a way "For to saue [his] soule."[103] And this act is coupled with the startling reversal of 7.109. Minstrels typically ask "largesse," a tip, for themselves, not others; the "good loos," the patronal praise which marks alliterative poetry, is expressed, not in panegyric, but in Will's usual metier, prayer, and requests for the patron's salvation.

This reversal can occur since, of course, the aristocratic patron has already given his "largesse" precisely in accord with the poet's lived biblical precept. Such precepts include that necessity which the very presence of the learned man and his fellow evangelical beggar-minstrels enacts, the command to give alms. One might compare both the instruction Holychurch appends to her passion narrative (1.171–74a) and the reference to Tobit as an appropriate poetic subject in the parallels to 11.32 (A 11.25, B 10.33) and at 11.70–80. But, in any event, Will here imagines a paradoxical return to the moral utterances also valued by the old poet of *Winner*: a face-to-face oral instruction which is also "literate," the product of "a lered man," a poet who has been schooled.

The "lunatyk lollares" (9.105–38) merely push this variety of argumentation a step further. These figures, like the hermit Will of passus 5, are not as they appear. Like Will, they look, as the noun which identifies them suggests, like hardy vagrants, people who ought to be at work. But Will now imagines himself in a guise far more perilous than earlier; when he is "In hele and in inwitt" (5.10), he is exposed to the regulations of the Statute of Laborers. The lunatic lollers—"in hele as hit semeth / Ac hem wanteth wit" (105–6)—incorporate a fantasy of self-defense which will avoid that previous discomfiture. If Will earlier encounters difficulty in arguing his claim, both eremitic and apostolic, to alms, this assimilation to the lunatic loller offers some hope: in spite of appearances, these figures cannot formulate for themselves even the imperative to survival, much less a means toward subsistence. They must truly represent a noble and licensed poverty, since their blight is divinely controlled and their state potentially blessed (cf. 9.116 and the conclusions Will draws, initially offered with some tentativeness, 117–18).

The naming of this group—"lunatyk lollares and lepares aboute" (repeated 9.137)—represents Will's final difficult (if not desparate) effort to distinguish himself from his look-alikes, the "lewede ermytes" who share his status. The generic nouns acknowledge connections with these offenders, while the qualifying adjective "lunatyk" attempts to define a licit subgroup.[104] But confusingly, the unqualified noun "lepare" here defines potential sanctity (perhaps recalling B 5.474–76, cf. 6.328–30) while such a qualified form as "ouer land strikare" (9.159), confusingly analogous to unqualified "lollare," indicates a person morally suspect (and its suspicious adjective is instructively a pun on the poet's name).

In the C version, which lacks Piers's statements at B 7.128–35, the lunatic lollers absorb a variety of concerns associated with Piers's quotation of the gospel command *ne soliciti sitis*. Will can identify the lunatics as deserving lollers, worthy of support, on the basis of their deprivation and their heedlessness about it, their mad refusal to take any interest in self-preservation. But this very insouciance goes further; rather than simply identifying a noncriminous version of a typically criminal activity, it becomes the basis for associating the figures with strongly positive values— predictably the apostolic status through which Will defines his eremiticism and the capacity for something like poetry (ultimately lunatics are "munstrals of heuene" [9.126], too).

Apostolic details, a full cento constantly echoic of Will's claims in C 5, litter the ten lines or so which most directly describe lunatic lollares. Just as these people are called "lollares," but are not, so also they fulfill numerous features of the apostolic life and yet are not apostles ("*as* his postles . . .

or *as* his priue disciples" 9.118). They walk, like Peter and Paul, but do
not perform the specifically apostolic offices, preaching and healing, described in Luke 9:2 (9.112–13). Yet their behavior recalls Will's apostolic
eremiticism; they literally fulfill the command of Luke 9:3, "Take nothing
for your journey; neither staff, nor scrip, nor bread, nor money; neither
have two coats" (9.119–20a; cf. 9.297). Nor, following Luke 10:4, do they
"carry . . . shoes," and they "salute no man by the way" (9.121–22). Thus, in
their blightedness, lunatic lollers exceed even the minstrel in his refusal to
flatter. They represent those *ydiotae* who comprised the primal Christian
community (Acts 4:13, and cf. 9.128a).

Yet however apostolic looking, hermit-/loller-like, or poetic lunatic
lollers may be, Will's possible assimilation to their state differs fundamentally from being "God's minstrel." That status respects and sanctifies what
Will has represented as a biographical self. But to become a lunatic loller
would be to disguise oneself once again, to take on a foreign habit: insofar as Will identifies himself with their state, he ostensibly surrenders that
one skill which has meant most to him earlier in the poem—his learning.
He thus returns (regresses?) to a moment like Prol. 2, in which a disguise
externally acceptable protects an unexaminable, and potentially dissolute,
interiority. To do this reverses the proud claims (5.92–101) for a noble interior masquerading in a bad cause. And we might consider that Will here
provides an ironic comment on that learning which shapes him and which
he cannot surrender, that it debilitates, is a madness. For that reading inheres in the transition at 5.33–35: schooling is an invisible maiming, in
which Will has lost his *lymes* in exchange for *lomes*, his prayerbook and,
what compels him more, his pen.[105]

Yet if Will voluntarily jettisons his overt claims to learning here, the
unique skills of lunatic lollers compensate, offer a very tentative gain in exchange for loss. For these figures' claim to anything like minstrel status,
to be "merye-mouthed men" or "bourdyors" (9.126–27), rests on higher
powers. Rather than either apostolic preaching[106] or fiddling up Good
Friday, "many tymes hem happeth / To profecye of þe peple, pleyinge, as
hit were" (113–14). Whatever their psychic blight, their want of wit implicitly renders them divine vehicles, possibly prophetic. Moreover, in this
process, they resemble Will in two other respects—their poetry shares the
same highly qualified value as "pleye" which Will admits when confronted
by Ymaginatif (B 12.20–24); and, like the satiric Will, their subject is contemporary conditions, "þe peple." Prophecy and corrective disrespect for

others seem linked traits; but such traits also accompany a highly qualified claim for poetic achievement.

In their ability to prophesy, perhaps antisocially, lunatic lollers might be construed as representing one powerful, but in *Piers* usually submerged, form of hermit work. The power to read the future and to advise their fellow Christians about it is typically associated with hermits, especially contemplatives with their direct line to divinity. For example, Wulfric of Haselbury was renowned for these skills; William Norham's prophecies could be construed of such potential power as to cost him his life; and prescient dream readers stock Malory's Grail quest.[107] And although Langland satirizes a fake lollare prophet (9.211), Margery Kempe's career routinely shows prophecy as a mode of eremitic contention: being chidden, having one's religious perquisites questioned, draws forth prophetic utterance as a form of self-defense; correspondingly, true prophecy provides the surest sign of innate sanctity.[108] Moreover, such predictive power often coexists with erratic behavior: Robert of Knaresborough, for example, feigns madness when introduced to King John (lines 755–60).

Of course, actions one might associate with lunatic lollers color Will's career through large stretches of the poem. Two extensive B version passages (Prol. 123–28 and 15.3–10) present behavior overtly lunatic. And at a variety of later points in C, culminating with his joining the few fools who enter Unity (21.61–67, 74–79), such associations recur; cf. 15.1–3, 18.179, 20.2–3. And in all versions, Will dabbles with problems of prophetic dreams (Prol. 217–18, 9.298–318, the latter newly resonant in C following this addition).

More to the point, the redefinition of the divine minstrel allows Will —whatever the surrenders of learning and seriousness of pursuit which he must make—a new, and more fully licensed, minstrel habit. For in the garb of a lunatic lollere Will still retains his entrée to aristocratic feasts (cf. 9.128–38, implicitly fulfilling Luke 10:5–7 once again). But his activity as lunatic, while it may still correspond to the highest—and if Rolle is any indication, most problematic—of hermit claims, would be exempted from that scrutiny which has made it so major a topic in the C version. "Me suffreth al þat suche sayen and in solace taketh" (9.131): the lunatic apparently resembles the licensed Renaissance fool, an antisocial figure who is no respecter of persons, a speaker of home truths which his rich host may not wish to hear. But even such satiric bluntness (a return to the "reasonable" poetic metier of 5.5) will be tolerated, if not heeded.

Moreover, license for lunatics extends beyond deregulated speech: "vnder godes secret seal here synnes ben keuered" (9.138). As lunatic, Will frees himself from those regulatory issues which establish, in the persons of Reason and Conscience, the very requirement of justifying one's status which in turn creates his peculiar self-representation. The cover of lunacy— another of Will's disguises, a concealment of the unlicensed yet learned self —would allow Will to follow that apostolic eremiticism he has chosen as his own, and to do so unqueried, unexamined. If there are indeed "synnes" associated with his behavior, they are the business of God, "abbot, prior, and provost of the cloister of his heart" ("abbas, prior, et prepositus claustri cordis sui," Camb. Reg., 304), not of human inquisitors. As lunatic, not only can Will achieve the status of satiric visionary which he has set out for himself all along, he can also achieve what he never has in the poem, the separation of poetic career from its now oralized medium. "Covered sins" allow a distinction far more valuable than all those Will has wrangled over in the past: his person, no longer interrogable and dismissable, stands apart from its sanctioning clothing and yet may persist, albeit in nonwritten form, in the process it wishes, poeticizing itself. Moreover, the poem can now triumph over the debilitating scrutiny to which its maker has been subjected, can now receive attention on its own merits. And since, as Will now argues, his work constitutes, in some indeterminate measure, divinely inspired prophecy, even if offered as "play," these merits might well be considerable.

But this final stage in Will's argument for apostolic poetry seems doubly compromised. On the one hand, "lunatyk lollares" are yet another self-serving fantasy, a way of imagining a self which could be thoroughly justified without external warrant or interference: such a view will only begin to unravel in the despair which overcomes Will in passus 11. Simultaneously, the very insistence upon the poem as an oral presence to a patronal audience conditions these claims: for the very presence of the poet immediately personalizes him, reveals precisely the extent to which he is an individual (even if one known, not suspiciously out of place, as in London) and not a transcendent voice. Thus the lollere disguise, not just not a madman but a covert learned man in drag, constantly undermines the less sophisticated claims of the *Winner and Waster* poet: such a doubly personalized poet can never voice Truth but only some highly limited and selected version. There will never be a stance, not even in the ancient and comforting alliterative festive community, totally justified in the way Will suggests.

Will's work in the poem—as hermit, apostle, and poet—thus enacts a retrograde swerve. In some sense, Langland represents himself as longing for an unrecapturable past which recedes from the present of his writing—the past of a learned (and ambitious) youth, of the stable social situation of the great hall, of a divine presence which justifies the individual's words and works (first to himself and then automatically to others). Within such a complex, Will's insistence upon his eremitic vocation remains central: perhaps his most retrograde move, a return past monasticism to the ancient apostolic life, it encapsulates the desire for a self stable in intention and act, anchored directly in divinity, and thus of unquestioned social validity. Yet this state itself, as I have described it, only recapitulates those difficulties which have rendered it initially attractive: engrossed within a discourse polyvalent and contentious, modern eremiticism has lost the very singularity which made it initially appear an attractive option. It has become the victim of regulation, not the freehold of the spirit. Finally, acting or living the past, the bible-life which Will most consistently associates with his vocation, proves an act which attains only distrust, not the ever receding Truth it was alleged to embody.

Notes

1. I was inspired to write this article and composed portions of it during the spring of 1990; the article in its present form was completed in 1991. I am especially grateful to my colleagues in the *Piers Plowman* annotation project—John Alford, Steve Barney, Andy Galloway, Traugott Lawler, and Anne Middleton—who got me started on the study and offered intensive feedback. For this publication I should have taken explicit account of the important works unavailable to me in composition: Nicholas Watson, *Richard Rolle and the Invention of Authority* (Cambridge: Cambridge University Press, 1991) and Derek Pearsall, " 'Lunatyk Lollares' in *Piers Plowman*," in *Religion in the Poetry and Drama of the Late Middle Ages in England*, ed. Piero Boitani and Anna Torti (Cambridge: D. S. Brewer, 1990), 163–78. However, as the years between composition and print appearance have lengthened, I have found myself unable to revise constructively what I had previously written and have finally determined to let it stand. *Mea maxima culpa.*

2. Most notably and explicitly Ymaginatif (at B 12.16–28). I discuss that passage in a companion paper, " 'Meddling with Makings' and Will's Work," in *Late-Medieval Religious Texts and Their Transmission: Essays in Honour of A. I. Doyle*, ed. A. J. Minnis (Woodbridge: D. S. Brewer, 1994), 85–94.

3. My unmarked citations always refer to Derek Pearsall, ed., *Piers Plowman, by William Langland: An Edition of the C-Text* (Berkeley and Los Angeles: University of California Press, 1978). I cite Langland's two earlier versions, as appropriate, from the standard Athlone editions, George Kane, ed., *Piers Plowman: The A Ver-*

sion (London: Athlone Press, 1960), and George Kane and E. Talbot Donaldson, eds., *Piers Plowman: The B Version* (London: Athlone Press, 1975).

4. See E. Talbot Donaldson, *Piers Plowman: The C-Text and Its Poet* (New Haven, Conn.: Yale University Press, 1949), 199–226.

5. This professional definition was first noted by Malcolm Godden; see "Plowmen and Hermits in Langland's *Piers Plowman*," *Review of English Studies* 35 (1984): 129–63; and *The Making of Piers Plowman* (London: Longman, 1990). But Godden simply assumes that hermits and plowmen are opposed and that the former are unequivocally associated with the life of contemplation, not that of labor. Following Godden, Vincent Gillespie, " 'Thy Will Be Done': *Piers Plowman* and the *Pater Noster*," in Minnis, ed., *Late-Medieval Religious Texts*, 95–119, assumes that Will is presented as a hermit.

6. Louis Gougaud, *Ermits et reclus: Études sur d'anciennes formes de vie religieuse* (Liguge: Abbaye Saint-Martin, 1928), 51, suggests that English interest in the topic was excessive; Paganus Bolotinus, "Le poème de Payen Bolotin contre les faux ermites," ed. Jean Leclercq, *Revue Bénédictine* 58 (1958): 52–86, inter alia, might suggest that such language forms a conventional discourse of complaint, particularly of a monastic sort.

7. For reasons outlined in " 'Meddling with Makings'," broadly, that hermits are supposed to be isolates and thus silent.

8. These include the following types of materials and specific texts:

a. *Ordo*s, liturgical formulae for the service consecrating a hermit: "Ad benedicendum heremitas," Bodleian Library, MS Tanner 5, pp. 95–98 (hereafter Tanner); Rotha Mary Clay, *Hermits and Anchorites of Medieval England* (London: Methuen, 1914), 199–202; "Forma et ordo qualiter heremita a seculi vanitate conuersus faciet professionem," and "Euery man that takith vpon hym the ordre of an herymyte," Bodleian Library, MS Rawlinson C.549, fols. 4–10, 10–11, + inserted fol. 10 bis. (hereafter Rawlinson); *Liber Pontificalis Chr. Bainbridge Archiepiscopi Eboracensis*, Surtees Society 61 (Durham: Andrews, 1865; hereafter Bainbridge Pont.); *Liber Pontificalis of Edmund Lacy, Bishop of Exeter*, ed. Ralph Baines (Exeter: Roberts, 1847; hereafter Lacy Pont.); "Ordo qualiter heremita facit professionem," Cambridge University Library, MS Mm.iii.21, fol. 193 (hereafter Mm.iii.21).

b. Rules for hermits: in Latin, "the Cambridge Rule" and "the Oxford Rule" (hereafter Camb. Reg. and Oxon. Reg.), both edited by Livarius Oliger, "Regulae tres Reclusorum et Eremitarum Angliae, saec. XIII–XIV," *Antonianum* 3 (1928): 151–90, 299–320, pp. 299–312, 312–20 respectively; the Middle English derivatives of the latter, "Pope off Rom that hyght Celestyn mad this maner off lyf that ys writtyne here ffor lyffing off hermyttis yat lyffis alone withowttynne certan Rewle gyvyne off holy Kyrke," British Library, MS. Sloane 1584, fols. 89–95ᵛ (hereafter Sloane); "Þe Reule of heremytis made and compiled of the blessed pope Celestyne þe v," British Library, MS. Additional 34193, fols. 131–36ᵛ (hereafter Additional); and Bristol Public Library, ms. 6, fols. 137ᵛ–40ᵛ (which I have not seen and know only from its incipit).

c. Records of consecrations in episcopal registers: *Episcopal Register of Robert Rede, Ordinis praedicatorum, Lord Bishop of Chichester, 1397–1415*, Sussex Record Society 8, 11 (London: Mitchell, Hughes, and Clark, 1908; hereafter Rede Reg.);

Register of Edmund Lacy, Bishop of Exeter, 1420–55, part 3, Devon and Cornwall Record Society n.s. 13 (Torquay: Devonshire Press, 1963; hereafter Lacy Reg.); *The Register of Thomas Bekynton, Bishop of Bath and Wells, 1443–1465*, Somerset Record Society 49–50 (London: Bucker and Tanner, 1834–35; hereafter Bekynton Reg.); *Registrum Thome Mylling, Episcopi Herefordensis*, Canterbury and York Society 26 (London: Canterbury and York Society, 1920).

d. General discussions, in the main of the twelfth century: Bernard of Clairvaux, "Epistola contra vitam heremiticam," in Jean Leclercq, *Études sur saint Bernard et le texte de ses écrits* (Rome: Curia Generalis Ordinis Cisterciensis, 1953), 138–39; Ivo of Chartres, "Epistola 192" and "Epistola 256," PL 162: 198–202, 260–62; Richard Methley, "Richard Methley: to Hew Heremyte A Pystyl of Solytary Lyfe Nowadayes," ed. James Hogg, Analecta Cartusiana 31 (Salzburg: Institut für englische Sprache und Literatur, 1977): 91–119; Peter Damian, "Epistola 6.12," PL 144: 392–96, and "Opusculum 15," PL 145: 335–64; Stephen of Muret, "Regula Sancti Stephani," PL 204: 1135–62; Stephen of Tournai, "Epistola 159," PL 201: 445–49.

9. Morton W. Bloomfield, *Piers Plowman as a Fourteenth-Century Apocalypse* (New Brunswick, N.J.: Rutgers University Press, 1962), 32.

10. Cf. Michel Foucault, *The History of Sexuality: Vol. 1, An Introduction*, trans. Robert Hurley (New York: Pantheon, 1978), 92–102.

11. Similarly Lawrence M. Clopper, "The Life of the Dreamer, the Dreams of the Wanderer in *Piers Plowman*," *Studies in Philology* 86 (1989): 261–85, at 275, n. 15. We disagree with Wendy Scase, *Piers Plowman and the New Anticlericalism* (Cambridge: Cambridge University Press, 1989), 138–46.

12. See Kathleen L. Wood-Legh, *Perpetual Chantries in Britain* (Cambridge: Cambridge University Press, 1965), passim, but especially 183, 185, 197, 198.

13. "Monachorum quattuor esse genera, manifestum est. Primum coenobitarum, hoc est monasteriale, militans sub Regula vel abbate. Deinde secundum genus est anachoritarum, id est heremitarum, horum qui non conversationis fervore novicio, sed monasterii probatione diuturna, qui didicerunt contra diabulum multorum solacio iam docti pugnare, et bene extructi fraterna ex acie ad singularem pugnam heremi, securi iam sine consolatione alterius, sola manu vel brachio contra vitia carnis vel cogitationum, Deo auxiliante, pugnare sufficiunt." Benedict of Nursia, *Regula*, ed. H. Rochais and E. Manning (Rochefort: La Documentation Cistercienne, 1980), 10.

14. See Scase, *Piers Plowman and the New Anticlericalism*, 125–26.

15. For the hermit's models, see, in episcopal *ordines*, Lacy Pont., 129; Tanner, 95; Rawlinson, fol. 5ᵛ; Clay, *Hermits and Anchorites of Medieval England*, 200 (and the discussion, 146); Bainbridge Pont., 140–41; Isidore of Seville, *Etymologiae*, ed. W. M. Lindsay, 2 vols. (Oxford: Clarendon Press, 1911), 7.13.3; Camb. Reg., 299; Paganus, line 68; and for discussion, Jean Leclercq, *Chances de la spiritualité occidentale* (Paris: Cerf, 1966), 248–51. On spiritual battle, cf. Benedict above; Leclercq, in *L'eremitismo in occidente nei secoli XI e XII*, Miscellanea del Centro di Studi Medioevali 4 (Milan: Vita e Pensiero, 1965), 39–40; Stephen of Tournai, cols. 446–47; Richard Methley, 112; and the *ordines* (which describe the lord as the hermit's shield): Clay, *Hermits and Anchorites of Medieval England*, 199; Rawlinson,

fol. 5; Mm.iii.21, fol. 193 rab; Bainbridge Pont., 288. The way of perfection connects a hermit's profession routinely with *contemptus mundi, paupertas*, the eschewing of property, and commands to an apostolic profession. Thus *paupertas* alternates with *castitas* as the center of a hermit's *propositum* in all *ordos*; cf. further Richard Rolle, *An Edition of the Judica me Deus*, ed. John Philip Daly (Salzburg: Universität Salzburg, 1984), 11; Oxon. Reg., 312–13 with citation of Matt. 19:21; and the two Middle English derivatives of this rule: Sloane, fols. 89–90; and Additional, fols. 131 ^{V}–32. Such claims to be a "verus pauper Christi," and thus an apostolic soul, underlie Will's claims against the friar at 15.87, 116.

16. At 312, thence Sloane, fol. 89; and Bristol Public Library, fol. 137 ^{V}.

17. The same apology appears at Clay, *Hermits and Anchorites of Medieval England*, 201. Similarly, at *Registrum Thome Myllyng*, 71, the bishop gives Thomas Simpson his habit "and, at the same time, we imposed on him a specific rule of living appropriate to such a habit" ("simul et certam vivendi rectam [sic: read "regulam"?] tali habitui convenientem eidem indiximus"): informatively, although "certa" ("specific"), this rule was not recorded. It thus sounds like the same quasi-official instructions of the two *ordos*.

18. I cite Henrietta Leyser, *Hermits and the New Monasticism: A Study of Religious Communities in Western Europe 1000–1150* (New York: St. Martin's, 1984), 8 (cf. 78).

19. "Coepit igitur leniter monere fratres de salute et profectu animarum suarum, proponens eis propriae voluntatis periculum, paucitatem fratrum, discipulos sine magistro, laicos sine sacerdote, suadens eos ad maiorem et ad meliorem formam religionis," cited by Hubert Dauphin in *L'eremitismo*, 283 n. 49.

20. Bernard of Clairvaux, "Epistola contra vitam heremiticam," 139. Cf. some further twelfth-century examples: Ivo of Chartres, "Epistola 256," PL 162: 260–62; in "Epistola 192," col. 200, he accuses renegade hermits of sarabaitism "so that they may live in private places according to a law they create themselves" ("ut in privatis locis proprio iure vivant"); Paganus, lines 1–3, etc.: "Outside any order, thus a criminal order" ("Ordinis expers, ordo nefandus"; a comparison with monks appears at lines 209–10).

21. Hermit lives ought to be particularly difficult to reconstruct (cf. Leclercq, in *L'eremitismo*, 28 and " 'Meddling with Makings,' " 85–87); the few hermit *vitae* are saints' lives. But at least one outstanding "lollare" career (in this case also Lollard), that of William Swinderby, can be tracked intermittently for about a decade, during which Langland was at work on the C version: see James Crompton, "Leicestershire Lollards," *Transactions of the Leicestershire Archaeological and Historical Society* 44 (1968–69): 18–24. Contrast Swinderby's varied and unregulated career with the regulated vicissitudes of Thomas Scrope; see Norman P. Tanner, *The Church in Late Medieval Norwich, 1370–1532*, Studies and Texts 66 (Toronto: Pontifical Institute of Mediaeval Studies, 1984), 59–60.

22. See the *quaestiones* printed by Oliger, "Regula reclusorum Angliae et Quaestiones tres de vita solitaria saec. XIII–XIV," *Antonianum* 9 (1934): 244, 257 (in both cases drawing on Aquinas, *Summa theologiae*, II ^{a} II ^{ae}, Q. 188, art. 8 [47: 218–22 in the Blackfriars edition]).

23. Richard Rolle, *The Fire of Love*, trans. Richard Misyn, EETS o.s. 106 (London: Methuen, 1914), 26/29–36.

24. Ibid., 29/14–17. Cf. Oxon. Reg., 315: "But he is not alone *that abideth in charity*, for *he abideth in God and God in him*, therefore with him" ("Sed non est solus *qui manet in caritate*, quia *in Deo manet et Deus in eo*, ergo cum eo," citing 1 John 4:16), perhaps Rolle-inspired.

25. "Soli Deo debet heremita obedienciam facere, quia ipse est abbas, prior, et prepositus claustri cordis sui. Episcopus tamen in cuius diocesi habitat vel patrono loci, si fuerit prelatus vel sacerdos bone discretionis, debet notificare vitam suam," Camb. Reg., 304–5; repeated at Oxon. Reg., 313 (thence, Sloane, fols. 90ᵛ–91; Additional, fol. 132), again probably from Rolle—see *The Melos amoris of Richard Rolle of Hampole*, ed. E. J. F. Arnould (Oxford: Blackwell, 1957), 147/27. And see also Wulfric of Haselbury, cited by Dauphin, in *L'eremitismo*, 286 and n. 57; and Arnould's appendix to *The Melos amoris*, 195–209. But Oxon. Reg., 313 (and Sloane, fol. 91; Additional, fol. 132ʳᵛ) also says that the hermit's *votum*, although properly to God alone, may be made to a bishop, and that the hermit may receive his habit from him.

26. See G. Morin, "Rainaud l'ermite et Ives de Chartres: Un épisode de la crise du cénobitisme au xiᵉ–xiiᵉ siècle," *Revue Bénédictine* 40 (1928): 102; and Rolle, *The Melos amoris*, 4/3.

27. For Rolle examples, see *The Fire of Love*, 29/1–2, 30/11–23; *The Melos amoris*, 23/20; for Peter Damian, see "Epistola 6.12," PL 144: 392–93.

28. Rainald, cited by Morin, "Rainaud l'ermite," 101.

29. See note 15 above. More directly in Stephen of Muret's "Regula Sancti Stephani," for Grandmont, PL 204: 1136, 1137, 1138; see the discussions of twelfth-century developments in M-D. Chenu, *La théologie au douzième siècle* (Paris: Vrin, 1957), 225–57; and Lester K. Little, *Religious Poverty and the Profit Economy in Medieval Europe* (Ithaca, N.Y.: Cornell University Press, 1978), 59–96.

30. Cf. Scase, *Piers Plowman and the New Anticlericalism*, 122–23.

31. I cite 12 Rich. II, c. 7, from *Statutes of the Realm* (London: HMSO, 1810), 2: 58. The relevance of this legislation to the passage has previously been noted by Anna P. Baldwin, *The Theme of Government in Piers Plowman* (Cambridge: D. S. Brewer, 1981), 101, n. 9; and Anne Middleton, "William Langland's 'Kynde Name': Authorial Signature and Social identity in Late Fourteenth- Century England," in *Literary Practice and Social Change in Britain, 1380–1530*, ed. Lee Patterson (Berkeley and Los Angeles: University of California Press, 1990), 56, n. 34 (see her considerably more detailed treatment elsewhere in this volume).

32. If he had, it would be that scroll given him by the bishop who had "licensed" him by blessing his habit; see further note 62 below.

33. On the sequential development of these texts, Aelred of Rievaulx's "De institutione inclusarum"—I cite Aelred of Rievaulx, *La vie de recluse*, ed. Charles Dumont (Paris: Cerf, 1961)—shapes the argument of Camb. Reg., in its turn revised into Oxon. Reg., from which three Middle English hermit rules "of Pope Celestine" were translated; see "'Meddling with Makings,'" 89–91. Oliger misdates the Latin texts; both manuscripts are fifteenth century (cf. the possible Rolle citations in notes 24 and 25 above), and the rules respond to impulses similar to Langland's poem.

34. Kempe frequently conceives her status as externally verifiable only by recourse to a textual locus; see such examples as *The Book of Margery Kempe*, ed.

Sanford Brown Meech and Hope Emily Allen, EETS 212 (London: Oxford University Press, 1940), 39/19–26 (and cf. 143/21–144/4), 47/26–35, 152/34–154/14.

35. Recall Scase, *Piers Plowman and the New Anticlericalism*, 125–26.

36. Which should probably be punctuated, "As ankeres, and eremites þat holdeth hem . . . " "Ankeres," by definition, are inclaustrated.

37. See David Aers, *Community, Gender, and Individual Identity: English Writing, 1360–1430* (London: Routledge, 1988), 26–33; and cf. the system of internal passports mandated by the 1388 Statutes.

38. See H. Mayr-Harting, "Functions of a Twelfth-Century Recluse," *History* 60 (1975): 337–52.

39. For examples of such extended pilgrimages outside the cell, see Rotha Mary Clay, "Further Studies on Medieval Recluses," *Journal of the British Archaeological Association* 3d ser. 16 (1953): 80 (a fifteen-month excursion in 1480); Tanner, *The Church in Late Medieval Norwich, 1370–1532*, 62 (a testamentary bequest in 1429 to enable a hermit to make a proxy pilgrimage for the deceased to Rome and Jerusalem); and the hermit who chaperones Margery Kempe to Ipswich (and later turns up at Sheen); *The Book of Margery Kempe*, 226/22–25, 228/22–33, 246/32–247/22.

40. Rolle, *The Fire of Love*, 32/1–8; similarly *The Melos amoris*, 152/17–27 and 155/26–30; and cf. *The Fire of Love*, 27/12 and 48/13, the last of which defines Active Life as running about.

41. See Rolle, *Judica me Deus*, 2; *The Fire of Love*, 35/21–24; *The Melos amoris*, 11/26–12/8.

42. Rolle, *The Fire of Love*, 35/21–22, like Walter Hilton's "De Imagine peccati," in Hilton, *Latin Writings*, ed. John P. H. Clark and Cheryl Taylor, 2 vols., Analecta Cartusiana 124 (Salzburg: Institut für englische Sprache und Literatur, 1987), 89/321–22; and Camb. Reg., 301, uses *discurrere* to describe the actions of vagrants (it also appears in Paganus's title, "Concerning false hermits who run about in their wanderings" ["De falsis heremitis qui vagando discurrunt"]); its contextual opposite is *sedere*.

43. Cf. Middleton, "William Langland's 'Kynde Name,'" 46, 59, n. 45.

44. Examples are absolutely legion; in *ordo*s, see Clay, *Hermits and Anchorites of Medieval England*, 199; Bainbridge Pont., 140–41; Lacy Pont., 130; Tanner, *The Church in Late Medieval Norwich, 1370–1532*, 96–97; Rawlinson, fols. 4ᵛ, 5, 6; Mm.iii.21, fol. 193; for pledges by individual hermits, see Lacy Reg., 88–89; Bekynton Reg., 121–22; Rede Red., 288–89. And one might compare the rigid opposition to sexual activity, expressed in variously misogynistic depictions at Camb. Reg., 303 and 307 (praise of chastity at 308), Rolle, *The Melos amoris*, 101/19–31; and persistently in *The Fire of Love*, 52/16–54/37, 65/31–66/16, 92/22–93/27, 94/32–95/13 (and note the four reproving women of 27/14–37, concluding with a typical self-defense, that Rolle was more interested in the food they might give him than in their bodies); Methley, 113–14. Note also the connection of hermits, chastity, and prophecy in Malory's Grail quest.

45. Tauno F. Mustanoja, "The Suggestive Use of Christian Names in Middle English Poetry," in *Medieval Literature and Folklore Studies: Essays in Honor of Francis Lee Utley*, ed. Jerome Mandel and Bruce A. Rosenberg (New Brunswick, N.J.: Rutgers University Press, 1970), 70.

46. As a hermit feminized by his reliance on a non-male/clerical conception of *ordo*, Will needs antifeminist discourse to reassert his resemblance to the male. Thus the various stock representations of Mede as unruly woman (including echoes in Reason's sermon at 5.128–35) are the obverse of Will's associations with that learnedness which defines the true *clericus*; see further below.

47. See Clay, *Hermits and Anchorites of Medieval England*, 88, 109. Several of Clay's testamentary examples, 109, prove very little: in their absence of reference to wives, they may record bequests of widowers (who professed after being bereaved). What then strikes one about them is the hermits' retention and/or amassing after profession of enough property to make a formal bequest necessary.

48. *Testamenta eboracensia: A Selection of Wills from the Registry at York*, Surtees Society 45 (Durham: The Society, 1836), 343.

49. See *The Book of Margery Kempe*, 23/9–25/19 and 179/6–181/15 respectively.

50. Cf. Clay, *Hermits and Anchorites of Medieval England*, 200, a prayer standard in the *ordos*: "may you deign to bless these garments which signify meekness of heart and contempt of the world, by which your well-disposed servant is visibly marked in keeping with his holy purpose" ("vt hec indumenta humilitatem cordis et contemptum mundi significandus, quibus famulus tuus sancto *visibiliter* est informandus proposito propicius benedicere digneris").

51. See " 'Meddling with Makings,' " and the references to the rather grudging acknowledgment of the ecclesiastical right to bless the new hermit's habit in Oxon. Reg. and its English derivatives, cited note 25 above.

52. For Rolle, see *Breviarium ad usum insignis ecclesie Eboracensis*, Surtees Society 75 (Durham: Andrews, 1880), cols. 790–91, previously cited by Godden, "Plowman and Hermits in Langland's *Piers Plowman*," 161–62; Kempe, of course, follows "normal procedure" in seeking ecclesiastical sanction for both vow and garb, e.g., with Repingdon of Lincoln at 34/9–24.

53. Cf. Paganus's evocation of the second passage at the start of his poem, esp. lines 1–3 and 11–13; and see Scase, *Piers Plowman and the New Anticlericalism*, 120–21.

54. Repeated at Additional, fol. 133; Sloane, fols. 91^V–92. Cf. Clay, *Hermits and Anchorites of Medieval England*, 202 (similarly Rawlinson, fol. 10): "A hermit is not permitted to wear linens, except for underpants; and he ought also to wear only sandals on his feet, always without socks" ("Lineis vti non licebit ei, exceptis femoralibus, pedulis eciam cum sotularibus solum vti debet, caligis semper omissis"). The English "Rule of St. Linus," printed in Oliger, "Regula reclusorum Angliae," 265, insists on a hairshirt and "schoen withowtyn hose"; the penitential Lancelot refuses a linen shirt in favor of retaining his hairshirt, Sir Thomas Malory, *The Works*, ed. Eugène Vinaver (Oxford: Clarendon Press, 1948), 1017/16–30 (see also 927/25–33, 931/7–10, 947/13–15). At least some of this material, like so much hermit discourse, appears to have entered English use through Aelred; cf. *De institutione*, 76, and its reflections at *Ancrene Wisse*, ed. J. R. R. Tolkien, EETS 249 (London: Oxford University Press), 214.

55. Repeated at Additional, fol. 133; Sloane, fol. 92. Also a topic of popular depictions, e.g., Joyce Bazire, ed., *The Metrical Life of St. Robert of Knaresborough*, EETS 228 (London: Oxford University Press, 1953), lines 561–62; the description

of Rolle cited in Hope Emily Allen, *Writings Ascribed to Richard Rolle Hermit of Hampole and Materials for His Biography*, MLA Monographs 3d ser. (New York: D. C. Heath, 1927), 526; Max Kaluza, ed., "The Eremyte and the Outelawe," *Englische Studien* 14 (1890): line 34; from Latinate tradition, cf. Peter Damian, "Opusculum 15," PL 145: 344, 353. In both Clay's *ordo* (199) and Rawlinson (fol. 4), the hermit comes to make his profession "nudis pedibus." But even this humble wear is not without its detractors. Among the more usual complaints about habits, monastics sneer that hermits confuse dirt and sanctity, underdress themselves to make an ostentatious show of holiness; see, e.g., Marbod of Rennes's admonition to Robert of Arbrissel, a famous hermit, "Epistola 6," PL 171: 1480–86, at col. 1483; or Oxon. Reg., 314 (citing Bernard).

56. "[C]um supertunice longe et clause non simplicibus sacerdotibus, sed doctoribus et viris preclaris in dignitate constitutis maxime conveniant," Wood-Legh, *Perpetual Chantries in Britain*, 247, n. 1.

57. Camb. Reg., 306; Oxon. Reg., 314. The complaint is an old one: cf. Paganus on hermits' desire to appropriate other people's clothes, including the adoption of ostentatious (flowing or particolored) habits, not the plain black (gray is the alternate color in English use), e.g., lines 35–38, 84, 112–16, 258, 274.

58. Note the popular discourse in which "friar" actually means "hermit" (a sense unrecognized by MED "frere" n., although sense 1 includes one or two examples applied to nonmendicant orders)—but not the reverse; thus a sign of the hermit's appropriation of title as well as habit: "How a Holy Hermit Prayed a Sinful Woman Pray to God for Him" [IMEV 971], in *The Minor Poems of the Vernon Manuscript, Part I*, ed. C. Horstmann, EETS o.s. 98 (London: K. Paul, Trench, Trubner, 1892), 145–49, lines 46, 47, 75; "The Kyng and the Hermyt" [IMEV 1764], in *Remains of the Early Popular Poetry of England*, ed. W. Carew Hazlitt (London: Russell Smith, 1864), 1: 11–34, lines 116, 244, 291, 309, 327, etc.

59. I take the "lollares" and "lewede ermytes" to be the same persons and believe that the word "lollare" should not be connected specifically with contemporary Lollard heretics. Notice the specificity of the behavior described in 5.29–31, without reference to any system of belief, and the discussions of Scase, *Piers Plowman and the New Anticlericalism*, 150–57, and of Middleton, in this volume.

60. Scase, *Piers Plowman and the New Anticlericalism*, 133, takes too broad a view.

61. "Det sibi episcopus in mandatis quod pro qualibet hora diei statuta ab ecclesia certum dicat numerum oracionum pro salute anime sue et omnium benefactorum suorum deuote impetranda, videlicet primo pro vesperis xx ᵃ Pater Noster cum totidem Aue Maria, pro completorio xiij Pater Noster cum totidem Aue Maria . . . ," *Benefactores* may in fact be the appropriate gloss for "frendes" (5.37); see MED "frend" n., sense 1(b). Cf. Donaldson's point, *Piers Plowman: The C-text and Its Poet*, 212–19, that Will prays both for the living (for their "good estate," their virtuous success in this world), as well as for specific persons in Purgatory.

62. "Si vero fuerit literatus, ita quod sciat dicere horas beate marie virginis cum vij psalmis et letania ac placebo et dirige pro defunctis, extunc cum qualibet horarum illarum dicat ter Pater Noster cum Aue Maria et cum dimidio nocturni Psalterii semel in die omnibus, aliis pretermissis." The Latin of Rawlinson (fol. 9 ʳᵛ) is virtually identical. This distinction between literate and illiterate offices appar-

ently derives from the sources of hermit regulation in orders for enclosed women; cf. Aelred, *De institutione inclusarum*, 66–68; *Ancrene Wisse*, 218–19. "Lewed" hermit offices comprise the full devotions enjoined in the Middle English "Rule of St. Linus," 263–64. The work survives in the autograph of the Norwich hermit Thomas Scrope; see note 21 above. Evidence for non-Latinate (indeed totally illiterate) hermits appears frequently in documents—usually in references to instructions repeated in "lingua materna" or to hermits who can only sign an "X" to the scrolls recording their profession. Similarly, Rawlinson adds to its Latin *ordo* vernacular instructions for the hermit, which originally included (on fol. 10) only "illiterate" devotions; a similar translation to provide the literate office as well was written out and tipped in later (the tab, fol. 10 bis). The producer of this manuscript at least originally felt that the Latin *ordo* provided adequate (and comprehensible) directions for literates, but not for others. Similarly, the English Waynflete Register, cited in Virginia Davis, "The Rule of St. Paul, the First Hermit, in Late Medieval England," *Studies in Church History* 22 (1985): 210, lacks the instructions for literates.

63. Which I discuss in "'Meddling with Makings.'" For the precise terminology, Will may, once again, rely on Statute language. To forestall wage inflation, Parliament requires open hiring meetings, to be held in a public place in boroughs; to these laborers are to "bear openly in their hands . . . their tools (=*lomes*" ("porte[nt] overtement en lour meyns . . . lour instrumentz," 25 Edw. III, c. 2.1; *Statutes*, 1: 311). Will's claim for an equality of manual and spiritual work is perhaps affirmed in B 6.247–49, lines revised out in the C version.

64. I quote 221, but cf. also Donaldson's citation from John of Bridlington (*Piers Plowman: The C-text and Its Poet*, 208–9), in which these prayers are encouraged as the offices of literate laity, with prayers analogous to those of "lewede ermytes" for the illiterate. Again, as Arundel pointed out to Adam Cressvill, hermit and lay status merge.

65. For the usual contents of *Horae* and a good introductory statement about their use, see Christopher de Hamel, *A History of Illuminated Manuscripts* (Oxford: Phaidon, 1986), 159–64. Such a regimen for the learned may be paralleled elsewhere, e.g., Peter Damian, "Opusculum 15," cols. 343–44, 350–52. The hermit rules are somewhat less specific: Camb. Reg., 307, for learned contemplatives, seems to assume regular canonical hours with the recitation of additional Paters, Aves, and Glorias; Oxon. Reg., 318–20 offers the same general materials the *ordo*s associate with learned hermits but disperses them peculiarly. It seems to assume canonical hours with additions; in the English versions (see Additional, fols. 134^V, 135, 136^V; Sloane, fols. 94^{rv}, 95^{rv}) the duties are redefined within the literate/illiterate terms provided by the *ordo*s.

66. Clay, *Hermits and Anchorites of Medieval England*, 200; similarly Tanner, 97; Rawlinson, fol. 7; Bainbridge Pont., 287; Lacy Pont., 130; and Methley, 118.

67. Both Latin rules enjoin overnight silence; see Camb. Reg., 306; Oxon. Reg., 316; Oxon. Reg., 319–20, and its derivatives provide hourly subjects from the life of Jesus for meditation (as, for example, does *The Mirror of St. Edmund*, a text that overtly adopts "religious" rules for lay use).

68. The exact reference of *opera misericordie* remains obscure. Given the frequent allusions to road work, including maintenance of bridges and of chapels,

the phrase may imply responsibility for hospitality ("Feed the hungry"). But these very labors are by their nature *elemosina* and probably qualify as "merciful works" (cf. the injunctions to merchants at 9.31–33 and the possible distinction between self-support and public activities in the commonplace formulation of Clay, *Hermits and Anchorites of Medieval England*, 202).

69. And, more important, they argue that labor in its alternation (its "meddling") with the other duties mentioned in the *ordo*s provides a double source of grace.

70. For the materials, see Camb. Reg., 302, 311–12; Oxon. Reg., 318; thence Sloane, fol. 93^{rv}; and Additional, fol. 133^V.

71. Rawlinson, fols. 9^V and 10^V (the latter English); cf. Clay, *Hermits and Anchorites of Medieval England*, 202; and the English Waynflete Register, cited by Davis, "The Rule of St. Paul, the First Hermit, in Late Medieval England," 212.

72. For documentary examples, see Clay, *Hermits and Anchorites of Medieval England*, 62; Tanner, *The Church in Late Medieval Norwich, 1370–1532*, 61–62; James Hamilton Wylie, *History of England Under Henry the Fourth* (London: Longmans, 1884–1898), 4: 144, n. 11 (a gift of logs for bridge repair); Davis, "The Rule of St. Paul, the First Hermit, in Late Medieval England," 212; Lacy Reg., 90 (an indulgence for gifts toward bridge repairs in Ottery St. Mary, apparently the responsibility of the just professed hermit Thomas Cornish). Rede Reg., 62–63 mentions a hermit who keeps a chapel; Clay, 50–52 has examples of hermits tending lighthouses in aid of sea travelers.

73. See *L'eremitismo*, 230; and cf. Elizabeth D. Kirk, "Langland's Plowman and the Recreation of Fourteenth-Century Religious Metaphor," *Yearbook of Langland Studies* 2 (1988): 1–21.

74. The latter, just as 9.151–52, neatly echoes the Commons petition of 1376, R. B. Dobson, *The Peasants' Revolt of 1381*, 2d ed. (London: Macmillan, 1983), 74; this text should, of course, be read against the satiric genealogy of "lewede ermytes" Will creates at 9.203–18: "Many of the said wandering labourers have become mendicant beggars in order to lead an idle life; and they usually go away from their own districts into cities, boroughs, and other good towns to beg, although they are able-bodied, and might well ease the commons by living on their labour and services."

75. "Parum autem prodest corporalis excercitacio ubi mens, a celestibus cogitandis distracta, in fantasmatibus fallibilium mundanarum rerum non metuit discurrere et oculum cordis ab intencione spiritualis gaudii gustus permittit evagare" (*The Melos amoris*, 23/36–24/3). For examples of the triad, see Rolle, *Judica me Deus*, 17/2; Hilton, "De Imagine peccati," *Latin Writings*, 105/532, and the explicitly entitled "Epistola de leccione, intencione, oracione, meditacione, et aliis" (215–43). "De Imagine," 87/266–70, also contains an extensive series of labors resembling those of the *ordo*s. Rolle's insistence on mental work implies his reliance on a doctrine of non-solicitousness about his "liflode"; see *The Melos amoris*, 24/3–25/18. Note the similar claim of Camb. Reg., 299 (although coexisting in the text with a command to labor: cf. Piers's "Ne *so* bisy be" B 7.123): "Many hermits fled the troubles of this world and God provided for them" ("Multi heremite fugerunt solicitudinem mundi et Dominus eius ministravit"), with a series of examples (including those at 17.9–16) and citation of Ps. 35: 26 (cf. 9.162a).

76. For these restrictions, see Oxon. Reg., 316–17; thence Sloane, fol. 92^V;

and Additional, fol. 133ᵛ; and in *ordos*, Clay, *Hermits and Anchorites of Medieval England*, 202; Rawlinson, fols. 9ᵛ–10. Piers knows at least portions of these hermit schedules; cf. 8.146 "þat eten but at nones," which corresponds to Camb. Reg., 307, Oxon. Reg., 318, explicates the regulations it finds in its predecessor: "the hermit should work with his hands at something for one period before his meal and another period afterwards" ("una vice ante prandium et alia vice post aliquid manibus operetur"). Rolle again proves an odd man out: although he decries work, he also decries fasting for the same reasons, as potentially disruptive of contemplation; see *The Fire of Love*, 25/28–26/18, which includes the argument that fasting is more deleterious than accidentally—once again, his hermit always intends to do well—exceeding moderate diet.

77. See respectively Robert of Knaresborough, lines 273–84 and "Kyng," lines 228–31, 286–87.

78. A point Leclercq notes, *L'eremitismo*, 37. Cf. *Ywain and Gawain*, ed. Albert B. Friedman and Norman T. Harrington, EETS 254 (London: Oxford University Press, 1964), lines 1671–708; the implicit description of Orfeo's banishment, A. J. Bliss, ed., *Sir Orfeo*, 2d ed. (London: Oxford University Press, 1966), lines 227–78; Malory, *The Works*, 927/29–31; and Chretien's *Perceval*, BN fr. 12576, lines 6499–6504.

79. Line 9.250 distinguishes some who "with þe furste sitteth," that is, don't wait for the call: "Amice, ascende superius" (contrast Rolle, *Breviarium*, col. 792, or Will and Patience in passus 15).

80. Cf. Oxon. Reg., 313–14, and note the moneyless "lunatyk lollares" at 9.110, 119. The rules ban monetary alms altogether, and generally hermits are encouraged not even to collect food beyond their personal needs. Although no one in *Piers Plowman* seems guilty of the self-restraint of seeking excess alms so as to distribute them to others, this is another kind of limitation inherent in a variety of eremitical discourses. But "excess," even if given away, may equally be construed as a form of solicitude: see Aelred, *De instititutione*, 48 (thence *Ancrene Wisse*, 212; and Camb. Reg., 310–11), with abundant twelfth-century parallels. Oxon. Reg., 314 acknowledges possible constrained reception of alms, and although refusing to accept this as a licit reason for carrying money, does allow such receipt: "If men should more willingly give the hermit alms than the needy, he should receive those in the name of God and give them to a poor man more needy than himself" (Si libencius dent homines elemosinam sibi quam indigentibus, recipiat illas in nomine Domini et det pauperi qui plus indiget").

81. The terms are exceptionally relevant to Langland's depiction of "goddes munstrals"; see below.

82. See Camb. Reg., 302, 311, the latter quoting Aelred, *De institutione*, 48; and Oxon. Reg., 314–15. And compare Kempe's various efforts at supporting herself, perhaps most notably in her Roman poverty, *The Book of Margery Kempe*, 93/20–94/7.

83. Cf. Paganus, lines 73–84, 211ff; and see Scase, *Piers Plowman and the New Anticlericalism*, 137.

84. "Ipse [Rolle] autem in prandio tam perfectus erat custos silencii, ut nec verbum quidem de ore eius procederet. Cum vero ad sufficienciam comedisset, surrexit priusquam mensa subtraheretur, et abire disposuit. Armiger autem qui eum

vocaverat dixit hoc non esse consuetudinis, et sic iterato eum residere coegit. Finito vero prandio iterum voluit abscessisse, sed armiger querens cum eo privatum habere colloquium ipsum detinuit" (*Breviarium*, cols. 792–93; see further 792–94). Its context requires some specification. Rolle's very *propositum heremite* is at stake here and animates his repeated effort to escape: at this moment, at the very inception of his career, he is terrified that his host will force him to return to his father and the life of the world. Of course, Kempe's efforts at "holy conversation," which I take up again below, are also relevant.

85. Cf. Margery Kempe's role as an efficacious orant for the souls of the dying, *The Book of Margery Kempe*, 53/29–54/7, 172/35–173/14. In addition, a good many of her prophetic efforts are associated with deathbed consolations, prognosis of diseases apparently mortal.

86. Among other examples in Rolle, see *The Fire of Love*, 26; *The Melos amoris*, 57/4–12. Compare Paganus's scathing attack on hermits who seek the urban "curiae" of the great, lines 85–90, 123–26, etc. However, Margery Kempe seems to have had minimal qualms on this score; cf., e.g., the reference to being in the household of Joan Beaufort at 133/22–134/12.

87. Cf. Rolle, *The Melos amoris*, 24/5–6: "Contemplation is also work" ("Est utique contemplacio labor"); contrast Camb. Reg.'s rejection of "spiritual work," above.

88. Cited, along with "pax huic domo" (Luke 10: 5) at Oxon. Reg., 316; thence Additional, fol. 133ᵛ.

89. For such querulous responses, see Michael G. Sargent, "Contemporary Criticism of Richard Rolle," in *Kartausermystik und -mystiker: Dritter Internaler Kongress über die Kartausergeschichte und -spiritualität*, Analecta Cartusiana 55 (Salzburg: Institut für Anglistik und Amerikanistik, 1981), 160–87; and Jonathan Hughes, *Pastors and Visionaries: Religion and Secular Life in Late Medieval Yorkshire* (Woodbridge: Boydell Press, 1988), passim.

90. Moreover, they dissipate any sense of penitential conclusion or advancement. The removal of Robert the Robber, whose *opera satisfactionis* close off the B Version, leaves the scene without a climax, potentially exemplifying that "roaming in remembrance" Anne Middleton discusses in "Making a Good End: John But as a Reader of Piers Plowman," in *Medieval English Studies Presented to George Kane*, ed. Edward Donald Kennedy, Ronald Waldron and Joseph S. Wittig (Woodbridge: D. S. Brewer, 1988), 247–50. See also my essay, "Robert the Ruyflare and His Companions," in *Literature and Religion in the Later Middle Ages: Philological Essays in Honor of Siegfried Wenzel*, ed. Richard G. Newhauser and John A. Alford (Binghamton, N.Y.: Medieval and Renaissance Texts and Studies, 1995), 81–96.

91. That instrument was losing its place of preeminence among royal stringmen during the reign of Edward II. Its leading role now passed to the ancestors of modern strings, fiddlelike instruments of greater range, the *vielle* and the *geige*; see Constance Bullock-Davies, *Menstrellorum multitudo: Minstrels at a Royal Feast* (Cardiff: University of Wales Press, 1978), 35 The verb "fithele" (7.107), which refers to these instruments, is surely, as Pearsall suggests, a figurative usage; cf. Donaldson's comment, 147, that Langland "is getting farther and farther from the reality of everyday entertainment" (which draws attention to Will's potentially real and

nonfigurative self-representation here). In fact, Langland imagines a return to a past (and glorious) age of true moral "making."

92. Scase, *Piers Plowman and the New Anticlericalism*, 149–50, believes otherwise; I address her views on the "Ilchester Prologue" in my *Pursuing History: Middle English Manuscripts and Their Texts* (Stanford, Calif.: Stanford University Press, 1996), 204–14. Associations of Will with a life of learning, rather than simple social commentary, form an initiative of the B Version—and, as we have seen, are elaborated and intensified in C.

93. Kempe's use of a vocabulary like "dalyawns" (e.g., *The Book of Margery Kempe*, 97/37) to describe her unlicensed holy speech resonates helpfully with Will's constantly conditioned description of his poetry as a form of "play." See further Anne Middleton, "Narration and the Invention of Experience: Episodic Form in *Piers Plowman*," in *The Wisdom of Poetry: Essays in Early English Literature in Honor of Morton W. Bloomfield*, ed. Larry D. Benson and Siegfried Wenzel (Kalamazoo, Mich.: Medieval Institute Publications, 1982), 116–19.

94. I concur with Middleton, "William Langland's 'Kynde Name,'" 57–58, rather than Clopper's suggestion, Clopper, "The Life of the Dreamer," 262–63, 272–76, that the poem executes a narrative loop. One might compare 5.2 with Wit's endorsement of sexuality at B 9.182–86a, a passage which suggests that the dreamer here is still *yong and yeep* (in contrast to 22.193–98, where he is rejected by his wife for impotence); in the C version (11.179–83), *Concupiscentia carnis* encourages similar behaviors.

95. See Thorlac Turville-Petre, "The Prologue of *Wynnere and Wastoure*," *Leeds Studies in English* n.s. 18 (1987): 20–21. I cite *Winner and Waster* from Thorlac Turville-Petre, *Alliterative Poetry of the Later Middle Ages: An Anthology* (London: Routledge, 1989), 41–66.

96. Ample evidence, signaled by the use of "whan" 5.1 (which implies a temporary residence) suggests that such a locale is not properly the dreamer's. Not only does the remainder of the "Visio" occur during a Malvern morning, but, as M. L. Samuels argues in "Dialect and Grammar," in *A Companion to Piers Plowman*, ed. John A. Alford (Berkeley and Los Angeles: University of California Press, 1988), 201–12, Langland's speech reflects the dialect of the same area, southwestern Worcestershire. Will is not in his home locale, as Middleton, "William Langland's 'Kynde Name,'" 58–60 trenchantly demonstrates.

97. In some sense, this forms the very metier of the poetry in Langland's first vision—where the entire career of Lady Meed narratively argues out the relevance of differing discursive contexts: biblical rhetoric (and if so, what passage?) or that practice associated with royal administration.

98. Cf. the numerous examples of the topos: the prologue to *The Wars of Alexander*, the opening scenes of *Gawain* and of *Morte Arthure*, the various feast scenes of *Cleanness*, the dinner cum council of *Siege of Jerusalem*, lines 949–1020.

99. The source also of 12.39–47 (from the related parable of Matt. 22) and of the subsequent C version expansion in 7.292–306.

100. The distinction answers that of 7.79, if one reads "Penaunse" there as enacted by the infirm of line 108.

101. See Scase, *Piers Plowman and the New Anticlericalism*, 63–64, etc.

102. Whether or not *Piers Plowman* coopts the space of gospel narrative, as David A. Lawton argues, "The Unity of Middle English Alliterative Poetry," *Speculum* 58 (1983): 72–94, the alliterative tradition generally may be typified by its swerve from overtly New Testament subject matter. The analogy of Margery Kempe is again worth pursuing here: she, too, faces modern resistance to gospel narrative at table (e.g., *The Book of Margery Kempe*, 65/33–36), yet simultaneously finds that an insistence on such T/truth(s) constructs a true feast (e.g., 140/21–23).

103. Cf. Rolle on the value of a domestic hermit to a rich man, *The Fire of Love*, 42/4–8 or Oxon. Reg., 315, on refusing to flatter. And, of course, Kempe ceaselessly rewards her various hosts and their households with such sharp words of correction (see, e.g., her rebuke of the rich man, 108/27–35).

104. Similarly the locution "godes boyes" (9.127); cf. the other uses of the noun, 9.194, 8.264 (and B 11.204), 20.98.

105. Cf. Stephen A. Barney, "The Plowshare of the Tongue: The Progress of a Symbol from the Bible to *Piers Plowman*," *Mediaeval Studies* 35 (1973): 261–93.

106. Which Will clearly has to avoid, since it requires examination and a license.

107. For Wulfric, see Mayr-Harting, "Functions of a Twelfth-Century Recluse," 341; and for William, Clay, *Hermits and Anchorites of Medieval England*, 158–60.

108. See, e.g., the confrontation with the unbelieving monk, *The Book of Margery Kempe*, 26/3–27/15.

2

Langland and the Bibliographic Ego

Kathryn Kerby-Fulton

I. Preface: Historical and Codicological Approaches
to Medieval Authorship

THIS ESSAY LOOKS AT Langland's C-text *apologia* in relation to the political conditions and conventions of medieval publication.[1] Langland inserted more plausible and extensive reference to his own authorship in the
apologia than he did in any other passage in the three versions of the poem,
yet little effort has been made to locate the historical and *bibliographical*
moment which might have prompted it.[2] The fact that we know so very
little about Langland might seem good reason for refraining from such an
attempt, but in fact I believe that we are beginning to know more than
we realize, thanks to some recent, though isolated, findings of textual,
dialectal, and codicological scholarship on the poem.[3] These fragmentary
findings can be gathered together to create the beginnings of a composite
picture with the help of evidence from two (mostly) unrelated fields. First,
although we still lack detailed codicological analysis of most *Piers* manuscripts, the burgeoning area of medieval "manuscript studies" has illuminated the production, marketing, and reception of many contemporary
texts for medieval readers, and some of these findings can be applied, by
extension, to Langland's case.[4] Second, Renaissance historicist criticism
offers a variety of concepts for the examination of authorship in a concrete
historical setting (it also offers a variety of blind spots, but these are at least
different from the habitual ones medievalists indulge, so they need not
trouble us overly here).[5] Both approaches, judiciously applied, can provide
practical insights into audience response and the authorial strategies of
publication and revision dictated by such response—problems raised tan-

talizingly but only abstractly by theorists like Jauss and Iser.[6] In particular, the present paper asks what the evidence for Langland's earliest readership can tell us about the circumstances in which he published the C-text. It will also ask what it was about the impact of his earlier poetry that induced him to add such an *apologia* to the final version of his poem. In short, what did he hope the *apologia* would *do* in a personal and political, rather than in an aesthetic sense?[7]

It is to Renaissance scholarship that medievalists must turn to find a sophisticated terminology for the study of politicized authorship. Emphasizing the political and social rather than the aesthetic aspirations of Renaissance poets, the impetus of historicist scholarship for well over a decade now, for better or for worse, has been to see poets as most often writing from precarious social positions, trying to win favor and patronage, and using the language of (for instance) love poetry to negotiate the economic, social, and polemical difficulties of their situations. Whatever one thinks of this impetus (and it has had many critics), one of its unquestionable and irreversible effects has been the shattering, for once and for all, of New Criticism's sanguine illusion that "author" and "persona" may be neatly distinguished one from another. At the same time and quite independently, manuscript studies have shown that medieval readers would not have recognized the New Critic's neat distinctions either. The upshot is that the poetic "I" speaker now stands in a more *historical* light than most medievalists have hitherto been comfortable discussing him (or her).[8] It is in this uncomfortable, more historical light (some might say half-light) that the present paper seeks to locate the "I" of Langland's *apologia*.

My own understanding of authorial goals and difficulties in the age before copyright has been greatly enhanced by three different concepts central to the work of Arthur Marotti, Annabel Patterson, and Joseph Loewenstein, respectively. Applying their concepts to medieval authorial history without committing anachronism is tricky, but well worth the risk. Take, for instance, Marotti's emphasis on the importance of a poet's first readers, that is, either his coterie or, to use Kane and Donaldson's less loaded term, his "group of supporters" (122, n.47) — the people who inevitably formed the immediate and intended audience of a pre-copyright writer. The presence of such readers has rarely been emphasized in Langland scholarship (Kane and Donaldson's timid reference to it is only elaborated in a footnote), but manuscript studies is slowly revealing that all medieval poets had such a group of immediate readers, and that the term "coterie" is not only applicable to court poets. What Marotti says of Sidney is, as we shall see, very suggestive even for a writer as different as Langland: "He thus invited his sophisticated readers to exercise their critical faculties to such a degree that the whole work must have begun to take the shape of a *metapoem, that is a literary work whose metacommunicative character made the relationship of poet and audience more important* than either the ostensible amorous subject-matter or its sociopolitical coordinates" (emphasis mine). Although we still know relatively little about Langland's closest and most sophisticated readers, there is enough evidence to suggest that *Piers*, too, was similarly coded in order to function as a "metapoem" for a group—how small?—of enviable intellectual agility. These and other questions about Langland's initial "group of supporters" will be discussed in sections V and VI below.

The necessity of encoding, of creating a metapoem, leads us to the question of Langland's relationship with political and ecclesiastical authorities, and the role of authorial intention, especially in the post-1381 world of literary London. Annabel Patterson's study of censorship in Renaissance literature[10] emphasizes the role of reader response, anticipated or actual, in the shaping of a literary work; for Patterson one of the most powerful tools authors used for controlling reader response was "functional ambiguity," a self-defensive authorial strategy of carefully coded communication with a select portion of the audience. This rhetorical strategy is at least as old as Quintillian, who had this advice for writers:

You can speak as openly as you like against . . . tyrants, as long as you can be understood differently, because you are not trying to avoid giving offence, only its dangerous repercussions. If danger can be avoided by some ambiguity of expression everyone will admire its cunning.[11]

Any writer who is self-conscious enough to offer a provocative exemplum or idea, and then expressly, indeed metadiscursively, state that he dares not interpret it, as Langland explicitly does in more than one instance, is certainly "not trying to avoid giving offence, only its dangerous repercussions."

This paper will argue that Langland feared the wrath of some of his readers, both those in authority and his social peers, after 1381, and that the C *apologia* attempts to use authorial intrusion into the text in order to negotiate these difficulties. Joseph Loewenstein coined the term "bibliographic ego" to describe the kind of authorial intrusion which serves to establish, protect, and/or market—not simply glorify—the author.[12] Putting a more practical construction on the long-denigrated "literary vanities" of Ben Jonson, Loewenstein describes Jonson's outbursts of bibliographic ego as

attempts to gain or regain control of both literary production and literary message in "a market place made harrowingly unstable by plague and
censor" (270). Moreover, Jonson's were times in which, like Langland's
own, everyone associated with a censored work—author, publisher, even
(in cases of heresy) an individual reader—could be punished by the authorities.[14] After having been censored and even imprisoned twice, Jonson
sought the means to secure support and protection for himself through the
strategy of self-representation in his own texts. What I wish to explore is
the possibility that Langland's *apologia* was meant to do something similar.

His *apologia*, as this paper will argue, was written in a particular historical context in response to the pressures, political, ecclesiastical and
authorial, created, among other things, by the misappropriation of his
poem by rebels in 1381.[15] Moreover, we know that the early dissemination
of *Piers* was problematic for Langland because the B-text upon which he
based his revisions was corrupt, and because parts of C were in circulation—whether by authorial sanction or not we do not know—prior to the
publication of the C-text.[16] Furthermore, as I shall argue, Langland's use of
distinctive conventions of *apologia* and, possibly, of literary mendicancy, in
conjunction with a new self-defensiveness and social conservatism, points
to his being concerned to present an authorial, rather than a simply fictional "I" (in this passage at least). Since we know little about Langland or
about the publication of *Piers*, much of what follows will be based on ex-
trapolation from what we know of the conditions of medieval publication
for other authors. This is, of course, in one sense very speculative, but informed speculation is the best we can do until further study of the poem's
textual and codicological problems reveals more. In the meantime we deal
in what Kane and Donaldson call "historical likelihood" (122).

The study of other poets of the Middle Ages about whom we know
more tells us that they wrote themselves into their texts in an age before
copyright for one of three reasons: (1) in an attempt to establish authorship, and sometimes to regain control of a text fraudulently disseminated
or otherwise misappropriated or interpreted; (2) in an attept to solicit patronage or other kinds of support; or (3) in an attempt to reenter a world
of offended readership. Recent textual work on *Piers*, when illuminated by
what we know of medieval anxieties about authorial credibility, political
sensitivity, and coterie circulation, can provide some clues to Langland's
situation at the time of publication of the C-text. What I hope to establish is the relevance of all three reasons in our thinking about the intended
function of the C-*apologia*.

II. Langland, Authorship, and Self-Representation in a Manuscript Culture

Recent studies of authorship and authorial self-representation in late medieval literature have shown that a significant shift in the medieval conception of the author occurs in the thirteenth century. Referring to Chenu's well-known account of the distinction between the *auctor* (meaning "one who produces") and *actor* (meaning "one who does or performs"),[17] De Looze explains that *actor* comes to replace *auctor*, and the latter becomes associated with *auctoritas*. The result was "an important shift in mentality" in which readers came to "relate the authority of a text to the personal experience of its author, making the authorial *vécu* an *authenticating feature*" (emphasis mine). Thus the blurring of author/persona distinctions which makes the reading of "Will" in *Piers Plowman* so difficult reflects, one assumes deliberately, the contemporary interest in "the authorial *vécu*." In fact, as marginal annotations in some Chaucer manuscripts show, later medieval readers were well aware of these concepts, and the fact that different annotators might use either *actor* or *auctor* in describing, say, the same narratorial voice in *Troilus*, suggests that our current difficulties in distinguishing *actor* from *auctor* in first-person narratives were shared by medieval readers.[18] *Piers* annotators (at least, those we know so far) were similarly divided on the subject.[19] However, there are many parallels in reader response to those turned up in an exhaustive study of the illustrated manuscripts of *The Divine Comedy*, showing that fourteenth-century readers read Dante's poem overwhelmingly as the authentic visionary experience of its author, evidence which independently corroborates De Looze's assertion.[20] Apparently when Langland wrote the *apologia* he was well aware of such readerly expectations.

This late medieval interest in, or expectation of, authorial authenticity is related to a more specific concern, especially in the marketing and reception of contentious literature, to authenticate, or at least scrutinize, the life of the author. Anne Middleton's essay in the present volume makes the intriguing case that Langland represented the *apologia* as a prosecution under the 1388 Statute of Labourers, and, moreover, that he likely did so in order to deflect the possibility of an even more dangerous prosecution at the hands of ecclesiastical authorities, newly alerted to Lollardy. Clearly, the *apologia* is played out as an interrogation under *something*—and something *public*, at that. The note of self-defensiveness is unmistakeable and it is also new—this is not the conventional self-deprecation of dream vision, nor is it the purely private self-excoriation of Imaginatif's rebuke in B (12.16–28). But this new self-defensiveness has been, as always in Langland, radically interiorized; his deft use of allegory conceals agency brilliantly, so we may never know for certain what institutional authority—or authorities—he is invoking in it or why. But whether Reason and Conscience "represent" secular authorities promulgating the 1388 Statute, or ecclesiastical authorities probating visionary claimants[21]—or both, or neither—it is clear that Langland is newly on the defensive here *as a public writer*. Publicity was a delicate matter for medieval authors: medieval visionaries, for instance, were never blamed for having visions, but rather for making them public, and ecclesiastical authorities probating visionaries were not much interested in the literary niceties of *actor/auctor* distinctions. Indeed, literature dealing with *probatio* issues, newly in circulation in England in the 1380s and 1390s, captures the mood of some of the revisions Langland made in the C-text, and some of the questions he has Reason and Conscience ask in the *apologia*.[22] Many of his C revisions, even to the opening of the poem, for instance, seem calculated to shift the genre of the poem from the *chanson d'aventure* style of B to something more like (though not yet entirely like) the autobiographical tendency in serious religious literature; such revisions seem generally aimed at toning down or cunningly obfuscating the radical tendencies of the "I" speaker. But whatever legislative or ecclesiastical factors lie behind Langland's extraordinary autobiographical defensiveness in the C 5 *apologia*, there can be no doubt that he is acutely and suddenly sensitive to audience response.

The fourteenth century was the period of new concern with bibliographical control, when authors "took an active part in the compilation of grand codices of their works, in editing *corpora* which were explicitly or implicitly analogous to their own lives, and even in the articulation of programs of manuscript illustration" (De Looze, 168). Authors explored the possibilities of "naming by not naming" in elaborate anagrams and acrostics (165), which depended for their intelligibility upon the readers' knowledge of the author's name—in other words, they were written for a known (and knowing) audience. In this period, then, there is a movement "vers la société de l'écriture," as Hult says,[23] a movement which is well established by the time Langland was writing. It seems, then, since Langland used these anagrammatic signatures, that he too was writing, in the first instance, for a known and knowing audience—at least, it is unlikely that he would have used these anagrams if he were unknown to those to whom he *wanted* to identify himself. Thus we do Langland an injustice by assuming that, because of his historical obscurity *to us*—or even to later medieval audiences—he had no immediate authorial circle who could appreciate the sophistication of his poetic strategies, or offer advice, as Hoccleve's literary friend does in his "Dialogue," about what is safe or unsafe to publish.[24]

That it should be somehow unusual to stress the historical reality of Langland's authorship of *Piers Plowman* is a peculiarity of *Piers* studies. It runs counter to an attitude built up over decades of well-intentioned scholarship on the poem, from the early authorship controversies which divided Langland into as a many as five authors, through the New Critical insistence that every "I" speaker has only aesthetic existence as a *persona*, to Deconstruction's view that Will functions merely as an "unstable analogy"[25]—whatever that may mean. The problem of (what we will for shorthand call) making *actor/auctor* distinctions in *Piers Plowman* has received extended discussion elsewhere, most recently and helpfully in Steven Justice's observation that in the *apologia* Langland must be either creating "what he takes to be a generalized portrait of authorship or offer[ing] his own authorship as a generalizable example of it."[26] What we need to take into account in deciding between Justice's two choices is that Langland's authorial portrait of Will shifted dramatically throughout the three versions of the poem, from the minstrel/scribe of A, to the poet who meddles with makings in B, to the defensively confessional but obliquely authoritative spokesman in C.[27] In the poem's final version, as we will see, he attains a kind of defensiveness and urgency which is hard to imagine as a merely *general* concern for the state of authorship. Langland refers explicitly in the *apologia* to audience reaction to his poetry (C 5.1–5), and I see no reason not to treat these remarks as authorially, that is, *bibliographically* relevant. Therefore, of the two choices Justice offers, I assume that Langland is working with his *own* authorial experience and doing so for particular purposes in the C-*apologia*, and that those purposes have to do with a combination of current affairs, personal history, and bibliographic concerns. *Piers Plowman* was not written by the fourteenth-century Zeitgeist, nor, I think, did Langland mean to give the impression it had been— although there were no doubt moments in 1381 and shortly thereafter when Langland may have wished the delusion possible.

Who, then, is the speaker of these lines of the C-*apologia*, appearing as the "Will" of the poem, and yet not the "Will" of the poem, as both *actor* and *auctor* at once? The whole passage strikes the reader (this reader, at least) as a new *metadiscursive* moment, when "in a self-conscious stance, . . . [the author] steps outside his text, names himself elliptically," thereby initiating "a metadiscursive dialogue with the reader or listener."[28] Brown, following Hult, explains that "in many medieval works, especially from the *Roman de la Rose* on, the presentation of the author occurs in a complex layering of subjectivities, which proceed from a kind of external authoritative figure . . . to a more internal fictional one. . . . Previously it [the self-conscious authorial voice] had been relegated to distinctly defined positions outside the text, to prologues and epilogues. . . . In the *Rose*, however, the persona of the first person voice is multiplied in an intricate meshing of narrative levels as the narrator occupies positions before, during, and after the recounted events" (112–13). So, too, in *Piers Plowman*, but never more so than in the *apologia*, which almost supplies the authorial prologue that, as Middleton has observed, the poem so oddly lacks.[29] The assumption underlying this paper, then, is that among the complex "layers of subjectivities" that make up the "I" speaker of the poem, the speaker of the *apologia* is much closer to the "external authoritative figure" than to the "more internal fictional one" Langland creates elsewhere, and that the reason for this is Langland's felt need at the historical moment of the C-text to communicate more directly—or at least to *appear* to do so[30]—with his public.

In emphasizing the historical aspect of the *apologia*, I have no wish to cast doubt on the semiotic significance of the passage as an elaborate form of authorial signature, so convincingly argued by Anne Middleton. Nor do I disagree with her view (though I will slightly qualify it) that it is anachronistic to treat such passages as "a primitive attempt at copyright."[31] But acts of medieval authorial self-representation were also usually meant to perform "real" as well as symbolic functions.[32] Although the signature in the *apologia* undoubtedly contains semiotic resonances, the passage *as a whole* appears to be a response, I believe, to very temporal events and anxieties. To understand it we must know the way in which Langland's poem impacted on its *first* audiences (the C-text was written for at least its *third*),[33] how Langland's revisions reflect that response and how the conditions of late fourteenth-century publication might have influenced Langland. In short, we need to consider the historical evidence as well as the semiotic. Only further (and massive) textual, codicological, and cultural work can really supply us with the evidence for these historical readings, and a single paper, obviously, is not going to go very far in any of these areas, but if it serves the purpose of engaging other scholars in these problems it will have done enough to satisfy its own author's bibliographic ego.[34]

We need, then, a very precise sense of the historical context of the C-text. The exceedingly topical nature of all three of Langland's texts is amply demonstrated by Langland's own revisions, which show him fine-tuning his C version in response to the most topical issues of the 1380s. As James Simpson has shown, Langland's poetry, which had been pushing the limits of official acceptability for many years, suddenly found itself seriously beyond them in 1382. The Blackfriars' Council of that year banned several ecclesiastical and theological opinions as heretical; among these Simpson cites three of which the B-text falls foul (#5, #17, #23).[35] What is interesting about these banned conclusions and the relevant passages Simpson cites from B is that if we take his suggestions one step further, and actually compare them with the corresponding passages in C, we find that in each case Langland made significant alterations in his final version so as to suppress the ideas most likely to offend.[36]

The first banned conclusion he cites is #5: "if a man were duly contrite, any exterior confession is superfluous or of no use to him," in relation to which Simpson draws our attention to B 11.80–82, which does indeed contain reference to this notion explicit enough, one assumes, to have gotten Langland into trouble. But the reference appears within an even larger passage of FitzRalphian antimendicantism, *all* of which is suppressed in the C version. The context is Will's complaint to the friar that he is interested only in the wealthy; he specifically asks the friar why "youre Couent coueiteþ to confesse and to burye/ Raþer þan to baptiʒe barnes," since a baptised man can "Thoruʒ contricion [clene] come to þe heiʒe heuene/— *Sola contricio [delet peccatum]*—/Ac [a] barn wiþouten bapteme may noʒt be saued" (B 11.76–77, 81–82). The complaint that the friars took up only the most lucrative kinds of pastoral work, notably confession and burying, was a well-worn plank of FitzRalph's platform.[37] When Langland revised this passage for C he removed lines 75–83, thus deleting not only the suggestion potentially offensive to the Blackfriar's Council conclusions that contrition is enough in itself, but also deleting the FitzRalphian attack, which suggests that he was becoming more cautious in his antimendicantism—either because of ecclesiastical concerns (the friars were formidable enemies) or because of a new appreciation for Franciscan spirituality (something which the major C-additions in 5 and 9 suggest)—or both.[38]

The second banned conclusion that Simpson cites is #17: "that temporal lords should be able, at their own judgement, to take away temporalities from habitually delinquent ecclesiastics, and that the people should be able to correct habitually delinquent lords at their own judgement." This no doubt accounts for an important C-revision which deletes Will's apparent approbation (B 10.336) for the role that lordship will play in despoiling the

monasteries, as prophesied in B 10.322–35 (cf. C 5.168–80). It is most interesting that he reacted to this particular ban by removing a remark which
was associated with the "I" speaker, but not by removing Reason's lengthy
prophecy to the same effect—this would seem to confirm that Langland,
like other medieval prophetic writers, thought prophecy a safer medium
than even fictional exposition (and that he, too, did not trust unfriendly
readers to make subtle *actor/auctor* distinctions). It might also explain why
Langland felt he could leave largely intact B 15.560–65 (the passage Simpson suggests in relation to this banned conclusion), because it too comes
in a prophetic context. This revision is also interesting in relation to Langland's apparent sympathy in all versions for the "gentle" classes.[39] We might
note that although he makes the suggestion in more than one place that the
clergy can be corrected, no one could accuse him of contravening the other
half of this banned conclusion, that *lords* may be corrected by the people.

The third banned conclusion which Simpson cites is #23: "That friars
should be constrained to acquire their food through the labour of their
hands, not through begging," to which he suggests that B 20.234–421
and 384–85 might prove offensive. Unfortunately, Langland seems to have
made no revisions to the last two passus of the poem, so a comparison with
C here would be fruitless. However, the C-*apologia* itself deals precisely,
although more widely, with this ecclesiological issue, asserting in the most
uncompromising terms, as we shall see below, the right of *all* clergy to live
without manual labour. Moreover, it is obvious that Langland was thinking a great deal about fraternal issues when writing the *apologia* because of
its close connections with the C 9 additions.[40]

In short, we are coming to be able to say something about what historical factors motivated some of Langland's revisions. The concerns of the
Blackfriars' Council, like the publicity his poem had received during the
Revolt, would seem to have been direct factors, as perhaps were the concerns of the decade with *probatio* (well represented in Middle English works
like *The Chastising of God's Children*) and with able-bodied mendicants (as
represented in legislation like the 1388 Statute).[41] Moreover, the poem's
handling both by its author and by its scribes during the 1380s and 1390s
suggests the sensitivity of its fabric to topicality (Langland himself removed the outdated reference to Chichester as mayor in the C-revision).[42]
From a historical perspective even the changes in his modes of signature
are significant, as we shall see. Middleton has pointed out that if Langland's signatures were meant to be records of authorship, they were "conspicuous failures," because even readers prior to the publication of C (i.e.,

the rebels) came to think of the poem's chief spokesman as Piers, not as William Langland[43]—a misreading they share with many C-range undergraduate essays today, one might add. The extent to which the "failure" of the more obscure C-anagram is in fact a form of what Annabel Patterson calls "functional ambiguity," motivated by the author's desire for a more select audience (i.e., a desire to reach an intended "public" and obfuscate an unwanted "audience," to use the terminology of another of Middleton's important articles)[44] will be discussed later in this paper. But clearly some group of people in the late 1370s and early 1380s, however small, knew that *Langland* was the author of this controversial poem, and these people likely knew him. As we are coming to understand from recent textual and codicological work, the initial audience of a Middle English poem was a very specific one, perhaps especially if a work was politically sensitive. As Malcolm Parkes has recently indicated with respect to the early circulation of Gower's *Vox clamantis*:

I suggest that these early surviving copies had been circulated to members of the circle of Gower's immediate friends and associates, who perhaps shared his political sympathies, and formed his first audience. . . . The subsequent pattern of scribal activity in these readers' copies becomes more intelligible when we remember the topical nature of Gower's writings: this is particularly evident in the Latin works where he could express his political views more freely in that language. . . . The owners of the manuscripts must have been persons who knew that Gower had revised his text (or, perhaps, revised his views). They wanted the revisions entered into their own copies . . . *as and when they got to know about them.* (my emphasis)[45]

No doubt medieval authors dreamed of reaching a wide audience eventually, just as modern ones do, but the technology of reproduction was slow and unreliable, the tendency toward scribal/editorial interference (or, if one prefers, "social authorship")[46] was rampant, and the size of literate communities with an active interest in Middle English literature was comparatively small (one notes, for instance, that Richard II owned no English books himself and that Chaucer's initial audience seems to have been a close circle of like-minded social peers).[47] Moreover, recent work on London book production in the decades just before and after the turn of the century shows a very small group of stationers, limners, and scriveners working cooperatively in close if not cramped quarters along the same street, copying all the major Middle English writers (including Langland) and even commissioning poetry from time to time.[48] The evidence, which of course is by no means all in, points toward a much more specific set of circumstances—literary, political and ecclesisastical—for the creation and early dissemination of Langland's poem than has hitherto been imagined. Publishing a large Middle English poem in late fourteenth-century London could not have been an *entirely* faceless activity, and there is every likelihood that Langland's anagrams were not failures in the immediate context for which they were produced. More likely, they were failures in certain quarters, and this was just what Langland intended—isn't it just as well for Langland after all that John Ball either did not know his name or chose not to use it if he did? It is this evidence—that is, what little evidence we have of this kind—that I wish to consider in what follows.

III. Establishing Authorship and the Bibliographic Ego in a Manuscript Culture

Even the existence of the printing press for more than a century by Jonson's time had not replaced the older means of transmission by manuscript, nor had it solved the problems of textual instability and literary property which had plagued medieval authorship. What Loewenstein says of Renaissance authors, then, is equally applicable to medieval authorship: "a Renaissance author never quite *owned* a literary work, or at least not a literary work as we now somewhat abstractly conceive it" (266), not having any right to control reproduction of the text either commercially or bibliographically. Piracy was still as common as it was in the medieval period of oral performance, and Loewenstein explains that "a market place made harrowingly unstable by plague and censor" generated special authorial concerns for literary property (270).[49] So it was not simply out of literary vanity that Jonson staged an authorial intrusion at the opening of *Bartholomew Fair* (1614) in which a scrivener, acting on behalf of the author, issues a legal contract which seeks satirically to overturn the current power structures of publication. As Loewenstein observes:

> He drives a hard bargain: the extent of a spectator's right of censure is to be kept proportionate to the price of his seat; the spectator is entitled only to is own opinion, and none other's; . . . and he is to protect the play from topical construction and the playwright from the sort of punitive censure that had already twice landed Jonson in prison. (267)

Similarly, in *Cynthia's Revels*, written when Jonson was seeking court patronage and release from the Grub Street world of Henslowe's enforced collaborations, he dramatized an autobiographical poet-figure, Crites, who begins as a persecuted but virtuous poet, and ends as a poet patronized by the gentle classes, not any longer a victim but "a legislator of aestheticized morals" (271).

This account of Jonson's experience gives us a window onto the instabilities of authorship before copyright,[50] instabilities which might have driven a writer to resort to such devices of authorial intrusion. But, although Jonson was the last author to write an "epistle mendicant" poem in the medieval style, and was to that extent a kind of latter-day Hoccleve, his experience is, of course, an anachronistic one for our purposes. Therefore in what follows the terms of reference for Jonsonian "bibliographic ego" have been significantly adapted and enlarged to suit medieval manuscript culture. For the purposes of the present study, the term "bibliographic ego" will be defined as any manifestation of authorial self-consciousness which serves to establish, protect, or market the author, usually involving some kind of authorial intrusion into the text itself. I take any of the following authorial strategies as evidence of a concern with bibliographic ego when it occurs *within the narrative framework of the text itself*:

1. revelation, direct or otherwise, of authorial identity;
2. authorial mention of previous works or of other data from the author's *"curriculum vitae"* which might serve to reaffirm his reputation, attract new patronage, or explain a new literary course of direction;
3. authorial concern about giving offense to readers, or about proceeding with publication or about the reliability of the means of literary (re)production;
4. the inclusion in the narrative of a metadiscursive moment in which the author is made actually present, whether by (i) a descriptive (verbal) self-portrait; (ii) a presentation portrait or an author portrait made at the author's request;[51] or (iii) inclusion of a passage in which the author's role *as speaker* in the text is emphasized;
5. the use of elements from the (originally monastic) tradition of *apologia*;
6. overt literary mendicancy, or the use of more subtle conventions from the genre of the "epistle mendicant" poem.

In most medieval writers such moments of bibliographic ego are more easily detected than they are in Langland (and in what follows I will thus have as much recourse to his colleagues as to him), but Langland exhibits— or *appears* to exhibit—all six of these characteristics in some form.

The first of these strategies, revelation of authorial identity within the text itself, needs no further explanation. For a contemporary instance of both the second and third, one might cite Chaucer's "Prologue to the Legend of Good Women" in which he has Alceste list, at great length, all his literary works to date (G-text, II. 402–20), some of which, indeed, have not survived. Chaucer was later to recast this list for somewhat different purposes in his ultimate manifestation of bibliographic ego, the "Retraction," but the "Prologue to the Legend" betrays more worldly concerns. Chaucer's playful authorial confessionalism pokes delicate fun at the all too real concern that an author's choice of "matere" will be offensive to some person in authority. At the same time it provides scope for some delicate grumbling about the plight of the poet in the world of courtly patronage: either, Alceste apologizes, the poet was too foolish to realize the harm his writings could do in the God of Love's domain, or he was asked to write on this subject by someone he dared not refuse:

> But for he useth bokes for to make,
> And taketh non hed of what matere he take,
> Therfore he wrot the Rose and ek Crisseyde
> Of innocence, and nyste what he seyde.
> Or hym was boden make thilke tweye
> Of som persone, and durste it not withseye;
> For he hath write many a bok er this. (G-text, 342–58) [52]

Moreover, Alceste's excuses to the God of Love on the poet's behalf are interwoven with allusions to the internecine tensions of court life, a world in which "Envye . . . / Is lavender in the grete court alway," never departing from "the hous of Cesar" in which she handles all dirty linen (G, 333–36). Alceste's intervention ostensibly gives the poet the chance to defend his motive for writing about false love, but one senses that the "Prologue" is not so much about the proprieties of love in the courtly world, as about the poet's status in that insecure atmosphere. [53]

Among other Middle English poets who use the technique of listing past works, or discussing them in relation to insecurities about new or past poetic directions, none springs more quickly to mind than the inveterate bibliographic egoist, Hoccleve, who devotes an entire poem ("Dialogue with a Friend") to the question of whether the poem he has just written (and the reader has just read) should be published, whether past poems have offended, and what topics might be suitable for new compositions. Langland's use of this second characteristic (allusion to previous writings in a current piece), however, is much more oblique than either Chaucer's or Hoccleve's. He alludes more than once to his own poetry within all three versions of his poem, and even in the C *apologia* to the impact of his writings (on local lollars and "lewede" hermits), but he never names or describes his works specifically. At least one early reader, John But, felt that the poem lacked sufficient internal reference to the writer's *oeuvre* and supplied a literary *curriculum vitae* for Langland in the epilogue he composed for the A-text.[54] With respect to the third characteristic (concern about getting into trouble), however, Langland needed no such assistance; he explicitly addresses his worries about giving offense to readers in Will's discussion with Leaute on poetic prudence in making ecclesiastical and political criticism public. In response to Will's wish ("Y wolde it were no synne . . . to seien þat were treuthe" (C 12.27)), Leaute gives him both encouragement and practical advice ("Thyng þat wolde be pryue publische thow hit neuere" (line 37)). Simpson calls this passage "powerful and largely well informed" on the subject of the legal constraints on satire in late fourteenth-century England (25), suggesting that in it Langland is overtly weighing the political dangers, just as he seems to be doing in the many passages in which he confesses that he is afraid to interpret or elaborate a point further.

The fourth strategy of bibliographic ego, the "presence" of the author in the text, generally manifests itself in devices like the dream vision prologue or in an (authorially directed) presentation or author portrait.[55] One of the more striking aspects of Langland's *apologia* is this "physical" presence of the author (or at least of the someone who claims to be *doing the writing*)—he describes himself in the most bodily fashion (his height, his weakness, his lassitude). Like so much else about the *apologia*, this recalls the kind of formal metadiscursive prologue which *Piers Plowman*, of course, had always lacked—that is, until this passage entered the final revision as surrogate. It is in such prologues that, in a tradition well established in the iconography of medieval book production, the author appears "physically" either in a presentation portrait, or, more commonly, an author portrait, often in an historiated initial in which, as Nichols has observed, the first letter of the first word the writer speaks is used to portray the "envoicement" of the text (141). It is no accident that the most elaborate physical description of Langland occurs in the *apologia*. This is indeed, to use Middleton's phrase, a rhetoric of presence,[56] but it is also an *iconography* of presence. Neither his allusion to his clerkish long robes, nor the fact that his self-portrait conjures up the medieval *ideal* of the clerk's physique can be accidental ("Y am to wayke to worche . . . / And to long . . . / as a werkeman eny while to duyren"; 5.23–25).[57] Here we have an author highlighting his physical similarity to the very clerkly characters who peer authoritatively out at the reader from historiated-initial author portraits, asserting their *auctoritas* by an iconography which links them implicitly with even the authors of the Bible.[58]

The fifth convention, the use of elements from a tradition of originally monastic *apologia*, is discussed in detail at the end of section IV, so it remains to explain briefly the sixth strategy, the use of overt literary mendicancy, or the more subtle use of conventions of literary *supplicatio*.[59] Poems written to entice patronage or payment, like Chaucer's "Complaint to his Purse" or Hoccleve's many delightful begging poems, were a well-recognized genre (the "epistle mendicant"), as were rhetorical applications of petitionary conventions within other genres—one thinks of the *epistola deprecatoria* of Heloise, which made authorial begging and authorial "presence" an art form.[60] The petitionary element within many longer medieval poems has been observed by Holzknecht, and more recently by Burrow,[61] but what will interest us here is how this mode is used in literature by two specific and often overlapping categories of medieval author: those publishing controversial works (in the political or theological spheres) and those who were writing, as we suspect Langland may have been, among the unbeneficed or underemployed clergy.

IV. Langland, the Conventions of Bibliographic Ego, and the Marginalized Writer

Many years ago Goldschmidt drew attention to the enormous obstacles to establishing authorship in pre-print culture: "Whoever enters upon any investigation in the field of medieval literature and bibliography cannot fail to be bewildered by the extraordinary uncertainty and elusive fluidity of the authors' names. Almost every other book seems to be known habitually under a name which cannot possibly be that of its true author."[62] Moreover, as Goldschmidt shows, in the chaos of medieval library designations a title such as "Sermones Bonaventurae," for instance, may mean as many as six different things to a contemporary reader, only one of which is what we would take the title to mean today, that is, sermons written by St. Bonaventure of Fidenza (d. 1274). So it comes as no surprise that medieval authors often sought some way of identifying themselves in their work. One of the cleverest instances in Middle English literature occurs early in the *Owl and the Nightingale*, in which the Nightingale proposes one Nicholas of Guildford (who is apparently the author) as adjudicator of their debate, to which the Owl agrees, noting that although he was wild in his youth (when he might have been disposed to support the nightingale), he is now grown to great discretion.[63] Not content with this self-recommendation, the author provided another, this time at the very end of the poem, spoken by the impartial Wren. This passage supplies Nicholas's address in some detail, presumably for the convenience of future patrons; he lives at Portisham in Dorsetshire, where he may easily be found because

> He naueþ bute one woning.
> Þat his bischopen muchel schame,
> An alle þan þat of his nome
> Habbeþ ihert, & of his dede. (1760–63)

Nicholas has only one living, to the shame of the bishops and others who should recognize his talent and promote him. The Owl adds that rich men are quick to hand out livings to their families, indeed, even to children ("An ȝiveþ rente litle childre" [1776]), while wise men such as Nicholas remain on the sidelines.

Like several of the other writers who availed themselves of these devices, including Langland himself, Nicholas wished to make a point about inequities in the distribution of benefices, and thus it is perhaps no accident that the bibliographic ego intrudes itself most often where poetry is at work in the pursuit of patronage or promotion. As John Burrow has observed, when a writer names himself in Middle English literature it is almost always in a petitionary mode: "Any such petition, whether to God or to some secular or ecclesiastical patron, would gain strength from a description of the petitioner's plight; but the really fundamental requirement was that the would-be beneficiary should be clearly and unambiguously identified—otherwise the favour might go to the wrong person" (38). Bibliographic ego, it seems, manifests itself in the Middle English period particularly among underemployed clerics.

Hoccleve, whose personal situation may have been much like what Langland describes in the *apologia*, tells us that he waited years for a benefice and finally gave up and married ("Regement," 1447–55). He expresses the same embitterment with those who are successful but serve so negligently that they do not care if "on þe hye auter it reyne or snewe" (1423),[64] echoing Langland's sentiment (and expression) precisely (cf. *Piers* B 10.318;

C 5.164). Langland, who may well have been in a similar position, awaiting a benefice, may have worked as a legal scribe for a period.[65] Hoccleve
worked as a clerk of the Privy Seal, and lamented the drudgery of the job,
with its endless hours of stooping and staring "uppon the schepys skynne."
This complaint, of course, is so commonly voiced by scribes and clerks as
to be conventional,[66] and so it may not have much autobiographical foundation in Hoccleve's case, but there can be little doubt that he seems to
have needed patronage for his poetry in order to fulfill his social, intellectual, and financial aspirations.[67] The large number of his begging poems
which survive, not to mention the extraordinary number of his holograph
manuscripts,[68] which have preserved his poetry from the textual fate of
Langland's and Chaucer's, are indicative of a studied and obviously successful bibliographic ego at work. He, too, advertises his name, literary
credentials, and address in a cunningly self-promoting dialogue in the *Prologue to the Regiment of Princes* with the old almsman, who insists that
Hoccleve is capable of writing a poem to win the favor of Prince Henry in
French, Latin, or English:

> Of alle thre þou oghtist be wele leerid
> Syn þou so long in hem laboured haast,
> Þou of þe þryue seel art old I-yeerid. (1856–58)

When Hoccleve demurs, pleading his lack of skill, the old man charges him
with having "foule . . . in waast / Despent" his time (1860–61), but suggests that he is simply being modest: "I trowe / Þou canst do bet þan þou
wilt do me knowe" (1861–62). Then (rather oddly, considering that they
have been in dialogue already for over 1,700 lines), the old man suddenly
asks his name:

> "What schal I calle þe? what is þi name?"
> "Hoccleue, fadir myn, men clepen me."
> "Hoccleue, sone?" "I-wis, fadir, þat same."
> "Sone, I haue herd, or this, men speke of þe;
> Þou were aqueynted with Caucher, pardee — ." (1863–67)

Hoccleve, like Nicholas, embeds the sense of an already-made reputation for himself right into his poem, the most important feature of which
at this stage of his career (judging by the elaborate way he advertises it)
seems to have been his association with Chaucer. Not only does he display

his connection with the right literary (and political) circles,[69] but he also identifies himself *openly* by his surname, not (as Langland does) by his baptismal name only. Moreover, he cunningly exploits the mimesis of actual conversation, with its tendency towards repetitiveness, to ensure that the name is well understood (Hoccleve's all-too-familiar sense of the vagaries of the means of production no doubt inspired him to this device, which gives any scribe struggling with an uncertain rendering of the name a second chance). Not for Hoccleve the coy anagrammatic strategies of the fourteenth century: Hoccleve was underpaid and underemployed, so this prologue was business. A misspent youth (which may be conventional)[70] and an underemployed adulthood (which isn't) seems to have been standard in these moments of bibliographic *supplicatio*.

So, too, in Langland. The *apologia* opens with explicit reference to the poet's address and implicit reference to his credentials as a poet with an established reputation for straight talk on lollars:

> Thus y awakede, woet god, whan y wonede in Cornehull,
> Kytte and y in a cote, yclothed as a lollare,
> And lytel ylet by, leueth me for sothe,
> Amonges lollares of Londone and lewede ermytes,
> For y made of tho men as resoun me tauhte. (5.1–5)

But as always in Langland, things are more complex. The address is a *past* address. The name is only cryptically mooted over a circuitous course of references to his being "long" (5.24) and wearing "longe clothes," culminating in "And so y leue yn London and opelond bothe" (44)—a pale reflection of the B-text's anagrammatized self-naming, it barely even qualifies as an anagram and would be useless as a form of authorial identification to anyone who did not already know who the poet was—indeed perhaps useless to anyone who did not know the B anagram. This, as I suspect, was precisely the point for Langland after 1381. But what this obfuscating little bit of self-advertisement does have in common with Nicholas of Guildford's and Thomas Hoccleve's (aside from the shared grumbling about corruption in church appointments, lines 70–81) is the suggestion that apparent indiscretions, both social and moral, belong to an earlier time, and that good judgment, both social and moral, belongs to the present man. The theme of self-improvement may be a convention of literary mendicancy, too, but the number of lines Langland devotes to it and the specificity of reference suggests that we are dealing here with more than convention in

his case. Moreover, since autobiography in a medieval text never exists for
its own sake, it seems likely that this *apologia* is poetry *at work*, poetry trying to achieve a specific end. There is the sense here that Langland is writing for an audience that already knows him, or knows *of* him, but which
requires some explanation of something which has displeased them.

That Langland's sense of his own authorship—and of the responsibility it entailed—weighed upon him in an entirely different way in the
period after the Peasant's Revolt cannot be doubted. One has only to look
at the transformation of B 12.1–28 into C 5.1–104 to see that Langland's
sense of authorial self had shifted from a self-absorbed concern with the
validity of "meddling with makings" (B 12.16) to an anxious defensiveness about the impact his message had already had.[71] By the time he wrote
these lines in C 5 he was an established author, part of a more politicized
world, and writing as (to use Middleton's distinction) an author not just
addressing an audience, but aware of a public. Moreover, by the time he
wrote these lines, two short portions of his C-text—one on clerical negligence, which escaped his hands even before the alliteration was perfected
(C Prol. 91–127), and a much longer piece on the differences between good
and bad beggars or lollars (C 9.66–281)—had already been in circulation
for reasons which are not yet clear.[72] One aspect of this change in situation
is that he suddenly found it necessary to defend himself against the charge
that his own life *appeared* no better than the lives of the "lollars" he had
criticized, and to this end he produced a defense of his own modus vivendi
owing much to the charismatic thought which had inspired his startling
description of the "good" lollars, God's "priuy disciples" (C 9.105–38), in
the prepublication circulation of the passage from C 9. This self-defense
takes up by far the largest portion of the *apologia* (most of lines 5–104,
but especially 35–52), and its intimate relation to the prepublication passage from C 9 suggests that the *apologia* was written in conjunction with
the "leaked" passage from 9—both of which suggest a special sensitivity to
audience reaction—and that it, too, may have been in progress early in the
C revision period.[73]

But perhaps most importantly for our purposes here, and most shock-
ingly for modern readers, he found it necessary to insert a reactionary
diatribe against social mobility, ostensibly as part of his defense against
Reason's suggestion that he ought to be performing manual labor in order
to justify his existence:

"And also moreouer me thynketh, syre Resoun,
Me sholde constrayne no clerc to no knaues werkes,

For by þe lawe of *Levyticy* þat oure lord ordeynede,
Clerkes ycrouned, of kynde vnderstondynge,
Sholde nother swynke ne swete. . . ." (5.53–57)

This much might be easily explained as a strict application of medieval estates ideology in order to get himself out of the tight corner Reason's question put him in, but it is given (for Langland) such an unusual emphasis
that one begins already to suspect that the poet's concern, in the immediate aftermath of the Revolt, is to be seen as upholding orthodox opinion
on the question of clerical labor. As we have seen in section II above,
Simpson has pointed out several passages in the B-text which could easily
be read as supporting conclusions banned either before or immediately
after the revolt of 1381, the most pertinent of which here is the conclusion
banned as heretical in the Blackfriars' Council of 1382: (#23) the belief
that friars ought to work manually (16). The *apologia* passage just quoted
is one of many C-text revisions which signals Langland's new awareness of
his dangerous political position, especially since as the passage continues it
becomes increasingly, and for readers accustomed to Langland's two previous texts, alarmingly shrill:

Hit bycometh for clerkes Crist for to serue
And knaues vncrounede to carte and to worche.
For sholde no clerke be crouned but yf he come were
Of frankeleynes and fre men and of folke ywedded.
Bondemen and bastardus and beggares children,
Thyse bylongeth to labory, and lordes kyn to serue. . . . (61–66)

It gets worse:

Ac sythe bondemen barnes haen be mad bisshopes
And barnes bastardus haen be erchedekenes
And soutares and here sones for suluer han be knyhtes
And lordes sones here laboreres and leyde here rentes to wedde,
For the ryhte of this reume ryden aȝeyn oure enemyes
. . . .
Popes and patrones *pore gentel blood refused*
And taken Symondes sones seyntwarie to kepe,
Lyf-holynesse and loue hath be longe hennes,
And wol, til hit be wered out, or oþerwyse ychaunged. (70–81;
  emphasis mine)

That this long passage is a response to the political situation the author of *Piers Plowman* found himself in after 1381 is a point which hardly
needs laboring. It seems to be an attempt to turn the tables on a certain
kind of reader and *reading* of his B-text; not only does it defend the current estates ideology (against readers like John Ball),[74] but it also implies
that the corruptions of the day are such that the socially privileged have
now become the *under*privileged, with its rhetorical assertion that "lordes
sones" have become the "laboreres" of the wealthy bourgeois (represented
by "soutares and here sones") because they have mortgaged their estates
to them in order to defend the realm (74–75). Now, Langland suggests,
it is "pore gentil blood" that is refused for patronage and promotion—
certainly, because of simony, a legitimate and traditionally Langlandian
concern, but, one senses, also because he finds it hard to accommodate the
shift from birth-based to wealth-based (or from agrarian to commercial)
systems of privilege. But even more significant than Langland's social conservatism, for our purposes here, is the personal edge to this passage—a
hint of bibliographic ego, to be precise, which has not been noticed before.
In this instance Langland seems to be writing himself into his text not so
much to claim "primitive copyright," but to reclaim an *intellectual* property.[75] The subtext here seems to be something like: "this poem is mine,
and although I have made mistakes in the past, and can easily be taken
for a lollar, nothing I've done would explain this degree of misappropriation, and so I'm stepping in to clarify how I really feel about these social
issues—and about myself."

Complicating our perception in the *apologia* are, of course, the ever-
shifting perspectives of autobiography (spiritual or otherwise) which make
this metadiscursive moment especially complex. The conventions of spiritual autobiography demand the confession of a conventionally misspent
youth, and Langland duly complies (5.6–9). But autobiography of any sort
is a genre in which the inexperience of earlier life is simultaneously relived
and filtered through the complexities of memory and experience:

> "When y ʒong was, many ʒer hennes,
> My fader and my frendes foende me to scole,
>
> . . . .
> And foend y nere, in fayth, seth my frendes deyede,
> Lyf þat me lykede but in this longe clothes." (5.35)

The statement works as both a defense of the past and a defense of the
present, and Langland seems to have wanted this ambiguity. It is a par-

ticularly bibliographic ambiguity. It is, generally speaking, unusual for a medieval writer to mention his or her childhood and education.[76] But the subject of the writer's inability to finish school for lack of funds does occur in some "epistle mendicant" poems, and for good reason: medieval students normally needed patronage of some sort to study.[77] Moreover, in authorial *apologia*, which is after all a piece of writing intended to defend the authoritative stance of its author, the author's educational history tends to come up because education (along with gender and social status) supplied the most obvious, *objectively* recognizable basis for claims to bibliographic authority in medieval society (those without the right combination of these attributes had to resort to more dubious claims, like divine inspiration). Thus it is no accident that in his *apologia* Langland identifies himself and his plight in the most social fashion—he is neither a manual laborer, nor a beggar; he is a learned man of respectable parentage (only such a "fader and . . . frendes" could or would send a son "to scole") who has simply fallen on hard times ("seth my frendes deyede . . ."). Thus he establishes, under the guise of excusing himself from manual labor, that his authority to speak is both socially and educationally derived. It is interesting that this fits quite closely with the information about the author given in the memorandum in Trinity College, Dublin MS 212, which says that Langland's father, Stacy de Rokayle, was of "gentle" birth ("fuit generosus"); however, unlike the Trinity scribe, Langland is not specific about either his own name or that of the "fader" he mentions.[78] This looks like a classic instance of what Annabel Patterson calls "functional ambiguity"—there is enough information in the *apologia* to establish a social and educational position without relinquishing a certain kind of privacy. There is not, that is, enough information for a noninitiate to construe the anagrammatic hints, but there is enough to reassure any concerned reader that the author is correctly socially positioned. The *apologia*, then, looks structured to do at least two kinds of work: to reassure that sector of his audience he wanted to keep (presumably an audience of respectable folk) and to put off that sector he did not (those like Ball and his correspondents).

However, there is further evidence of Langland's specifically bibliographic concerns in this passage and that lies in his use of some of the conventions of traditional authorial *apologia*. This was originally a monastic form of apologetics, and especially (for historical reasons) a Benedictine form, which arose during the centuries when Benedictinism and its defenders were most under fire from the newer orders.[79] It is well exemplified in twelfth-century Benedictine writers like Rupert of Deutz and Abelard, both controversialists who also turned to authorial apologetics at points of crisis in vocation. These conventions seem to be used particularly at a stage in which the writer—marginalized, like Rupert, or in disgrace, like Abelard—is seeking to defend a damaged sense of authority (Rupert) or to make a self-defensive reentry into a circle of antagonized colleagues or unreceptive readers (Abelard). This is how later, nonmonastic writers would use these conventions as well, especially when the piece of writing they were publishing (or had published) was controversial. For instance, in Langland's London, Hoccleve used the same conventions of *apologia* and, more broadly, bibliographic ego, to plead for patronage and later to reestablish his credibility after a nervous breakdown had rendered him a questionable acquaintance in social and literary circles. Very little scholarship has been written on the history of the authorial *apologia* in the Middle Ages, but what follows reveals enough parallels between disparate monastic and secular writers, I believe, to suggest that certain conventions had distinctive bibliographic resonances for medieval authors.

Langland's *apologia* is formulated heavily upon two important biblical parables (with incidental citation of two more),[80] both of which recur in medieval bibliographical apologetics. The first is the parable of the pearl of great price (Matt. 13:45–46) and the second is the parable of the unjust steward (Luke 16:1–8). In the first, Christ explains "simile est regnum coelorum homini negotiatori quaerenti bonas margaritas. Inventa autem una pretiosa margarita, abiit, et vendidit omnia quae habuit, et emit eam." [The kingdom of heaven is like to a merchant seeking good pearls, Who, when he had found one pearl of great price, went his way and sold all that he had and bought it]. This parable supplies the otherwise entirely suspect metaphor of mercantile speculation which Will uses both to explain his unfruitful past and to convey a (still slightly suspect) sense of expectation about his future. Will confesses:

> That y haue ytynt tyme and tyme myspened;
> Ac ȝut, I hope, as he þat ofte hath ychaffared
> And ay loste and loste, and at þe laste hym happed
> A bouhte such a bargayne he was þe bet euere. . . . (5.93–96)

The second parable supplies the biblical justification for Will's firm rejection of manual labor, and even, although more problematically, for his denial that he lives by begging. The unjust steward, finding that he has been caught out by his master, exclaims: "fodere non valeo, mendicare erubesco" [to dig I am unable, to beg I am ashamed] (Luke 16:3). In Will's response to Reason's query as to why he is not serving the community with manual labor, he echoes the parable,[81] and in doing so he describes himself in the most physical fashion, drawing an actual self-portrait which would underline the metadiscursive nature of the moment, especially (we assume)[82] to those who actually knew "Long Will":

> Y am too wayke to worche with sykel or with sythe
> And to long, lef me, lowe to stoupe,
> To wurche as a werkeman eny while to duyren. (5.22–24)

This is the same self-deprecating image of a talented, learned man down on his luck which haunts the petitionary apologetics of many medieval writers, like Abelard, Rutebeuf, or Hoccleve.[83] Abelard cites the unjust steward's words in the *Historia Calamitatum* to explain why he returned to teaching at a moment of vocational crisis (one of many) when he allowed the Paraclete, his hermitage refuge from his academic enemies, to develop into a monastic school: "Tunc autem precipue ad scolarum regimen intolerabilis me compulit paupertas, cum 'fodere non valerem et mendicare erubescerem'" [At that time, unbearable poverty compelled me to run a school since to dig I would not have been able, and to beg I would have been ashamed].[84] This quotation arises in the midst of Abelard's exultation over his literary and theological enemies, whom he portrays as lamenting, in a metaphor quintessentially epitomizing the bibliographic egoist he was: "We have tried to blot out [extinguere] his name and we have made it better known" (Muckle, 59; Monfrin, 94, 1105). As McLaughlin has argued, Abelard wrote his *Historia* as an epistolary *consolatio* (directed to an "unknown friend," but like most monastic letters, intended for wide circulation). His purpose was not only to defend past indiscretions, but also to prepare his readers for a new one (he was shortly to resign as unhappy abbot of the troubled St. Gildas, violating yet again the monastic ideal of *stabilitas*) and to canvas support for a change of position and, he hoped, a change of fortune (468).

Even more striking, however, as a manifestation of bibliographic ego is the instance of Rupert of Deutz's use of the pearl of great price parable in a very similar moment of authorial defensiveness. As John van Engen has said, commenting on the parallels to Rupert's apologetics in Abelard, Otloh of St. Emmeram and Suger of St. Denis, the fact that monastic *apologia* is largely a Benedictine genre is historically explicable:

On reflection it may not be so surprising that Black Monks were the first to compose such apologias. New monks and new masters had still to make their way, and they did so in good part by attacking what had gone wrong in the recent past. Black Monks were compelled thus to defend either the appropriateness or the quality of their work as scribes, teachers, administrators, and theologians, tasks in which they had often led the way for almost two centuries. (349)

Rupert's *apologia*, which is an early and influential instance of the genre, takes up the entire first book of his *Commentary on the Rule of St. Benedict*, which in manuscript is called "Liber de apollogeticis suis."[85] In a remarkable passage Rupert describes his plight as a marginalized writer, never having attended the Schools, and yet daring to comment upon and even contradict the Fathers in his prolific writings. The issue for his enemies was the source of his *auctoritas*. In desperation, apparently, Rupert resorted to two strategies for self-defense in his *apologia*: he gave an account of his childhood as an oblate which kept him "detained" [*detentus*] in the cloister from the earliest time, and prevented him from seeking the "pearls" of the Schools; and second, he made a claim to visionary inspiration for his unusual knowledge.[86] In the flamboyantly self-deprecatory style of authorial apologetics, he describes himself as the *pauper* of Ecclus. 13.29, a verse which he uses to sum up how he is perceived by his enemy theologians: "Pauper locutus est et dicunt 'Quis est hic? Et si offenderit, subvertent illum'" [The poor man has spoken and they say: "Who is this? And if he offends (literally "stumbles"), they will overthrow him"] (PL 170, col. 480A). For Rupert the theologians who attack him are like the rich merchants (*divites negotiatores*) of Matthew's parable who have wandered in search of "margaritas poetarum atque philosophorum," until at last they found the one truly good and precious pearl, Holy Scripture— would that they might possess it "ad perfectum," he exclaims (480B). If they lack perfection, however, he lacks the authority bestowed by scholarly experiences, having stayed at home like Jacob with his mother Rebecca, contemptible in the eyes of those who ask "Quis est hic? Scribit enim et loquitur, loquitur et scribit, qui magistros et praeceptores nostros saltem videre nunquam dignus fuit. Inde etiam pauper ego, quia saltem chartulas, quibus inscriberem, habere vel acquirere vix potui." [Who is this? For he writes and speaks, he speaks and writes who was never even worthy to see our masters and teachers. From that time indeed I was a pauper, because I was scarcely able even to acquire parchment with which to write] (480C). But two things, Rupert goes on to say, have improved the lot of the *pauper*: first, a visionary experience of Christ, from whose golden body (*totum aureum*) the living waters of Wisdom flowed into Rupert, making him rich (480CD), and second, the patronage of Abbot Cuno, who has protected and supported him throughout his recent authorial trials. Through these events his fortunes have begun to turn; patronage is now the instrument, as it were, of God's grace. Addressing Cuno directly, he explains that it was through his patronage that "it began to be accomplished from that time (*ex tunc*) that to write and by writing" he was able "to pour back the living waters" which had flowed down to him, and "money was not absent nor parchment (*membranula*) lacking." Divine wisdom, he concludes from his vision, is "a rich man, he has gold and silver enough" (col. 481A).[87]

There are many interesting things in this passage. Rupert is an early example of a developed "bibliographic ego"; he turns to his own early autobiography and to visionary experience to defend his writing from a marginalized position, and then to transcend it. He uses the parable of the pearl merchant defensively, just as Langland does, to describe a lifelong search for wisdom by a path his critics think inferior or dubious; he never-theless commends his enemies for their search and even for their findings, wishing only that they could use these pearls "ad perfectum." As in Lang-land's passage, the parable is connected with perfection in the (initially) monastic sense,[88] but the dubious element in both Rupert's and Lang-land's uses of the parable would have been suggested to medieval minds by the merchant metaphor it contained.[89] Accused of novelty and heresy, unpopular in his extreme Gregorian reformist stance, and finally having found a patron who was powerful enough to protect him from the slings and arrows of fellow theologians and imperial appointees opposed to the Gregorian party, Rupert developed a kind of bibliographic ego, writing himself, a list of his publications, and a defense of those which had come under fire, into his next work, a commentary on the *Rule*. (The pliability of medieval sense of genre is nowhere more evident than in such "outbursts of autobiography," as Robert Brentano so vividly calls them, noting that autobiography nearly always had to be disguised as another genre.)[90] Even the practical details of Rupert's means of production, such as his difficulty in attaining parchment, come to light in this extraordinary metadiscursive moment. Most interesting is the unabashed use of the language of money (in effect, of patronage) to describe divine grace—a feature which has dis-turbed critics of Langland's *apologia*, who have not perhaps understood the conventions which gave rise to it. Rupert's *apologia*, as John van Engen has said, is not so much the product of the much-vaunted rise of the individual in the twelfth century as of a peculiarly Benedictine defensiveness, and, I would add, an authorial defensiveness common to those clerics who dared to take up reformist or controversial themes throughout the later Middle Ages. The practical reality was that they needed patronage urgently.

Writers who were bringing the concerns of interclerical controversy before a vernacular audience were obviously especially unpopular with colleagues, and needed the patronage of someone powerful, often a secular lord. A good instance of this is Lodewijch van Velthem, who in 1316 undertook a continuation of the moral-didactic poet Jacob van Maerlant's *Spieghel Historiael*, translating into Flemish for the first time Hildegard of Bingen's inflammatory prophecies on the chastisement of the clergy. In his study of Beguine history Ernest W. McDonnell summarizes van Velthem's *apologia* in this way:

> As Van Velthem begins to recount Hildegarde's prophecies, he points out "that the clergy have heretofore been covered," but that there is no use in concealing "those things that must happen." He "will thus write boldly and acquaint the laity with the revelations." At the same time he hopes "that some lord will reward him" for uncovering these hidden things "since it has been so difficult to put such matters in Flemish." He was already being "slandered by those who thought he was after them" especially for the two chapters criticizing the friars. The entire chapter 15 is both a statement of purpose and a petition for patronage.[91]

Van Velthem was in fact rewarded with a benefice by a nobleman, one of whose tenants had initially suggested the project of the continuation. The parallel with Langland is suggestive (and interestingly the memorandum in Trinity 212 places him in just such a social circle), although we know nothing for certain of Langland's patron or protector,[92] other than the "historical likelihood," as Kane and Donaldson might say, that he had one.

In the publication of such works, everything about the writer—his education, vocation, modus vivendi—came under scrutiny. As Nicholas Watson has shown, in the most detailed study to date of authorial defensiveness in a medieval author, Rolle was hounded by such scrutiny from without, and by near-paranoic insecurities from within. In a passage from the *Incendium amoris*, strikingly like the one we have just examined in Rupert, Rolle writes of himself:

> And then, assumed into the fiery heaven, [the lover] received wisdom and subtlety, so that he knew how to speak among the chatterers and put forward boldly whatever he thought it necessary to say, although previously he was regarded as stupid and feeble, and perhaps even was so. But those taught by acquired not infused wisdom and swollen up with intricate arguments mock, saying: "Where did he learn? Which doctor [*a quo doctore*] has he heard?" They do not reckon that lovers of eternity are taught by an inner doctor, so that they can speak more eloquently than those who were taught by people who have all the time been studying for futile honours.[93]

At a moment of vocational crisis, brought on by having authored controversial theological or ecclesiastical writings, all these writers draw upon a
tradition of monastic *apologia* which, by Langland's time (or indeed, even
Rolle's), had escaped the confines of the cloister and found itself in the vernacular literary world.

Thus it is that the complaint of the unjust steward was adopted by
Hoccleve not long after Langland had used it (and perhaps with Langland's precedent in mind). In *La Male Regle* he complains that his annuity
has not been paid, and that his salary for his work at the Privy Seal is insufficient; he tells himself that to "stele, for the guerdoun is so keene, / Ne
darst thow nat, ne begge also for shame."[94] And again, in the Prologue to
his *Regement*, the most elaborate metadiscursive interlude a medieval author ever wrote, Hoccleve asks the sympathetic old almsman: what can a
man of decent social standing do in such straits?

> Wyth plough can I not medle, ne wyth harowe,
> Ne wot nat what londe good ys for what corne;
> And for to lade a cart or fyll a barowe,
> (To whyche I never used was to forne)
> My bak vnbuxum hath swych swynke forsworne. (981–85)

The answer, as the old man advises Hoccleve, is to write a poem and seek
patronage. The parable seems to recur in such bids for poetic patronage: it
was also invoked by the Archpoet in a poem for his patron on the woes of
the starving and overworked poet in which he complains that he cannot
dig for a living "quia sum scolaris," and because his father is of the knightly
class.[95] The translator of *The Orcherd of Syon* also alludes to the parable in a
way which strongly suggests that it had become attached to authorial cries
for support, moral as well as economic: "Grete leborer was I neuer, bo-
dili ne gostli. I had neuer grete strenþe myztli to laboure wiþ spade ne wiþ
shouel. Þerfore now, deuoute sustern, helpep me wiþ preiers."[96] The translator defines his labor as *labor of the pen*, and, as Denise Despres points out,
as valid work in "þis gostli orcherd." Here the allusion becomes simply a
vehicle of authorial modesty *topos*, and one wonders whether the motif of
laziness in the C 5 *apologia* is not also part of the same convention.

These instances, taken together, suggest that Langland's invocation of
the parable may have as much or more to do with the business of authorship as with imputations of physical laziness (self-inflicted or otherwise);
in fact, it may have little to do with questions of helping with any *literal*

harvest at all.[97] He uses it to make clear that he wishes to be counted as part of the clerical club, that is, among those who wield the pen, not the scythe; the "prymer," not the spade.[98] But whether Langland was seeking patronage or not (or, since the *apologia* is set in the past, whether he is describing a time when he *was* seeking patronage or not) in the suggestive final lines of his *apologia* (92–102) is very difficult to say. The primary thrust of these lines is spiritual and confessional in the most literal sense: "and so y beknowe / That y haue ytynt tyme and tyme myspened" (92–93). But the "myspened" launches that deluge of troublesome economic metaphors in which he hopes eventually to be like the trader who "ofte hath ychaffared / And ay loste and loste," but who finally hits upon "suche a bargayn" that all his losses will be forever offset—a hope deferred breathlessly over five lines (94 to 99), and bolstered by the Latin cue references for two parables which use the metaphor of accidental good fortune as an analogy for the finding of salvation (Matt. 13:44 and Luke 15:10). These refer respectively to salvation as a treasure buried in a field, and to the woman who lost the coin; when added to the allusion to the pearl of great price already suggested, the passage takes on a distinctly "venture capital" flavor. The fashion recently has been to read these lines as cynical and self-parodic, but this may be yet another instance of the twentieth-century penchant for over-ironizing medieval texts: the conflation of spiritual grace with good fortune in patronage has precedents in other instances of bibliographic *apologia*, as we have already seen. In fact, in the very decade in which Langland was working on the C-text, we have another example of this blend in the political apologetics of the unlucky and untalented Thomas Usk. As Paul Strohm has recently remarked, "many of the promises of reward within the *Testment* come to seem double-sided, referring not only to heavenly but to worldly matters as well."[99] Whether Langland belongs in company of strategizing egoists of the likes of Usk is a matter for (wild) speculation which need not detain us here,[100] but it is clear that Langland, too, knew of the long-established tradition of authorial apologetics which deliberately mixes economic and spiritual metaphors for practical purposes. Representing himself as something of an underachiever in either area, Will's highest hopes "of hym þat is almyghty" are for a "gobet of his grace," a meek and moving climax to the *apologia* (100–101), which surely, as A. C. Spearing has suggested, "spiritualizes the idea of profit much more than it mercantilizes the [idea of] heavenly reward."[101] This self-effacing tug at the sleeve of one who is Almighty (and perhaps simultaneously of one who is simply almighty) makes quite clear that neither does its "subject" beg nor is he vocationally or physically suited to manual labor, and that he is still awaiting the "bargain"—whether spiritual or vocational is a moot point—which will put an end to everything his critics regard as dubious about his life. But whatever he intended this passage to actually *do* in the 1380s, our job is to be alert to its many resonances, including the *bibliographic* ones—and to be aware of how medieval conditions of publication might have influenced his decision to write such an *apologia*, and put it to work.

V. Medieval Publication Habits and the Early Transmission of *Piers Plowman*

What did "publication" mean in Langland's context, and in what sense might any medieval author be said to have an audience? Publication, for a late medieval author, was no longer necessarily an oral event.[102] The earlier method is well, if somewhat flamboyantly, exemplified by Giraldus Cambrensis, who threw three lavishly supplied parties at the time of the first public reading of his *Topographia hibernia*, as he himself tells us in a fit of bibliographic ego of the most obvious kind:

When in process of time the work was finished and corrected, and not wishing to place the candle which he had lit under a bushel but to lift it aloft . . . , he determined to read it before a great audience at Oxford, where, of all places in England, the clergy were most strong and pre-eminent in learning. And since his book was divided into three parts [*distinctiones*], he gave three consecutive days to the reading, a part being read each day. On the first he hospitably entertained the poor of the whole town [*pauperes omnes oppidi totius*] . . . , on the morrow he entertained all the doctors of the divers faculties, and those of their scholars who were best known and best spoken of; and on the third day he entertained the remainder of the scholars together with the knights of the town and a number of citizens. It was a magnificent and costly achievement, since thereby the ancient and authentic times of the poets were in some manner revived.[103]

As Coulton pointed out long ago about this passage, Giraldus was so immensely proud of these proceedings not because oral publication was unusual, but because "Giraldus knows of no one who has dared and afforded to practise it on such a scale." But for most authors, Coulton continues, "no 'public' in the modern sense was possible as yet; even down to the end of the Middle Ages it must be mainly a public of private benefactors. He who has not a patrimony must get a patron."[104] In this regard it may be no accident that Langland chose to publicize his *loss* of patrimony in the *apologia*, and then, as we have seen, to follow it up with his oblique use of what may be the "double-sided" language of patronage mendicancy.[105]

In formal situations in which a patron was involved, the copy went first to the patron, whose responsibility it apparently was to oversee its sending forth "into the public (*in publicum*)," in Boccaccio's words to Madonna Andrea Acciaioli, into whose hands he first placed his *De Claris Mulieribus*.[106] He tells her that if the work is "sent out (*emissus*) under your auspices it will go free, as I think, from the insults of the malicious," a comment which underlines the patron's role as moral, not simply financial, supporter. In a letter accompanying the presentation copy of his *De Casibus Virorum Illustrium* to Maghinardo dei Cavalcanti, he writes, "While reading it do not disdain to correct whatsoever is not fitting. Then, when it shall seem well, share it with your friends (*hoc inter amicos communices*), and finally send it forth to the public (*emittas in publicum*) under your name" (419). The role of the author's or patron's friends comes up again and again in such letters, giving an important clue to the intended and immediate audience in the author's mind. In many cases, the work might not ever go beyond a fairly close-knit circle, even a work by a prominent writer; nor is there any guarantee that a long work might be known in its entirety even to that circle. As Beverly Boyd has recently remarked of the *Canterbury Tales*, "In all likelihood, [they] were not known as a unit by Chaucer's public or by his friends, the materials existing separately or in clusters, sometimes in more than one version, borrowed back and forth by individuals in more than one attempt to put together a unified work."[107] The fact that some very early readers of *Piers* are aware of more than one version of the poem may be (slight) evidence that the text's dissemination took place from a knowledgeable reading group, although other explanations are possible.[108]

Where no patron was involved, the situation seems less clear. Judging from evidence which comes mainly from fifteenth-century London, sometimes an agent acted as publisher—either an enterprising stationer, or a "publisher" like the enigmatic man of letters, John Shirley (d.1456), who so shamelessly promoted Lydgate's works, advertising in the versified tables of contents to his manuscripts the poet's availability to future patrons: "his thred bare coule . . . why nill ye se / and reward his pouerte?" (lines 42–44). Shirley prepared manuscripts or had them prepared, providing them with rubrics and marginal apparatus, and perhaps running a "samplecase" lending system to advertise his wares: "thus haue I them in ordre sete / [þat] fere were eft // now here ben mette / I meane [þe] copyes // ne douteth noughte // In sondry place haue I them soughte" (lines 15–18).[109] Of Langland's method of publication we know very little, beyond Kane and Donaldson's evidence that he used a commercial scribe to publish the B-text in its first phase, and, much more speculatively, Robert Adams's view that the rubrics of *Piers Plowman* were supplied by a scribe or editor.[110] If this is the case, it would likely have been a "publisher" like Shirley who, exceedingly early in the transmission of the poem, began this remarkably tenacious tradition of *ordinatio*, although it must be said that the rubrics we have received are *utterly unlike* anything normally added by a "publisher" such as Shirley, or by any annotating scribe whose job it was to prepare a MS of the poem. After one has studied the nonauthorial rubrics and marginal guides generally supplied by scribes (like, for instance, John Cok, who prepared several such manuscripts, some for Shirley, and who even once copied a fragment of *Piers Plowman*), one is tempted to say that the rubrics are likely not editorial because (*lectio difficilior*) they are so unhelpful for a superficial reading of the poem.[111]

However, the apparent anonymity which surrounds the publication of Langland's texts and even the ownership of *Piers* manuscripts links the poem with the publishing of more socially or politically sensitive works than those of Chaucer or Lydgate. Sometimes a work was put out through an agent in order to preserve anonymity, as we know to be the case with Osbern Bokenham's *Legendys of Hooly Wummen*, which was published anonymously at Bokenham's request by a protégé, Thomas Burgh, since he feared the "right capcyous and subtyl wyttys" of Cambridge.[112] In the areas of theological or ecclesiastical writing especially, many medieval authors feared the criticisms of church authorities and scholars, while political writers feared secular authorities and the powerful—in such instances conventions like the encoding of an author's name, or the comment that the writer will submit the work to correction, take on new meaning. The Prologue to *Richard the Redeless*, a poem clearly written for polemical purposes, draws quite unsubtly upon the latter bibliographic convention, because it is trying so self-consciously to pass as a work secretly circulated to a select few *before* going forth to the public:

And if ჳe ffynde ffables . or ffoly ther-amonge,
Or ony ffantasie yffeyned . that no ffrute is in,
Lete ჳoure conceill corette it . and clerkis to-gedyr,
And amende that ys amysse . and make it more better:

ffor ʒit it is secrette . and so it shall lenger,
Tyll wyser wittis . han waytid it ouere,
That it be lore laweffull and lusty to here.[113]

It seems that political verse was especially carefully circulated in its prepublication state—although the comment "ffor ʒit it is secrette" was simply
tactical (and probably disingenuous) in *Richard*. In any event, this passage and the Prologue to *Richard* generally display a metadiscursive authorial concern with the conventions of publishing political verse in late
fourteenth-century England. They remind the reader of a real world of
publication dangers, conveying precisely that use of "functional ambiguity" and authorial apologetics which many of Langland's more controversial passages do, especially those which teeter uneasily on the brink of
open dissent (although one feels that the *Richard* author is simply *using* the
conventions of political coyness, rather than drawing upon them in serious need, as Langland must have done).

Even when a work was not politically volatile, the moment of its
going forth into public was an anxious one, much commemorated in the
ubiquitous "Go, little book" motif[114] and in expensive author presentation
portraits. The biggest reason for the anxiety of this moment, beyond the
obvious ones which authors in any age would feel, was that it was the last
moment during which the author could assert real control over the state of
the text in a manuscript culture: no medieval author could be certain that a
text, once it left his hands or the hands of the scribe he'd supervised, would
ever be copied the same way twice. Authorial anxiety about maintaining
textual integrity, especially in instances where a work invited scribal "participation" by its polemical nature, as *Piers* did, can only be imagined. This
factor, coupled with a traditional prejudice against authorship, particularly
in monastic circles (where it was viewed as a mark of presumptuousness)
drove many authors to pretend that their works had never been intended
for publication, but had been surreptitiously "leaked."[115]

Although an author's claim that the text had been released without
his (or her) approval was often a form of modesty *topos*, many apparently
genuine instances can also be documented. As Bennett has said, "The author's rights in his work seem to have been very nebulous" (173). Most
often it seems to have been a friend or member of the author's literary circle
who leaked a text before the author was really ready to proceed to publication. Petrarch, Boccaccio, and Dante all complained of this violation.
Petrarch wrote to Boccaccio in 1363 complaining that his friend, Barbato

di Solmona, who had pestered him since 1352 for a copy of *Africa*, had broken his promise not to circulate the 34 verses he had given him. Root summarizes the letter: "From that day Petrarch never entered the library of a *litterato* without finding his poor verses, the native rudeness of which had been made worse by the corruption of the copyist."[116] Since Petrarch's reluctance to publish his *Africa* is a certainty (he never did), this complaint must represent more than convention, and, as Root has noted, several copies of the thirty-four verses still exist in manuscript. Petrarch's original letter of 1352 to Barbato di Solmona cites particularly his concern that the work was "unripe" for publication, adding that he would not send it "especially since it could not be retrieved once it has made a public appearance and since my judgement daily undergoes extraordinary change." Similarly, Boccaccio suffered a larger premature breach of promise when his friend Hugo de Sancto Severino surreptitiously circulated his *De Genealogia Deorum*, which had been entrusted to him only upon the condition that Hugo would not allow another copy to be made until Boccaccio could give him his final corrections. Revealingly, Boccaccio says, "And what is most grievous to me, I hear that it has been spread abroad (divulgatus) among many, not by my liberality but as the gift of another; so that all hope is take from me of making over into something better an imperfect work."[117]

A similar leakage process may account for the prepublication circulation of either or both passages from the C-text identified by Scase (C Prol. 91–127 and C 9.66–281), but it may especially account for C Prol. 91–127 (on negligent clergy using the exemplum of Ophni and Phinees, sons of the High Priest, Heli), which is definitely unfinished because it lacks alliteration. As Derek Pearsall has said in his discussion of its appearance in the Ilchester MS, the passage gives us a glimpse of "the poet in his working-clothes, knocking out his first version, half-prose, half-verse, of a not very familiar biblical story."[118] The Ilchester MS was written by Doyle and Parkes's Scribe D, who is of particular significance as an early copyist of *Piers*, having connections both in the London book trade before the turn of the century and also with Southwest Worcestershire. What is remarkable about the passage on Heli's sons he preserves (and about its companion, C 9.66–281, on true and false beggars) is that, as Scase has shown, they contain *none* of the B-text material interlineated with the lines new to C one normally finds in the C textual tradition. However, they are both preceded and followed by a few contextualizing lines from the B-text (not just where they appear in the Ilchester MS, but in HM 114, the other MS containing these two passages in this uninterpolated form, as well).[119]

This should tell us something about Langland's revision process prior to the (full) publication of C. What the evidence seems to suggest is that Langland wrote these two passages *without* having had extended recourse to his B copy in order to work out exactly how the new material might be integrated with the old. He did, however, before they escaped his hands (either as unsanctioned leakage or by his own decision to circulate them) know *where* he wanted to insert them in his B-text. As Donaldson showed, Langland probably worked with loose sheets (on which the new lines were written) and cues for insertion.[120] What these pieces of textual evidence point toward is Langland's preoccupation with writing new material composed quite independently from his B-text, but meant ultimately for insertion in it, to strengthen and clarify it, so to speak, on very topical issues—issues, moreover, which his poem had partly helped to make topical. The subjects of these "independent" passages give us some clue about Langland's concerns prior to the final publication of C, and as such, they are interesting as attempts to deal with issues raised by Wyclif and the Rising of 1381: the C 9 passage is an extended attempt to differentiate the beggars and "lollares" (who were threatening to the social structure) from the "deserving poor" and the legitimate lollars (who in Langland's opinion were not). In the latter group, he is especially concerned to distinguish the lunatic lollars, God's "priue disciples" (9.118), who for Langland were living witnesses to a latter day *vita apostolica*. The passage on Heli's sons attacks the negligence of priests and prelates, particularly where they encourage devotion to false relics because it profits them "into pursward" (C Prol. 101). But both passages deal with the issues in a very Langlandian way, motivated as they are primarily by reformist initiative and his relentless quest for true spirituality, not simply by ecclesiastical politics. The latter is not a Wycliffite attack on images (although it could easily be taken for one), but an attack on shrines set up on false premises—the fact that it escaped his hands in an unfinished state suggests how interested some of his readers were in his opinion on a very, very current issue. One can easily imagine these passages being used or adapted as broadside material.

Moreover, the C 9 passage, especially, shows that Langland was responding to the new jargon of what Scase calls "anticlericalism," but which I would prefer to call interclerical controversy (the word "lollar" was likely being used controversially as early as 1382).[121] Langland provides his own definition of the word in this new passage (C9.213–218), a word which he had used without defining in the B-text, in fact, and which in C he defends (at least apparently) on the basis of a traditionally *English* usage ("As by þe Engelisch of oure eldres, of olde mennes techynge," 214)—a point which suggests that he is *now* aware of an alternative use based on a new borrowing from Dutch ("lollaert"), and no doubt of the foreign interclerical controversies which gave rise to it.[122] The prepublication circulation of these passages, then, establishes that Langland was writing from a position on the cutting edge (so to speak) of ecclesiastical disturbances, and that he was regarded as such by readers who valued his responses to current issues enough to snap them up even before they were finished. This gives us a different view of Langland's situation while writing C, during which he was obviously surrounded by some sort of coterie, and responding to new ecclesiastical and political concerns minute by minute while still trying to hang on to Langlandian ideals (and perhaps some sense of English linguistic traditions) in the midst of interclerical furor. One thinks of the situation Hoccleve portrays in his *Series* poems, in which he dramatizes a member of his coterie beating down the door just as he finishes a poem, and then spending the next poem giving the poet unsolicited advice on its suitability for publication. If any one in Langland's coterie raised the spectre of such (absurd) audience sensitivity as Hoccleve's friend does in "Dialogue with a Friend," it seems hardly surprising that Langland was driven to write an *apologia*, ultimately defending and revising the way his poem had impacted on its initial audiences.

Were the passages leaked? We may never know. Wendy Scase has gone so far as to argue that the defensiveness of the C5 *apologia* was a result of audience criticism of these passages (462–63), which is possible, but could be unnecessarily specific; the *apologia* may simply represent a further (or another) evolution of the same response to topical concerns; that is, that he initially thought of the obliquely defensive strategy of distinguishing good and bad "lollars," and then hit upon the idea of a self-portrait portraying his own difficulties. We do know that the leaking of topical material could be a serious problem for authors dealing in controversial theological wares; Pecock complained that some of his writings:

ben runne abrood and copied aȝens my wil and myn entent, as y haue openli prechid at poulis, and þat bi vncurtesie and vndiscresioun of freendis, into whos singuler siȝt y lousid þo writinges to go, and forto not haue go ferþir into tyme þei were bettir examyned of me and approvid of my lordis and fadreis of þe churche, y wole to be as noon of myn; but in as moche as in me is, y wole þei be rendrid up aȝen, and bettir formes of þe same be to hem deliuered, whanne dewe deliueraunce þerof schal be made.[123]

Pecock was so concerned about the work's going into circulation before it had been "bettir examyned of me and approvid of my lordis and fadris of þe churche," that he "openli prechid at poules," publicizing the leak and going so far as to deny his authorship of these works, which, he writes, "y wole to be as noon of myn." Pecock's sensitivity on this point may give us some insight into Langland's situation between the publication of B and C—precisely the time during which Lollardy first rears its head—as we have seen some of what Langland felt free to criticize or represent in B he clearly felt uneasy about in C, and in the C-revisions we see him struggling to clarify his reformist stance and his position on social issues by revisions aimed at affirming orthodoxy without giving up the prophetic and charismatic beliefs he so cherished.

It seems, then, that there was for medieval authors a kind of intermediate stage between composition and formal publication in which the work might circulate among a few friends from whom the author was hoping for approval, correction, or constructive criticism. But what kind of control could a medieval author exert after publication? Inevitably even the most careful authors found themselves having to issue corrections, and in this the relative narrowness of the circle that constituted any medieval author's initial audience was an advantage. Petrarch's letters contain several remarks about his attempts to insert corrections after the publication of a text, a process which involved sending the corrections to friends who owned copies of his work, or having someone (in one instance Boccaccio) read the corrected version aloud while Petrarch himself inserted the changes in several copies before him.[124] One finds a similar phenomenon in Gower MSS, in which there are several instances of the same hand correcting more than one copy of the *Vox Clamantis* (the same *correcting* hand appears in as many as four MSS; moreover, up to three correctors have contributed emendations in each of four MSS at different times).[125] It looks from this evidence as if members of his coterie sometimes employed the same scribe to make corrections—corrections which are interesting in themselves because they reflect changes in Gower's political views (the fact that the *Vox* was in Latin, of course, allowed a "safe" range of circulation for potentially controversial opinions). The pattern of scribal activity in *Vox* MSS, then, reflects the topical nature of Gower's poems and suggests that owners wanted copies corrected when they became aware of his change of views. Moreover, the fact that some of these changes were inserted after Gower's death suggests a great deal about the control that Gower, and later his literary executors, exercised over the textual qualities of his works. It also tells us a great deal about the closeness of Gower's immediate readership. However, with writers like Petrarch and Gower we have full-fledged humanist literary circles drawn together, no doubt, by a humanist (or consciously classicizing) concept of authorship. To what extent is this model of authorship relevant to Langland?

There is no doubt that Langland's authorial self-concept was much more traditionally Anglo-Saxon in character. (We have just noted an instance of his respect, or at least, appearance of respect, for "þe Engelisch of oure eldres, of olde mennes techynge" (9.214)). In the A-text the authorial role projected into the text is virtually that of the alliterative scop.[126] After telling Will that love is "þe plante of pes," Holy Church adds that he should "preche it in þin harpe/ [Þer] þou art m[er]y at mete, ʒif men bidde þe ʒedde" (A 1.137–38). Later in the poem, in a split reflecting the as yet unstable connection between the recitation of poetry and the writing down of it, the role of Will as author is momentarily and metadiscursively projected as almost purely scribal in nature:

> Þanne were marchauntis merye; many wepe for ioye,
> And ʒaf wille for his writyng wollene clopis;
> For he co[pie]de þus here clause þei [couden] hym gret mede.
> (A8.42–44)

This is a striking moment of bibliographic awareness. The merchants are relieved and delighted because Piers's pardon has made room for them (admittedly in the margin) in a covenant of salvation with Truth. Will's role in the drama is that of a legal scribe (which may have been Langland's means of livelihood for some time), but, of course, he is also the poet who is composing the entire poem. These two very different senses in which Will is a writer[127] simultaneously capture, first of all, the as yet imperfect transition between oral and written discourse, and, second, the visionary-reformist voice which is part of Langland's complex authorial voice. In religious visionary genres generally, the authorial role is always conceived as scribal, because the source of the inspiration must be seen to be divine (St. John, the archetype of all medieval visionaries, is told, "What thou seest, write in a book," Apoc. 1:11).[128] Moreover, as Nichols has recently shown, the connection between the oral and written aspects of a poet's work from the thirteenth century onward is evident in features of manuscript preparation which stress the "envoicement" of the text (i.e., those features which stress "the poetic voice to be a dual phenomenon of writing and speaking," 139). Nichols provides instances of this in some dramatic author portraits from troubadour manuscripts of the thirteenth and fourteenth centuries, one of which captures the duality of Langland's authorial self-concept in his earliest text precisely: the troubadour poet is shown declaiming *from his desk*, with the hand holding his pen raised in an oratorical gesture.[129] Similarly, it may be no accident that the only two manuscripts of *Piers Plowman* which contain illustrations (of the poem itself) have historiated initials at the opening of the Prologue containing an "author" portrait.[130] Clearly the problems of *auctoritas* raised by the authorial voice in the poem did not go unnoticed by those preparing copies of the poem. The supervisor of the Corpus MS chose as the poem's single illustration a reassuring portrait of the dreamer as, one might say, a scholar and a gentleman, even adapting the first word of the poem to accommodate it. Moreover, the supervisor of Douce 104, as Linda Olson has pointed out, chose the splendidly self-referential strategy of using the clerkly dreamer's long body to "historiate" the initial "Y" of the poem's first word.[131] While clerkly author portraits are commonplace in obviously clerkly texts (especially bibles, commentaries, and the like), their presence in vernacular English poems is rarer,[132] which makes its use in the two *Piers* manuscripts interesting.

In the B-text a more modern concept of authorship is already emerging: although he has not yet found it necessary to spiritualize minstrelsy in order to justify its use even as an image (as in C), the poet is portrayed as self-absorbed in his concern with the validity of "meddling with makings"[133] and with the dangers to the poet of adopting a forthright stance as social and ecclesiastical critic (B 11.91–106a). These authorial images shift again in the C-text to a new confidence in the power of his writing, a new self-defensiveness about his own life and means of livelihood in relation to his prophetic gifts, and a new anxiety to control the reception of his text to avoid future political (and ecclesiastical) misappropriation. These shifts are dramatic, and suggest that as his revisions progressed he gave increasing attention to authorial self-image. Loewenstein suggests how difficult circumstances bred a heightened sense of authorial self-image and literary property in early seventeenth-century London; similarly, even if Langland's sense of authorship was not such as might have been fostered by humanism, it seems that both traditional alliterative images of authorship and the politicized environment in which his B-text was read made him authorially aware enough to produce the C *apologia* and to take care that the C version would never undergo the same process of corruption and misappropriation. (And, given the relative stability of the C tradition, he would seem to have been more successful here, although the overseeing of C's publication, so far as we know, was as likely the responsibility of literary executors as of

Langland).[134] However, the awareness came too late for B—what, exactly, did Langland find when he returned to B to begin the revision process?

Bennett once speculated about what happened during Langland's revision process as follows:

Langland is not likely to have had a clean copy of the poem in his possession. Indeed, if he had had one it would not have been easy for him to rewrite and to change the place of so many passages. With his 'foul papers,' however, he could rearrange, rewrite, and in the course of time produce a very different 'edition' from his original (A) text. It is much more difficult to account for the changes if the reworking was done (whether by the author or by another person) on the A or B texts as we now have it. (177)

But rearranging and revising from his foul papers could not account for the making of C, since, as Kane and Donaldson have shown (121), we know that "the C-reviser's B" was corrupt, and that Langland was forced to make some of the revisions he made in order simply to deal with the corruption before him—never mind carrying out his *intended* strategy for revision, which, even though it was inconsistently applied, had some very consistent purposes.[135] (Perhaps the most important of these is the spiritualizing tendency which transforms and refocuses the more worldly B-text, mitigating and translating into another sphere many of the political problems B had raised.) Bennett's opinion was so authoritative for Kane and Donaldson that it was one of the things which initially inhibited them from coming to the conclusion to which they found all the evidence pointed.[136] They explain:

And for the opinion that Langland would more easily have made changes on 'foul papers' than a fair copy we can discover no reason: it seems simply mistaken. For an author's own fair copy is at least as likely as not to have been unbound; thus there would be no necessary physical difficulty about rearranging its contents. And its clean margins (probably handsomer than those in surviving manuscripts, which are often cropped) would as any author knows not merely accommodate but actively invite additions and substitutions. (122)

But what fair copy was Langland working from, if not from his "foul papers" in revising B? It cannot have been his *own* fair copy he worked from, even though Kane and Donaldson imply in the above quotation that his final revision process *was* carried out on his "fair copy." One could assume—if Langland were following the process Chaucer describes in his poem, "Adam"—that "his corrected version of the scribal copy would supersede his own autograph,"[137] but this would account for only a small portion of the corruption in the C-reviser's B. As Edwards and Pearsall say of the text resulting from the process Chaucer describes, "it would contain the 'mistakes' (i.e., scribal and original errors unnoticed by the author in revision) that constitute the reason for distinguishing, in textual criticism, between scribal archetype and author's text" (259). Kane and Donaldson do suggest that the "copying in the first phase was professional" (124); however, the nature and extent of the corruption they reveal in the C-reviser's B is unlikely to have gone unnoticed in a copy which Langland had had made and *corrected himself*. This could be explained two ways. The first explanation would be that he (whether through poverty or some accident) did not have access to *either* his scribal archetype or his "foul papers"—which involves a double loss of some sort (we know, for instance, that Machaut normally had or had access to both kinds of copy).[138] But such a theory, of necessity, suggests that he also did not have access to a manuscript from among his "group of supporters," that is, a manuscript which had not yet undergone the kind of corruption process which Kane and Donaldson found in the C-reviser's B. (We know, for instance, from the work of Parkes and other scholars, that had Gower suffered such a double loss, *at least* three or four friends could have supplied a relatively recently corrected copy). This seems unlikely, however, given that it would appear from what we have seen so far that Langland was not working in total isolation. Kane and Donaldson say that Langland did not check his "C-reviser's B" before proceeding—but does this mean he had nothing to check it against? Or does it mean that Langland's standards of textual management (and those of his friends) were radically different from those of his more humanist contemporaries? The character of his C-revisions is perplexing on this point because of the sometimes sloppy, sometimes minute, obviously unfinished revision process it betrays. Although Kane and Donaldson have probably overemphasized aesthetic motivations for Langland's revisions, they have produced enough unquestionable evidence of aesthetic concern on his part to suggest that he cared deeply about his art, as well as about his politics, ecclesiology, and spirituality.

What is clear from the pattern of the revisions is that Langland never intended the kind of minute and complete revision which might begin with checking an entire manuscript (assuming he had something to check it against). As Pearsall explained in his edition, "The C-reviser seems to have worked piecemeal, outward from certain cores of dissatisfaction, rather than systematically through B from beginning to end" (10). The suggestion here, then, is that certain aspects of the poem as it stood (e.g., in relation to current affairs) disturbed him, and to these problems must be added the problem of a faulty base text; as Kane and Donaldson say,

he visibly reacted to many of the readings which we, for distinct modern editorial reasons, have identified as archetypally corrupt in B. The impression given is that when he did so this was not because he was aesthetically dissatisfied with what he believed he had earlier written but because he sensed that what lay before him was not as he had written it, was in an alien *usus scribendi*. (125)

Langland's perception of this "alien *usus scribendi*," I believe, provides another way of explaining why he used neither his foul papers nor his scribal archetype, nor even the reliable copy of a close literary friend: that is, he chose not to use them, compelled by the need to revise and correct a form of the text that was *already abroad*.

We know that although his B was corrupt, it was closer to the archetype than any existing B-MS today (Kane and Donaldson, 121–22). Perhaps it was close enough to make working with it bearable, and he thought he could rely on his memory for the rest (medieval memories, of course, were much more highly developed than our own, and Kane and Donaldson have shown that *some* of the evidence of his revision process suggests that he was groping back from a memory of what he had once written).[139] But given the political circumstances (i.e., the misappropriation of his reforming plowman, converted into political revolutionary by the rebels, and the hostilities that his poem had engendered both as a result of this misappropriation and by virtue of its uncompromising reformist stance), it also seems possible that he decided to work with the corrupt B *because it was the version already abroad*. The fact that in some places he was relying on memory would not necessarily contradict this premise, especially given the somewhat looser standards of textual management that certain aspects of his revision habits suggest. Interestingly, Petrarch defended the revision, correction, and republication of verses published when he was "young and immature" on the grounds that, although he would prefer to destroy them, since they had already been published (*"in publicum exivissent"*), they were long since distributed among his friends in faulty copies, and only reissuing them could salvage (or attempt to salvage) the situation (Root, 425). Clearly Langland, too, was aware of both the circulation of faulty copies and of political misreading of his work, and he may have seen these as overlapping problems. Petrarch's testimony shows that medieval authors were quite aware of faulty copies, and concerned about them; perhaps Langland began working with the corrupt B expecting (and dreading,

as one would) to see serious corruption on every leaf he turned up—a corrupt version of one's work would be a compelling object for any author.
But whether or not he began by trying to find the key to the misappropriation of his work, there is no doubt that some of the revisions he made on
the basis of that B-text were motivated by the corruption he found there,
as well as by political and ecclesiastical concerns, and that they show a serious attempt to *prevent* such misunderstanding of his text in the future.[140]

Whatever the reasons, he became intensely, though not systematically,
interested in revising and correcting a corrupt copy, and the result was the
C-text as we now have it, in which "errors" were allowed to stand in certain patches (including the entire last two passus) which the archetypal C
inherited along with its substantive revisions. Medieval authorial concerns
about resecuring control of a published text and about authorial responsibility—indeed, liability—for political repercussions obviously played a
large part in Langland's thinking. We still know relatively little about the
state of the earliest texts of *Piers Plowman* in circulation, but we know
that all three versions were very rapidly disseminated.[141] The Z-text provides an excellent example (and fortunately, probably an extreme one) of
the extent to which the authorship of the poem was a "social authorship."
Perhaps written sometime between 1376 and 1388, the degree of scribal
interference in or contribution to (depending on one's textual ideology)
Langland's A-text it sports is revealing evidence of what was happening to
Piers Plowman in the hands of a receptive (far too receptive) audience.[142]
Until further detailed textual and codicological work is completed, we will
be unable to do more than theorize about the evidently extraordinary circumstances of the C-revision. But we need to start looking at historical,
and not only aesthetic explanations (as important as Kane and Donaldson
have made these) of the evidence we already have, and for direction in interpreting what further textual and codicological work may tell us.

VI. Langland's Earliest Readers and the
Question of Patronage

Kane and Donaldson have attempted to quash, as a corollary of their findings about the "C-reviser's B," the perhaps romantic notion held by earlier
scholars that Langland could not afford a fair copy of his own poem, proposing instead on the basis of "historical likelihood" that he had "a patron
or group of supporters" (122). Following John Burrow, they note that

Langland's public was not of the marketplace or innyard; from its character his poem was directed to persons of education and therefore of some standing. This implies a patron or patrons, and the presumption is that one of these will have paid for making a necessarily postulated first, clean, scribal copy from which not only the MS tradition of B, but also—all hypotheses apart—the tradition of C XXI and XXII must descend.[143]

To think of Langland as having a patron is jolting—but given the historical evidence that Kane and Donaldson cite and the evidence slowly being gathered in Middle English manuscript studies, one realizes that perhaps it is naive to imagine him *not* having (or seeking) a patron. The cost of producing a book the length of *Piers Plowman*, even without elaborate decoration, was very high.[144] Even though recent studies of unbeneficed clergy (if indeed that is what Langland was) have shown less evidence of the widespread poverty among this class that scholars once imagined, it seems unlikely that a clerk in minor orders (and therefore unable to perform the most lucrative job open to unbeneficed clergy, saying masses in a chantry) could easily sustain the cost of issuing three successive versions of a long poem.[145]

Langland, then, must have had patronage of some sort, as well as some "group of supporters." Clearly he was circulating his poetry to someone. He must have had a "coterie," or if not a coterie, in the conscious, humanist sense that one associates with Petrarch and Boccaccio, or Chaucer and Gower, at least a group of interested friends or colleagues. Langland's poetry certainly lacks the *overt* features of coterie writing, like Chaucer's explicit naming of friends in an envoy or even within the text of a larger poem, like *Troilus*. However, the political nature of the poetry Langland was writing might well explain its superficially "impersonal" aspect. Moreover, the poem does furnish some tentative evidence of in-joking: for instance, Langland's reference to the greedy friar at the Feast of Patience as "þis iurdan" (15.92) may be a punning reference to Friar William Jordan, a well-known Dominican opponent of Uhtred de Boldon.[146] This is not precisely the same kind of thing as, for instance, Chaucer's punning reference to "Vache" supplied in the envoy attached to "Truth,"[147] but it is an indication of shared literary experience of precisely the type we would expect Langland's associates to trade in: that is, a knowledge of the latest ecclesiological polemics. Nor is this the *openly* shared literary experience we see in Chaucer's casual allusion to the Wife of Bath in "The Envoy to Bukton,"[148] and with good reason. The kind of literary wares Langland is dealing in— interclerical polemics, reformist prophecy, and theological controversy—

are not such as one would openly advertise in connection with named contemporaries. But there can be little doubt of the existence of coded writing in the poem: to begin with, *Piers Plowman* contains enough scholarly cruxes, the solutions to which, judging by scribal puzzlement, have not been lost recently.[149] Its prophetic passages also abound in obscurities which Langland must have expected *some* readers to be able to construe (or more precisely, decode).[150] Medieval prophecies, both religious and political, are notoriously difficult; even medieval readers complained of their obscurity, and interest in them has been declared "slightly unusual" by a recent historian of medieval reading habits.[151] What evidence we have regarding their genesis (and it is still not enough) suggests that they were usually produced for some immediate, knowledgeable, and often secretive audience who *did* understand them.[152] In fact, the inclusion of prophecy at all in his poem, especially the sophisticated brand he chose, links Langland with a somewhat dangerous, and certainly secretive world (or even underworld) of pseudonymous attribution and cautious transmission.

The fact that we know so little about Langland today may have as much to do with this aspect of his work as it does with the games of "naming and not naming" which so many fourteenth-century writers engaged in. It is striking that we usually know who the poets who indulged in such literary games *were* (i.e., by external evidence) in a way that we do not know who Langland was.[153] Moreover, the prophecies, along with other passages in the poem, show every evidence of operating for a dual audience —those "in the know" and those who are not (for whom they still function, but less satisfactorily). Langland, as we have seen, made use of "functional ambiguity" and other strategies for communication with a stratified readership (like the encoding of prophecies) in periods of political or ecclesiastical authoritarianism. Even the dullest reader would have picked up the sense of a second agenda by the end of the Prologue, where Langland tantalizes us with the first of many "if I dared, I'd interpret" comments: "What þis meteles bymeneth, ȝe men þat ben merye, / Deuyne ȝe, for y ne dar, by dere god almyhten" (217–18). Unfortunately, this is not the place for a detailed analysis of Langland's many teasing ambiguities, in which he skillfully both says and does not say what he wants, frequently using the interface between latin and Middle English to help "grade" the degree of radicalism on view for two different audiences.[154] But as any close study of this aspect of his work indicates, Langland always provides himself with the minimum amount of cover—sometimes it is the merest figleaf—to disguise otherwise explicitly dangerous and unacceptable comments or information; even the care he takes in his self-naming suggests this, as we have seen.

There have been very few studies of Middle English coterie writing, but from what we know, Langland's poetry appears to lack only the most obvious features of such literature, such as the explicit naming of colleagues. Interestingly, most evidence for coterie writing comes not so much from the court (as parallels with Renaissance poets might lead us to suspect), but rather from the civil service. Perhaps the best example is Hoccleve's following at the Privy Seal, but as Lenaghan has said of Chaucer's "The Envoy to Scogan," "the social context . . . is the civil service of Richard II, a bureaucracy of clerks and a fellowship of gentlemen,"[155] implying that even Chaucer's was to some extent a coterie of the "workplace." Hoccleve's coterie seems to have centered around the Privy Seal and Chester's Inn; he playfully mentions two younger colleagues, "Prentys and Arondel," for instance, when speaking about his reluctance to part with his pillow after a night of reveling ("Male Regle," lines 319–25). The tone of the reference indicates that they were primary among his readership (important here as well is his later testimony in the "Complaint" to the steadfast friendship of his fellow clerks during and after his illness). In fact, as a number of scholars have recently shown, civil servants and scriveners were an important primary and secondary audience for Ricardian and Henrician vernacular poetry generally.[156] Another instance of coterie readership involving just such a group occurs in marginal apparatus of the *Omne Bonum*, in the authorially created annotations to the work, written between 1360 and 1375 by James le Palmer, Treasurer's scribe in the Exchequer of Edward III. Le Palmer explicitly addresses some of his annotations to fellow officers in the Exchequer: for instance, besides the entry entitled "Clericus venator," he wrote, "Note here that hunting is forbidden to clerks and this goes against [hoc facit contra] W. de Hanley."[157] Le Palmer's extensive knowledge of the literature of clerical controversy, canon law, and moral issues generally suggests the kinds of intellectual interests (and humor) he shared with his colleagues, and it suggests further that the reading of such a workplace coterie might not be restricted to "literary" interests at all.

Of course we know nothing for certain of Langland's "workplace," but it seems likely that he was situated among the unbeneficed and underemployed clergy who earned a livelihood by a variety of lesser clerical jobs, including saying prayers and legal secretarial work. This is precisely the kind of group—educated, frustrated, and underemployed—who might take an interest in his work, although his immediate circle of readers may have included clerks with better positions and prospects, too.[158] If, then, he had a group of supporters, as seems entirely likely given the complex layering of response at which the poem so obviously aims, who were the readers on the top layer? We can only speculate, but they are a readership to be envied, since it is highly unlikely that Langland wrote in a vacuum, wondering whether any reader would ever appreciate his verbal agility and multivalent ambiguities. (Certainly, the evidence provided by many of his scribes indicates that not all medieval readers were so capable.) If, as he tells us, even the "lewede ermytes" of Cornhill were aware of his written criticisms of them and their ilk (5.3–5), a group of more learned Londoners (and West Midlanders) must have been, too.

Among the readers and owners during Langland's lifetime, we know of two politically active—not to say sensationally active—ones: John Ball, of course, must have shared or discussed his reading of the poem with others, because his allusions to *Piers* in the rebel letters would make little sense if he had simply gleaned them privately. Ball's letters conjure up images of *Piers* conventicles, on the model of Lollard ones, and suggest a mixed stratum of readers and *hearers*.[159] How accurate this image is is difficult to say, but we need not assume that all such readers read (or heard) Langland as radically as Ball did. Second, we know that Thomas Usk, originally a scrivener (executed in 1388) quotes and borrows from the C-text fairly extensively (see below).[160] Another, less dramatic, but apparently sociopolitically motivated, reader is William Palmere,[161] rector of St. Alphage, Cripplegate, who bequeathed a copy of the poem in his will in 1400. A man of slightly democratic impulses, as Wood has noted, he asked to be buried in the churchyard among his parishoners, not in the chancel, and perhaps more surprisingly, he bequeathed his copy of *Piers* to one of the few women known to be in Langland's audience, Agnes Eggesfeld.[162] However, that other women were in Langland's immediate audience is quite likely: the *apologia* refers to visits "now with hym, now with here" (line 51), and if this is not simply for the convenience of alliteration, it suggests a mixed clientele who may have been willing to hear more than prayers from their visitor. Wood concludes that the fact that Palmere "possessed a copy of the poem as early as 1400 in London brings us a little closer to the audience for whom Langland wrote. His poem was known and valued apparently by both sexes, in the town where the author had worked and taught. Perhaps William Langland . . . sat down to supper with the rector of St. Alphage" (86).

Usk and Palmere are most certainly—and Ball, possibly—London readers, and early ones at that. But political radicals and progressive clerks are not the only two groups who took an interest in the poem. As Turville-Petre has reminded us, the immediate audience for Langland's poem, as for other alliterative poetry, was likely to have been "the gentry . . . knights, franklins, and the clergy, the educated men often with positions of local authority."[163] And to this should be added Anne Middleton's observation that what the medieval audience of *Piers*, diverse as it is, invariably has in common was that "their customary activities involve them in counsel, policy, education, administration, pastoral care—in those tasks and offices where spiritual and temporal governance meet" ("Audience and Public," 104). However, among pre-1400 readers (and possible readers), two overlapping subgroups from those Middleton has distinguished stand out strikingly, the significance of neither of which has been recognized: civil servants and scribes. Both groups link Langland's poem directly to the London, and in a few cases, West Midlands literary community, and if such links are evident during a period for the most part of which we assume Langland was alive (i.e., 1369–1400), perhaps they shed some light upon his immediate circle. That Langland had such a literary community among pre-1400 readers is apparent from examining not just the kinds of readers we know by name from this period, but the kind of response they made to the poem.

Among very early readers is John But (or someone calling himself by that name), whose knowledge of the poem in more than one version Anne Middleton has recently shown to be so sympathetic. He may or may not be identifiable: one possible identification is with a king's messenger of that name, a civil servant, whose work would have taken him to and from London; moreover (if the identification is accurate), he apparently had links to Gloucestershire as well. By the 1380s this John But was likely, as Middleton suggests, "close to the west-south-west midlands area from which the C text appears to have been disseminated." However, other identifications are equally possible, and it is also entirely likely that But was a code name.[164] A second pre-1400 reader, likely from Langland's native area, is the Ilchester redactor, who took such an intelligent (not to say creative) interest in his work on the poem. Both readers add something to the poem's textual history which we have from no other source.[165]

Among readers associated, so far as we know, just with London, Usk

is perhaps most significant. Thomas Usk was originally a scrivener, hired
by the mayor, Northampton, and his faction "to write thair billes."[166] But
despite his unfortunate political career, his literary appreciation of Langland manifested itself in numerous echoes and borrowings in the *Testament*—some, like his reworking of the C-text's Tree of Charity passage,
quite extensive—and this may have been in progress as early as 1384.[167]
Usk was probably on the periphery of Chaucer's acquaintances among the
royal faction. Paul Strohm writes of him that he may have heard Chaucer's
works read,

since he was in and about London in the 1380s, was hand in glove with Brembre
(after 1383), and even gained provisional and ill-fated admission to the royal faction
between autumn 1387 and his death in 1388. More probably, though—given his
role as a rather shadowy and Pynchonesque inhabitant of what Chaucer probably
considered a political demimonde—he encountered Chaucer's works in manuscript
form. While working on his *Testament of Love* between late 1384 and mid-1387, he
may have had access to Chaucer's *Boece.* . . . , and he refers to Chaucer's *Troilus*.[168]

He certainly knew (indeed plundered) Chaucer's translation of Boethius
and the *Troilus*, also, like Langland's C-text, *very, very* recent works when
Usk was writing the *Testament*.[169] Obviously, Usk was in touch with the
newest works of *both* Chaucer and Langland in the mid-1380s—which suggests a number of things, in particular, a London literary community small
enough to share the quick dissemination (either by public recitation or by
efficient manuscript production) of *substantial* literary texts.

Usk's witness, then, is valuable as an indicator of a pre-1400 London
vernacular literary circle, a circle which manuscript studies is increasingly
revealing to be very small indeed. As V. J. Scattergood has shown, with respect to the poetry of Gower and Chaucer, "there is no evidence that the
merchant class were part of it,"; nor indeed were the aristocracy, for

from the evidence of books owned by the aristocracy it appears they preferred
literature in Latin and French on a variety of serious subjects, but that for entertainment they relied almost exclusively on romances; the career diplomats, civil
servants, officials and administrators, on the other hand, appear to have been open
to the new, serious-minded poetry . . . often written in the vernacular.[170]

Scattergood goes on to cite Sir John Clanvowe, who attacked "the values
of the court and the literature which sustains these values," all of which
suggests that the readership for serious vernacular literature in London in
the 1380s was largely made up of scribes and civil servants, as well as some

progressive clergy and members of the knightly class (like Clanvowe). The narrowness of this circle in what was after all still, by modern standards, a very small city, suggests that most vernacular writers and readers were likely to be acquainted. There is every chance that Chaucer and Langland knew each other's works (and possibly each other personally). Schmidt suggests that Chaucer's Plowman was inspired by Piers, and more recently Helen Cooper has argued very plausibly that Chaucer probably knew at least the A-text.[171] Moreover, Hoccleve, although a much younger man, was like Usk a clerk, and like Chaucer a civil servant; there are indications internal to his poetry (a few of which we have seen) that he may have known the C-text of *Piers Plowman*.[172] If this surmise is correct, we have another instance of a scrivener-civil servant who is also (or would be) a writer himself, reading both Langland and Chaucer. Hoccleve was educated in London's Inns of Chancery in the 1380s and began work in the Office of the Privy Seal Easter 1387. As Tout, and more recently Richardson, has shown, the lively social and intellectual life of the inns were a breeding ground for literary men during the period Langland was writing and for centuries afterward (one thinks of John Donne). Noting that two such men, Richard Sotheworth and John Stopyndon, civil servants and clerks of the royal Chancery, were early owners of Chaucer's works, Richardson says that the inns were filled with "young men who hoped to make their way in life through the use of the written word. They were united, whatever their grade, by the study of the English writ system and the medieval dictamen or art of letter-writing."[173] We know on the basis of internal evidence that Langland may have worked as a legal scribe himself, and John Fisher has recently tentatively connected several *Piers* manuscripts with evidence of Chancery production.[174] In fact there can be little doubt that some *Piers* MSS were produced by such young men. Doyle mentions, for instance, the Duke of Westminster's MS, an A and C conflation "which is written in an elegant set secretary of the kind employed by Privy Seal and some other official scribes at the beginning of the fifteenth century, with bastard anglicana rubrics, coloured initials, parasigns and line-fillers; it is simplest, though not necessary, to guess that this may have been so commissioned and executed in that milieu" (46).

To think of Usk, But (whoever he was), and possibly Chaucer and Hoccleve, along with an unknown number of civil servants and scribes[175] in Langland's first audience not only dilutes the chiefly religious image of his audience that modern scholars cherish, but it also links Langland's poem—and possibly Langland himself—more firmly with London literary

circles. What is striking about four of Langland's early London readers—
Usk, and (possibly) But, Chaucer, and Hoccleve—is that all apparently
"made" (in the Middle English sense) a literary response to it. Moreover,
John Ball's response was "literary" as well: he created a sequel, after a fashion, in which Langland's protagonist was the star player.[176] All this literary
activity, even leaving aside the appearance of early *Piers* tradition poems
like *Pierce the Ploughman's Crede* (whose author also knew London), suggests a literary community of some sophistication and with rapid habits of
dissemination.

The association of Langland's poem with this community is further
suggested by what Doyle and Parkes have established about the scribe of
the important University of London C-text, the "Ilchester MS"; he was
a specialist (so to speak) in Middle English texts because he made a stag-
gering eight copies of Gower's *Confessio*, two of the *Canterbury Tales*, and
one of Trevisa's *On the Properties of Things*—expensive manuscripts written
and illuminated, apparently, in London. The Ilchester MS is of special significance because it contains, along with HM 114, the passages of C which
circulated prior to C's publication. Scribe D, as Doyle and Parkes call him
for his stint on the Trinity Gower, was active in the late fourteenth and
early fifteenth centuries, although the Ilchester MS is known to be among
his early pieces of work. As Jeremy Smith has explained in his analysis
of Scribe D's dialect, "Given the origin of the C-texts of *Piers Plowman*
in the S[outh[W[est] M[idlands], it is appropriate that D should start
his copying career by producing such a text [i.e., as the Ilchester *Piers*]."
Smith goes on to explain that the linguistic profile of Scribe D is entirely
consistent with what we know of "reasonably educated men" who came
up from the provinces seeking their fortunes, Dick Whittington style.[177]
Moreover, the decoration of Ilchester also points to the fact that it was one
of D's first pieces, perhaps done as early as the 1380s.[178] Clearly Ilchester
was copied during Langland's lifetime or very shortly thereafter. The professionalism of the Ilchester MS, and the fact that Scribe D is known to
have subsequently copied Gower and Chaucer in even more lavish editions, and to have worked, on at least one occasion, with the scribe of
Ellesmere and Hengwrt (Scribe B), suggests that, between the two of
them, either they, or the stationer for whom they worked, were in touch
with sources of some of the best Middle English exemplars of the Ricardian poets.[179] Not only did Scribe D have access to some very good exemplars, but his links (or his boss's) with London literary circles have been
illuminated further: one of his colleagues on the Trinity Gower was, of

course, Hoccleve, who was moonlighting from the Privy Seal as Doyle and Parkes's Scribe E. Christianson has shown what a close-knit community the scribes, stationers, limners, and parchment makers of late fourteenth-/ early fifteenth-century London were—indeed, of necessity, since they were mainly cramped together in Pater Noster Row. That stationers, who were of course in a good position to know what kinds of books were selling, could be actively involved in the literary community appears (at least by the early fifteenth century) in the evidence that one of them commissioned a poem from Hoccleve.[180] That Hoccleve may have known the C-text of *Piers* has already been suggested; that one of his fellow scribes on the Trinity Gower had already copied a C-text of *Piers* is beyond doubt. Although it is clear from Doyle and Parkes's evidence that Hoccleve could hardly have done his share of the copying on the same premises (i.e., at the next desk) as his colleagues, it is not unreasonable to assume that "young men who hoped to make their way in life through the use of the written word," to cite Richardson again, might have spoken of literary matters to one another, especially given that vernacular literature was such a minority interest. The significant point here is that within Langland's lifetime and not long after his death, his work can be associated with the same kind of readership and distribution center as Chaucer's and Gower's,[181] giving us a glimpse of the literary marketplace within the London literary community itself in which he was copied and read.

To sum up, then, among his "group of supporters" could no doubt be counted reform-minded, beneficed clerics like William Palmere, interested in social and ecclesiological issues; unbeneficed clerics ("clerical proletariat") serving as chantry priests, parish clerks, secretaries, beadsmen, legal scribes or clerks (like Usk and Hoccleve); and perhaps various civil servants like John But, interested in moral and political questions (there can be a good deal of overlap among these categories, of course). But what of his patron(s)? If one takes the analogy of Chaucer, whose "group of supporters" or literary circle included men like Gower and Strode—men similar in social class and education, but whose patrons (insofar as we know) would have included men of much higher rank, like John of Gaunt—then we must look to classes more wealthy and influential than those we've been describing. Two likely types present themselves. Langland's (relative) deference to monks (in comparison that is, to his severity upon the other orders of regular and secular clergy), might indicate a monastic patron of some sort: copies of the poem like the one in the Vernon MS, and the one possibly owned by the Oxford black monk, John Wells (the Z-text), might support an early Benedictine connection (certainly Wells himself was influential in his order).[182] Second, his patron(s) may have come from the "gentle" classes. There is a variety of evidence in the poem of Langland's sympathy for the well-born: for instance, in his C 5 diatribe against the upward mobility of "bondmen's barnes," as we have seen, he seems to be speaking for two victimized groups: a "clerical proletariat" of qualified, unbeneficed clergy passed over because of nepotism and simony, and a group of "pore gentel blood" (line 78) who have mortgaged the family farm, so to speak, to fight for the realm.[183] Moreover, if what the Trinity College, Dublin, 212, note says about him is true, Langland himself came from a background which would have made the seeking of patronage from a local lord quite natural.[184] Among other instances of Langland's pro-"gentel" stance, one might cite the prophecy that the monasteries will be reformed by a king acting with the barons (B 10.322–35; C 5.168–80), after which, in the B-text, Will innocently asks, " 'Thanne is dowel and dobet', quod I, 'dominus and kny3thode?' " (B 10.336). This comment, as mentioned above, disappears in the C-text, along with a number of other inflammatory remarks, probably in deference to the conclusions of the Blackfriar's Council of 1382.[185]

The most striking instance, however, of Langland's special respect for knighthood is his treatment of the knight in the ploughing of the half-acre episode. Although Langland's knight is stereotypically courteous ("as his kynde wolde," C 8.161), his slightly democratic inclinations (he is willing to help Piers plow) — cannot have been so commonplace:

"Ac on þe teme trewely tau3t was I neuere.
[Ac] kenne me," quod þe kny3t, "and [I wole konne erie]."
(B 6.22–23)

Such an inclination has to be muted in the more politically sensitive C-text:

"Ac on þe teme treuely ytauhte was y neuere.
Y wolde y couthe," quod the knyhte, "by Crist and his moder;
Y wolde assaie som tyme *for solace as hit were.*" (C 8.20–22;
emphasis mine)

Most interesting, however, is that in both texts Langland is careful not to show his knight in a battle unworthy of a man of his status, that is, in a confrontation with Wastour (C 8.161 ff.). Unfit, by nature of the very courtesy and respect which Langland so pointedly attributes to him, to deal with so outrageous a phenomenon as Wastour, Langland relieves the knight of this unpleasant task by having Piers call in the impersonal protagonist, Hunger, to do the job. This is the same strategy which, as Greenblatt has shown, certain Renaissance poets used, perhaps for the same reasons; the closest parallels to Langland here are in Sidney and Spenser, both, incidentally, poets seeking court (or courtly) patronage. When Artegall is faced with a "lawlesse multitude" seeking revenge, he is at a loss, "For loth he was his noble hands t'embrew/ In the base blood of such a rascall crew," but equally fearing that "shame would him persew" if he retired, he sends in Talus to deal with the situation. As Greenblatt observes, "Artegall takes the nobler course which is to persuade and to negotiate; the violence . . . is the prerogative of Talus who can no more receive dishonor than can a Cruise missile."[186] Like Spenser, Langland attributes the victory over unworthy adversaries to a "mechanical monster,"[187] but for Langland (unlike his more complacent Renaissance counterpart), the matter does not end there—in fact, Langland's social sympathies, so evident elsewhere, have usually led readers to ignore this kind of parallel with overtly deferential courtly writers.

We are, of course, in no position to speculate upon who among the knightly class might have read or supported Langland's poetry, but the existence of a group of Ricardian knights with reformist sympathies has been long established, and it is easy to imagine that a knight of the mental stamp of Sir John Clanvowe, for instance, would have been very interested in what Langland was writing. Like the poet, he shared much common ground with Lollard thinkers, but his extant writings are entirely orthodox. Like Langland, he uses what Scase calls "the new language of anticlericalism" unusually sympathetically.[188] However, for the kind of financial support and protection that Langland may have needed, it seems possible that a magnate rather than a knight played the role of patron.[189] Our best guess (and it remains a guess) is that one of the Despensers may have helped him; one small clue pointing in this direction is the relationship between the very early and avid dissemination of the poem in Ireland, and the important role of the Despensers there.[190]

Of course, none of this is evidence that Langland had a knightly or (more likely) baronial patron, but it does suggest where his sympathies lay. Nothing could have been easier than for him to have drawn, as even some contemporary religious writers did, a portrait of a cruel landlord-knight, but there is nothing of this sort in *Piers Plowman*.[191] In recent years much has been done to illuminate the production and readership of manuscripts of Middle English literature, especially of collections of secular literature.[192] It is instructive that little of what has been turned up helps us to understand what kind of person would have read or supported the publication of *Piers Plowman*—certainly not the bourgeois or "upwardly mobile" audience for romance, courtly lyrics, and unadventurous piety who seem to have been entirely conservative in their tastes (one thinks immediately of Robert Thornton). Rather, Langland's audience seems to have been made up of a diverse group of disenfranchised or underemployed clerks, progressive or satirically inclined clergy, legal scribes, civil servants, and unknown knightly or "gentel" readers. However, he seems not to have been uniformly pleased with each of these groups of readers—he appears not to have been appealing, in his C 5 *apologia*, to the John Balls or even the Thomas Usks among them. If his intent in the *apologia* is not simply to seek political safety under the shelter of a hastily worked up social conservatism—which seems very un-Langlandian and inappropriate in any case for insertion in what remains largely a B-text—then it may have been something much more local (in the first instance) he was trying to achieve by adding this remarkable moment of bibliographic self-revelation. In addition to all the devices for self-preservation and promotion we have seen to be so delicately managed in the passage, he appears to have been trying to gain back the good will of the two groups about whose welfare he is so exercised in this lengthy and enigmatic response to Reason: unbeneficed clergy and "pore gentel[s]." Moreover, the fact that he makes this case in a format so very laden with the conventions of "bibliographic ego"—that he presents himself momentarily as "the author's author"—seems (to this reader at least) to suggest that prominent among the audience to whom the *apologia* is addressed are those capable of "making" themselves—the Buts, Chaucers, Hoccleves, and Ilchester redactors who responded so intelligently and creatively to his poem.

Notes

1. During its five-year gestation period, this article has been read with unusual care by some of the scholars whose literary and historical sensibilities I most trust and admire. Gordon Fulton read the entire essay in its earliest phase with his usual wisdom and incisive literary sense, recommending some imperative revisions; among medievalists I'd especially like to thank Derek Pearsall, Tony Spearing, Nicholas Watson, and Anne Middleton for detailed and serious commentary. Penn Syzitta's reader's report for the press was also very helpful, and made me re-

think some of my positions (although I hope he will forgive me for digging in my heels on most of them). Among the students who have offered keen comment, I'd like to thank especially Andrew Murray and Linda Olson. Linda also took on the tedious job of initial copyediting, a task she carried out with equanimity and good humor. My greatest debt here, however, is to Steven Justice, who first provoked and then inspired this paper with his God-given enthusiasm. His support has been crucial in luring me back from the far reaches of religious history to the study of literature once again—and in making the journey home worthwhile.

2. Langland's *apologia*, for the purposes of this article, refers to the passage found in C 5. 1–108; all citations of the C-text are from Derek Pearsall, ed., *Piers Plowman, by William Langland: An Edition of the C-Text* (Berkeley and Los Angeles: University of California Press, 1978); citations of the B-text are from George Kane and E. Talbot Donaldson, eds., *Piers Plowman: The B Version* (London: Athlone Press, 1975); citations of the A-text are from George Kane, ed., *Piers Plowman: The A Version* (London: Athlone Press, 1960). Along with the essays in the present volume (especially Anne Middleton's, which also addresses the historical context of the *apologia* very specifically), on the *apologia* and biographical questions see E. Talbot Donaldson, *Piers Plowman: The C-Text and Its Poet* (New Haven, Conn.: Yale University Press, 1949); George Kane, *The Autobiographical Fallacy in Chaucer and Langland Studies* (London: H. K. Lewis, 1965); Anne Middleton, "William Langland's 'Kynde Name': Authorial Signature and Social Identity in Late Fourteenth-Century England," in *Literary Practice and Social Change in Britain, 1380–1530,* ed. Lee Patterson (Berkeley and Los Angeles: University of California Press, 1990), 15–82; David Lawton, "The Subject of *Piers Plowman*," *Yearbook of Langland Studies* 1 (1987): 1–30; Ralph Hanna, III, *William Langland* (Aldershot: Variorum, 1993); J. A. Burrow, *Langland's Fictions* (Oxford: Clarendon Press, 1993). Other studies will be cited individually in what follows. My concern with historical and biographical aspects of the *apologia* had its beginnings in Kathryn Kerby-Fulton, " 'Who Has Written this Book?': Visionary Autobiography in Langland's C-Text," in *The Medieval Mystical Tradition in England*, ed. Marion Glasscoe, Exeter Symposium, vol. 5 (Cambridge: D. S. Brewer, 1992), 101–16, which mentions other studies not specifically noted here.

3. Among the most important are the studies by A. I. Doyle and M. B. Parkes, "The Production of Copies of the *Canterbury Tales* and the *Confessio amantis* in the Early Fifteenth Century," in *Medieval Scribes, Manuscripts and Libraries: Essays Presented to N. R. Ker*, ed. M. B. Parkes and Andrew G. Watson (London: Scolar Press, 1978), 163–210; A. I. Doyle, "Remarks on Surviving MSS of Piers Plowman," in *Medieval English Religious and Ethical Literature: Essays in Honour of G. H. Russell*, ed. G. Kratzmann and James Simpson (Cambridge: D. S. Brewer, 1986); A. I. Doyle, "The Manuscripts," in *Middle English Alliterative Poetry and Its Literary Background*, ed. David Lawton (Cambridge: D. S. Brewer, 1982), 88–100; Derek Pearsall, "The 'Ilchester' Manuscript of *Piers Plowman*," *Neuphilologische Mitteilungen* 82 (1981): 181–92; Wendy Scase, "Two *Piers Plowman* C-Text Interpolations: Evidence for a Second Textual Tradition," *Notes and Queries* 232 (1987): 456–63; M. L. Samuels, "Langland's Dialect," *Medium Ævum* 54 (1985): 232–47; George H. Russell, "Some Early Responses to the C-Version of *Piers Plowman*,"

Viator 15 (1984): 275–303; Ralph Hanna, III, "Studies in the Manuscripts of *Piers Plowman*," *Yearbook of Langland Studies* 7 (1993): 1–25; and for a review of the most recent work see Kathryn Kerby-Fulton, "*Piers Plowman* Scholarship: Some Recent Studies," *Modern Language Review* 91 (1996): 691–96.

4. A disproportionate amount of the scholarship on late Middle English manuscripts to date is concerned with fifteenth-century secular texts (particularly romance); however, for a convenient recent overview of the field, complete with detailed bibliography, see Jeremy Griffiths and Derek Pearsall, eds., *Book Production and Publishing in Britain, 1375–1475* (Cambridge: Cambridge University Press, 1989); more specific studies will be cited below.

5. The study of medieval authorship has been heavily dominated so far by medieval *theory* of authorship, which is not all the same as study of the *practical* aspects and difficulties of authorial work; see Alastair J. Minnis, *Medieval Theory of Authorship: Scholastic Literary Attitudes in the Late Middle Ages*, 2d ed. (Philadelphia: University of Pennsylvania Press, 1988). Minnis's work has limited application for the study of *politicized* authorship (that is, authorship outside of humanist or scholastic circles) one finds in *Piers Plowman* (see note 13 below). For a discussion of some of the blind spots of "vintage" New Historicism, see Lee Patterson, *Negotiating the Past: The Historical Understanding of Medieval Literature* (Madison: University of Wisconsin Press, 1987), 41–76; for more recent critiques, see notes 7 and 32 below.

6. For Wolfgang Iser's theory, see *The Implied Reader: Patterns of Communication in Prose Fiction from Bunyan to Beckett* (Baltimore: Johns Hopkins University Press, 1974); for Hans Robert Jauss's theory, see *Toward an Aesthetic of Reception*, trans. Timothy Bahti (Brighton: Harvester, 1982); for a discussion of problems of application in both, see Robert C. Holub, *Reception Theory: A Critical Introduction* (New York: Methuen, 1984).

7. As Barbara Newman says of New Historicist approaches: "Older literary scholarship was overwhelmingly concerned with *meaning*—that is, with deciphering the explicit and implicit statements made by texts through an exploration of their linguistic and symbolic contexts. New Historicism, in contrast, concerns itself above all with *function*—the place occupied by a given text with respect to wider social practices and its utility to particular audiences"; Barbara Newman, "On the Ethics of Feminist Historiography," *Exemplaria* 22 (1990): 705. It is the historical *function* of the *apologia* which interests me here.

8. Medievalists have been heavily influenced by Leo Spitzer's seminal essay, "Note on the Poetic and the Empirical 'I' in Medieval Authors," *Traditio* 4 (1946): 414–22; see Burrow's assessment and critique, "Autobiographical Poetry in the Middle Ages: The Case of Thomas Hoccleve," *Proceedings of the British Academy* 68 (1982): 389–412. Hoccleve, thanks to the ground-breaking work of Burrow, has since become a kind of safe haven for medievalists with historical or historicist designs on authorship questions; see, for instance, Derek Pearsall's superb article, "Hoccleve's *Regement of Princes:* The Poetics of Royal Self-Representation," *Speculum* 69 (1994): 386–410.

9. Arthur Marotti, "'Love Is Not Love': Elizabethan Sonnet Sequences and

the Social Order," *ELH* 49 (1982): 406; see also Arthur Marotti, *John Donne: Coterie Poet* (Madison: University of Wisconsin Press, 1986); Arthur Marotti, *Manuscript, Print and the English Renaissance Lyric* (Ithaca, N.Y.: Cornell University Press, 1995).

10. Annabel Patterson, *Censorship and Interpretation: The Conditions of Writing and Reading in Early Modern England* (Madison: University of Wisconsin Press, 1984). Patterson describes the impact of audience response "mak[ing] itself heard inferentially, in the space between what is written or acted and what the audience, knowing what they know, might expect to read or see" (63).

11. Cited by A. Patterson, 14–15, from *Institutio Oratoria*, IXii67; Patterson does not cite either a translator or an edition, but the Latin text can be found in the edition by M. Winterbottom (Oxford: Clarendon, 1970) II, 504.

12. Joseph F. Loewenstein, "The Script in the Marketplace," in *Representing the English Renaissance*, ed. Stephen Greenblatt (Berkeley and Los Angeles: University of California Press, 1988), 265–76; originally published in *Representations* 12 (1985): 101–14.

13. See especially James Simpson, "The Constraints of Satire in 'Piers Plowman' and 'Mum and the Sothsegger,'" in *Langland, the Mystics and the Medieval English Religious Tradition: Essays in Honour of S. S. Hussey*, ed. Helen Phillips (Cambridge: D. S. Brewer, 1990), 11–30; natural disaster also contributed to instability during the time of the composition of the poem; see Robert Worth Frank, "The 'Hungry Gap,' Crop Failure, and Famine: The Fourteenth-Century Agricultural Crisis and *Piers Plowman*," *Yearbook of Langland Studies* 4 (1990): 87–104.

14. Loewenstein, "The Script in the Marketplace," 269. I assume that Justinian was the original source for this idea—"si quis ad infamiam alicuius libellum aut carmen scripserit, composuerit, ediderit, dolove malo fecerit quo quid eorum fieret." *Institutes*, IV, tit. iv, ed. J. A. C. Thomas (Amsterdam: North Holland Publishing, 1975); thus Milton threatened Alexander More, "If I find that you wrote or contributed one page of this book, if I find that you published it, or procured or persuaded anyone to publish it, you alone will be the author of the whole work, the culprit and the crier. Read the *Institutes* of Justinian, book 4, concerning injuries, tit. 4. 'If any, to the infamy of another, shall write, compose, or publish any libel or poem or history, or with evil intent shall cause any such to be done, &c.' Other laws add: 'Even though he publish under the name of another, or without a name.' And they all decree that he shall be considered and punished as the author." *The Complete Prose Works of John Milton*, 4:ii (New Haven, Conn.: Yale University Press, 1968), 712–13. I am grateful to Tim Haskett for advice on Justinian and other medieval legal matters, and to Terry Sherwood for pointing out this passage in Milton to me. On the life-and-death matter of book authorship, ownership, and readership for Lollard heretics, see Anne Hudson, "Lollard Book Production," in *Book Production and Publishing in Britain 1375–1475*, ed. Jeremy Griffiths and Derek Pearsall (Cambridge: Cambridge University Press, 1989), 125–52; Anne Hudson, *Lollards and Their Books* (London: Hambledon Press, 1985). It should be pointed out, however, that the organized and deliberate repression of (especially vernacular) literature was a gradual phenomenon, which did not reach its peak until 1409, long after Lang-

land's C-text had been published. See Nicholas Watson, "Censorship and Cultural Change in Late-Medieval England: Vernacular Theology, the Oxford Translation Debate, and Arundel's Constitutions of 1409," *Speculum* 70 (1995): 822–64.

15. Anne Hudson has recently argued, in "Piers Plowman and the Peasants' Revolt: A Problem Revisited," *Yearbook of Langland Studies* 8 (1994): 85–106, that it is the B-text which embodies Langland's response to the revolt of 1381. For reasons which will become apparent in the present study, I find the arguments for the C-text more convincing than those she advances for B.

16. On the corruption of the "C-Reviser's B," see Kane and Donaldson, 98–127; on the parts of C in prior circulation, see Scase, "Two *Piers Plowman* C-Text Interpolations."

17. Lawrence De Looze, "Signing Off in the Middle Ages: Medieval Textuality and Strategies of Authorial Self-Naming," in *Vox intexta: Orality and Textuality in the Middle Ages*, ed. A. N. Doane and Carol Braun Pasternak (Madison: University of Wisconsin Press, 1991), 165; see also M-D. Chenu, "Auctor, actor, autor," *Archivum Latinitatis Medii Aevi (Bulletin du Cange)* 3 (1927): 81–86; Minnis, *Medieval Theory of Authorship*, 26 and 157.

18. C. David Benson and Barry Windeatt, "The MS Glosses to Chaucer's *Troilus and Criseyde*," *Chaucer Review* 25 (1990): 33–53; see, for example, the annotations to Book II, lines 1–52 (pp. 38–39) or compare those to III 1324, 1331, with those to III 1408 (pp. 38–39, 44). This is interesting for Langland scholars because we now know that *Piers* and the *Troilus* were read by many of the same readers (in some cases the same individuals), as early as the first decade they were produced. The evidence for this will be presented in Kathryn Kerby-Fulton and Steven Justice, "Langlandian Reading Circles, and the Civil Service in London and Dublin, 1380–1427," *New Medieval Literature* 1 (1997).

19. *Piers* annotators were much less likely to use formal literary (and humanist) terminology than Chaucer readers, but they were very interested in authorial issues, and some, like the annotator of Bodleian Library Douce 104, see the "I" of the *apologia* as distinctive from the "I" elsewhere in the poem; see Kathryn Kerby-Fulton and Denise Despres, *Iconography and the Professional Reader: The Politics of Book Production in the Douce Piers Plowman* (Minneapolis: University of Minnesota Press, 1997).

20. P. Brieger, "Pictorial Commentaries to the *Commedia*," in *Illuminated MSS of the Divine Comedy*, ed. P. Brieger, Millard Meiss, and C. S. Singleton (Princeton, N.J.: Princeton University Press, 1969), 1:88–89.

21. The passage may also owe some of its elements, for instance, to the process of *probatio* interrogation: *probatio*, or the testing process which ecclesiastical authorities used to validate medieval claims to visionary experience, accounts in part for the preoccupation with authorial authenticity which seasoned readers of visionary writing brought to their reading. See Kerby-Fulton, "'Who has Written this Book?': Visionary Autobiography in Langland's C-Text," 101–16.

22. I am thinking here of literature like *The Chastising of God's Children* and the *Epistola solitarii*, Alphonse of Pecha's defense of Bridget of Sweden's visions; the former has usually been dated to shortly after 1382 (see Kerby-Fulton, "'Who has Written This Book?': Visionary Autobiography in Langland's C-Text," 103–4),

though Roger Ellis and Nicholas Watson have both suggested to me that its references to Bridget as "seint bride" might suggest a date after *1391*; however, as many holy women who were never canonized were popularly given the title of "saint," this may or may not be significant to the dating of the text.

23. David F. Hult, "Vers la société de l'écriture," *Poétique* 50 (1982): 155–72.

24. Middleton, "William Langland's 'Kynde Name': Authorial Signature and Social Identity in Late Fourteenth-Century England," 15–82; for Hoccleve's "Dialogue with a Friend," see Thomas Hoccleve, *Selected Poems*, ed. Bernard O'Donoghue (Manchester: Carcanet, 1982), 32–46.

25. Lawton, "The Subject of *Piers Plowman*," 1–30.

26. Steven Justice, *Writing and Rebellion: England in 1381* (Berkeley and Los Angeles: University of California Press, 1994), 128, n. 53 (more fully quoted below). Deconstruction brought about a renewed interest in authorial presence and authorial signature in medieval literature, but it made speaking of the actual historical author as appearing within the poem unfashionable. However, recent study of self-referential passages in many medieval poems has established beyond doubt that there is often an element of autobiographical authenticity (see Burrow, "Autobiographical Poetry in the Middle Ages: The Case of Thomas Hoccleve," 389–412, for example). This is especially true of the Ricardian poets who were writing during the transition period between public performance of poetry by the poet himself and the development of anonymous private reading (the difference between audience as listeners and as page-turners). Although George Kane's warning of the dangers of autobiographical fallacy is still salutary, so is Burrow's warning of the dangers of falling into the other extreme, which he calls the "conventional fallacy" (the belief that because something is conventional, it must necessarily be untrue). Justice tried to negotiate the stand-off between Kane's warnings against "autobiographical fallacy" and Burrow's warnings against "conventional fallacy" by reading Will as:

> a place-holder designating authorial agency. The importance of this point for the understanding of Langland is that he has constructed the figure of Will so as to embody certain problems of literary form and authority as generalizable problems of authorship itself; and so the question of how Will's reported career fits with Langland's is *only* the (here unimportant) question of whether Langland is creating what he takes to be a generalized portrait of authorship, or offering his own authorship as a generalizable example of it. (emphasis mine)

This lucid juxtaposition brings us (thankfully) beyond the extremes of fallacy wars with the insightful observation that it is *authorship*, more than autobigraphy, which is at stake in this passage. However, the comment arises only in passing in Justice's wider discussion of Langland's most sensational early readers (the rebels of 1381) and he thus has the luxury of leaving the remaining question hanging. There can be no "only" about the question here, however, and I will argue on the basis of the social and bibliographical sensitivities Langland displays that it is indeed a portrait of his *own* authorship that Langland is offering up for public inspection.

27. See section V below; and see Ralph Hanna's essay in the present volume

on the conventions of the *alliterative* poet's self-representation, which are especially relevant to the A-text.

28. David F. Hult uses the term "metadiscursive dialogue" in his discussion of *Roman de la Rose*; *Self-Fulfilling Prophecies: Readership and Authority in the First Roman de la Rose* (Cambridge: Cambridge University Press, 1986), 113; the quotation from Brown comes from Cynthia J. Brown, "Text, Image, and Authorial Self-Consciousness in Late-Medieval Paris," in *Printing the Written Word: The Social History of Books, circa 1450–1520*, ed. Sandra Hindman (Ithaca, N.Y.: Cornell University Press, 1991), 111.

29. Anne Middleton, "The Audience and Public of *Piers Plowman*," in *Middle English Alliterative Poetry*, ed. David Lawton (Cambridge: D. S. Brewer, 1982), 101–23.

30. Metadiscursive moments are always structured so as to *appear* to be (whether they are or not) a more direct communication between author and audience; I take moments in which an author refers explicitly to audience reaction as *more* direct (if not *direct*) in this sense; take, for instance, the following metadiscursive moment from "The Book of Privy Counselling": "I merueyle me sometyme whan I here sum men sey (I mene not simple lewid men & wommen, bot clerkes [& men] of grete kunnyng) þat my writing to þee & to oþer is so harde & so heiȝ, & so curious & so queinte, þat vnneþes it may be conceivid of þe sotelist clerk or wittid man or womman in þis liif, as þei seyn. Bot to þees men most I answere & sey þat it is moche worþi to be sorowid, & of God & his louers to be mercyfuly scornid & bitterly reprouid, þat now þees dayes generaly niȝhond alle . . . ben so bleendid in here coryous kunnyng of clergie & of kynde þat þe trewe conceite of þis liȝt werk . . . may no more . . . be conceyuid of hem in soþfastnes of spirit." Cited from "The Book of Privy Counselling," in *The Cloud of Unknowing*, ed. Phyllis Hodgson, EETS os. 218 (London: Oxford University Press, 1944; italicized abbreviations normalized), 137. In another metadiscursive moment the same author also lists his previous works without bothering to mention his name, which he assumes readers already know (see 154; I would like to thank Nicholas Watson for pointing out this passage to me). Langland's metadiscursive moments may owe as much to this tradition of religious prose and its conventions of "direct" author-audience address, as to the more obviously "fictional" traditions of Chaucerian poetry.

31. In "Authorial Signature," Middleton comments that, because anagrammatic signatures like Langland's "*appear* to derive their legibility from a stable social medium, one normally expects to find them in writers who in fact have a fairly secure and enduring institutional base of operations and are known by name and literary reputation over a considerable period of time to their primary audience— particularly court or coterie poets." As she goes on to say, momentarily anticipating the present study, this "suggests that the question of Langland's immediate circle and his following may require considerable reexamination" (36). Despite the somewhat ahistorical nature of her topic, Middleton's essay does a great deal to pull consideration of the question of Langland's authorship back to historical perspectives, and she concludes by affirming that Langland's practice of self-representation is "based on a rhetoric of presence, on resistance to the independent intelligibility of texts without reference to their authorship" (75). But she explicitly rejects the

view that authorial self-naming can be discussed "as if it were a primitive attempt at copyright" or as if "the author is in effect naming his price and attempting to control in his absence from the means of reproduction transactions in what he has made" (26). It is only the development of mechanical reproduction, she argues (echoing prominent historians of print culture) which allows for such ideas of literary property, and she concludes that "In late medieval literary texts, internal signature regulates, I shall argue, proprieties that are in the first instance *grammatical* and *ontological* rather than *economic*" (27; emphasis mine). I would agree that the establishing of a sense of "primitive copyright" is not Langland's chief aim (in fact he is in one sense trying to do almost the reverse, as we shall see). But two points need to be made: (1) it is not so easy to dismiss economic factors from instances of medieval authorial self-identification; (2) neither economic nor grammatical and ontological considerations can adequately explain Langland's *apologia*. However, Middleton is quite rightly here pointing to an important difference between modern notions of copyright and medieval senses of authorial property (most medieval authors' sense of literary property seems to derive from a feeling of *intellectual* and *social* responsibility, rather than from economic motives). But I would also argue that historians of print culture have for too long overemphasized the differences, assuming a naive simplicity in medieval concepts and conditions of publication. In fact, upon closer examination, medieval authors appear to have had quite a sophisticated sense of literary property. Certain medieval authors betray a surprisingly formal sense (given the means of production) of what publication meant; they had anxieties about "going to press" (to use an anachronistic phrase), and perhaps most importantly a weighty sense of literary property based on authorial accountability, which is hardly surprising in an age when, as Anne Hudson says, books could be a matter of life and death to writers and owners alike. And, of course, the publication of any piece of medieval writing could have an economic dimension if it involved the conventions of literary mendicancy or bids (covert or otherwise) for patronage. Recent work in manuscript studies has even revealed some other economic aspects of medieval authorship, such as evidence of the commercial commissioning of work in the London book trade and evidence of the advertising of literary works and authors (see below, sections IV and V). Although much remains to be uncovered about book production in the 1380s, certainly by the beginning of the fifteenth century the world of a London author was closer to the world of Ben Jonson's literary entrepreneurship than historians of print would have us believe. Of course, Middleton's concern in her essay is largely (and appropriately for her topic) with the multiple meanings made by the signatures, for instance A 2.118's play on "longe launde," which is the strip of land a plowman works (50). This sort of *assimilatio* of a poet's name or the personal details of his life to symbolic significances is well attested (see Middleton on Antoine de la Sale, 54), but it does not mean that the poet should be reduced to an ahistorical symbol for modern readers.

    32. Cf. Gabrielle M. Spiegel, "History, Historicism and the Social Logic of the Text," *Speculum* 65 (1990): 85. "Only after the text has been returned to its social and political context can we begin to appreciate the ways in which both language and social reality shape discursive and material fields of activity. In the end, what this means is acknowledging that cockfights are something more than sym-

bolic gestures. It does not deny that the Balinese cockfight also possesses symbolic dimensions, but its full meaning as a social activity is not exhausted in its symbolic significance." (The allusion is to Clifford Geertz's classic study, "Deep Play: Notes on a Balinese Cockfight," in *The Interpretation of Cultures* [New York: Basic Books, 1973]).

33. As Derek Pearsall has indicated, what we are really up against in modern attempts to fix the textual state of works like the *Canterbury Tales* and *Piers Plowman* is a medieval authorial habit of "composition and recomposition." Derek Pearsall, *The Life of Geoffrey Chaucer* (Oxford: Blackwell, 1992), 188. He elaborates: "There is no 'first edition', released for publication by the author, followed after a due interval by a 'second edition' containing his revisions. The process of composition and recomposition may well be continuous, with versions of the text at any stage 'leaking' into circulation" (189). For a discussion of one aspect of first audience impact (of the B-text) and Langland's response in revisions to C, see Justice, *Writing and Rebellion: England in 1381*, chaps. 3 and 5, respectively.

34. Aside from the historical studies in the present volume, and those already cited, see Lawrence M. Clopper, "Need Men and Women Labor? Langland's Wanderer and the Labor Ordinances," in *Chaucer's England: Literature in Historical Context*, ed. Barbara A. Hanawalt (Minneapolis: University of Minnesota Press, 1992), 110–29; one could also point to an explicitly New Historicist piece like John M. Bowers, "*Piers Plowman* and the Police: Notes Toward a History of the Wycliffite Langland," *Yearbook of Langland Studies* 6 (1992): 1–50, which has both the strengths and weaknesses of its genre.

35. Simpson is citing these conclusions from W. W. Shirley, ed., *Fasciculi zizaniorum magistri Johannis Wyclif cum tritico*, by Thomas Netter, Rolls Ser. (London, 1858), #5: "Item quod si homo fuerit debite contritus, omnis confessio exterior est sibi superflua vel inutilis" (494); #17: "Item quod domini temporales possunt ad arbitrium eorum auferre bona temporalia a viris ecclesiasticis delinquentibus; vel quod populares possint ad eorum arbitrium dominos delinquentes corrigere" (495–96); #23: "Item quod fratres teneantur per laborem manuum, et non per mendicationem, victum suum acquirere" (496).

36. Anne Hudson, *The Premature Reformation: Wycliffite Texts and Lollard History* (Oxford: Clarendon Press, 1988), 408, lists the C-revisions pertinent to Lollardy, but suggests that the evidence for or against the influence of Lollardy on his revision strategy is inconclusive. For a much fuller discussion of the passages in question, see Linda Olson, "William Langland's *Piers Plowman*: Spiritual Revisions in the Age of Wyclif," unpublished paper, which I am grateful to be able to cite.

37. Wendy Scase, *Piers Plowman and the New Anticlericalism* (Cambridge: Cambridge University Press, 1989); Kathryn Kerby-Fulton, *Reformist Apocalypticism and Piers Plowman* (Cambridge: Cambridge University Press, 1990).

38. See Lawrence M. Clopper's essay, this volume, with references to his previous work on the subject of Langland's Franciscanism.

39. See section VI below.

40. See section III below, and Kathryn Kerby-Fulton, *Reformist Apocalypticism and Piers Plowman*, 142–46.

41. See note 22 above.

42. See Derek Pearsall, this volume; for an instance of scribal sensitivity, see Pearsall, "The 'Ilchester' Manuscript of *Piers Plowman*," and see Kathryn Kerby-Fulton (with Steven Justice), "The Ilchester Manuscript of *Piers Plowman* and London Book Production," in *Essays in Honour of Derek Pearsall*, ed. Alastair Minnis, forthcoming.

43. Middleton, "Authorial Signature," Middle English 25.

44. Middleton, "The Audience and Public of *Piers Plowman*," 101–23.

45. Cited from Parkes's essay: "The Production, Dissemination and Revision of the Earliest Manuscripts of the Works of John Gower," presented at the Sixth York Manuscripts Conference, July 5–8, 1991. I am most grateful to Professor Parkes for sending me a photocopy of his earlier version and for his advice. For a revised and expanded version of this paper, now published, see note 125 below, and page 98 for this quotation.

46. L. Patterson, *Negotiating the Past: The Historical Understanding of Medieval Literature*, 79 and n. 8.

47. V. J. Scattergood, "Literary Culture at the Court of Richard II," in *English Court Culture in the Later Middle Ages*, ed. V. J. Scattergood and J. W. Sherborne (London: Duckworth, 1983), 29–43; Paul Strohm, *Social Chaucer* (Cambridge, Mass.: Harvard University Press, 1988); and for a recent assessment see Pearsall on Chaucer's audience in *The Life of Geoffrey Chaucer*, 178–85, and the bibliography listed there.

48. See Doyle and Parkes on the scribes of the Trinity Gower; and see C. Paul Christianson, "A Community of Book Artisans in Chaucer's London," *Viator* 20 (1989): 216.

49. Printers did give some revision rights to authors, but these were very limited; see Loewenstein, "The Script in the Marketplace," 266. On piracy in medieval oral performance, see H. J. Chaytor, *From Script to Print: An Introduction to Medieval Vernacular Literature* (London: Sidgwick and Jackson, 1966), 123–28. On literary property see also Gerald L. Bruns, "The Originality of Texts in a Manuscript Culture," *Comparative Literature* 32 (1980): 113–29, and the note below.

50. The first attempt to prosecute for copyright violation occurred in relation to Bunyan's *Pilgrim's Progress* in 1679 (see J. H. Baker, *An Introduction to English Legal History*, 3d ed. (London: Butterworth's, 1990), 515. On copyright, see Elizabeth Eisenstein, *The Printing Press as an Agent of Change* (Cambridge: Cambridge University Press, 1979), 120–21; David Pottinger, *The French Book Trade in the Ancien Régime* (Cambridge, Mass.: Harvard University Press, 1958), 95; Frederick Seaton Siebert, *Freedom of the Press* (Urbana: University of Illinois Press, 1952), 64–65. On censorship, see Pottinger, *The French Book Trade in the Ancien Régime*, 55–60, 72–76; A. Patterson, *Censorship and Interpretation: The Conditions of Writing and Reading in Early Modern England*; for medieval England specifically, see Simpson, "The Constraints of Satire in 'Piers Plowman' and 'Mum and the Sothsegger,'" 11–30; Hudson, *Lollards and Their Books*, especially 189–90.

51. Author portraits confer *auctoritas* (one thinks of the ubiquitous author portraits of biblical authors in medieval bibles, for instance). It is often impossible to know in many cases who is responsible for the inclusion of an author portrait in a MS, but in instances where concern for authorial credibility is a factor, even

a scribe or owner may direct the placement of such a portrait, which involves a kind of vicarious concern for "bibliographic ego," another aspect of "social authorship." This concern arises especially in the production of controversial literature: one might note, for example, the instance of portraits of Wyclif in historiated initials, either as author (e.g., Prague University Library MS VIII C3, fol. 2r) or as "anti-author" (e.g., Merton College 319, fol. 41r). Both illustrations are reproduced in *Wyclif and His Followers: An Exhibition to Mark the 600th Anniversary of the Death of John Wyclif: December 1984 to April 1985* (Oxford: Bodleian Library, 1984) as cover illustration and as #89, respectively.

52. Geoffrey Chaucer, *The Riverside Chaucer*, ed. Larry Benson (Boston: Houghton Mifflin, 1987); all citations, unless otherwise indicated, are from this edition.

53. Chaucer plays off some of the same concerns in lyrics like "Lenvoy de Chaucer a Scogan" and "Complaint of Chaucer to his Purse."

54. On John But, see Anne Middleton's excellent study, "Making a Good End: John But as a Reader of *Piers Plowman*," in *Medieval English Studies Presented to George Kane*, ed. Edward Donald Kennedy, Ronald Waldron, and Joseph S. Wittig (Woodbridge: D. S. Brewer, 1988), 243–66; see also Kerby-Fulton and Justice, "Langlandian Reading Circles" and see below, Section VI.

55. See especially Brown, "Text, Image, and Authorial Self-Consciousness in Late-Medieval Paris," 103–42, and also Stephen Nichols, "Voice and Writing in Augustine and in the Troubadour Lyric," in *Vox intexta: Orality and Textuality in the Middle Ages*, ed. A. N. Doane and Carol Braun Pasternak (Madison: University of Wisconsin Press, 1991), 137–61.

56. See note 31 above.

57. Compare Chaucer's Clerk: "As leene was his hors as is a rake / And he nas nat right fat, I undertake / But looked holwe, and therto sobrely," *General Prologue*, lines 287–89; and his physical (and vocational) opposite, the Monk, *General Prologue*, lines 200, 205.

58. A very common subject for historiated initials in medieval bibles is an author portrait; see, for instance, the selection of illuminated bibles described in M. B. Parkes, *The Medieval Manuscripts of Keble College, Oxford: A Descriptive Catalogue* (London: Scolar, 1979), e.g., MS #20 or #69.

59. See J. A. Burrow, *Thomas Hoccleve*, ed. M. C. Seymour, vol. 4 of *Authors of the Middle Ages* (Aldershot, Hants: Variorum, 1994), 6, for a discussion (with regard to the amount of petition and complaint in Hoccleve's poetry) of the legal genre of *supplicatio*.

60. R. W. Southern, "The Letters of Abelard and Heloise," in *Medieval Humanism and Other Studies* (New York: Harper and Row, 1970), 86–104.

61. Karl J. Holzknecht, *Literary Patronage in the Middle Ages* (New York: Octagon, 1966); John A. Burrow, *Medieval Writers and Their Work: Middle English Literature and Its Background 1100–1500* (Oxford: Oxford University Press, 1982), 38–46.

62. See E. P. Goldschmidt, *Medieval Texts and Their First Appearance in Print* (London: Oxford University Press, 1943), 87, for an interesting list of instances: e.g., Walter Map's work found under the name of St. Jerome; Nicholas of Cusa's

found under the name of Petrarch, and so on; for his discussion of the six possible medieval interpretations of the book title "Sermones Bonaventurae," see 98.

63. *Owl and the Nightingale*, ed. E. G. Stanley (London: Nelson, 1960), lines 186–214. On this passage see Burrow, *Medieval Writers*, 39–40.

64. Thomas Hoccleve, "Regement of Princes," in *Hoccleve's Works*, ed. F. J. Furnivall (London: Kegan Paul, 1897).

65. See Pearsall, this volume.

66. See Marc Drogin, *Anathema: Medieval Scribes and the History of Book Curses* (Totowa, N.J.: Allanheld and Schram, 1983), 15–25, for several instances.

67. Prologue to Hoccleve, "Regement of Princes," line 1014. On the nature of Hoccleve's work, see H. S. Bennett, *Six Medieval Men and Women* (New York: Atheneum, 1960), 78; Burrow, "Autobiographical Poetry in the Middle Ages: The Case of Thomas Hoccleve," 389–412; Burrow, *Thomas Hoccleve*, 6.

68. On Hoccleve's holographs, see Anthony G. Petti, *English Literary Hands from Chaucer to Dryden* (Cambridge, Mass.: Harvard University Press, 1977), 55; Judith A. Jefferson, "The Hoccleve Holographs and Hoccleve's Metrical Practice," in *Manuscripts and Texts*, ed. Derek Pearsall (Cambridge: D. S. Brewer, 1985), 95–109; Doyle and Parkes, "The Production of Copies of the *Canterbury Tales* and the *Confessio amantis* in the Early Fifteenth Century," 182–83, plates 53 and 54.

69. On Hoccleve's Lancastrian associations, see Sylvia Wright, "The Author Portraits in the Bedford Psalter-Hours: Gower, Chaucer, and Hoccleve," *British Library Journal* 18 (1992): 190–201, where the Bedford Psalter-Hours, in which (Wright argues) Hoccleve is pictured three times, is described as containing a "national portrait gallery of Lancastrian friends and foes concealed in the initials of carefully selected texts" (190).

70. See *Piers* 1.139–40, and Pearsall's note to those lines.

71. Kerby-Fulton, "'Who Has Written This Book?': Visionary Autobiography in Langland's C-Text," 101–16.

72. Scase, "Two *Piers Plowman* C-Text Interpolations," 456–63. See also Kerby-Fulton (with Justice), "Ilchester Manuscript of *Piers Plowman*."

73. See section V below, and see Middleton's essay in this volume, in which she argues that the *apologia* was the last thing added to the C-text. For reasons which will become clear, I would argue that (at least part of) the *apologia* was in process not long after the Revolt of 1381, though it may have taken its final form (a form which may have been importantly influenced by the 1388 Statute) much later on, as Middleton suggests. In any case, the *apologia* must have been in circulation by the time *Pierce the Ploughman's Crede* was written (which could have been as early as 1393 or as late as 1401), because the *Crede* author apparently imitates it in a passage against the upward mobility of the lower classes (more vicious, however, than Langland's); see *Crede*, 744–62, in Helen Barr, ed., *The Piers Plowman Tradition* (London: Dent, 1993), 92–93; compare the *apologia*, lines 53–81. Textual evidence from the long-awaited Athone Press edition of the C-text may shed new light on this question, and to some extent all attempts to address it in the interim must be regarded as speculative.

74. On Ball's reading of *Piers Plowman*, see Justice, *Writing and Rebellion: England in 1381*, chap. 3.

75. See section II, note 31 above.

76. Nicholas Orme, "Langland and Education," *History of Education* 11 (1982): 251–66.

77. See William J. Courtenay, *Schools and Scholars in Fourteenth-Century England* (Princeton, N.J.: Princeton University Press, 1987), 120, where he comments: "For those who did not inherit their social contacts by being born into a prominent, aristocratic family, the link between the university and public society had to be forged, first by finding a patron before or while still at the university, and secondly, and more importantly, by becoming part of the patron's extended *familia* soon after graduation."

78. The memorandum reads: "Memorand*um* quod Stacy de Rokayle pater will*ielm*i de Langlond qui stacius fuit generosus & morabatur in Schiptou*n* vnder whicwode tenens d*om*i*n*i le Spenser in co*m*itatu Oxon*iensi* qui p*re*d*ictus* will*ielm*us fecit librum qui vocatur Perys ploughman," fol. 89v; cited from George Kane, *Piers Plowman: The Evidence for Authorship* (London: Athlone Press, 1965), 26.

79. See especially John van Engen, *Rupert of Deutz* (Berkeley and Los Angeles: University of California Press, 1983), 349; Mary M. McLaughlin, "Abelard as Autobiographer: The Motives and Meaning of his 'Story of Calamities,'" *Speculum* 42 (1967): 463–88.

80. For a parallel discussion of these, see Middleton's essay in this volume.

81. As he does later in another significant waking episode, his encounter with Need at the beginning of 22.

82. It is always possible, of course, that Langland was actually short and fat, and that the portrait was meant to be comically dissimilar; however, the physical details of Chaucer's self-portraits confirm the portrait of him commissioned by Hoccleve specifically to "putte othir men in remembraunce / Of his persone" (Hoccleve, "Regement," 4.994–95; see Pearsall, *The Life of Geoffrey Chaucer*, "Appendix 1: The Chaucer Portraits"), so there seems little reason to question this aspect of Langland's self-portrayal either.

83. For Rutebeuf, see Holzknecht, *Literary Patronage in the Middle Ages*, 202; for Abelard and Hoccleve, see below; see also Middleton's essay in the present volume.

84. Abelard, *The Story of Abelard's Adversities*, trans. J. T. Muckle (Toronto: Pontifical Institute of Mediaeval Studies, 1964), 60. The Latin text is from Abelard, *Historia calamitatum*, ed. J. Monfrin (Paris: Vrin, 1967), 94, lines 1109–11. For a parallel discussion of this passage, see Middleton, this volume.

85. See van Engen, *Rupert of Deutz*, 347. Rupert of Deutz, *Commentary on the Rule of St. Benedict*, is edited in PL 170, col. 480A–81A, from which the quotations below are translated.

86. See van Engen, *Rupert of Deutz*, 346, for discussion and for references to parallel passages elsewhere in Rupert's works, and see Robert Lerner, "Ecstatic Dissent," *Speculum* 67 (1992): 35–57.

87. The full passage concerning (and addressed to) Cuno is: "Et si alii cuilibet hoc ridiculum forte aut infantile videtur, at saltem tibi jucundum esse et venerabile videri debet, per quem fieri coeptum est ex tunc, ut scribere et scribendo refundere volenti vivas aquas de illo charactere aureo in me decurrentes, nummus non dees-

set, menbranula non deficeret, ut dicere possim: Quia sapienta Dei Christus revera, secundum auream visionem illam, dives est, et auri atque argenti satis habet."

88. See Morton W. Bloomfield, *Piers Plowman as a Fourteenth-Century Apocalypse* (New Brunswick, N.J.: Rutgers University Press, 1962), chap. 2, on the monastic origins of Langland's concept of perfection.

89. On disdain of merchant classes see Jacques Le Goff, "The Town as an Agent of Civilisation," in *The Fontana Economic History of Europe: The Middle Ages*, ed. Carlo M. Cipolla (Glasgow: Collins/Fontana Books, 1972), 111; and see Pearsall, this volume.

90. Brentano's remarks are from Robert Brentano, "Autobiography and Memory: Some Late Medieval Examples," Plenary address, Medieval Academy of America (Boston, March 31, 1994).

91. Ernest W. McDonnell, *The Beguines and Beghards in Medieval Culture* (New York: Octagon, 1969), 293; Hildegard herself came from a powerful family, a factor which has often been overlooked in discussions of her extraordinarily courageous stance on ecclesiastical reform.

92. It is entirely possible that the Despensers acted in this capacity for him.

93. Nicholas Watson, *Richard Rolle and the Invention of Authority*. (Cambridge: Cambridge University Press, 1991), 140, with full Latin text.

94. Hoccleve, *La Male Regle*, in *Selected Poems*, lines 367–68.

95. "Archicancellarie, vir discrete mentis," in Heinrich Watenpuhl and Heinrich Krefeld, eds., *Die Gedichte des Archpoeta* (Heidelberg, 1958), 4 stanza 18; discussed by Holzknecht, *Literary Patronage in the Middle Ages*, 201; and by Middleton, in the present volume, note 57.

96. Phyllis Hodgson and Gabriel M. Liegey, eds., *The Orcherd of Syon*, EETS o.s. 258 (London: Oxford University Press, 1966), 16, lines 15–20; I am grateful to Denise Despres for letting me read prior to publication her paper, "Ecstatic Reading and Missionary Mysticism: *The Orcherd of Syon*," in *Prophets Abroad: The Reception of Continental Holy Women in Late-Medieval England*, ed. Rosalynn Voaden (Woodbridge: Brewer, 1996), 141–60.

97. See 5.7–9, and Middleton's essay, this volume, for the view that Langland uses the 1388 Statute of Laborers as a pretext here; equally relevant may be the metaphorical harvest that Christ alludes to in his comment to the disciples, "The harvest indeed is great, but the labourers are few" (Luke 10:2).

98. He makes a similar metadiscursive move, asserting his membership among the clergy, at C 15.79–80.

99. Paul Strohm, "Politics and Poetics: Usk and Chaucer in the 1380s," in *Literary Practice and Social Change in Britain, 1380–1530*, ed. Lee Patterson (Berkeley and Los Angeles: University of California Press, 1990), 104. Usk, of course, was among Langland's first readers; see VI below.

100. See Kerby-Fulton and Justice, "Langlandian Reading Circles."

101. Private communication; I would like to thank Professor Spearing once again for his thoughtful comments.

102. See Paul Saenger, "Silent Reading: Its Impact on Late Medieval Script and Society," *Viator* 13 (1982): 367–414; Robert K. Root, "Publication Before Printing," *PMLA* 8 (1913): 431.

103. Trans. by H. E. Butler from Giraldus's *De Rebus a se Gestis*, Rolls Ser. I (1861), 72, in Giraldus Cambrensis, *The Autobiography of Giraldus Cambrensis* (London: Jonathan Cape, 1937), 97, with my insertions from the Latin text. Coulton (see next note) assumed that the "pauperes" entertained on the first day were poor scholars, a logical assumption since it is difficult to know what the (general) poor would have made of the oral recitation of a Latin text; however, the passage as a whole does not support this view.

104. G. C. Coulton, *Medieval Panorama* (New York: Collins, 1961), 226–27.

105. Strohm, "Politics and Poetics: Usk and Chaucer in the 1380s," 104.

106. Root, "Publication Before Printing," 419. See also S. J. Williams, "An Author's Role in Fourteenth-Century Book Production," *Romania* 90 (1969): 437, citing Machaut's apology to his lady that a rondeau he has written containing an anagram of her name has had nonetheless to be given *first* to his patrons.

107. Beverly Boyd, "The Infamous B-Text of the *Canterbury Tales*," *Manuscripta* 34 (1990): 235.

108. See especially Middleton, "Making a Good End: John But as a Reader of Piers Plowman," 243–66.

109. E. P. Hammond, *English Verse Between Chaucer and Surrey* (New York: Octagon, 1965), 196–97, both citations from BL, Add. MS 29729 (I have expanded the superscript abbreviations Hammond retained). On stationers' activities in London, see Hammond, *English Verse Between Chaucer and Surrey*; on Shirley, see the latest discussion, Julia Boffey and John J. Thompson, "Anthologies and Miscellanies: Production and Choice of Texts," in *Book Production and Publishing in Britain 1375–1475*, ed. Jeremy Griffiths and Derek Pearsall (Cambridge: Cambridge University Press, 1989), 279–315; see also A. S. G. Edwards, "John Shirley and the Emulation of Courtly Culture," in *The Court and Cultural Diversity*, ed. John J. Thompson (Cambridge: Boydell and Brewer, forthcoming), which summarizes the previous scholarship; our knowledge of such "publishing" activities is still scanty and comes mainly from the fifteenth century, which makes its relevance to Langland problematic.

110. See Kane and Donaldson, 124; Robert Adams, "The Reliability of the Rubrics in the B Text of *Piers Plowman*," *Medium Ævum* 54 (1985): 208–31; Robert Adams, "Langland's *Ordinatio:* The *Visio* and *Vita* Once More," *Yearbook of Langland Studies* 8 (1994): 51–84.

111. On Cok, see A. I. Doyle, "More Light on John Shirley," *Medium Ævum* 30 (1961): 98–99; George Russell, "As They Read It," *Leeds Studies in English* n.s. 20 (1989): 173–87; the *Piers* fragment he copied, and for which he supplied an elaborate rubric, appears in Gonville and Caius MS 669*/446. For the kinds of marginal guides usually supplied by *Piers* scribes, see Russell, "Some Early Responses to the C-Version of *Piers Plowman*," *Viator* 15 (1984): 295–303; Carl Grindley, "From Creation to Desecration: The Marginal Annotations of *Piers Plowman* C Text HM 143" (master's thesis, University of Victoria, 1992); Marie-Claire Uhart, "The Early Reception of *Piers Plowman*" (Ph.D. diss., University of Leicester, 1988); Kathryn Kerby-Fulton and Denise Despres, *Iconography and the Professional Reader*.

112. Bokenham is cited in H. S. Bennett, "The Production and Dissemination of Vernacular Manuscripts in the Fifteenth Century," *The Library* 5th ser 27 (1947): 174; on Bokenham and Burgh's MS, see also A. I. Doyle, "Publication by Mem-

bers of the Religious Orders," in *Book Production and Publishing in Britain 1375–1475*, ed. Jeremy Griffiths and Derek Pearsall (Cambridge: Cambridge University Press, 1989), 118–19 and n. 42; Bokenham's *Legendys* were edited by M. S. Serjeantson, for EETS o.s. 206 (1938).

113. Walter W. Skeat, ed., *The Vision of William concerning Piers the plowman, in Three Parallel Texts* (London: Oxford University Press, 1886), Prologue, lines 57–63; see Barr, 103 and note to line 61 on *Richard* as thinly veiled propaganda justifying the deposition, see George Kane, "Some Fourteenth-Century Political Poems," in *Medieval English Religious and Ethical Literature: Essays in Honour of G. H. Russell*, ed. Gregory Kratzman and James Simpson (Cambridge: D. S. Brewer, 1986), 90.

114. Holzknecht, *Literary Patronage in the Middle Ages*, chap. 7, "The Epilogue Excusatory and the 'Go, Little Book' Formula." See also Samuel Moore, "Patrons of Letters in Norfolk and Suffolk, c. 1450," *PMLA* 28 (1913): 199.

115. For a graphic instance of a writer combatting the monastic prejudice against authorship, see the autobiography of Guibert de Nogent, *Monodiae*, conveniently trans. in Guibert of Nogent, *Monodiae*, in *Self and Society in Medieval France: The Memoirs of Abbot Guibert of Nogent*, trans. John F. Benton (New York: Harper, 1970); on the conventions of modesty and "leakage," see Ernst Robert Curtius, *European Literature in the Latin Middle Ages*, trans. Willard R. Trask (Princeton, N.J.: Princeton University Press, 1953), 83–85, 517; instances of this attitude appear well into the Renaissance; see, for example, the Preface to Sir Thomas Browne, *Religio medici*, ed. James Winny (Cambridge: Cambridge University Press, 1963), 1–2; on the question of leakage in relation to the "composition and recomposition process" of medieval authors such as Chaucer, Gower, and Langland, see Pearsall, *The Life of Geoffrey Chaucer*, especially 188–89.

116. Cited in Root, "Publication Before Printing," 421; the quotation from the letter of 1352 below is from the translation of Francis Petrarch, *Rerum familiarum libri*, trans. Aldo S. Bernardo (Albany: State University of New York Press, 1975), 152.

117. Cited in Root, "Publication Before Printing," 421.

118. Pearsall, "The 'Ilchester' Manuscript of *Piers Plowman*," 192.

119. Scase, "Two *Piers Plowman* C-Text Interpolations: Evidence for a Second Textual Tradition," 460. On the (physical) format in which these passages were released, see Kerby-Fulton (with Justice), "Ilchester Manuscript of *Piers Plowman*."

120. Donaldson showed that in the case of the passage on Heli's sons, Langland had to change the pronouns of B Prol. 95–99 from third person to second person—changes which a couple of MSS (X and B 2) betray. He would then "cue his insertion into the text by correcting the first pronoun of the line which would follow it. The insertion itself was, as I have already suggested, probably written on a sheet of paper and its position in the text marked by an arrow." Donaldson, *Piers Plowman: The C-Text and Its Poet*, 246. Interestingly, Scase has shown that two other MSS, H 2 and E, have the cue lines *only* (i.e., they do not also have the passages they once cued for insertion). In the case of one of these MSS, some prior ancestor no doubt had the cue lines written in its margins with a mark for insertion, but the loose sheet accompanying the cue had been lost, so the scribe inserted the cue without its accompanying text.

121. Scase, *Piers Plowman and the New Anticlericalism*, 152. For the argument

that Langland's etymology for the word is original to him, see Middleton, this volume.

122. Pearsall, note to 5.2; and Gordon Leff, *Heresy in the Later Middle Ages: The Relation of Heterodoxy to Dissent c. 1250–c. 1450* (Manchester: Manchester University Press, 1967), 319, 599.

123. Cited in Bennett, "The Production and Dissemination of Vernacular Manuscripts in the Fifteenth Century," 173; from Reginald Pecock, *The Donet*, ed. Elsie Vaughan Hitchcock, EETS o.s. 156 (London, 1921), 6–7.

124. Root, "Publication Before Printing," 422.

125. See M. B. Parkes, "Patterns of Scribal Activity and Revisions of the Text in Early Copies of Works by John Gower," in *New Science Out of Old Books: Studies in Manuscripts and Early Printed Books in Honour of A. I. Doyle*, ed. Richard Beadle and A. J. Piper (Aldershot, Hants: Scolar, 1995), 81–121; Doyle and Parkes, "The Production of Copies of the *Canterbury Tales* and the *Confessio amantis* in the Early Fifteenth Century," 200.

126. See also Hanna's paper in this volume. On A's priority, see note 129 below.

127. The difference between "scriptor" and "auctor" in Bonaventure's terminology; see Minnis, *Medieval Theory of Authorship*, 94.

128. See Kerby-Fulton, *Reformist Apocalypticism and Piers Plowman*, 80–81.

129. See Nichols, "Voice and Writing in Augustine and in the Trobadour Lyric," Fig. 8.1, p. 140 of MS New York, Pierpoint Morgan Library M819. In spite of Jill Mann's recent argument in "The Power of the Alphabet: A Reassessment of the Relation between the A and B Versions of *Piers Plowman*," *Yearbook of Langland Studies* 8 (1994): 21–50, I persist in believing that A is the earliest version of the poem.

130. Or "dreamer portrait" (i.e., "actor" rather than "auctor") if one prefers; the MSS are Corpus Christi College, Oxford 201 and Bodleian Library Douce 104. The figure in Douce is undoubtedly a clerk; the figure in Corpus is dressed in a conflation of the clerkish russet and gentlemanly garb; his clothing is similar to that of the knight on fol. 35v of Douce; both portraits are sensible and sensitive renderings of the dreamer. Kathleen Scott, it should be noted, registers surprise that a MS made in Essex (Corpus) and one made in Ireland (Douce) should *both* choose to render the author-dreamer similarly, but I would suggest that there may be author-portrait conventions at work here (see Derek Pearsall and Kathleen Scott, *Piers Plowman: A Facsimile of Bodleian Library, Oxford, MS Douce 104* (Cambridge: D. S. Brewer, 1992), xxxix; for clear reproductions of both portraits, see Kathleen Scott, "The Illustrations of *Piers Plowman* in Bodleian Library Douce 104," *Yearbook of Langland Studies* 4 (1990): figs. 1 and 2. See also the portraits of Chaucer in historiated initials reproduced in M. C. Seymour, "MS Portraits of Chaucer and Hoccleve," *Burlington Magazine* 124 (1982): 618–23.

131. Linda Olson's unpublished paper is entitled, "A Fifteenth-Century Reading of *Piers Plowman* and the Tradition of Monastic Autobiography."

132. See, however, the clerkly author portrait at the opening of *Laʒamon's Brut* in MS BL Cotton Caligula A IX, fol. 1r, reproduced as a frontispiece to Bruce Dickens and R. M. Wilson, eds., *Early Middle English Texts* (London: Bowes and Bowes, 1951).

133. See Hanna, this volume; Kerby-Fulton, " 'Who Has Written This Book?' ": Visionary Autobiography in Langland's C-Text," 101–16.

134. George Kane, "The Text," in *A Companion to Piers Plowman*, ed. John A. Alford (Berkeley and Los Angeles: University of California Press, 1988), 183.

135. See Kane, "The Text," 175–200. Nicholas Watson informs me that there is an example of dittography in both Julian of Norwich's short and long texts, which might suggest that Julian, too, used a scribal copy for revision.

136. "We did not come easily or quickly to this position" (Kane and Donaldson, 121), and see their explanation, p. 122.

137. A. S. G. Edwards and Derek Pearsall, "The Manuscripts of the Major English Poetic Texts," in *Book Production and Publishing in Britain 1375–1475*, ed. Jeremy Griffiths and Derek Pearsall (Cambridge: Cambridge University Press, 1989), 259; John Gower, *English Works of John Gower*, ed. G. C. Macaulay (London: Oxford University Press, 1900–1901), cxxx.

138. See Williams's comment on the question of Machaut's own copies of his work: "The passage seems to imply the existence of *two* manuscripts, one of them Machaut's 'livre ou toutes les choses sont que je fis onques,' and the other the *copy* he has had made for one of his lords." Williams, "An Author's Role in Fourteenth-Century Book Production," 444.

139. For example, Kane and Donaldson, 126, n. 64.

140. See, for instance, Kane and Donaldson, *Piers Plowman: The B Version*, 126, on this kind of preventative revision generally, and the instances they give of scribal censorship (e.g., 102–6). Anne Middleton has kindly informed me that she has discovered several more.

141. Kane, "The Text," 175–200; the A-text, however, seems to have remained a coterie text, probably brought into wider circulation by the success of B and C.

142. Unfortunately, I cannot agree with Rigg and Brewer's theory that Z is authorial, but this only changes, rather than mitigates, the fascination of the text (my reasons for rejecting their theory are detailed in Kathryn Kerby-Fulton, "*Piers Plowman*," in *The Cambridge History of Medieval English Literature 1066–1547*, ed. David Wallace (Cambridge: Cambridge University Press, forthcoming). On Z, see the recently issued facsimile, Charlotte Brewer and A. G. Rigg, *Piers Plowman: A Facsimile of the Z-Text in Bodleian Library, Oxford, MS Bodley 851* (Woodbridge: Boydell and Brewer, 1994), and for the opposing view, see Hanna, "Studies in the Manuscripts of *Piers Plowman*," 1–25.

143. Kane and Donaldson, 122, n. 47; on patronage generally, see especially Kate Harris, "Patrons, Buyers and Owners: The Evidence for Ownership, and the Role of Book Owners in Book Production and the Book Trade," in *Book Production and Publishing in Britain 1375–1475*, ed. Jeremy Griffiths and Derek Pearsall (Cambridge: Cambridge University Press, 1989); Pearsall, *The Life of Geoffrey Chaucer*, 181–90; Ralph Hanna, III, "Sir Thomas Berkeley and His Patronage," *Speculum* 64 (1989): 878–916.

144. For examples of the cost involved in medieval book production, see A. I. Doyle, "The Work of a Late Fifteenth-Century English Scribe, William Ebesham," *Bulletin of the John Rylands Library* 39 (1957): 298–325; or Bennett, "The Production and Dissemination of Vernacular Manuscripts in the Fifteenth Century," 174 (on Bokenham).

145. See note 34 below; but see Norman Tanner, *The Church in Late Medieval Norwich, 1370–1532*, Studies and Texts 66 (Toronto: Pontifical Institute of Mediaeval Studies, 1984), 56, for evidence that some clerks in minor orders were comparatively well off.

146. See Pearsall's note to 15.92.

147. For a full discussion of the textual and historical evidence, see George Pace and Alfred David, eds., *The Minor Poems, A Variorum Edition of the Works of Geoffrey Chaucer*, vol. 5 (Norman: University of Oklahoma Press, 1982) especially 65, n. to line 22, on "þou Vache"; and 150 on the context of "Scogan."

148. Pace and David, *The Minor Poems*, 148, line 29 and n.

149. See, for instance, the variants generated by some of the obscure prophecies in the B-text; for discussion of some modern scholarly attempts to crack these prophetic codes, see Kerby-Fulton, *Reformist Apocalypticism and Piers Plowman*, 14–17, and 171–72 on the likelihood of a Joachite "code" for 3.477–81; and Andrew Galloway, "The Rhetoric of Riddling in Late-Medieval England: The 'Oxford' Riddles," *Speculum* 70 (1995): 68–105.

150. See John Erghome's (partly satirical) prologue to the pseudonymous Bridlington prophecies, for medieval methods of decoding political prophecy, in T. Wright, ed., *Political Poems and Songs*, Rolls Ser., vol. 14 (London: Longmans, 1859), 123–215.

151. K. W. Humphreys, "The Library of John Erghome and Personal Libraries of Fourteenth-Century England," in *A Medieval Miscellany in Honour of Prof. John le Patourel*, ed. R. L. Thomson (Leeds: Leeds Philosophical and Literary Society, 1982), 106–23.

152. Not enough work has been done on the reception of prophecy, but see Marjorie Reeves, *The Influence of Prophecy in the Later Middle Ages: A Study in Joachimism* (Oxford: Clarendon Press, 1969), on the Joachite circle surrounding Hugh of Digne; on other instances of reception, see Morton W. Bloomfield and Marjorie Reeves, "The Penetration of Joachism into Northern Europe," *Speculum* 29 (1954): 772–93; Robert E. Lerner, *The Powers of Prophecy: The Cedar of Lebanon Vision from the Mongol Onslaught to the Dawn of the Enlightenment* (Berkeley and Los Angeles: University of California Press, 1983).

153. See De Looze's discussion of Machaut and others, "Signing Off in the Middle Ages," 168–69.

154. Kerby-Fulton, *"Piers Plowman."*

155. Pace and David, *The Minor Poems*, 150.

156. See Scattergood, "Literary Culture at the Court of Richard II"; Malcolm Richardson, "The Earliest Known Owners of *Canterbury Tales* MSS and Chaucer's Secondary Audience," *Chaucer Review* 25 (1990): 17–21; Strohm, "Politics and Poetics: Usk and Chaucer in the 1380s," 83–112.

157. Lucy Freeman Sandler, *"Omne bonum: Compilatio* and *ordinatio* in an English Illustrated Encyclopedia of the Fourteenth Century," in *Medieval Book Production*, ed. Linda L. Brownrigg (Los Altos, Calif.: Anderson-Lovelace, 1990), 189 and fig. 4, portraying the entry and its note with the accompanying caricature of a clerk with a minute fox amidst the robes of his skirt.

158. Hanna, *William Langland*, 23–24.

159. On Ball's reading of Langland, see Justice, *Writing and Rebellion: En-*

gland in 1381. On Lollard conventicles and book owners (some of whom were illiterate), see Hudson, "Lollard Book Production," 125–521. Usk, too, may have been a hearer; see Kerby-Fulton and Justice, "Langlandian Reading Circles."

160. See Donaldson, *Piers Plowman: The C-Text and Its Poet*, 18–19; and Kerby-Fulton and Justice, "Langlandian Reading Circles," and below.

161. On Palmere, see Robert A. Wood, "A Fourteenth Century London Owner of *Piers Plowman*," *Medium Ævum* 53 (1984): 83–89; Bowers, "*Piers Plowman* and the Police: Notes Toward a History of the Wycliffite Langland," 23, seems to think that Palmere had Lollard leanings, but his views could also be explained by orthodox reformist concerns not unlike Langland's own.

162. Another woman, Anne Fortescue, an early sixteenth-century reader, left marginalia beside a number of passages in the poem, particularly those on marriage (now Bodleian Library Digby 145); Liverpool University Library Chaderton F48 appears to have been owned by a woman, and a few other MSS contain the names of women; see Kerby-Fulton, "*Piers Plowman*."

163. Cited in John A. Burrow, *Essays on Medieval Literature* (Oxford: Clarendon Press, 1984), 115, from Thorlac Turville-Petre, *The Alliterative Revival* (Cambridge: Cambridge University Press, 1977), 46.

164. For the theory that "But" is a code name for a member of Langland's coterie, see Kerby-Fulton and Justice, "Langlandian Reading Circles." For possible identification of But with the king's messenger, see Middleton, "Making a Good End: John But as a Reader of Piers Plowman," 266, but finding the right John But in the historical records remains problematic, a factor which makes all these comments tentative; for all the possible candidates, see Hanna, *William Langland*, 28–31.

165. The Ilchester redactor's contribution will be discussed further below (and in relation to HM 114's); But's, of course, is the epilogue he created for the A-text, which reports the author's death (see Kane's edition, Appendix, 427–31). Unfortunately, a detailed study of the manuscript evidence for earlier ownership of the poem is beyond the scope of the present paper, which is mainly concerned with known literary readers; for more detailed discussion, see Kerby-Fulton and Justice, "Langlandian Reading Circles" and "Ilchester Manuscript of *Piers Plowman*."

166. Cited from Usk's *Appeal* (R. W. Chambers and Marjorie Daunt, eds., *A Book of London English* (Oxford: Oxford University Press, 1931), 23) by Strohm, "Politics and Poetics: Usk and Chaucer in the 1380s," 85.

167. The question of Usk's use of Langland is complex (much more complex than the three suggested borrowings listed by Sr. Mary Acquinas Devlin in 1928; see Donaldson, 18–19); for a more detailed discussion, see Kerby-Fulton and Justice, "Langlandian Reading Circles."

168. Paul Strohm, *Social Chaucer* (Cambridge, Mass.: Harvard University Press, 1988), 75–76.

169. The *Boece* and *Troilus* were probably both written between 1382 and 1386 (see Chaucer, *Riverside Chaucer*, xxix).

170. Scattergood, "Literary Culture at the Court of Richard II," 40.

171. Helen Cooper, "Langland's and Chaucer's Prologues," *Yearbook of Langland Studies* 1 (1987): 71–81; A. V. C. Schmidt, ed., *The Vision of Piers Plowman: A Critical Edition of the B-Text* (London: J. M. Dent, 1978), xvi.

172. I have based this suggestion on internal evidence in Hoccleve's autobio-

graphical verse, too complex for presentation here, but which will be discussed further in Kerby-Fulton and Justice, "Langlandian Reading Circles"; however, see above.

173. Richardson, "The Earliest Known Owners of *Canterbury Tales* MSS and Chaucer's Secondary Audience," 19.

174. See Pearsall, this volume; and John H. Fisher, "*Piers Plowman* and the Chancery Tradition," in *Medieval English Studies Presented to George Kane*, ed. Edward Donald Kennedy, Ronald Waldron, and Joseph S. Wittig (Woodbridge: D. S. Brewer, 1988), 267–78; Doyle and Parkes, "The Production of Copies of the *Canterbury Tales* and the *Confessio amantis* in the Early Fifteenth Century," 163–210.

175. Many scribes and civil servants, of course, were clerks awaiting benefices, like Hoccleve; see A. K. McHardy, "Careers and Disappointments in the Late Medieval Church: Some English Evidence," *Studies in Church History* 26 (1989): 111–30; R. N. Swanson, "Chaucer's Parson and Other Priests," *Studies in the Age of Chaucer* 13 (1991): esp. 41–61.

176. See Justice, *Writing and Rebellion: England in 1381*, ch. 3.

177. Jeremy J. Smith, "Linguistic Features of Some Early Fifteenth-Century Middle English Manuscripts," in *Manuscripts and Readers in Fifteenth-Century England: The Literary Implications of Manuscript Study*, ed. Derek Pearsall (Cambridge: D. S. Brewer, 1983), 110–11. The relation of Scribe D to the Ilchester redactor will be the subject of Kerby-Fulton (with Justice), "Ilchester Manuscript of *Piers Plowman*."

178. The fact of its being a C-text, of course, means that it likely postdates 1387, although Francis Wormald noted the similarities between Ilchester's "daisy-bud" decoration and those found in a Winchester document of 1380 (Doyle and Parkes, "The Production of Copies of the *Canterbury Tales* and the *Confessio amantis* in the Early Fifteenth Century," 105 and n. 78).

179. A similar case occurs during the second quarter of the fifteenth century, when HM 114 was made (the other MS containing prepublication material); its scribe, who can be identified in two other Middle English MSS, one a *Troilus* for which he supplied missing passages, "must have had access to a wide range of sources, not least of alliterative verse" (Doyle, "Remarks on Surviving MSS of *Piers Plowman*," 410).

180. Thomas Marlburghe requested a poem on the Virgin from Hoccleve; see C. Paul Christianson, "A Community of Book Artisans in Chaucer's London," *Viator* 20 (1989): 216.

181. See Edwards and Pearsall, "The Manuscripts of the Major English Poetic Texts," 257–78.

182. Doyle cast doubt on the relevance of Wells's ex libris inscription to the portion of Bodley 851 containing the A-text of *Piers* (Doyle, "Remarks on Surviving MSS of Piers Plowman"), and Hanna has made further arguments for the independent production of Z's booklets (Hanna, "Studies in the Manuscripts of *Piers Plowman*," 1–25). However, the fact that this copy of the poem, with its C-continuation, was part of a much-used communal book at Ramsey Abbey at least by the mid-fifteenth century is beyond doubt. See Rigg's introduction to Brewer and Rigg, *Piers Plowman: A Facsimile of the Z-Text in Bodleian Library, Oxford, MS Bodley 851*. The MS testifies to Benedictine tolerance for satire (and prophecy),

even when directed against the Benedictines themselves, as do other comparable monastic collections; see, for instance, A. G. Rigg, *A Glastonbury Miscellany of the Fifteenth Century* (Oxford: Oxford University Press, 1968). A surprising number of *Piers* MSS can be associated with Benedictine convents or owners; see Hanna, *William Langland*, 34–35.

183. At least some of Langland's readers shared his sympathy: the Douce 104 annotator summarized this passage with the marginal note "houu pore gentill beþ refusit" (fol. 22); see also Pearsall's note to 5.73.

184. On MS Trinity College, Dublin, 212, see St. John Brooks, "The *Piers Plowman* Manuscripts in Trinity College, Dublin," *The Library* 5th ser. 6 (1951): 141–53.

185. See conclusion #17, discussed above. Donaldson also noted the pro-knighthood stance of the C-text; see 108–9.

186. Stephen Greenblatt, "Murdering Peasants: Status, Genre and the Representation of Rebellion," in *Representing the English Renaissance*, ed. Stephen Greenblatt (Berkeley and Los Angeles: University of California Press, 1988), 1–29, citing Spenser's *Faerie Queene* from *The Works of Edmund Spenser*, ed. Edwin Greenlaw et al. (Baltimore: Johns Hopkins, 1932–1957), Book 5, canto 2, 52–55.

187. Greenblatt, "Murdering Peasants," 23.

188. Note Clanvowe's use of the term "loller" in John Clanvowe, *The Works of Sir John Clanvowe*, ed. V. J. Scattergood (Cambridge: D. S. Brewer, 1975), lines 510–19; and see Scattergood's comment, p. 20.

189. Much remains to be done on late medieval English patrons and patronage, but see Hanna, "Sir Thomas Berkeley," and see Richard Firth Green, *Poets and Princepleasers: Literature and the English Court in the Later Middle Ages* (Toronto: University of Toronto Press, 1980).

190. See Kerby-Fulton and Despres, *Iconography and the Professional Reader*.

191. Although Piers's advice to the knight at 8.35–38 gestures in the direction of such abuses. For a contemporary allusion to the typically oppressive landlord knight, see *Ancrene Wisse*, ed. J. R. R. Tolkien, EETS o.s. 249, 46, lines 26–32.

192. Most of the scholarship done so far has focused on manuscripts containing romances and lyrics; see Griffiths and Pearsall, eds., *Book Production and Publishing in Britain, 1375–1475*, for an overview of recent work on manuscripts of all types.

3

Langland's Persona: An Anatomy of the Mendicant Orders

Lawrence M. Clopper

NEARLY ONE HUNDRED YEARS AGO J. J. Jusserand pointed to a problem that arises as a consequence of thinking of *Piers Plowman* as an antifraternal poem. Why did William Langland make his Dreamer an itinerant beggar at the same time that he singled out the mendicant orders as the most immoral of the clergy?[1] Jusserand also argued that the "goddes mynstruls" of the C-text were derived from Francis's *joculatores dei*, "minstrels of God," without offering any explanation for why the poet should include in his poem ideal types of those persons whom he most despised. There matters seem to have stood until the publication of Konrad Burdach's *Der Dichter des Ackermann aus Böhmen und seine Zeit* in 1932.[2] Burdach had an intimate knowledge of Franciscan materials and demonstrated a number of parallels between ideas and wording in Langland's poem and Franciscan documents and mentality. His most important contribution was to substantiate the Franciscan character of the Rechelesnesse who makes his appearance in the latter portions of the first Inner Dream of the C-text (11.167–13.213); Rechelesnesse, Burdach argued, was a personification of the Franciscan understanding of *ne soliciti sitis* [be not solicitous (for your life, etc.)].[3] Donaldson cited Burdach's and Jusserand's contributions in his discussions of Rechelesnesse and the minstrel imagery.[4] Although Donaldson recognized the problematical nature of Rechelesnesse, he found no fault with the statement on Christ's poverty,[5] and he acknowledged the Franciscan character of "goddes mynstruls" in his authoritative treatment of the minstrel imagery. Nevertheless, he did not discuss the larger issue of why a poet antagonistic to friars should incorporate these favorable Franciscan images and themes into his poem.

The unexplained presence of a positive Franciscanism seems not to
have affected most critics' opinion that all of the friars in the poem are portrayed negatively. Robert Frank, however, warned against assuming that
the portrait of the friars at the beginning of the *Vita* was irrelevant satire.
On the whole, he said, "they are treated respectfully." [6] Nevertheless, Frank
regarded most portraits of the friars, and especially that of Nede before the
last vision, to be negative ones. Subsequent readers seem to have rejected
Frank's cautionary note about the friars in passus 8; instead, they continue
the tradition that all friars are treated negatively. [7]

There can be no doubt that Langland attacks friars—or at least that the
voices of the poem do. There are those friars who gloss the gospel as they
please in order to get copes and secure themselves. There are those who
beg clamorously for more than they need. There is the confessor who offers
Mede absolution if she will endow a window. There is the friar confessor
who is solicitous of burying laypeople in the friars' cloisters—but only if
there is a testamentary gift. There is Sir Penetrans Domos who slithers into
the Vnite of Conscience and poisons it. And when the king acts against the
Cart of Liar, Falseness flees first to the friars, and Liar eventually comes to
reside with them as well. On the other hand, Francis is invoked positively
four times in the B-text: when Resoun lists him with Benedict and Bernard
as founders who can correct a covetous clergy (4.121); when Anima says
that Charity was once found in a "freres frokke . . . in Frraunceis tyme"
but rarely since (15.230–31), and later when he lists Francis among those
founders of religious orders who show the way to poverty and perfection
(15.421); and in the final passus when Conscience first welcomes the mendicants into Vnite as long as they adhere to their rule and follow Francis
and Dominic in leaving all concern for *dominium* [possession] of land
and lordship (20.244–52). Moreover, the radical theory of Christ's poverty
that Rechelesnesse advances and which is specifically Franciscan in character is never disputed by anyone in the poem, and the absence of solicitude
he preaches is later personified in Patience and affirmed by Patience and
Anima. At the same time that the poem attacks some mendicant practices, it advocates a mendicant reformist agenda, one that is Franciscan in
character. [8] We can resolve the problem noted by Jusserand once we realize
that we have mistaken as antifraternal critique Langland's reformist rhetoric. We have erred in our judgment of Langland's relation to the friars,
I believe, because from the time of the poem's recovery in the sixteenth
century antifraternalism has been thought to be one of the distinguishing
features of Wyclif's polemic, hence the presumption that Langland was

an early follower of Wyclif and a proto-Protestant.[9] We now know considerably more about external critics of the friars such as William of St. Amour and Richard FitzRalph and the larger antifraternal debate, and I think we have begun to recognize the reformist voices within the Franciscan order primarily as a result of work on Olivi, Ubertino da Casale, and others.[10] Both the external critiques and the Franciscan ideal are central to *Piers Plowman* as a whole. Although some accusations are clearly modeled on those made by Richard FitzRalph[11] and others echo the language and imagery of William of Saint Amour, there are also sections, some quite extensive, that struggle with the concept of evangelical poverty and provide a stringent Franciscan definition of the key terms. Other events illustrate a concern with the granting of privileges to the friars and the consequent disruption of the church, which were of regard to both external and internal critics.[12] All of these seem intended to hold up a mirror for the friars in order that they may see how they have abandoned their rules and, consequently, their providential mission. Wille the Wanderer, a bold itinerant beggar who justifies his life according to apostolic principles, is one site at which external critiques and mendicant idealism clash.[13]

Before presenting my analysis of Langland's persona, I would like briefly to characterize the mendicant orders, especially as they appear within antifraternal polemic.[14] It is a common observation that mendicant critics attacked the four orders indiscriminately. This undifferentiated assault seems particularly obvious in the writings of Wyclif and the English tract writers, persons who were uninterested in distinctions between the orders since their view was that all orders—including the monastic ones—were unauthorized by the scriptures. However, if we look at the other two historically prominent antimendicant writers—William of St. Amour and Richard FitzRalph—we see that there is acknowledgment of difference among the mendicant orders. William of St. Amour borrowed scriptural and apocalyptic language to warn against Sir *Penetrans Domos*, the precursors of Antichrist in his polemic. But in some of his writings he specifies these enemy camps as *pseudophropehtae* [false prophets] and *pseudopredicatores* [false preachers], using the first as a code name for the Franciscans with their prophetic speculations and the second for the Dominicans who were known for their preaching missions.

Richard FitzRalph makes a more decisive distinction between teachings unique to the Franciscans and practices common to all four orders in his *Defensio curatorum*.[15] At a crucial moment in his sermon he says that he will now turn to speak particularly to the Franciscans because they began the cause against him in London and urged the other orders to it and because the Franciscans dispute more than any others the perfection of the gospel and how it stands in "willful begging."[16] FitzRalph insists that the practice of begging among the four orders is pernicious for a variety of reasons, but he is particularly offended—indeed appalled—by the Franciscan argument that willful begging is authorized by the actions of Christ and the apostles, who possessed nothing either individually or in common (*nihil in mundo habere proprium aut commune*) and who, consequently, depended upon the alms of the faithful for their daily needs. Only the Franciscans used this phrase, with its total repudiation of *dominium*, to assert the absoluteness of Christ's poverty.[17] If their thesis were correct, then it would imply that it was illegitimate for the church to have *dominium* of sacred precincts, lands, and other provisions necessary to its functioning. The Franciscan position with regard to Christ's poverty threatened the entire church hierarchy, FitzRalph believed, and had to be condemned. I might add that the thesis, as FitzRalph phrases it, had been condemned by John XXII earlier in the century; it was one that the Franciscan order had argued but had been enjoined no longer to teach.[18] FitzRalph claims to have recently heard a friar preaching the condemned thesis; thus, he is implying that the justification of mendicant begging is based in a heresy.

The practice of begging was especially troubling to critics of the friars since it seemed to contravene canon law and ecclesiastical practice with regard to the establishment and maintenance of religious institutions. Monasteries could not be founded without endowments to provide for their needs; clerics were not allowed to take major orders unless they were provided for by the bishop or by private patrimony. To claim that one could live on alms, with only meagre endowments, seemed reckless. Furthermore, there was the danger that the taking of alms would defraud the legitimate poor, and, more perversely, the critics said, the friars justified taking alms by claiming poverty when it was manifest to all that they lived in rich palaces and dwellings.[19]

Many of these discontents are reflected in *Piers Plowman* but the matter of begging is central, for there are, the narrator complains, "friars and faitours" who beg beyond their needs. These "friars and faitours" are often linked with "Bidders and beggares," those who ask ("bid") for alms without need.[20] "Faitour" is also a word used in the statutes to refer to those

who aid and abet illegal activity.[21] To Langland, some friars are "faitours,"
therefore, not just because they deceive with their begging beyond need
but because they abet men in their sins when they take money for penance
and allow the sinner to remain in debt while the friar lives off the other
man's goods (20.284–93). All of these beggars and friars deceive when they
"bid" without need. The Bible forbids such begging (7.89), for need alone
justifies begging (line 84), and it is need that brings the true beggar pardon (lines 100–106), for God stands "borgh" for true beggars' debts.[22] The
legitimacy of begging, therefore, is defended on two points: The true beggar may beg if he has need; and if he *receives* but does not *ask*, does not
"bid" for alms. He may pray ("bid") but not demand ("bid") alms. The
distinction is consistent with Franciscan reformist thought but is subtler
in English than in Latin. Ubertino da Casale uses a vocabulary that distinguishes two legitimate forms of alms-taking (*accipere/recipere* and *petere*)
from solicitous begging (*queror*).[23] "Questing" for alms, sepulchre, and the
like is a sign of cupidity; since Ubertino also strongly opposed the friars'
or their intermediaries' involvement in litigation, "questing" for alms undoubtedly connoted for him the same avidity he associated with going to
court. Langland has conflated the two kinds of begging in the term "bid"
in order to suggest the ease with which begging can move from "accepting" or "praying for" alms to "questing." Langland's discussion of begging
challenges individual friars—and others like them—to ask whether they receive and pray for necessary alms or quest for superfluities. The subtle distinction is that between being solicitous and unsolicitous, between using
and possessing the world, between being reckless by bringing oneself into
debt and being "recheles."

The "recheles" or unsolicitous person is reckless in a positive sense insofar as he risks his physical well-being when he relinquishes *dominium* of
things in this world for a greater good, his salvation. Indeed, there are a
number of statements in the poem that argue that the greatest perfection
is to be without possession of goods. Holy hermits are said to forsake land
and lordship (C 9.201–2) whereas, according to Dame Study, "flatereres"
and "fooles" prefer "lond and lordshipe on erþe" (10.5–16). Rechelesnesse
says that "Vch a parfit preest to pouerte sholde drawe" (C 13.99) and that
those who would be perfect must forsake possession (11.272). Patience says
that those who leave lordship gain heaven by right, for such a person is
"sib to god hymself" (14.258–73). Anima asserts that Charity has no rents
because he is provided for by *Fiat voluntas tua* [thy will be done] (15.176–
80). And *Liberum-arbitrium* [Free-will] claims that he who has land and

lordship shall be poorest in power at his parting hence (C 16.159–60). But the greatest eulogy of poverty is Patience's when he tries to get Haukyn to relinquish his concern for the morrow, for, he says, "shal noon faille of þyng þat hem nede / *Ne soliciti sitis &c; Volucres celi deus pascit &c.; pacientes vincunt &c.*" [Be not solicitous, etc; (Behold) the birds of the air . . . your heavenly Father feeds them; the patient are victorious] (14.29 ff.).

In the C-text, it is Rechelesnesse who, while personally a failure in attaining the ideal, presents the pre-Johannine Franciscan proposition that "perfect poverty" is to be without *dominium* either personally or communally.[24] When Richard FitzRalph disputed the Franciscan teaching on Christ's absolute poverty, he cited Solomon's text, "Give me neither riches nor poverty," as authority for a middle way of clerical poverty.[25] The church was not required to be without appropriate means of support; if it had no endowments, how could it perform its apostolic mission? The mendicant counterargument was that Christ was *mendicus*, according to His statement in Psalm 39:18, "*Ego sum pauper et mendicus*" ["I am poor and needy as a beggar"],[26] and the Franciscan interpretation had been that he called his disciples to a life of poverty without *dominium* individually or in common, according to the verse in Matthew, "If you would be perfect, go and sell all that you have."[27] Rechelesnesse follows the Franciscan line of argument when his praise of poverty leads to the assertion that "parfit pouerte" consists in being without possession, and that this life is most pleasing to God, *Pauper ego ludo dum tu diues meditaris* [Poor, I play, while you being wealthy brood]:

Alþou3 Salomon seide, as folk seeþ in þe bible,
Diuicias nec paupertates &c [Give me neither beggary nor riches],
Wiser þan Salomon was bereþ witnesse and tau3te
That parfit pouerte was no possession to haue,
And lif moost likynge to god as luc bereþ witnesse:
Si vis perfectus esse vade & vende [&c] [If you wish to be perfect, go
    sell (what you have and give it to the poor)]
And is to mene to men þat on þis moolde lyuen,
Whoso wole be pure parfit moot possession forsake
Or selle it, as seiþ þe book, and þe siluer dele
To beggeris þat begge and bidden for goddes loue.
For failed neuere man mete þat my3tful god serueþ;
As Dauid seiþ in þe Sauter: to swiche þat ben in wille
To serue god goodliche, ne greueþ hym no penaunce:

Nichil impossibile volenti, [Nothing is impossible to him who wills it]
Ne lakkeþ neue*re* liflode, lynnen ne wollen:
Inquirentes autem dominum non minuentur omni bono. [They who
 seek the Lord shall not be deprived of any good] (lines 270–82)

Rechelesnesse indicates the mendicant bias to the argument when he rejects the Solomonic text.[28] "Parfit pouerte" is to have *no* possession or
dominium. Rechelesnesse reads the verse *Si vis perfectus esse* literally: Those
who would be "pure parfit" (note the emphatic modifier) must abandon
possession or sell their goods and give the proceeds to beggars. Langland
makes "perfect" a synonym of "pure," and "poverty" an analogue of "perfection" when he has Rechelesnesse parallel "parfit pouerte was no possession to haue" (line 272) with "Whoso wole be pure parfit moot possession
forsake" (line 276) and give it to beggars. Therefore, "pure parfit" and "perfect poverty," though differently phrased, point to the same phenomenon.

 Monastic commentators—and the other three mendicant orders as
well—read the text *Si vis perfectus esse* less stringently: Those who would be
perfect leave personal for communal *dominium*; goods need not be literally given to beggars but may be offered to the institution the initiate seeks
to enter. However, it is clear that Rechelesnesse is not talking about lives
secured by communal ownership of goods or the possession of anything;
rather, he is making the claim, as the Franciscan *Rule* stresses, for those
who are unsolicitous of even daily sustenance (lines 279–82). We can see
the distinction in the lines that follow because there he turns to the clergy
who are permitted to be waged in order that they can perform their function (lines 283–317) whereas in the allegory of the last passus Conscience
argues that the friars should not be waged because it will increase their
numbers (20.268–69).

 The pre-Johannine Franciscan character of the argument is indicated
by the phrase "parfit pouerte," a term that denotes renunciation of everything both individually and in common. In commenting on chapter 6 of
the Rule of 1223, the Four Masters had said that when Francis told the
brothers they were to appropriate nothing for themselves and that when
he described their poverty as the most exalted kind, he distinguished imperfect from perfect poverty:

There are two forms of evangelical poverty: imperfect poverty which, with poverty
of spirit, retains no temporal superfluities but only that which is necessary; and
perfect poverty which, with poverty of spirit, retains neither superfluities nor the
necessities of life as one's own but depends upon God's provision. This poverty

is called mendicity. This is the poverty of the brothers minor, as a consequence of which they are told to go seek alms with confidence.[29]

"Perfect poverty," therefore, is not just the renunciation of superfluities so that one only retains necessities (i.e., commons); it is the renunciation of personal *dominium* over all things individually and in common as a consequence of which one may go beg and be confident of the result. It is not, however, just absence of material goods; it is absolute poverty linked to absence of solicitude (note the references to poverty of spirit). A similar point is made in Hugh of Digne's commentary on the same chapter where he equates *paupertas altissima* [highest poverty] with *caritas perfectissima* [most perfect charity]. He defines "perfection of poverty" as literal adherence to the command, *Si vis perfectus esse*, and this in turn is equated with the renunciation of possession *in proprio et in communi*.[30] We routinely find similar expressions about "perfect poverty," and often the quotation from the Four Masters, in Franciscan defenses and discussions of poverty up to the time of John XXII's *Cum inter nonnullos* (November 1323), the bull that condemned the Franciscan notion of Christ's poverty.[31]

The phrase "perfect poverty" is peculiarly Franciscan. No other mendicant order makes such a claim about its or Christ's poverty; indeed, Aquinas specifically rejected the Franciscan interpretation, so it is not surprising that we find not a single instance in the entire *Index Thomisticus* of any combination of "perfect" and "poverty."[32] Furthermore, it was a Dominican who had accused a Franciscan lay brother of heresy for teaching this theory of Christ's poverty, as a consequence of which the Franciscan order was drawn into a papal inquiry which resulted in John XXII's ruling that "to persist in teaching that Christ and the apostles were without *dominium in proprio et in communi* was heretical."[33] The use of the phrase "parfit pouerte" indicates that the Franciscan view Rechelesnesse espouses is one that the order had been forced to relinquish under the rulings of John XXII in the early part of the century. It is *not* the official teaching of the order in Langland's day; it is the teaching of the order prior to John's ruling. It can be found in the pre-Johannine writings of Pecham and Bonaventure and the Spirituals, but it is no longer an orthodox teaching of the order's concept of poverty[34]; it is the false doctrine FitzRalph claimed a friar had preached not long before.

Having said that Langland has Rechelesnesse advance a condemned doctrine, I want to add that it is done covertly. Langland does not use the condemned phrase; rather, he uses a code word, "perfect poverty," that stands for the condemned teaching. Thus Langland is obedient to the papal bull while still intruding the teaching into his text. However, only Franciscans or persons thoroughly familiar with Franciscan teaching would recognize the import of the code word, "perfect poverty." This usage gives evidence that there is a targeted audience to whom Langland speaks by code in order to remind them of what their order once stood for.

No figure later in the poem disputes Rechelesnesse's characterization of Christ or the absoluteness of His poverty; indeed, Patience and Anima continue the discourse on poverty in a nuanced Franciscan fashion.[35] Further, Patience himself exemplifies patient poverty in the highest degree when he combines perfect patience with perfect poverty, as he does in the banquet scene and in his apostolic itinerancy in the scene that follows. However, in making this claim, I do not mean to suggest that only the Franciscans exhibit "patient poverty"; rather, "patient poverty" is an essential characteristic of "perfect poverty." There is no simple equation in the poem between the two, for Patience himself makes a distinction between degrees of perfection of poverty when it is suffered by the involuntary as opposed to the voluntary poor. Patience insists that the involuntary patient poor achieve salvation by "trewe riȝte" because Christ Himself provided this example of patient poverty:

in þat secte oure saueour saued al mankynde
Forþi [al] poore þat pacient is [of pure riȝt] may cleymen,
After hir endynge here, heueneriche blisse. (14.259–61)[36]

Patience's greater promise, however, is to those who, having land and *dominium*, give them up:

Muche hardier may he asken þat here myȝte haue his wille
In lond and in lordshipe and likynge of bodie
And for goddes loue leueþ al and lyueþ as a beggare. (14.262–64)

Note the last few words. Patience is not making the claim that all those who are voluntarily poor—the monastic and secular clergy who give up private ownership for ownership in common—will be saved by right but that those who give up all possession and *live as beggars*. Ultimately, Patience's thesis is based on the Franciscan interpretation of the first Beatitude as a *promise* of heavenly reward. Francis had said that *altissima paupertas* made his followers the heirs and kings of the kingdom of heaven (*Rule of 1223*, cap. 6), and the commentators linked this *altissima paupertas* to the Beatitude: *Beati pauperes spiritu, quoniam ipsorum est regnum caelorum* [Blessed are the poor in spirit for theirs is the kingdom of heaven (Matt. 5:3)].[37] The Franciscans seem to have routinely read the Matthean version as if it were Luke's "Blessed are the poor, for yours is the kingdom of heaven." John Pecham had to defend this peculiarly Franciscan gloss on the Matthean Beatitude against the Dominican Robert Kilwardby's charge that scripture does not say "*beati pauperes rebus sed spiritu*" [blessed are the poor in things but in spirit]. Pecham cited the gloss: "*paupertas spiritualis duas habet partes, rerum abdicationem et spiritus contritionem*" [poverty of spirit has two parts: the renunciation of things and spiritual contrition]. Therefore, he argued, "*beati pauperes spiritu*" implicitly says "*beati pauperes rebus*."[38]

In the passages cited earlier we see that Langland, like FitzRalph and others, attacks the friars when they beg without need, but, unlike these critics, he at the same time praises those who live as "true" beggars, those who renounce *dominium* of land and lordship out of love for God, as Francis and Dominic are said to have done (20.252). The central point of Langland's attack on the friars, I believe, is not that it is illegitimate for them to beg—the antifraternal argument—but that most beg solicitously and for more than they need, which is part of the internal critique of Franciscans like Ubertino, Bonaventure, and Pecham.

Although I believe the poem to be couched primarily in Franciscan language, imagery, and polemic, Langland does not ignore the other mendicant orders; indeed, he seems to hold Dominic in high regard (see 20.251–52, where he is paired with Francis) and refers favorably to the eremitical life on a number of occasions (e.g., Prol. 25–30; 15.269 ff). It appears then that Langland used Franciscan language to appeal first and most narrowly to that order but framed the issues so that the other three mendicant orders would recognize them as well.[39] Since all four orders were understood to be begging orders—as opposed to endowed ones— the major distinctions among them were between an itinerant and a reclusive/contemplative life. As we shall see, these idealized lives were replaced in actuality by communal life within towns and cities where the friars devoted themselves to service to the laity.

Since the Dominican order was founded to combat heresy and to teach the orthodox faith, its members were itinerant and lived on alms.[40] However, the Dominican Constitutions were modeled on the rule of the Premonstratensian Canons, which provided for a communal life that served the laity; thus, the order was a hybrid of monastic organization and the parochial life of the secular clergy. Given the Dominican commitment to teaching, the order had schools and procedures for the education and licensing of preachers and, consequently, was allowed to accumulate possessions necessary to the fulfillment of their mission. The initial objective was not to reside at the home friary but to travel about wherever there was need; as the order developed, however, there were restrictions placed on itinerancy so that many friars were limited to the friary and its immediate environs while others were licensed to travel only within certain geographical limits.

The Franciscan order was not founded as a learned order.[41] Francis's first followers were laymen who were encouraged to exhort men to penance more by example than by words. These brothers were not authorized to preach but to testify by works.[42] Francis, himself, was ambivalent toward learning, noting at one point that a person who clung to his own opinions had not entirely left the world.[43] He conceded the value of learning insofar as it encouraged the desire for salvation, but felt that the reenactment of the poor life of Christ and his disciples had greater power to call people to penance. However, with its remarkable success, the order immediately began to attract priests and scholars, with the result that it took on an external character much like that of the Dominicans. Schools were established, books and other necessities were accumulated, and allowances were made to enable persons to have more than their daily necessities. Nevertheless, Dominican and Franciscan ideologies continued to differ because of the characters of their founders and because of their understanding of the nature of their own and Christ's poverty until John XXII's rulings, which made the Franciscan order externally and institutionally much like that of the Dominicans. There was friction and competition between the two orders, yet both the Dominican and Franciscan rules and legislation required that brothers welcome and act charitably toward members of the other order.[44]

Both the Dominican and Franciscan orders stressed their itinerancy, but we must remember that ideology is not always reflected in practice. "Itinerancy" came to be conceived more as living according to need than as extensive traveling about. Francis, for example, did not forbid dwellings to his followers as long as they lived in them as strangers and pilgrims (*advenae et peregrini*; see the *Testament*). The friar, therefore, could be an itinerant in the town or city where he sojourned; he need not be a pilgrim of the foot. Nevertheless, critics of the Franciscans and Dominicans focused on itinerancy as a sign of aberrancy, idleness, and irregularity, for monks, who were bound to place, had labeled such itinerant "monks" *gyrovagues* and *sarabaites*.

The Carmelites and the Friars Hermits of St. Augustine emerged from groups that antedate the Franciscan and Dominican orders; however, they did not achieve the organization and unity of rule of the itinerant orders until the mid-thirteenth century.[45] Both were committed to some form of the Rule of St. Augustine, but their rules and constitutions were refined under Dominican advisors with the result that there is a Dominican character to their mission which enabled them to move quickly from their early wilderness sites into the cities and universities. The movement from remote areas into towns and cities created divisions within both orders, for the change seemed to some to violate the eremitical character of their foundations. Neither order centered on a charismatic founder such as Dominic or Francis; instead, the claim to ancientness and tradition was made to the figures of Elijah and his companions (by the Carmelites) or to Augustine or, more significantly, to the early desert fathers (by the Augustinians). Both foundation myths evoke images of heroic struggle in the wilderness, a struggle that had to be internalized and memorialized by these urban dwellers. Like the itinerancy of the Franciscans and Dominicans, the eremitism of the Carmelites and Augustintian Friars was often more ideology than practice.

The difference between ideology and practice or ideal and reality is one subject of Langland's persona. I wish to argue that Langland very carefully created the Wanderer as a persona who conflates images of the two principal kinds of mendicity, the itinerancy of the Franciscans and Dominicans and the eremitism of the Austin Friars and Carmelites. These two sets of orders provide different models of the apostolic life, the one imitating Christ's sojourn in the desert, the other His (more important) itinerant ministry. Insofar as the Wanderer, or Wille, is represented as a failure in the pursuit of the life of perfection, the persona projects the principal shortcomings of all the mendicant orders: they are wanderers and idle beggars. More important, the persona is deeply conflicted, for while the Franciscans' and Dominicans' itinerancy is part of their vocation, there are indications in the poem that Langland believes that eremites are to be settled. The persona is an "heremite, vnholy of werkes," in part then, because he wanders about. But the persona does not fulfill the apostolic role of the itinerant Franciscans and Dominicans either, for he confesses himself an idler, a "faitour" or deceiving beggar, and a wanderer rather than a pilgrim. Although the Wanderer is a failure at both forms of mendicancy, the construction of the narrator implies the ideal—itinerancy for the first two orders, a settled life of penance for the latter two—but this distinction also may suggest that Langland hierarchizes the two kinds of mendicant life, itinerancy over eremitism. I deduce this relative valuation from the few negative comments the poet makes specifically about the Augustinian friars and the general complaint that hermits violate the ideal of the early desert fathers by wandering around and living near cities and busy thoroughfares.[46] On the positive side, Langland produces images of rightly motivated itinerant teachers throughout his text: Patient Poverty, Conscience (when he leaves the banquet with Patience and at the end of the poem), the Samaritan, and Piers.

That the narrator is conflicted is apparent from the opening lines of the poem: He says,

I shoop me into [a] shrou[d] as I a sheep weere;
In habite as an heremite, vnholy of werkes,
Wente wide in þis world wondres to here. (Prol. 2–4)[47]

The second of these admissions is straightforward: He has dressed himself in hermit's garb in order to wander about like those "Grete lobies and longe . . . [who] / Shopen hem heremytes hire ese to haue" (Prol. 25–30, 53–57). The first admission, however, is more problematical. Skeat defended the argument that "sheep" meant "shepherd" on the basis of the C-MSS readings and contemporary usage, but subsequent editors have remained skeptical and tend to read the line as parallel to line 3.[48] They regard the "shroud of a sheep" as the sheepskin garment of the hermit and understand the two lines together to signify that the Wanderer is a wolf in sheep's clothing. But I think the lines can be read literally: He dressed himself as a sheep, that is, as an apostle. The relevant verse, Matt. 10:16: "Behold, I send you out as sheep (*oves*) in the midst of wolves," is preceded by the apostolic counsels, which I give here in the shortened version of Luke 10.3: "Go your way; behold, I send you out as lambs (*agni*) in the midst of wolves. Carry no purse, no bag, no sandals; and salute no one on the road."[49]

The reference to "sheep" would have been evocative for Franciscan readers because of a story about Francis in which they figure (*Leg. maj.* 9.8). Bonaventure tells us that when Brother Illuminatus and Francis set out on the saint's third attempt to preach the faith to the pagans, they met two lambs as they went on their way. Francis was overjoyed at the sign and recalled the quote from Matthew. Shortly thereafter, men from the sultan's army fell upon them like wolves, and the meeting with the Sultan, which follows, illustrates the divine inspiration the apostolic man receives when confronted by his persecutors. But the sheep also signifies patience (the very antithesis of Wille's questing), for, as Bonaventure says in one of his sermons, the sheep is the most patient of animals and sustains all patiently. For that reason, it signifies Christ: "As a sheep led to slaughter" (Isa. 53:7); and in Matthew 10: "Behold, I send you," etc. [it is] as if he said: 'See that you have patience like the sheep and that you sustain all patiently.'"[50] Similarly, Pecham advises the brothers: "When you go through the world, do not judge: e.g., do not put yourself above others, but exhort. I send you as sheep, not *ledentes* ("doers of harm," from *laedo*?). Pacific . . . modest . . . mild . . . humble . . . honestly speaking to all . . . and, by the example of Christ and the disciples, not riding [but walking]."[51] The "shroud" our "shep" wears would also help construct the image of an apostolic man because a "shroud" may be a priestly or ecclesiastical garment (*MED* sb1 ab). The garment Wille wears is later said to be a russet robe (8.1), that is, a poor quality of gray wool, which is also the garb of the Franciscans.[52] When the Wanderer goes out as a sheep and a hermit, therefore, he brings before his mendicant audiences the two figures that signify the itinerant Dominicans and Franciscans and the eremitical Augustinians and Carmelites. The Wanderer's confession that he dressed himself as a "shep" and was a hermit "vnholy in werkes" raises the question whether he is as false an apostle as he is an eremite.

One of the most dramatic moments in which these ideologies and polemics clash is the interrogation of Wille by Reson and Conscience in the biographical passage (C 5). The inquiry opens with an examination according to the provisions of the labor statute to determine whether Wille is a cleric or a layman, a point that seems difficult to resolve.[53] In addition, the discourse is carried out within the topic of whether one can legitimately beg if one is physically capable of labor. This topic is not restricted to the question of the obligations of the commons versus those of the clergy, for begging by the friars had raised the issue of whether it was legitimate for clerics to beg.[54] The shift from the Labor Statute to this latter topic is indicated when Reson says:

> For an ydel man þow semest,
> A spendour þat spene mot or a spille-tyme,
> Or beggest thy bylyue aboute at men hacches
> Or faytest vppon Frydayes or feste-dayes in churches,
> The whiche is lollarne lyf, þat lytel is preysed

There ryhtfulnesse rewardeth ryht as men deserueth.
Reddet unicuique iuxta opera sua. [He will repay everyone according
to his works] (lines 26–32)

Although we might at first assume that "lollarne lyf" is a pejorative term
suggesting the life of an idler, we should recall that Langland later makes
a distinction between two kinds of "lollares": "lunatyk lollares and lepares
aboute," who are God's privy disciples, and "lollares and lewede ermytes,"
who are simply idle wasters. Both are "lollares," and the slippery use here of
"lollarne lyf" anticipates the elaborate distinction made later at C 9.61–281.

The movement of the statement is very subtle, as if to indicate how
difficult it is to distinguish idleness from appropriate beggary, the very
issue at hand with regard to Wille. First, Reson says that Wille looks
like a waster and idler, but then asks whether he begs his "bylyue" from
other men. The word "bylyue," which Langland elsewhere identifies with
belief, the substance of Faith, implies that he begs his necessities. Compare 5.7, 13.217, and 14.38, where it means "creed" or "belief," with 19.235
and 20.7, where it denotes "sustenance." Begging for necessities is acceptable, but the connotation quickly turns negative when Reson asks whether
Wille "faiteth" on Fridays, for, as we have seen, the verb "faiten" means
"to deceive," especially "to beg deceptively." It would appear that the "lollarne lyf" referred to in the next line is one involving "faiting," the reason
for which it is little praised, except that the final line rewrites the passage
to suggest that the "lollarne lyf" is one of such hardship that it is little
praised because "ryhtfulnesse rewardeth ryht as men deserueth," which,
along with the Latin, suggests that there is a strict celestial justice that
dispenses meager portions to those who follow the hateful "lollarne lyf."
I think the alternatives—"Or beggest"/"Or faytest," one appropriate, one
not—are both contained within this instance of the use of the "lollarne
lyf" because Wille has already told us that he lived on Cornhill "yclothed
as a lollare . . . / Amonges lollares of Londone and lewede ermytes." The
question is whether the "lollarne lyf" is legitimate *for Wille.* Embedded
in Reson's question about begging, then, is another one: Do you merely
use or do you actually *live* the "lollarne lyf"? Are you a "lollare" or simply
"yclothed as a lollare"?

At this juncture Wille claims that he was sent to school until he knew
what holy writ meant, implying that he is clergy. Acknowledging that he
has lost his patronage, he nevertheless continues that if he should live by
labor, then he should live by that labor (= clergye) which he knows best,
for *In eadem vocacione in qua vocati estis* [Remain in the calling to which you

are called (1 Cor. 7:20)]. This choice of text is explosive since FitzRalph had used the verse to launch his assault on the friars for *not* having remained in their calling.[55] But it is also a text that Francis had recalled to insist that friars be allowed to remain in their simpleness and poverty.[56] The Wanderer's use of the verse is clearly sophistical and hypocritical since he later admits to the principal charges brought against him when he says he has "ytyht tyme and tyme myspened" (1.93; cf. lines 7–9). But in the passage immediately following the verse, *In eadem vocacione*, he presents himself as one who observes the apostolic counsels: he is at times itinerant, echoing the requirement that the apostles travel about, and, like them, he carries no "bagge" or "botel" but begs with his "wombe" only. In effect, he presents himself as one of the "luntyk lollares" who are later described as observers of the apostolic counsels:

> Hit aren his postles, suche peple, or as his priue disciples.
> For a sent hem forth seluerles in a somur garnement
> Withoute bagge and bred, as þe book telleth:
> *Quando misi vos sine pane et pera* [When I sent you forth without
>   bread or bag].
> Barfoot and bredles, beggeth they of no man.
> And thauh a mete with the mayre ameddes þe strete,
> A reuerenseth hym ryht nauht, no rather then another.
> *Neminem salutaueritis per viam.* [Salute no one on the road]
>   (C 9.18–25).

In a subsequent defense in the biographical passage, Wille claims to live a life without solicitude, for, he says, men should not live by bread alone, as the *Pater noster* witnesses: "*Fiat voluntas dei*—þat fynt vs alle thynges" (5.87–88). But this remark only causes Conscience to question whether this is another subterfuge for illicit begging:

> By Crist, y can nat se this lyeth;
> Ac it semeth no sad parfitnesse in citees to begge,
> But he be obediencer to prior or to mynistre. (lines 89–91)

This query also has explosive repercussions, for it recalls the argument monastics, in particular, made about the mendicant orders and secular canons in the early years of polemic. "Minister" is the term used by the Franciscans for the superiors of their order, those who impose obedience on the brothers. "Prior" might suggest "abbot," the head of a monastery, but since it is used in a context that questions the appropriateness of "monks" living in cities, I suspect Langland may have had the secular canons particularly in mind, for the older monastic orders had used the argument that "monks" should not live in cities first against the secular canons and later against the mendicants.

The monastic charge against the mendicants was that they were gyrovagues in their wandering, but even worse, they and others like them were sarabaites who lived without a rule near or in cities where they begged for more than they needed in order to live in idleness.[57] According to Benedict, the Sarabaites are the worst kind of monks. They are

unschooled by any rule, untested, as gold is by fire, but soft as lead, living in and of the world, openly lying to god through their tonsure. They live together in twos or threes, more often alone, without a shepherd in their own fold, not the Lord's. Their only law is the pleasure of their desires, and whatever they wish or choose they call holy. They consider whatever they dislike unlawful.[58]

Cassian's more detailed portrait emphasizes that Sarabaites prefer "to put on the show of evangelical perfection rather than to take it up for what it really is. Their incentive to act in this way is envy, as well as the praises heaped upon those who prefer the utter poverty of Christ to all the riches of the world." They hurry to bear the name of monk but have no interest in monastic discipline. Their "withdrawal from the world is for the sake of public show and is something done before men's eyes. Or else they remain in their own houses, enjoy the name of being monks, and continue to do what they always did. Or else they build cells for themselves, give them the title of monasteries, and then freely live in them as they choose. They never fall in with the gospel commands not to be concerned about one's daily bread and not to be taken up with worldly affairs. . . . Their special concern is to be free of the yoke of elders, to be free to do what they themselves wish, to travel out, to wander wherever they please, to do what takes their fancy." They do not gather money or goods for the poor or the church but collect and save money to satisfy their own desires.[59]

We might compare this portrait with the confession by Haukyn, Wille's alter ego, that he is

Yhabited as an heremyte, an ordre by hymselue,
Religion saunȝ rule [and] resonable obedience;
Lakkynge lettrede men and lewed men boþe;
In likynge of lele life and a liere in soule;

· · · · · · · · · · · · ·

Boldest of beggeris; a bostere þat noȝt haþ,
In towne and in tauernes tales to telle
And segge þyng þat he neuere seiȝ and for soþe sweren it.
(13.284–304)

Kathryn Kerby-Fulton has suggested to me that this characterization of
Haukyn may indulge in anti-Rollean satire; however, insofar as Haukyn is
an alter ego of Wille, it also participates in the discourse on gyrovagues
and sarabaites.

   We can see these issues brought forward in Piers's elaboration of
the distinction between "bidders and beggars" and "lollares and lewede
ermytes" on the one hand, and "Godes munstrals" and "lunatyk lollares
and lepares aboute" on the other. The first group are "beggares with
bagges" who could labor but who "lollares lyf *vsen*" and thus "Lyuen aȝen
goddes lawe and þe lore of holi churche" (my emphasis; 9.98–104). The
second group are, to Piers's thinking, God's "postles," His "priue disciples"
(line 118). They beg of no one and are no respecters of persons:

> *Quando misi vos sine pane et pera.* [When I sent you forth without
>   bread or bag]
> Barfoot and bredles, beggeth they of no man.
> And thauh a mete with the mayre ameddes þe strete,
> A reuerenseth hym ryht nauht, no rather then another.
> *Neminem salutaueritis per viam.* [Salute no one on the road]
>   (lines 121–23)

The first text is used by friars to characterize the apostolic, and to justify
the mendicant, life; the second is the apostolic counsel to salute no one
on one's way (Luke 10:4). The Wanderer, in fact, seeks to represent himself as such a "fool," and is regarded as a "fool," because he was "looþ to
reuerencen / Lordes or ladies or any life ellis, / As persons in pelure wiþ
pendauntȝ of siluer" (15.1–7).

   "Priue disciples," Piers continues, should be called to the feast and
aided,

> For hit aren merye-mouthed men, munstrals of heuene,
> And godes boys, bourdyors, as the book telleth.
> *Si quis videtur sapiens, fiet stultus vt sit sapiens.* [If anyone thinks he is
>   wise, let him become a fool that he may be wise]

. . . .

Ryht so, 3e ryche, 3ut rather 3e sholde
Welcomen and worschipen and with 3oure goed helpen
Godes munstrals and his mesagers and his mery bordiours,
The whiche arn lunatyk loreles and lepares aboute,
For vnder godes secret seal here synnes ben keuered.
For they bereth none bagges ne boteles vnder clokes,
The whiche is lollarne lyf. . . . (lines 126–40a)

"Boys" and "bourdyors" are normally derogatory terms, so the suggestion here is that the "munstrals of heuene" seem somehow disreputable yet
have transformed that quality into the wisdom of fools. The caesura in line
140a marks the distinction between these "lunatyk lollares" who follow
the apostolic counsel not to take purse nor bag (Luke 10:4: *Nolite portare
sacculum, neque peram*) and the "lewede ermytes" of lines 140b and following who travel about in order to "lache men almesse," to eat and drink to
their fill, and to return to their cotes at night and thereby live in idleness
and ease on others' labors (lines 140–52). I think that Langland makes the
distinction at the caesura in order to suggest how subtle the dividing line
between the two groups is.

Nevertheless, there are some outward signs by which the two can be
discerned. "Lewede ermytes" live by the highway and in cities; they beg in
churches:

Al þat holy ermytes hatede and despisede,
As rychesses and reuerences and ryche menne almesse,
Thise lollares, lache-draweres, lewede ermytes
Coueyten þe contrarye, for as coterelles they libbeth.
For hit ben but boyes, bollares at þe ale,
Noyther of lynage ne of lettrure, ne lyf-holy as ermytes
That wonede whilom in wodes with beres and lyons.
Summe hadde lyflode of his lynage and of no lyf elles
And summe lyuede by here lettrure and labour of here handes
And somme hadde foreynes to frendes þat hem fode sente
And briddes brouhte somme bred þat they by lyuede.
Althey holy ermytes were of heye kynne,
Forsoken lond and lordschipe and alle lykynges of body. (lines
190–202)

I think that here Langland attacks both unauthorized hermits and the
Austin Friars who, after the Grand Union, followed the Franciscans and

Dominicans into the cities. Holy hermits renounced possessions and *dominium* to live in penance in the wilderness. The "lewede ermytes" live by the highways. They once labored but ceased when they saw friars living better from begging than they did by their craft:

> at the laste they aspyde
> That faytede in frere clothinge hadde fatte chekes.
> Forthy lefte they here labour, thise lewede knaues,
> And clothed hem in copes, clerkes as hit were,
> Or oen of som ordre or elles a profete,
> Aȝen þe lawe of Leuey, yf Latyn be trewe:
> *Non licet uobis legem voluntati, set voluntatem coniungere legi.* [It is not
> lawful to make the law conform to your will but for you to
> conform your will to the law] (lines 207–12)

These "lollares and lewede ermytes" do not perform the religious observances imposed on all men and women (lines 213–39); rather, they remain in bed until noon when they come out dressed as religious in search of alms:

> Ac aboute mydday at mele-tyme y mette with hem ofte,
> Come in his cope as he a clerk were;
> A bacheler or a bew-pere beste hym bysemede,
> And for þe cloth þat keuereth hym ykald he is a frere,
> Wascheth and wypeth and with þe furste sitteth. (lines 246–50)

Before this laborer became a "lollare and lewede ermyte," he acted more humbly and lived a simple moral life:

> Ac while a wrouhte in þe world and wan his mete with treuthe
> He sat at þe syde benche and at þe seconde table.
> Cam no wyn in his wombe thorw þe woke longe
> Ne no blanked on his bed ne whyte bred byfore hym. (lines 251–54)

The "lollares and lewede ermytes" feign themselves fools; they come in the garb of friars to deceive the people with their "faiterye." They are like gyrovagues and sarabaites.

Bonaventure and other mendicants recognized the seriousness of the charge that their life of mendicity was unauthorized; consequently, they

answered that they were not gyrovagues or sarabaites because those were
bad monks and hermits. The mendicants, by contrast, followed the apostles
in their itinerancy and went into cities (rather than into the wilderness),
just as had the apostles, because that was where there was greatest need.[60]
Indeed, John Pecham says that not all gyrovagues are to be condemned, for
Paul was sometimes one; however, properly motivated itinerants should
not be called gyrovagues but *rotae Domini* (citing Gregory on Daniel 7:9:
"Those who go about preaching are the wheels on the fiery chariot").[61]
More interestingly, reformers within the Franciscan order and those who
were persecuted seem to have used the name as a badge of their persecu-
tion. John of St. Victor says that in the south of France and northern Italy,
persons committed to a life of poverty and mendicancy were maligned
as *sarabaitae* but popularly called "spiritual."[62] And Angelo Clareno's *Expositio regulae fratrum minorum* cites John Cassian's *favorable* view of the
original Sarabaites who, like the Franciscans, were without solicitude for
the morrow (160–61).[63] Finally, the name is used in a positive sense in the
English tract, *Leaven of Pharisees*: The speaker complains that hypocritical
clergy "pursuen to þe deþ pore freris serabitis, þat kepen fraunseis reule
and testament to þe riȝte vndyrstondynge and wille of fraunceis wiþouten
glose of antecristes clerkis."[64] The Wanderer pursues a similar line of argument when he responds to Reson and Conscience; he implies he is neither
a gyrovague nor a sarabaite but one who follows the apostolic counsels
and begs without "bagge or botel but [his] wombe one" (line 52).

I believe that we can read "lollares and lewede ermytes" in the C-text
additions as contemporary names for sarabaites and gyrovagues, respectively, and that Langland wants to distinguish them from God's privy disciples, the "lunatyk lollares and lepares aboute," for the same reasons that
Bonaventure and others rejected the monastic argument that the mendicants were bad monks. Although I do not believe that "lunatyk lollares"
is a code name for Franciscans alone, I think the description is intended
to remind the Franciscans of the evangelical life to which the Franciscans
vowed themselves and which justified their itinerancy and mendicity. What
distinction, then, is Langland trying to make? I think the discussion of this
passage has been hampered by scholars' failure to focus on the fact that
"lollares" is the key term in both formulations. To be sure, there has been a
lengthy debate on whether "lollare" is equivalent to "Lollard," but the critical consensus has been that Langland is not a Wycliffite and that the passage
is intended to repudiate Lollard sympathies.[65] Wendy Scase has recently argued that Langland's coinage was overwhelmed by later usage of the term
"Lollard," and that all Langland originally meant by the term was "loller,"

or idler.[66] A second tendency has been to make the opposition one between "lunatyk" and "lollare," thus suppressing the fact that "lollare" is a definer of both groups under discussion.[67] My point is that both groups are "lollares"; that is, neither group works; nor are they stable since the "ermytes" are "lewede" because they wander about, yet the "lunatyk lollares" follow the apostolic counsel to be itinerant. The primary opposition, therefore, is between "lunatyk" and "lewede." As I have just suggested, the "lewede" are persons who are ignorant of their vocations; like the gyrovagues and sarabaites, they adopt the outer appearance of religious but observe no rule.

What, then, does "lunatyk" signify? It would be easy enough to read "lunatyk lollares" as mad persons or, as Derek Pearsall has recently suggested, as mental incompetents.[68] But if either is the case, why are they called "lollares"? Neither the mad nor the mentally incompetent were required to labor for their necessities, for they were wards of the state and appropriate objects of charity. By contrast, the "lunatyk lollares" are said to be legitimate accepters of alms because they are like apostolic men and women. Unlike disabled and poor laborers, they appear to be in health, and thus appear able to provide for themselves—but they do not:

> And ȝut ar ther oþere beggares, in hele, as hit semeth,
> Ac hem wanteth wyt, men and women bothe,
> The whiche aren lunatyk lollares and lepares aboute,
> And madden as þe mone sit, more other lasse.
> Careth they for no colde ne counteth of non hete
> And aren meuynge aftur þe mone. (lines 105–10)

Although they might seem to be merely insane, they are not. Line 105 says they seem to be in health but "want wit." By contrast, Wit says, 9.68–72, that "[Fauntes and] fooles . . . fauten Inwit" and that the church, consequently, is obliged to provide for them.[69] I take the "more other lasse" in line 108 to qualify the first part of the line and to suggest that the "lunatyk lollares" appear rather than are mad; they have Inwit but "want wit." They are imprudent. The lines following 108 tell us in what senses they "want wit" or are "mad": they have no regard, no solicitude, for the world and their well-being. They are not lunatics, for if they were the mentally incompetent of any kind, they would be classed with the other disabled who are legitimate recipients of alms. Statute 17 Edward II, cap. 10, gave the crown jurisdiction over lunatics and idiots, which means that they were regarded as unable to provide for themselves, not that they were able-bodied laborers. Since both the state and the church regard the insane or the incompetent as wards, there is no need for Langland to defend them; consequently, "lunatyk lollares" cannot refer to the mentally incompetent. Furthermore, if they were simply the insane, there would not be much point in designating them "lollares," which suggests they could but do not work. The key distinction is between kinds of "lollares"—all give up labor, but some are merely idlers while others are "lunatyk."

"Lunatyk lollares" are like *viri apostolici*, for they follow the evangelical counsels. They go "forth seluerles in a somur garnement / Withoute bagge and bred, as þe book telleth / *Quando misi vos sine pane et pera*" [When I sent you without bread and bag (Luke 9:3; lines 119–20)]. This text is one of the three Francis found when he sought scriptural sanction for his life of poverty (*Leg. maj.* 3.3), and it is frequently cited by mendicants as evidence that Christ and the apostles were without possession and, therefore, that a life of voluntary poverty without manual labor was sanctioned by the gospels.[70] Like the apostles, "lunatyk lollares"

> . . . moneyeles þey walke,
> With a good will, witteles, mony wyde contreyes,
> Riht as Peter dede and Poul, saueþ þat þey preche nat
> Ne none muracles maken—ac many tymes hem happeth
> To profecye of þe peple, pleyinge, as hit were. (lines 110–14)

It should be clear from this passage that the "lunatyk lollares" are not clerics in any simple sense; they neither have nor exercise the office of preaching. They may be lay people but, if so, they are not "lewede." They may be unlettered; they appear mad or foolish to others. Nevertheless, God provides their necessities and sometimes fills their mouths with prophecies. I think that Langland has deliberately made the "lunatyk lollares" enigmatic; they are images intended to recall the *apostolici* for friars and others. They are reminders of how the apostles must have appeared to the rich of this world and to the "clerkes of þe lawe" who opposed them much like the priest does Piers.

Langland's basic distinction is between those who are "lunatyk" and those who are "lewede." Both are "lollares," but the "lewede ermytes," "bidders and beggares," and even "friars and faitours," are merely idlers and deceivers. They *use* the "lollarne lyf" in order to be idle whereas the "lunatyk lollares" do not care and do not labor, the combination of which *manifests* their absence of solicitude. The "lunatyk lollares" are sapiential men and women who prophesy apparently as much through their absence of solicitude as through any words they may utter: *Si quis videtur sapiens, fiet stultus vt sit sapiens* [If anyone thinks he is wise, let him become a fool that he may be wise (line 127)]. They are the humble voluntary poor who beg, not with bags or bowls or by asking, but by their obvious need alone. Because they live in conformity with Christ's injunctions to the apostles, they are His "priue disciplis," and He sustains them in their adversity.

In the biographical passage, Wille claims to be a "lunatyk lollare" but he suggests there and in the opening lines that he is a "lollare and lewede ermyte," an idle "shep" and an "vnholy eremite." These false religious had been classically (re)conceived within monastic circles as the gyrovague and sarabaite, respectively. Beneath the tarnished image of these two, however, lies the potential ideal of the apostle and hermit described by Bonaventure. The persona, therefore, is the site of a number of conflicts: he represents himself in pursuit of apostolic and eremitical perfection, yet confesses his failures in both as a result of which he is accused (intertextually) by external critics of not remaining in the calling to which he has been called but instead of being a gyrovague and sarabaite, both of which roles he more or less confesses to in the opening lines of the poem and the biographical passage.

But there is one further wrinkle in that Francis was at various times an itinerant and a hermit. After he renounced the world before the Bishop of Assisi, he went to the Portiuncula, where he remained as a hermit for several years (*Leg. maj.* 2.8), and toward the end of his life he moved to a cave on Mount Averna, the hilltop where he had earlier received the stigmata.[71] However, near the beginning of his new life, he had consciously chosen to live among men rather than retreat into solitude. We are told that Francis,

a true servant of Christ, refused to trust in his own opinion or in the suggestions of his companions; instead, he sought to discover God's will by persevering prayer. Then, enlightened by a revelation from heaven, he realized that he was sent by God to win for Christ the souls which the Devil was trying to snatch away. And so he chose to live for the benefit of his fellow men, rather than for himself alone, after the example of Him who was so good as to die for all men. (*Leg. maj.* 4.2)

This apostolacy remained his perferred form of life, and the image that he presents to the brothers is that they are pilgrims and strangers having no permanent abode. If we narrow our focus to the figure of Francis, then, we see that Wille does not entirely satisfy either form of life that Francis had followed.

The two modes of living represented in the narrator are not given

equal weight, for, like Francis, Langland hierarchizes the apostolic over the
eremitical life. I think our poet privileges the two preaching orders, the
Franciscans and Dominicans, because they are itinerant and thus closer to
his models of Christ and His apostles. The function of the two eremitical
orders, the Augustinians and the Carmelites, is to exhibit poverty and repudiation of the world by retreat from the society of men. Their origins
are to be found in John the Baptist or the early desert saints, but neither
is a life established by Christ except insofar as he sojourned briefly in the
wilderness before taking up his itinerant ministry. This relative valuation
of mendicant lives is suggested by the praise of Francis and Dominic, the
absence of the name Carmelite in the text (whereas the other three are included), and the occasional ridicule of Augustinian claims to sanctity and
primacy of foundation. The principal positive images of apostolic men
in the text are itinerants who teach: Patient Poverty, Conscience after he
leaves the banquet and again at the end of the poem, and the Samaritan.
Piers is a much more complicated figure, a teacher whose first "pilgrimage" is remaining on his half-acre to plow but who subsequently renounces
everything to become itinerant. Later he is called a palmer (C 15.34), and in
the final passus Grace goes as "wide as þe world is wiþ Piers to tilie truþe"
(19.333). On the other hand, itinerant hermits, whether of the mendicant
orders or self-constituted, are frequently ridiculed; indeed, the poem chas-
tises them for living near highways (C 9.192–203) and going from one city
to another (Prol. 53–57). By contrast, Langland never ridicules the Franciscans and Dominicans for residing in cities, a common complaint of their
critics. The function of the hermit, it seems, is to show his renunciation by
retreat and stability in the wilderness.

We can see the relative values of the two ways first in Anima's illustration that the mendicant orders had their foundational origins in the desert
and early saints even though he at the same time snidely attacks the Austin
Friars for their claim of institutional origin in Paul the Hermit, and second,
in another bit of anti-Augustinian satire in which Imaginatyf ridicules the
notion that the Austin Friars were at the nativity of Christ.

Anima's evocation of the desert fathers and early saints is significant
because it—somewhat covertly—argues that the foundational authority
for the mendicant orders of the later Middle Ages were the apostles and
premonastic saints who withdrew to the wilderness. The matter of origins
is of great significance in the debate about the legitimacy of the mendicant
orders; often, critics of the friars called them "new orders," suggesting,
since novelty is always bad, that the vocations were without authority. The

monks, critics of both the secular canons and the friars, had appealed to the apostolic life of Christ and the apostles as their model, stressing that monks recreated their *conversatio* and lived with communal possession of goods as had the members of the early church.[72] The friars used, among other arguments, a variant of the monastic justification for their own lives. The Franciscans and Dominicans pointed to the poverty of the early church and the itinerancy and preaching of the apostles as their models. But religious orders could also cite the desert fathers as exemplars for their way of life as Benedict did when he associated his monks with the coenobitic saints and as the eremitical friars did when they invoked the early hermits.

The debate about appropriate lives of perfection provides the background for Anima's praise of the desert fathers and early saints:

[Lo!] in *legenda sanctorum*, þe lif of holy Seintes,
What penaunce and pouerte and passion þei suffrede,
In hunger, in hete, in alle manere angres.
Antony and Egidie and oþere holy fadres
Woneden in wildernesse among wilde beestes,
Monkes and mendinaunt3, men by hemselue
In spekes and spelonkes; selde speken togideres. (15.269–75)

He claims that none of these ever took food from beasts of prey but were fed by the birds or, in Egidius's case, by a hind. Similarly,

Poul *primus heremita* hadde parroked hymselue
That no man my3te hym se for mosse and for leues.
Foweles hym fedde, fele wyntres wiþall,
Til he foundede freres of Austynes ordre, [or ellis freres lyen].
    (lines 286–89)

The section in brackets appears only in MS B, though it is entered by a later hand in MS Bm. There is a corresponding passage in C 17.13–16 in which *Liberum-arbitrium* says that Paul founded the order "or elles þey [= the "frere Austynes"] gabben." I think Langland believes the story of Paul the Hermit, but I suspect he doubts that he literally founded the Augustinian order if for no other reason than Paul died c. 340, some years before Augustine's birth and nearly sixty years before Augustine wrote his rule. The notion that Augustine was a hermit also rather strains the imagination. Thus, the claim to ancient origin struck many as preposterous since, as an institution, the Order of Hermits was not created until 1256, the year of the Grand Union.

The passage continues that Paul, after preaching, made paniers and that Peter and Andrew fished for their food; yet Mary Magdalene lived on roots, the dew, but mostly through the "[meditacion] and mynde of god almyghty" (lines 290–95).

The passage as a whole names three kinds of vocations among the early saints: monks, hermits, and "mendinaunt3." Although the last word is used as a general term for beggar in Langland's culture, it also denotes begging friars. Since the passage goes on to talk about the apostles who labored for their necessities, as opposed to these saints who did not, we can see that the discourse is focused on the issue of the legitimacy of begging when one could labor for one's needs, a topic in the antifraternal debates. Anima, therefore, provides a foundation for all three vocations. The friars used much the same argument in order to justify their dependence on begging rather than on manual labor. The aside about the founding of the Austin Friars, clearly a pejorative statement, indicates the concern for origins, for if one could show that one were founded before the monastic orders, then one had answered the charge that the friars were "new orders."[73] The Franciscans and Dominicans, however, never claimed that they were founded in the early days; to the contrary, these orders answered the criticism that they were "new orders" by claiming that they were "renewing orders."[74] Their spiritual origins, not their institutions, were established within the primitive church; they propose to return to, to renew, those apostolic and saintly lives.

In a brief and obscure aside, Imaginatyf also ridicules the Austin Friars' preposterous claims to early foundation by rejecting the notion that they could have been at Christ's birth. He says,

If any frere were founde þere I ȝyue þee fyue shillynges!
Ne in none [beggers] cote [n]as þat barn born,
But in a Burgeises place, of Bethlem þe best:
Set non erat ei locus in diuersorio, et pauper non habet diuersorium
[But there was no place for them in the lodging place, and a pauper
    does not have a lodging place]. (12.145–47)[75]

This statement is very unusual since it seems to defy the scriptural statement that Christ was born in a stable because there was no place in the inn. At first, I took the remark, odd though it is, as another of Langland's attacks on friars, but the "bet" that the friars were not at the birth seems gratuitously snide.

The other curious element in Imaginatyf's remark about Christ's birth is that He was born in a burgess's "place," not a "beggers cote." The remark has been interpreted as an instance of Langland's desire to dissociate Christ from beggars and mendicancy.[76] The Latin quoted at the end of the passage comes from Luke 2:7 (*non erat ei locus in diuersorio*), to which Imaginatyf adds the comment, *et pauper non habet diuersorium*. If the Latin text is intended to nail down the argument of the preceding three lines, then it would appear that finding no place in an inn confirms that Christ *was* born a beggar because a beggar has no *diversorium*. But this conclusion would seem to contradict the assertion that Christ was not born in a "beggers cote" but a "Burgeises place." If there were no place in the inn (*diversorium*), then what is the "Burgeises place"?

One's first guess is that the "place" is a merchant's palace or mansion (a *domus*); however, such an understanding ill fits the larger context. The speaker, Imaginatyf, is in the midst of his defense of "clergye." He says that the prophets and patriarchs reproved the knowledge ("science") of "kynde witted" men who had not been converted to the way of truth (12.136–38, and see the preceding discussion). Then the passage segues into a historical prophetic voice: The Holy Ghost shall cleave heaven and love leap out and "clennesse" receive it and clerks "fynde" it, *Pastores loquebantur ad inuicem* [The shepherds said to one another, let us go to Bethlehem (lines 139–41)]. Imaginatyf says that he does not speak of rich men, nor of those who were "riȝt witty," nor of lords who were ignorant, but of the "hyeste lettred oute, / *Ibant magi ab oriente*" [The magi came from the east]. These two scriptural figures, *pastores* and *magi*, are picked up after the lines that concern us and identified as "pastours" and "poetes" (line 148). Only after the annunciation to *pastores* and *magi* did "Clerkes" come with their presents (lines 153–55). Clearly, Langland is reading *magi* as visionaries ("poetes" and *vates*) and not as kings, and he insists that the news was first sent to shepherds, not "lered" men, clerks, or even magi. The implication is that the word was first made known to the ignorant, simple shepherds and then to the magi in order to make the point that "clergye" is valued but that it is not to be valued most. The aside about the friars not being there, consequently, takes place in the context of whom Christ first appeared to.

Given the emphasis on the simple and poor, it seems even more strange that Imaginatyf should then remark that Christ was born in a "Burgeises place," if we are to understand the place to be a rich house. The "place," therefore, is not a palace or mansion but a place (*platea, piazza, Platz*), an open space. The Franciscan Lyra says that the *diversoria* were filled with great men, but, even though Joseph was of a noble kind, they were poor, and thus the savior was born in a lesser place.[77] Lyra thus seems to make a distinction between the great and lesser *loci* within the *diversorium*, the emphasis in his reading being on *locus* rather than *diversorium*. This distinction also appears in Bonaventure's commentary on Luke: first, he says, "*Et reclinavit eum in praesepio* [and she laid him in a manger], *non in cubiculo* [= room, bedchamber]," and then moves from the deficient bed (*defectus lectulus*) to the deficient abode (*defectus habitaculus*), citing the verse, *Quia non erat eis locus in diversorium* [because there was not a place for them]. He comments that a *diversorium*, according to Isidore, is a place where many persons convene, since according to Bede, it has several openings, for it is an open space (*platea vacua*) between two walls or streets (*duos vicos*) and is open at the entrance and exit, but is covered above to protect people from the elements, so that the citizens might come together there. Here Mary gave birth because they had no room (*domum*) in which they might have been housed.[78] Similarly, in remarking on the season of Christ's birth, Bonaventure says that God placed the idea of taking the census in the emperor's thought in order that Mary travel to Bethlehem and there give birth *in diversorio* (meaning, apparently, a place in the larger structure but not in a *domum*).[79] Pecham repeats the idea in his commentary on the rule when he's defending the greater needs of the larger numbers of friars and says that Christ was content to be born *in diversorio et praesepio* but gathered his disciples in a large room for the Last Supper.[80] We have misread Langland's statement, as we may have misread Luke, when we assume that it is the *diversorium* that had no room, whereas these commentators understand the verse to say that there was no room (*locus, domus*) in the *diversorium* and therefore Joseph and Mary had to sleep in the public place (the courtyard within the larger structure).

Both the B- and C-texts also insist that Christ was not born in a "beggers cote." Besides wishing to stress that, unlike foxes who have holes to hide themselves in, Christ had nowhere to lay his head—a common mendicant trope to assert Christ's utter poverty—Imaginatyf seems intent on rejecting the notion that Christ was born in a "cote." I suspect that the choice of this word is directed particularly toward the eremitical mendicants, who (supposedly) lived in simple, often separate dwellings (= cotes), rather than toward the Dominicans and Franciscans, who lived communally in friaries.

The logic of Langland's argument in this section is that Christ appeared first to shepherds and magi—but not friars—and that He was not born in a beggar's cote; nor was He born in a room in an inn, because *pauper non habet diuersorium*. Rather, He was born in the town "place," which suggests He was a *pauper*, as Langland's gloss on Luke 2:7 implies. The purpose of the remark is not to deny Christ's poverty or His mendicancy, but to deny that friars were present at His birth and thereby to make a joke of the eremitical orders' claims to ancient foundation. We might also observe that the arguments Imaginatyf uses to set up the Austin Friars are those of Lyra, a Franciscan, and Hugh of St. Cher, a Dominican. They have textual hegemony here.

Langland seems to have constructed his persona as an itinerant eremite dressed in gray russet in order to show how difficult it is to remain true to the primitive rules of both the itinerant and eremitical orders; in addition, the characterization would remind his Franciscan readers that Francis was a mendicant and a hermit, for both of which lives Francis acts as an exemplar. No matter how we ultimately regard Wille, his itinerancy is obviously illegitimate because it is improperly motivated. The text elsewhere suggests that itinerancy is justified when one renounces everything and is unsolicitous of the morrow, but the Wanderer admits to disguising himself in order to seek out "wonders." In addition, if he were actually a hermit, then he would violate the eremitical rules when he became itinerant or would make himself one of those self-proclaimed hermits who were often suspect because of their wandering. When we look at the persona with regard to the four mendicant orders, he can be read as a negative reminder for all four. However, it seems to me that it is a more negative image for the eremitical orders since itinerancy, at least according to Langland, is a violation of their rules whereas itinerancy is part of the vocation of the two preaching orders. On the other hand, we can also look at the persona as a construct of Francis's two callings, mendicant and hermit, and thus a composite figure that would be particularly rich for Franciscan readers, for even though Wille may be a failure in his calling, he projects the potential for reform. We can read the poem as Wille's meditation on the difficulties of living the ideal he aspires to, of recording the ease with which one can move from the ideal to its failure. By raising the issue of whether the Wanderer himself is a "lunatyk lollare" or a "lollare and lewede ermyte," he crystallizes the issue for his readers. Rather than personally accusing his (unreformed) reader, he asks the reader to meditate on his own life. Langland's "spiritual autobiograpy" thus evokes a spiritually autobiographical response in his readers.

The Wanderer is certainly poorly motivated and hypocritical, but potentially his itinerant/eremitical life is justified if he learns patient poverty and undertakes to do whatever is required of his calling; thus, the figure reminds Langland's Franciscan readers of how easily one can fail at the same time as it suggests the ideal image that in this world they are to be strangers and pilgrims. Langland's persona is a voice crying in the wilderness—but first it cries to itself that others might hear.

Notes

1. J. J. Jusserand, *"Piers Plowman," a Contribution to the History of English Mysticism,* trans. M. E. R. (London: Unwin, 1894), 70, n. 1. Walter W. Skeat remarked on the contradiction as well but it would appear that John Bowers, Wendy Scase, and Kathryn Kerby-Fulton are the only ones to have focused on it in recent years. See Walter W. Skeat, ed., *The Vision of William concerning Piers the Plowman, in Three Parallel Texts* (London: Oxford University Press, 1886), 2.xxxvii; John M. Bowers, *The Crisis of Will in Piers Plowman* (Washington, D.C.: Catholic University of America Press, 1986), 165–89; Wendy Scase, *Piers Plowman and the New Anticlericalism* (Cambridge: Cambridge University Press, 1989), 161–73; and Kathryn Kerby-Fulton, *Reformist Apocalypticism and Piers Plowman* (Cambridge: Cambridge University Press, 1990), 116–32. David Lawton has presented a wide-ranging analysis of the conflicts within the persona in David Lawton, "The Subject of *Piers Plowman,*" *Yearbook of Langland Studies* 1 (1987): 1–30.

2. Konrad Burdach, *Der Dichter des Ackermann aus Böhmen und seine Zeit,* vol. 3, part 2 of *Vom Mittelalter zur Reformation: Forschungen zur Geschichte der deutschen Bildung* (Berlin: Weidmannsche Buchhandlung, 1932), 140–371.

3. Citations will be from the B-text unless otherwise noted: George Kane and E. Talbot Donaldson, eds., *Piers Plowman: The B Version* (London: Athlone Press, 1975); and Derek Pearsall, ed., *Piers Plowman by William Langland: An Edition of the C-Text* (Berkeley and Los Angeles: University of California Press, 1979).

4. E. Talbot Donaldson, *Piers Plowman: The C-Text and Its Poet* (New Haven, Conn.: Yale University Press, 1949), 146–47, 171–74.

5. Donaldson remarked several times in my presence that he "did not see what was wrong with Rechelesnesse's statement." I think he remained puzzled by Langland's decision to give this statement to a figure so problematical as the C-Rechelesnesse.

6. Robert Worth Frank, *Piers Plowman and the Scheme of Salvation* (New Haven, Conn.: Yale University Press, 1957), 48–49.

7. The most detailed analysis of Langland's traditional antifraternal views is Penn R. Szittya, *The Antifraternal Tradition in Medieval Literature* (Princeton, N.J.: Princeton University Press, 1986), 247–87; for the figure of Nede, see Robert Adams, "The Nature of Need in *Piers Plowman* XX," *Traditio* 34 (1978): 273–301.

8. See my essay, Lawrence M. Clopper, "Langland's Franciscanism," *Chaucer Review* 25 (1990): 54–75. Although Kerby-Fulton, *Reformist Apocalypticism and*

Piers Plowman, indicates that she is not concerned to establish sources for *Piers Plowman*, her chapter on Joachite apocalypticism (pp. 162–200) lays the groundwork for the argument that Langland was profoundly influenced by Franciscan reformist apocalypticism; her larger point, however, is that *Piers* is reformist, not simply antifraternal.

9. John Bale, *Scriptorvm illustrium maioris Brytannie quam nunc Angliam & Scotiam uocant*. (Basel: Ionnem Oporinum, 1557?), 474; on the poem's reception, see John N. King, "Robert Crowley's Editions of *Piers Plowman*: A Tudor Apocalypse," *Modern Philology* 73 (1976): 342–52.

10. Particularly valuable for William, FitzRalph, and Wyclif is Szittya, *The Antifraternal Tradition in Medieval Literature*. For Olivi, see David Burr, *Olivi and Franciscan Poverty: The Origins of the* usus pauper *Controversy* (Philadelphia: University of Pennsylvania Press, 1989); and for Ubertino da Casale, see P. Anicetus Chiappini, "Communitatis responsio 'Religiosi viri' ad Rotulum Fr. Ubertini de Casali," *Archivum Franciscanum Historicum* 7–8 (1914–1915): 654–75 [7], 56–80 [8], the materials on Casale edited by Franz Ehrle, "Responsio" and "Rotulus," in *Archiv für Litteratur- und Kirchengeschichte des Mittelalters* 3 (1887): 51–89, 93–137, and Charles T. Davis, "Le pape Jean XXII et les spirituels: Ubertin de Casale," in *Franciscains d'Oc: Les spirituels ca. 1280–1324*, ed. Edouard Privat (Toulouse: Centre d'Etudes Historiques de Fanjeaux, 1975), 263–83.

11. Frank, *Piers Plowman and the Scheme of Salvation*, 106–7, n. 2, 110, n. 6, and 115–16; Szittya, *The Antifraternal Tradition in Medieval Literature*, 280–83; Scase, *Piers Plowman and the New Anticlericalism*, passim; and Kerby-Fulton, *Reformist Apocalypticism and Piers Plowman*, 150–53, 160.

12. FitzRalph makes the granting of the privileges of hearing confession, right of sepulture, and preaching the center of his critique of the friars; the desire for these privileges, he argued, violates the mendicant rules and interferes with ecclesiastical rights. But some mendicants also deplored the avidity with which right of sepulture was exercised and warned against improper granting of penance (e.g., Ubertino da Casale, "Rotulus [ed. Franz Ehrle]," 114; see also Olivi's comments, in P. Damasus Laberge, "Fr. Petri Ioannis Olivi, OFM: Tria scripta sui ipsius apologetica annorum 1283 et 1285," *Archivum Franciscanum Historicum* 28 (1935): art. 12, pp. 378–81, and his quoting of Bonaventure as one of his authorities, 380; for which see Bonaventure, Epistle 2, *Epistolae officiales*, in *Opera omnia*, ed. Quaracchi fathers (Quaracchi: College of St. Bonaventure, 1882–1902), 8.470–71. Hugh of Digne draws a sharp line between the Franciscan mission to evangelize and to provide normal pastoral care when he quotes Paul (1 Cor. 1:17), "*Non misit nos Christus baptizare sed evangelizare*" ["Christ did not send us to baptize but to evangelize"]; Hugh of Digne, *Hugh of Digne's Rule Commentary*, ed. David Flood, OFM (Rome: College of St. Bonaventure, 1979), 191.

13. I have discussed the life of the Dreamer, and his claims to perfection, in Lawrence M. Clopper, "The Life of the Dreamer, the Dreams of the Wanderer in *Piers Plowman*," *Studies in Philology* 86 (1989): 261–85. The present essay responds to Lawton's suggestion, in Lawton, "The Subject of *Piers Plowman*," 1–30, that the persona is the site of a variety of discourses, though I find the subject more integrated than Lawton does.

14. The following discussion is based on a more detailed analysis in my forthcoming book, Lawrence M. Clopper, *"Songes of Rechelesnesse": Langland and the Franciscans* (Ann Arbor: University of Michigan Press, 1997).

15. Richard FitzRalph, *Defensio curatorum*, ed. Melchior Goldast, *Monarchia S. romani imperii*, II (Hanover: Conrad Biermann, 1614). See also John Trevisa, trans., *Defensio curatorum*, in *Dialogus inter Militem et clericum*, EETS o.s. 167 (London, 1925). The passage discussed below occurs at *Defensio* 1402 (Trevisa, 70). For FitzRalph, see Katherine Walsh, *A Fourteenth-Century Scholar and Primate: Richard FitzRalph in Oxford, Avignon, and Armagh* (Oxford: Clarendon Press, 1981), 349–451; Szittya, *The Antifraternal Tradition in Medieval Literature*, 123–51; James Dawson, "Richard FitzRalph and the Fourteenth-Century Poverty Controversies," *Journal of Ecclesiastical History* 34 (1983): 315–44; and Janet Coleman, "FitzRalph's Antimendicant 'Proposicio' (1350) and the Politics of the Papal Court at Avignon," *Journal of Ecclesiastical History* 35 (1984): 376–90.

16. FitzRalph, *Defensio curatorum*, 1405–8 (Trevisa, 80–89). Trevisa translates FitzRalph's *spontanée* as "willful"; like the phrase "begged by the mouth," the word choice is intended to suggest that someone verbally requested something rather than that he was an obvious and passive object of charity. Such begging is "voluntary" as opposed to "necessary," so the implication is that willful begging defrauds the rightful poor. Richard Maidstone, like other friars, defined *spontanée* as begging for necessities; Arnold Williams, *"Protectorium pauperis*, a Defense of the Begging Friars by Richard of Maidstone, O. Carm," *Carmelus* 5 (1958): 153.

17. Malcolm D. Lambert, *Franciscan Poverty: The Doctrine of the Absolute Poverty of Christ and the Apostles in the Franciscan Order 1210–1323* (London: SPCK, 1961), 208–46.

18. Thomas Turley, "John XXII and the Franciscans: A Reappraisal," in *Popes, Teachers and Canon Law in the Middle Ages*, ed. James A. Sweeney and Stanley Chodorow (Ithaca, N.Y.: Cornell University Press, 1989), 74–88.

19. Here is another point at which external and internal critiques coincide. In his first letter after his election, Bonaventure lists sumptuous buildings among numerous other abuses within the order, Epistle 1, *Epistolae officiales*, in Bonaventure, *Opera omnia*, 8.468–69; in his second letter he reduces the greatest abuses to three, one of which is sumptuous dwellings. Similarly, in his *Tractatus pauperis* John Pecham calls friars' dwellings *monstra*; he complains that friars beg importunately and live in excessive buildings; John Pecham, *Tractatus de paupertate*, ed. C. L. Kingsford et al. (Aberdeen: Aberdeen University Press, 1910), 36, 85.

20. The poet uses the formula "friars and faitours" or variants of it in order to point to friars who have deceived with their begging at 2.183 (see variants); 6.72; 10.72; 13.242; and C 9.208. Elsewhere, he uses "faitours" to mean "beggars who deceive the almsgiver" (2.183; 6.121, 183; 9.196; 15.215; 20.5; and C 9.64), "faiten" to mean "to beg by deception" (Prol. 42 [the textual variants]; 7.95; 10.39; and C 5.30; 9.100) and "faiterie" to mean "deception" (11.92; and C 8.138). The poet uses the alliterative pairs, "bidders and beggars" and related expressions in passages where he is discussing false beggars (Prol. 40–45; 6.203; 7.65–69; 13.241–42; 15.205–8; and C 6.49). Other passages in which some form of the two words appear together stress the reckless condition of begging (3.219; 7.81, 84–86; and 15.227, 256 [elaborated in C 16.369–71]).

21. *Rotuli parliamentorum* (London: HMSO, 1783), 2.332, for 1376; and John A. Alford, *Piers Plowman: A Glossary of Legal Diction* (Cambridge: D. S. Brewer, 1988), 54 ("faitour") and 56 ("fautor").

22. Lines 76–83; and see the Samaritan's remark at 17.320 for the general principle: "His [the sinner's] sorwe is satisfaccion for [swich] þat may no3t paie."

23. Ubertino da Casale, "Responsio [ed. Franz Ehrle]," 69, 81, and "Rotulus [ed. Franz Ehrle]," 104–7. Rigorists and moderates alike argued that brothers should not show signs of solicitude in their begging; they ought not to be clamorous in asking for alms; they ought not to make signs to induce people to give them alms (e.g., Pecham, *Tractatus pauperis*, 63). Ubertino says that voluntary poverty consists in being content with few and vile things, not *importune extorquens* [extorting importunately], as a result of which secular people, seeing *importunos petetores* [importunate beggars] and the defection from poverty, give less to the friars; Ubertino, "Responsio [ed. Franz Ehrle]," 3.70. For similar sentiments, see Peter John Olivi, *Peter Olivi's Rule Commentary*, ed. David Flood (Wiesbaden: Franz Steiner, 1972), 165; and Angelo Clareno, *Expositio regulae fratrum minorum*, ed. P. Livarius Oliger, OFM (Quaracchi: College of St. Bonaventure, 1912), 22. The community responded to the criticism in the Constitutions of Perpignan (1331) by distinguishing appropriate from "*indecens*" forms of begging; P. Saturninus Mencherini, OFM, "Constitutiones generales ordinis fratrum minorum a capitulo Perpiniani anno 1331 celebrato editae," *Archivum Franciscanum Historicum* 2 (1909): 419. In his response to the papal bull *Ad conditorem* (1322) the Franciscan Provincial Minister, Richard Conington, said that "*petant humiliter*" ["they should ask (for alms) humbly"] was to be understood in two ways: as an obligation not to ask *litigando nec veniendo quasi ex iure* [as if it were owed or came by right]; and as informing the brothers they are not to beg *importune nec elate* (= wildly, from *effero*; see P. Albanus Heysse, "Fr. Richardi de Conington, OFM. Tractatus de paupertate Fratrum Minorum et Abbreviatura inde a Communitate extracta," *Archivum Franciscanum Historicum* 23 [1930]: 355). Friars might accept (*accipere, recipere*) alms, but ought not to solicit them. They might pray (*petere*) for necessities, but not demand them. The monks charged that it was all right to receive (*accipere, recipere*) but not to beg (*petere*) alms because canon law said that churches and monasteries were to be endowed in order to perform their functions. Bonaventure lashed out at this absurd distinction on the grounds that the possessioners had less need than the friars who had given up everything. See his *Quaestiones disputatae de perfectione evangelica*, q. 2, art. 2, concl., in *Opera omnia*, 5.141–42. For the general principle of receiving (*accipere*) alms, see Pecham, *Tractatus pauperis*, 25–27, 32.

24. In the B-text the passage under discussion occurs within the first Inner Dream in a passage that is not clearly assigned to a speaker (see 11.154 ff.). It is presented in an "authoritative" voice, possibly an "authorial intrusion," but I understand the discussion of Christ's poverty to be part of the Dreamer's debate with his friar-confessor and the whole sequence to be a kind of interior monologue.

25. FitzRalph, *Defensio curatorum*, 1394–95 (Trevisa, 47). FitzRalph was following earlier critiques of the mendicant teaching on poverty. Pecham cites the Solomonic verse as the first of the critics' charges and responds to it first since it is necessary to establish poverty as the foundation of the evangelical life; Pecham, *Tractatus pauperis*, 23–24.

26. The text is usually cited to establish Christ's poverty and often plays a role in the larger argument that Christ begged. Bonaventure, *Quaest. disp.*, q. 2, art. 2.9, in *Opera omnia*, 5.137, cites the *Glossa Ordinaria* on the following terms: a *pauper* is one who does not have sufficient for himself; a *mendicus* is one who asks from another or who lives on what is others. Cf. Richard of Maidstone, Carm., in Williams, "*Protectorium pauperis*: A Defense of the Begging Friars by Richard of Maidstone, O. Carm," 148–49, 156, and Aquinas, *Contra impugnantes dei cultum et religionem*, in *Opera omnia* ed. Dominican brothers, vol. 41A (Rome: Sancta Sabina, 1970), 78/745–49; and Thomas Aquinas, *Summa theologiae*, ed. Blackfriars fathers (Cambridge: Blackfriars, 1964–1976), II-II, q. 187, art. 5, sed contra. The text was important because it clearly identified Christ as a *mendicus*. If Christ was a *mendicus*, then it was legitimate for friars to be *mendici* and to beg for alms. William of St. Amour rejects the mendicant argument; see John V. Fleming, "The 'Collations' of William of Saint-Amour against S. Thomas," *Recherches de théologie ancienne et médiévale* 32 (1965): 134; and *Quaestio reportata de mendicitate cum annotationibus Gulielmi de S. Amore*, ed. F. M. Delorme, OFM, in Bonaventure, *Collationes in Hexaëmeron* (Florence: College of St. Bonaventure, 1934), 334–35.

27. Bonaventure, *Quaest. disp.*, q. 2, art. 1, sed c. 1, in *Opera omnia*, 5.128, 131; and see art. 2, ad 14, 5.146; Aquinas, *Contra impugnantes dei cultum et religionem*, cap. 6.12–15, 270–77. Like other Franciscans, Walter Chatton uses the text to establish the absolute poverty of Christ; Decima L. Douie, "Three Treatises on Evangelical Poverty by Fr. Richard Conyngton, Fr. Walter Chatton, and an Anonymous from MS. V III 18 in Bishop Cosin's Library, Durham," *Archivum Franciscanum Historicum* 25 (1932): 37–38.

28. Scase, *Piers Plowman and the New Anticlericalism*, 57–58, says that Langland fuses FitzRalph's position (lines 270–71) with the mendicant one (the remainder); however, the logic of the argument is that a wiser one, Christ, dismisses the Old Testament statement of Solomon.

29. "Ad quod videtur dicendum, quod cum sit duplex necessitas paupertatis evangelicae, sicut dicunt sancti, paupertas imperfecta, quae cum paupertate spiritus nihil retinet superfluum temporale, sed solum retinet quod est necessitatis; alia vero est paupertas perfecta, quae cum paupertate spiritus nec superfluum nec necessarium vitae retinet tanquam proprium, sed ex Dei provisione pendet, quae paupertas dicitur mendicitatis. Haec videtur paupertas fratrum minorum, quae hic determinatur. Unde attenditur in duobus: unum est, ut non recipiant fixum aliquid, sicut redditum; et hoc est quoniam *tanquam peregrini et advenae in paupertate debent Domino* famulari. Aliud est, quia debent habere paupertatem quantum ad usum, ut taliter sint pauperes quod etiam sint mendici. Unde etiam additur: *Vadant pro elemosina confidenter*"; P. Livarius Oliger, ed., *Expositio quatuor magistrorum super regulam fratrum minorum (1241-1242)* (Rome: Edizioni di Storia e Letteratura, 1950), 157–58.

30. Digne, *Hugh of Digne's Rule Commentary*, 159.

31. E.g., Clareno, *Expositio regulae fratrum minorum*, 174–76; and Ubertino da Casale , "Rotulus [ed. Franz Ehrle]," 114–15. On the notion in Bonaventure, see Aidan Carr, OFM Conv., "Poverty in Perfection according to St. Bonaventure," *Franciscan Studies* 7 (1947): 313–23, 415–25.

32. In the early phase of the mendicant-secular debate at the University of Paris, Aquinas defended a position nearly indistinguishable from that of Bonaventure; see Aquinas, *Contra impugnantes dei cultum et religionem*. cap. 6: "Utrum liceat religioso omnia sua relinquere ita quod nihil sibi possidendum remaneat nec in proprio nec in communi" ["Whether it is allowed for a religious to leave all that he has so that he reserves no possessions for himself either in person or in common"]. However, in what appears to be a direct response to Bonaventure, he later argued that it was neither possible nor desirable to renounce all things *in proprio et in communi*. See Aquinas, *Summa theologiae*, II-II, qq. 185–87; and Edouard-Henri Weber, *Dialogue et dissension entre St. Bonaventure et St. Thomas d'Aquin. . . . Paris (1252–1273)* (Paris: Vrin, 1974). All orders under the rules of St. Benedict or some form of the Rule of St. Augustine, that is, all monastic orders, canons, and the three non-Franciscan mendicant orders, acknowledged the legitimacy of ownership in common.

33. Lambert, *Franciscan Poverty: The Doctrine of the Absolute Poverty of Christ and the Apostles in the Franciscan Order, 1210–1323*, 223–25, 235–36.

34. An interesting illustration of the change in the Franciscan stance is the tract by William Woodford, OFM, in which he cites John's rulings against Wyclif's theory of *dominium*; Eric Doyle, OFM, "William Woodford's 'De dominio civili clericorum' against John Wyclif," *Archivum Franciscanum Historicum* 66 (1973): 49–109, esp. 67–69.

35. See 14.258–73 (where Christ is said to come in the sect of poverty) and 15.165 ff. (where the theological virtue of Charity is identified with poverty). The last is a typical Franciscan trope; for example, Hugh of Digne had equated *paupertas altissima* [highest poverty] with *caritas perfectissima* [most perfect charity] (above), and Bonaventure had said that poverty was the first condition of perfection (and thus equivalent to the two friars' Dowel) and, at the same time, the highest manifestation of Charity or perfection (Anima's Dobest). See Bonaventure's comment: "Paupertas spiritus, quae includit paupertatem et humilitatem, est fundamentum perfectionis evangelicae et etiam consummatio eius" ["Poverty of spirit, which includes poverty and humility, is the foundation of evangelical perfection and also its consummation"], *Comm. in Luc*, Bonaventure, *Opera omnia*, 7.175b; see also *Apol. paup*, Bonaventure, *Opera omnia*, 8.280a. For brief discussion, see Jacques-Guy Bougerol, *Lexique Saint Bonaventure* (Paris: Éditions Franciscaines, 1969), 105. Donaldson, *Piers Plowman: The C-Text and Its Poet*, 170, 175–78, and Frank, *Piers Plowman and the Scheme of Salvation*, 70–75, have shown that the poem identifies patient poverty with Charity. Aquinas thought the Franciscans' emphasis on poverty extreme and rejected the equation of poverty and Charity; see Aquinas, *Summa theologiae*, II-II, q. 186, art. 8.

36. "Sect" is part of the Franciscan vocabulary. See, Ubertino da Casale, "Rotulus [ed. Franz Ehrle]," 132, where he quotes Bonaventure to the effect that those who commit themselves to the sect of Christ in extreme poverty [Christum in extrema paupertate sectari] abdicate everything. The *Rule of 1223*, cap. 5, says that brothers may accept anything necessary, but they should do so humbly, as is fitting of the servants of God and followers (*sectatores*) of most holy poverty. K-D emend "of pure riʒt" from C 16.100 for the alliteration, but the B-MSS have the

same sense: "Forþi [al] poore þat pacient is ⟨may cleymen and asken⟩, / After hir endynge here, heueneriche blisse."

37. The Four Masters cited the Beatitude in their definition of "perfect poverty," so later commentators elaborated the significance (e.g., Pecham, *Expositio super regulam fratrum minorum*, 6.25, in Bonaventure, *Opera omnia*). Francis's statement also draws on James 2:5: "*Audite fratres mei dilectissimi, nonne Deus elegit pauperes in hoc mundo, divites in fide, et haeredes regni, quod repromisit Deus diligentibus se?*" [Listen, my beloved brethren, has not God chosen those who are poor in this world to be rich in faith and heirs of the kingdom which God promised to those who love him?]; see Bonaventure's Epiphany sermon, Bonaventure, *Opera omnia*, 9.147.

38. *Tractatus contra fratrem Robertum Kilwardby, OP*, in Pecham, *Tractatus pauperis*, 142. For further discussion of the treatment of the beatitudes by Franciscans and others, see Lawrence M. Clopper, "*Patience*: Meditations on a Whale and a Woodbine," *Mediaevalia* 14 (1991 for 1988): 164–66.

39. In making this claim I do not mean to argue that Langland did not also direct his poem to a yet larger public; the apostrophes to lords and to clergy and the delineation of the roles of members in each estate indicate that Langland hoped for a broader reform than that of the mendicants alone. Nevertheless, within the total readership are narrower ones, and Langland's concern for these specialized vocations affects not only the content of the poem but also the ways that Langland constructed his narrator, the Wanderer of the waking moments.

40. William A. Hinnebusch, OP, *The History of the Dominican Order* (New York: Alba House, 1966–1973); G. R. Galbraith, *The Constitution of the Dominican Order, 1216 to 1360* (Manchester: Manchester University Press, 1925); and for the rule, see Raymond Creytens, OP, "Les Constitutions des Frères Prêcheurs dans la rédaction de S. Raymond de Peñafort (1241)," *Archivum fratrum predicatorum* 18 (1948): 5–68.

41. A standard history is John Moorman, *A History of the Franciscan Order from Its Origins to the Year 1517* (Oxford: Clarendon Press, 1968).

42. He said, "omnes tamen Fratres operibus praedicent" ["however, all brothers should preach by their works" (that is, by example)], *Rule of 1221*, cap. 17; and see 2 Celano 142.189, both in Marion A. Habig, ed., *St. Francis of Assisi: Writings and Early Biographies*, 4th ed. (Chicago: Franciscan Herald Press, 1983).

43. Bonaventure, *Legenda major*, 7.2.

44. Despite the friction between the orders, the Dominican Constitutions required their brothers always to welcome the Franciscans, Dist. 2, cap. 13, and Franciscan ones ordered the corrollary; Assisi, 1354, cap. 4, item 13; in Michael Bihl, "Statuta generali ordinis edita in capitulo generali an. 1354 Assisii celebrato," *Archivum Franciscanum Historicum* 35 (1935): 35–112, 177–253.

45. A succinct description is given by David Knowles, *The Religious Orders in England*, 2 vols. (Cambridge: Cambridge University Press, 1948–1955), 1.194–201. Standard histories are Francis Roth, OSA, *The English Austin Friars: 1249–1538*, 2 vols. (New York: Augustinian Historical Institute, 1966); Aubrey Gwynn, *The English Austin Friars in the Age of Wyclif* (London: Oxford University Press, 1940); and Patrick McCaffrey, *The White Friars: An Outline of Carmelite History with Special Reference to the English Speaking Province* (Dublin: M. H. Gill, 1926).

46. I should acknowledge here that my argument pertains to the construction of the persona insofar as the persona is the site of mendicant debates. Langland also is critical of those itinerant hermits who do not belong to the orders of Augustinian or Carmelite friars. For this tradition, see Ralph Hanna's essay in this volume and Kathryn Kerby-Fulton's discussion of the itinerant eremitical ideal; Kathryn Kerby-Fulton, "A Return to 'The First Dawn of Justice': Hildegard's Visions of Clerical Reform and the Eremitical Life," *American Benedictine Review* 40 (1989): 383–407. It will be apparent to readers of Ralph Hanna's essay and my own where our differences lie. I think that by focusing on the Dreamer as itinerant (and disreputable) hermit, Hanna makes the portrait more negative than I do. I believe that Langland wished to force his readers to meditate on the various ideals of mendicancy and thereby to acknowledge the difficulty of achieving them. By this strategy he *invites* his mendicant readers to reform themselves.

47. Elsewhere he refers to himself as a "mendynaunt" (13.3). He goes about in a "habite as a heremite"; he "roams about" "yrobbed in russet" (= gray wool [see 15.167]; 8.1), a garment like that worn by the Franciscans.

48. Skeat, *The Vision of William concerning Piers the Plowman, in Three Parallel Texts*, 2.2; but see J. A. W. Bennett, ed., *Piers Plowman, Prologue and Passus I–VII of the B Text* (Oxford: Clarendon Press, 1972), 80. Derek Pearsall, *Piers Plowman, by William Langland: An Edition of the C-Text*, seems to genuinely offer the two alternatives (27). Ralph Hanna takes it as a witty reference to Wille's "sheep-garb."

49. Given the construction of the Good Shepherd in Christ's parable and the glosses upon it, the C-MSS "shepherd" would effectively identify the Wanderer as an "apostle" as well.

50. *Sermones de B. Virgine Maria, De Purificatione*, Sermon II, in Bonaventure, *Opera omnia*, 9.648.

51. Pecham, *Tractatus pauperis*, 50; he cites Luc. x:[3], but reads *oves* for *agni*: " 'Ecce ego mitto vos sicut' etc. Oves dico."

52. 15.167; and at C 9.246–50 the "lollares and lewede ermytes" are said to dress themselves in such a way that they will be mistaken for friars.

53. See my essays, Clopper, "The Life of the Dreamer, the Dreams of the Wanderer in *Piers Plowman*," *Studies in Philology* 86 (1989): 261–85; and "Need Men and Women Labor? Langland's Wanderer and the Labor Ordinances," in *Chaucer's England: Literature in Historical Context*, ed. Barbara A. Hanawalt (Minneapolis: University of Minnesota Press, 1992), 110–29; and also Anne Middleton's essay in the present volume. Kathryn Kerby-Fulton has pointed out the similarity between the examination of the Wanderer in C 5 and the interrogation by probators to determine whether a visionary's life was proper and the visions God-sent; see Kathryn Kerby-Fulton, " 'Who Has Written This Book?': Visionary Autobiography in Langland's C-Text," in *The Medieval Mystical Tradition in England*, ed. Marion Glasscoe, Exeter Symposium, vol. 5 (Cambridge: D. S. Brewer, 1992), 101–16.

54. Szittya, *The Antifraternal Tradition in Medieval Literature*, 47–50, 126–28, 141–43 et passim.

55. Richard FitzRalph, *Proposicio: Unusquisque*, ed. L. L. Hammerich in *The Beginning of the Strife Between Richard FitzRalph and the Mendicants* (Copenhagen: Levin and Munksgaard, 1938), 53–73. FitzRalph said he did not wish to dispute

the legitimacy of the mendicant orders but to return them to their rule. Whether FitzRalph was sincere or not, the verse has the effect of bringing forth all the accusations of the antimendicants regarding what constitutes the mendicant rules and the *vita apostolica* [apostolic life].

56. Bonaventure, *Legenda Major* 6.5; 2 Celano 109.148.

57. On the issues of the conflict, see Yves Congar, "Aspectes ecclésiologiques de la querelle entre mendiants et séculiers dan la seconde moitié du XIIIe siècle et le début du XIVe," *Archives d'histoire doctrinale et littéraire du moyen âge* 28 (1961): 80–83, and the works cited there. Scase, *Piers Plowman and the New Anticlericalism*, stresses the gyrovague associations in Langland's persona, but several times also alludes to the sarabaites (see 126–27, 131–32, 151–52).

58. Cap. 1; the translation is Anthony Meisel and M. L. del Mastro's (New York: Image Books, 1975), 47.

59. Cassian, *Conferences*, 18.7; the translation is Colm Luibheid's (New York: Paulist Press, 1985), 188–90.

60. Bonaventure, *Apologia pauperum* 12.11, in *Opera omnia*, 8.319–20; and *Quaest. disp*, q. 2, a. 3, ad 12, in *Opera omnia*. 5.164.

61. *Tract. paup*, cap. 8, in F. M. Delorme, "Trois chapitres de Jean Peckam pour la défense des ordres mendiants," *Studi francescani* 29 (1932): 177–78.

62. Etiénne Baluze, *Vitae paparum Avenionensium*, ed. G. Mollat (Paris: Librairie Letouzey and Son, 1914–1927), 1.20.

63. Clareno, *Expositio regulae fratrum minorum*, 160–61.

64. F. D. Mathew, ed., *The English Works of Wycliffe Hitherto Unprinted*, EETS o.s. 74 2nd rev. ed. (1902), 12.

65. Early scholars noted a resemblance between Wyclif and Langland, but most followed the lead of J. J. Jusserand in proclaiming him a "faithful son of the church"; Jusserand, *"Piers Plowman," a Contribution to the History of English Mysticism*, 148–50. For the suggestion that Langland added the "lollare-"passages in order to distinguish himself from the Lollards, see Pearsall, *Piers Plowman, by William Langland: An Edition of the C-Text*, 15–16. The most systematic analyses of the case against Langland's Lollardy are Christina von Nolcken, *"Piers Plowman*, the Wycliffites, and *Pierce the Plowman's Creed," Yearbook of Langland Studies* 2 (1988): 71–102; and Pamela Gradon, "Langland and the Ideology of Dissent," *Proceedings of the British Academy* 66 (1980): 179–205.

66. Scase, *Piers Plowman and the New Anticlericalism*, 125–37. For a basic sense of the term, see Skeat, *The Vision of William concerning Piers the Plowman, in Three Parallel Texts*, 2.126, note to lines 213 and 218, who points out that English "loller" (see line 214) existed independently of Lat. *lollardus*, though the two were mixed together in the Wycliffite period; and see Pearsall, *Piers Plowman, by William Langland: An Edition of the C-Text*, 15–16, and his note to 5.2 (p. 97).

67. Scase, *Piers Plowman and the New Anticlericalism*, 125–37, believes that they are lunatics and that it is their lunacy that distinguishes them from the "lollers," those who do not labor. But she never explains why the insane would be apostolic, and she suppresses the "loller" part of their name. Langland's distinction is not between "lollers" and "lunatyks"; it is between two kinds of "lollares." Kerby-Fulton, *Reformist Apocalypticism and Piers Plowman*, 72–74, regards the "lunatyk lollares"

as perfect *viri apostolici* who prophesy (wise fools) but implies they are imbeciles or literal fools; however, she also believes the distinction arises in the context of the visionary convention of authorial self-denigration—that the visionary feels he is mad rather than inspired.

68. Derek Pearsall has argued that the "lunatyk lollares" are not madmen but the feeble-minded; Pearsall, *Piers Plowman, by William Langland: An Edition of the C-Text*, note to 11.105 (p. 165); Derek Pearsall, "'Lunatyk Lollares' in *Piers Plowman*," in *Religion in the Poetry and Drama of the Late Middle Ages in England*, ed. Piero Boitani and Anna Torti (Cambridge: D. S. Brewer, 1990), 163–78. Given the Franciscan regard for the feeble-minded and simple—e.g., Brother Giles (Bonaventure, *Legenda Major*, 3.4) and John the Simple (2 Celano 143.190)—Pearsall's interpretation merits attention. However, if the "lunatyk lollares" are simply or only the feeble-minded, there would seem to be no necessity for them to labor and hence no point in calling them "lollares." I will argue below that the "lunatyk lollares" are voluntary poor whereas the feeble-minded would presumably be among the involuntary poor.

69. The consensus seems to be that "Inwit" (Inner Wit) is the part of the Reason (*ratio*) that contains a certain knowledge of natural law (= prudent self-survival). It is not a deliberative faculty, like Conscience; rather, it is more like the instinctual knowledge of animals; A. V. C. Schmidt, "A Note on Langland's Conception of 'Anima' and 'Inwit,'" *Notes and Queries* n.s. 15 (1968): 363–64; Britton J. Harwood and Ruth F. Smith, "Inwit and the Castle of Caro in *Piers Plowman*," *Neuphilologische Mitteilungen* 71 (1970): 648–54; Ernest Kaulbach, "*Piers Plowman* B.IX: Further Refinements of Inwitte," in *Linguistic and Literary Studies in Honor of Archibald A. Hill*, ed. Mohammed Ali Jazayery, Edgar C. Polome, and Werner Winter (The Hague: Mouton, 1979), 103–10; and, the important preliminary study, Randolf Quirk, "Langland's Use of 'Kind Wit' and 'Inwit,'" *Journal of English and Germanic Philology* 52 (1953): 182–88.

70. E.g., Bonaventure, *Quaest. disp*, q. 2, art. 2, sed c. 3, in *Opera omnia*, 5.136.

71. Francis also wrote a brief description, "Religious Life in Hermitages," for those brothers who wished to live together in small numbers.

72. M.-H. Vicaire, OP, provides an extensive treatment of various orders' claims to the apostolic life in *L'imitation des apôtres: Moines, chanoines, mendiants (IVe–XIIIe siècles)* (Paris: Éditions du Cerf, 1963).

73. See, for example, Katherine Walsh, *The "De vita evangelica" of Geoffrey Hardeby, O.E.S.A. (c. 1320–c. 1382): A Study in the Mendicant Controversies of the Fourteenth Century* (Rome: Augustinian Historical Institute, 1972), 55–56; and Skeat's note on Paul the Hermit; Skeat, *The Vision of William concerning Piers the Plowman, in Three Parallel Texts*, 2.224.

74. See, for example, John Pecham's assertion that the Franciscan *Rule* is not a *Regula aut vita nova res* but *renovata*; *Expositio super regulam fratrum minorum* 1.3, in Bonaventure, *Opera omnia*, 8.393.

75. Kane and Donaldson restore "beggers" from the other MSS; only MS W reads "burgeises." C 14.89–91 retains the first line and then reads: "Ne in no cote ne caytyfs hous Crist was ybore / But in a burgeis hous, the beste of þe toune." The Latin is omitted.

76. Pearsall, *Piers Plowman*, 238, and Schmidt, *The Vision of Piers Plowman*, 338, provide standard glosses; and see David Fowler, "Editorial 'Jamming': Two New Editions of *Piers Plowman*," *Review* 2 (1980): 235; see also Kane and Donaldson, *Piers Plowman*, 115, 195, for discussion of the textual problem, and Scase, *Piers Plowman and the New Anticlericalism*, 75–76, for the relation of the verse, and this passage, to the matter of Christ's poverty.

77. Nicholas of Lyra, *Postillae perpetuae in Vetus et Novum Testamentum* (Rome, 1471–1472), unpaginated: "quia non erat ei locus in diuersorio. est enim diversorium hospitalaria ad quam diuertunt uenientes ab extra ad hospitandum. ciuitas autem Bethleem tunc erat plena, populo qui uenerat ad predicatam professionem: & illa qui erant potentiores occupauerunt loca majora. & ideo Ioseph qui licet esset de nobili genere ut predictum est: non tamen erat de ditioribus: & ideo ita paruum locum habuit."

78. Bonaventure, *Opera omnia*, 7.47: "Propter *defectum lectuli* subdit: *Et reclinavit eum in praesepio*, non in cubiculo ita ut vereficaretur illud Matthaei octavo [20]: "Vulpes foveas habent" [etc]. Propter *defectum habitaculi* subdit: *Quia non erat eis locus in diversorium*. *Diversorium* namque secundum Isodorum dicitur, eo quod diversi ibi conveniant, et hic est locus patens; secundum Bedam vero, eo quod diversa habeat orificia; nam est platea vacua inter duos vicos, habens introitum et exitum ad utrumque, et propter intemperiem aeris superius cooperta, ut ibi cives convenire ad colloqunedum possint. Hic peperit virgo Maria, quia non habebant domum, in qua possent hospitari."

79. Bonaventure, *Collationes*, 16.16. Elsewhere Bonaventure uses the fact of Christ's birth *in praesepio* as evidence of the poverty of his parents (e.g., *Apol. paup.* 77). The Dominican Hugh of St. Cher, 61.40v, cites Isidore and the gloss from Bede, and also says that Christ was born *in diversorio* in order to teach people to seek *diversoria, non palatea* [palaces], in this world. The passage from Bede is not cited in the *Glossa ordinaria*.

80. Bonaventure, *Opera omnia*, 8.343.

4

Langland's London[1]

Derek Pearsall

It may be that the first sketch of the poem was composed in that locality [the Malvern Hills], but we must not be misled into supposing that the poem has much to do with Worcestershire. It is clear, both from very numerous allusions and from the whole tone of the poem, that the place the poet knew best and most delighted to describe was the city of London. It cannot be too strongly impressed upon the reader (especially as the point has often been overlooked) that one great merit of the poem consists in its exhibition of *London* life and *London* opinions; and that to remember the *London* origin of, at any rate, the larger portion of the poem, is the true key to the right understanding of it.[2]

Everything that Skeat says about *Piers Plowman* is worth attending to, and the comment quoted above, from his note to C Prol. 6 (C 1.6, in Skeat's passus numbering), makes a good introduction to an essay on Langland's London. What Skeat says is broadly true, at least of the literal level of the poem, but he exaggerates, for two reasons: one is that Skeat, like most late nineteenth- and early twentieth-century readers of the poem, was thinking principally of the *Visio* of B (Prologue and Passus 1–7), where London (including Westminster) is much more prominent than in the rest of the poem; further, he wanted to correct the common misapprehension that a poem about a ploughman that began on the Worcestershire hills would be a predominantly rural poem, and for this reason he overstated the case. As often, Skeat was saying what was useful and needed to be said at the time. It may still need to be said, but there are many qualifications to be made. The argument that follows is tentative, but I have found it necessary to stress that Langland, though he is conscious of and minutely attentive to the economic and political life of the city, chooses agrarian models for his allegorical ideals of community. The patterns of commercial practice, city and guild government, and social relationship to which he gives such vivid and localized expression are not absorbed into his traditional and idealizing cast of mind, and London remains, in epitome, the problem that the poem does not solve.

London—its streets, people, trades, churches, and courts of law—is a strong physical presence in the early part of the poem. The opening, it is true, is archetypally rural, and the dreamer's presence in the Malvern Hills and his vision of "a fair feld ful of folk" (Prol. 19) in which the first people he identifies are ploughmen (Prol. 22) contribute much to the initial rural impression—even though a "feld" is not necessarily a meadow.[3] But very soon we are amongst those who have chosen "chaffare" (33), with all its doubtfully licit prosperity, and by lines 83 and 89 London has been named as the place where priests go to sing for simony, abandoning their parishes for the sweetness of silver (Chaucer surely remembered this passage in describing what his good Parson did not do), and the place where bishops and other high ecclesiastics run the government finances and courts of law "in þe cheker and in þe chancerye" (91), likewise to the neglect of their pastoral responsibilities. The A-text refers even more specifically to the bishops and bachelors of divinity who become "clerkis of acountis" (A Prol. 91) and to the archdeacons and deacons who "ben ylope to lundoun . . . / And ben clerkis of þe kinges bench þe cuntre to schende" (94–95). The "route of ratones" who come running in B and C (165) to complain about the court cat who tyrannizes over them is Langland's mild image of a crowd of Londoners and parliamentarians, excited by events in the Westminster ("Good") Parliament of 1376. The reasonably tongued "ratoun of renoun" (176) mentions in passing the "colers of crafty werk" that knights and squires wear about their necks in the streets of cities and towns: he wants to hang one on the cat's neck, with a bell on it, but the dominant image evoked is of those bodies of armed retainers, wearing the collar and livery of a great lord, who at times helped to make the streets of London a regular battlefield. John of Gaunt kept a posse of such retainers about him in London in the late 1370s.[4]

When the "feld ful of folk" dissolves into a blur of crowded impressions and a chorus of street cries at the end of the Prologue, both agricultural and urban workers are referred to, but the latter predominate, especially victuallers ("bakeres and breweres, bochers and other," 222) and textile workers ("webbesteres and walkeres . . . taylers and tanners," 223–24). A distinction between agricultural and urban workers cannot be strictly maintained, since the city of London was a small smoky town of

50,000 inhabitants at most, many of whom had business outside the walls, and an hour's walk in almost any direction would take one into the country; nor are urban workers necessarily London workers; but for the most part, given the poet's occasional specificity and general experience, I think the reference is to town and especially London life. The final picture of cooks and taverners shouting their wares at the doors of their respective establishments (227–31) is at any rate a vivid and particular impression of London life.

Whenever the poem descends to detail of social and economic life, and especially social and economic malpractice, it focuses on London. So in Passus 1, in the discourse of Holy Church, London is out of focus, though it is there by implication in Holy Church's hopeful allusion to the role of the mayor as a mediator between king and commons (1.156), which would be most relevant, if literally relevant at all, to the Mayor of London, and perhaps to those delicate occasions when the king held the pleas of his crown at the Tower of London, within the city, in the presence of the Mayor of London and the "Barons" of the city.[5] Such occasions would act as a reminder that, in the last resort, the mayor needed the king's support and goodwill; but they would not disguise the greatly increased power that had accrued to the mayor in the thirteenth and fourteenth centuries (largely at the expense of the sheriffs, who were king's officers), and the fact that the mayor now commanded a jurisdiction that rivaled that of the Chancery and the Common Pleas.[6] Langland tends always to want to restore power to an idealized king and to give to the king a quasi-divine status, rather than to negotiate among these fragmented and competing jurisdictions.

In Passus 2–4, the narrative of Lady Meed, London is omnipresent, both the city and Westminster. These are the passus in which *Piers Plowman* seems most fully a London poem, most fully engaged in the world of urban corruption, and it is worth quoting Yunck, the historian of the traditions of venality satire, who remarks that, whatever debt Langland had to those traditions, "this attention to municipal graft is a relatively new element in the satirical theme."[7] So those who run excitedly about Meed include specifically London groups such as the "vokettes of the Arches" (2.61) as well as general urban traders, "brokeres of chaffares,"/ Vorgoers and vitalers" (2.60–61). Later, when Falseness, Guile, and Liar run away terrified, having heard of the king's threats, it is the London streets that they take refuge in. The first goes to the friars, the second is looked after by merchants, who set him up like an apprentice to sell goods in their shops (2.222–24), while Liar goes "Lorkyng thorw lanes, to-logged of moneye" (226), and gets work with pardoners, physicians, "spysours" (grocers), minstrels, and messengers (229–38).

In the account of the appearance of Meed at the king's court in Westminster, there is an important digression, much expanded in C (3.77–126), which is packed with London allusion. Seemingly prompted by his criticism of the friars' ostentation in glazing and building their churches, the poet passes on to fraudulent traders, such as "bakeres and breweres, bocheres and cokes" (3.80), who "rychen thorw regraterye" (82) (retail-trade profiteering, including "forestalling") and build high timbered houses and buy up tenements. These are the men who "don most harm to þe mene peple" (81) since it is the poor "þat parselmele mot begge" (86) and who are therefore most vulnerable to profiteering and to the use of false weights and measures. An interesting addition in C (90–107) speaks of the prayers of the poor for vengeance which will sometimes seem to be answered by the great fires that sweep through the close-packed wooden-framed tenements of the city:[8]

> Al this haue we seyn, þat som tyme thorw a breware
> Many burgages ybrent and bodies þer-ynne,
> And thorw a candle clemynge in a cursed place
> Ful adoun and forbrent forth alle þe rewe. (104–7)

Poor as well as rich die in these disasters, the poet tells us, perhaps as a way of emphasizing the indivisibility of the community, in suffering as in true and false dealing. But the immediate impetus of the passage is the biblical text (Job 15:34) that he was already chewing over in A and which still occupies his ruminations: "Ignis deuorabit tabernacula eorum qui libenter accipiunt munera" (C 3.123a). The target is the "mayres and oþer stywardes" (122) who accept bribes from unsuitable candidates for the freedom of the city (108–14),[9] but the punishment has been extended to those who give the bribes as well as those who take them, and is also suggested to be generally appropriate to all those who lead bad lives (if, that is, the "cursed place" is a brothel).

There is much else of London, and of Westminster too, in these passus, and many reminders of how sharp and specific Langland can be when he is dealing with London malpractices and London government, as well as with the mayor's role, responsibilities, and failings—and how broad and unspecific he is, by contrast, when talking of the problems of national government and the solutions to them.[10] It is noticeable too, in a poem so redolent of London, how readily and ubiquitously the world of agricultural life and labor reasserts its traditional images in the allegory of the poem. The image of the millennial world to come, at the end of Passus 3, is and apparently must be of a rural world, in accordance with the text of prophecy: "Conflabunt gladios suos in uomeres et lancias in falces" (3.460a). And the complaint of Peace against Wrong at the beginning of Passus 4 is of rape, highway robbery, purveying, blackmail, and "protection," all of them principally exurban crimes against the king's peace, clearly defined as wrong, where the tangle of malpractice and sharp practice in the commercial city, some of it newly invented, seems resistant to the traditional kinds of lawmaking. In fact, a whole new body of law for the regulation of commerce, especially international commerce, was in the making, the "law merchant," but Langland shows no interest in it and little awareness of its existence.[11]

The poet gives an evocative picture of his life in London in the "*Apologia pro vita sua*" that he adds in C. He lives in Cornhill, he tells us, with his wife Kit, among "lollares of Londone and lewede ermytes" (5.4), himself "yclothed as a lollare" (5.2). Though it would not be wise to take entirely on trust what the poet says about his own life,[12] there is no reason to assume that what he says about the facts and experience of his own life is untrue. There are times when allegorical and narrative demands will override such a simple fidelity. The attribution to Will, for instance, of traits of personality is more likely to be a tactical move than a form of self-expression: the "combative animus" that Langland assigns to Will may, as Anne Middleton points out, be "a kind of enabling gesture which permits a particular kind of turn in the development of an episode."[13] But where such conditions do not operate, we may assume that what he says is by and large true. What he says about the reception given to his "makynges"[14] by his neighbors has certainly the ring of authenticity; Cornhill had something of a reputation as a resort of vagabonds, and its pillories and stocks were famous. There was a large general market that specialized in second-hand clothes, such as those that came from hastily broken-up estates: the "upholderes on þe hulle" who did the selling are mentioned in this context in 12.217, and it is evident from *London Lickpenny*, a lively early fifteenth-century portrait of the predatory city (the author of which knew a version of *Piers Plowman*), that many of the goods would have fallen off the back of the medieval equivalent of the proverbial lorry.[15] The city ordinances contain particular prohibitions against the "Evynchepynge" at Cornhill, held by candlelight, where dealers would pass off old clothes as new and sell stolen goods.[16]

In the allegorical scene that follows, the poet is walking in the country when he meets with Conscience and Reason. The walk is biographically plausible (it is not a dream), given the closeness of the country and the city, and given Langland's mode of employment. The prayers and other services that he performed for people, visiting them every month or so (5.50), took him on a wide circuit, and he had a large "parish," extending well beyond the city walls, as he himself makes clear: "And so y leue yn London and opelond both" (5.44).[17]

But Reason's interrogation, it may be noticed, concerns itself almost exclusively with the agricultural work that Will might more properly be doing, and in this respect it may echo the questioning directed at idle laborers with regard to the provisions of the Statute of Laborers.[18] In Reason's long list of legitimate occupations, only those who "shap shon or cloth" (5.18) are possibly urban workers, and the reason for the absence of the vigorous industrial and commercial life of the city is suggested in Reason's final question, when he asks whether Will can do "eny other kynes craft þat to þe comune nedeth" (20). It is difficult for Reason (or for the justices responsible for enforcing the Statute of Laborers) to think of London work as being in any way related to the common good: the only true work is on the land or in occupations directly supportive of agricultural activity. After Will has defended his way of earning his livelihood, Conscience's reproach is pointed: "it semeth no sad parfitnesse in citees to begge" (90). It is as if Conscience, like Wordsworth in *The Old Cumberland Beggar*, could have tolerated the occasional picturesque rural beggar, but systematic conspicuous begging in the city, like Will's, or such as was now becoming common with the increase in the number of the chronic urban poor, upsets him.[19]

Nevertheless, despite the recurrent shifting of his gaze from the confusion of the London streets, and the problems that its commercial life set to a traditional morality, Langland is constantly making those casual references, both literal and figurative, to London streets, scenes, places, and people that bespeak a familiar intimacy. Tyburn, the place of public execution outside the city at what is now the Marble Arch, at the junction of Oxford Street and Edgware Road, is twice mentioned (6.368, 14.129), St. Paul's three times, twice specifically with reference to the preaching at St. Paul's Cross (11.56, 15.71; cf. also B 10.46), and the Thames is commonly employed as a synecdoche for "a lot of water" (6.335, 14.104, B 15.338). Two local and perhaps apocryphal people who had a reputation as "wicches" are mentioned, "the soutere of Southewerk" (6.83, B 13.340) and "Dame Emme of Shordych" (B 13.339; cf. C Prol. 226): both, it appears, operated in the "twilight" area just outside the city walls and probably dispensed sexual and contraceptive advice and performed abortions.

The same casual intimacy of London reference is found in the account of the confessions of the Seven Deadly Sins that follows close after the autobiographical digression: Envy refers briefly to the time he spent among merchants, "nameliche in Londone" (6.96), where he was specially valued for his skill in dispraising the goods of others, and Covetousness and Gluttony are primarily London portraits. These two seem appropriate as the sins of the city, avaricious getting and wasteful spending, or, as they appear in another, nearly contemporary, London poem, winning and wasting.[20] The density of London reference in Langland's portrait of Covetousness is somewhat diffused in C, which conflates the confession with predominantly agricultural material (e.g., 6.260–71) drawn in from Haukyn's later confession in B 13, but much of the confession has to do with offenses against lawful trading practices, such as the use of false weights and measures, which are the regular concern of London city and guild ordinances.[21] Some extraordinarily devious and subtle malpractices are described, especially the devices for cloth-stretching (6.215–20), almost as if Langland had inside knowledge (from his wife?). Mrs. Covetyse, also known as "Rose þe regrater" (6.232), was a "webbe" (221), like the Wife of Bath, and was similarly in the way of being a small capitalist as a *femme sole*, with "spynnesteres" (222) working for her.[22] She knew all the tricks of the trade, as also in her other business as a brewer, where she had long "holde hokkerye" (233), that is, employed others ("hucksters") to sell her ale door to door—a practice forbidden in the city ordinances.[23]

The confession of Gluttony is a London tavern scene crowded with characters from inside and outside the city like a Brueghel townscape, many of them with personal names. They include a female shoemaker, a warrener or gamekeeper, a tinker, a hackneyman, a needle-maker, a prostitute from Cock's Lane, a parish clerk, an idle priest, a Flemish prostitute, a hayward, a hermit, the Tyburn hangman, a ditch-digger, porters, pick-purses, bald tooth-drawers, a rubible-player, a rat-catcher, a street-cleaner, a rope-maker, a thatcher (?), a female pewterer, a garlic-seller, a Welshman, a heap of upholders, a cobbler, and a butcher. Something of the pullulating life of the city comes over, though I cannot, hard as I try, agree with David Aers in admiring the vitality of the scene as a kind of celebration of an anti-establishment counterculture.[24] The energy of the tavern scene is not expressed in boisterous bonhomie and good-natured drunkenness but principally in a game ("þe newe fayre," 377) that seems to have been a cheap confidence trick and in violent farting and vomiting. I am sure that Langland regarded Glutton's tavern as the very sump of the den of iniquity that was London, and he throws into it, with deliberate indiscriminateness, both the criminal and the criminalized classes and also those in regular but poorly paid urban employment.

In this connection, it is interesting to try to distinguish his opinions from those of the 1929 editor of the London city records, whose description of the London unemployed, underemployed, and misemployed reads like the guest list at Glutton's tavern:

Beneath the steady hard-working men of the crafts there was a mass of destitution, misfortune and rascality, housed in broken-down tenements, in rents, slums and alleys. There was a poverty-stricken class of casual labourers, whose scanty possessions are revealed by inquests; of the blind, lame and diseased whose misery evoked the pity of testators; of pickpockets and thieves who lurked within the shadow of pentices; sharpsters and tricksters who haunted the taverns; loose and disorderly women of every degree; drunken and dishonest chaplains and broken soldiers. This class may have been to some extent recruited from idle and workless apprentices and journeymen, but mainly it was a class, which from want of character, physique and opportunity had no means of self-improvement and no understanding of or desire to participate in the privileges of citizenship.[25]

One recognizes a familiar voice, and takes reassurance from the fact that Langland, though he does not offer a more discriminating account of or insight into the economic circumstances that produced such a class, at least has the exercise of a compassionate and energetic humanity that preserves him from such patronizing and sanctimonious complacency.

The confession of the sins is followed by a return to the countryside, and there, if we are anywhere, we remain for most of the rest of the poem, though the changing nature of the poem and its concentration upon inner rather than outer realities means that references to the literal world are in any case more infrequent and problematic. The thousands in search of Truth go blustering over dales and hills (7.159), and Piers Plowman's proposed itinerary takes the pilgrims through a farmed and forested agricultural landscape to the castle of Truth, almost as in an allegorical romance. Those who refuse to go on the journey are a cutpurse, an ape-keeper, and a wafer-seller (7.283–5), and might be meant as typical of the entertainers and predators that London, especially, encouraged. The ideal community that Piers tries to set up is, inevitably, an agricultural one, in which roles are figured on the basis of feudal and manorial relationships, and in which women, instead of working commercially and independently as brewsters, websters, spinsters, and souteresses, are specifically told to make the cloth that is needed for immediate agricultural purposes, or by their husbands and families, or by the church (8.7–14). Piers's wife, meanwhile, cooks up soups for the agricultural workers (8.182). When Piers is putting the people to work, it is to all kinds of agricultural jobs that he directs them and to "alle kyne trewe craft þat man couthe deuyse" (8.200). The former are specified, in detail; the latter are left unspecified, since Langland knows what problems he will have once he mentions crafts and trades that do not have directly to do with consumption. Those who are excluded from Piers's community are the traditional "crafts of folly,"[26] the juggler, the prostitute, the dice-player, and the bawd (8.71–5), and those who threaten the community are itinerant laborers and out-of-work soldiers ("Wastor," 149, and the "Bretener," 152). The real enemies of Piers's community, the merchants and traders who operate the elaborate machinery of the money economy, are not mentioned at all, even though they have been a preoccupation in previous passus and even though their activities have rendered Piers's ideal world obsolete.

Langland casts a last look at the world of London commerce in the Pardon episode, before he abandons it more or less completely. Merchants appear only in the margin of the document of the Pardon (9.22–6), presumably because they are not a recognized estate of society, but they have a special letter sent to them under Truth's secret seal (9.27–42) which says they may practice their trade, that is, buying goods and selling them again at a profit, but must devote their profits to good works. The merchants are overjoyed at the approval given to their activities (9.41), not surprisingly, given that the traditional view of men of business, as expressed in the *Elucidarium* of Honorius of Autun, was that they could hardly be saved since they lived by cheating and profiteering.[27] Finance and trade appear to be driven by the appetite for gain, not by the service of the common good and the needs of consumers, and cannot in themselves be legitimated. But a sacramental notion of the unity and indivisibility of society can solve the problem by requiring that profits beyond a certain level be returned to the community in almsgiving and charitable works. This is the late medieval view, necessitated by altering economic circumstances and developed, for instance, by Aquinas, whose views are briefly summarized by Tawney:

It is right for a man to seek such wealth as is necessary for a livelihood in his station. To seek more is not enterprise, but avarice, and avarice is a deadly sin. Trade is legitimate: the different resources of different countries show that it was intended by Providence. But it is a dangerous business. A man must be sure that he carries it on for the public benefit, and that the profits which he takes are no more than the wages of his labour.[28]

This is what Piers's Pardon allows: merchants can buy and sell freely and "saue þe wynnynges" (9.29) as long as they use them to endow hospitals, repair highways and bridges, succour the poor, and to support all the other good causes that regularly benefit from merchants' bequests and the charitable works financed by craft guilds.[29] Langland says nothing on the awkward question of what constitutes a reasonable competence for one's livelihood in one's station; nor does he explain how legitimate buying and selling at a profit can always be distinguished from "regraterye," the predicting, creating, and exploiting of shortages to increase profit, the practice excoriated by himself and in the city and guild ordinances;[30] nor does he wish to think of trade as anything more than a primitive form of barter or exchange. These were the terms in which Conscience had earlier exonerated merchants, declaring that "marchandise is no mede," since "hit is as a permutacoun apertly, on peneworth for another" (3.312–13). Langland's reluctance to recognize that this is not what merchants actually do, or to confront in any way the changed world of investment finance, is to be contrasted with the cool insouciance of Chaucer, who has the merchant of the *Shipman's Tale* declare roundly that, for merchants, "hir moneie is hir plogh" (*Canterbury Tales*, VII.288).[31] Langland might have understood this axiom of capitalism, but he never acknowledged it.

There is little further allusion to the London world of money and commerce in the Pardon episode, and the expanded meditation in the C-text on the suffering of poor people and "the wo of this wommen þat wonyeth in cotes" (9.83) allows only one brief reference, though that a passionately particular one, to the characteristic part-time ill-paid urban occupations of those women,

> Bothe to carde and to kembe, to cloute and to wasche,
> And to rybbe and to rele, rusches to pylie. (9.80–81)

By the end of the passus, we are back in the Malverns, and the roaming of the *Vita* is all through traditional woods and wildernesses (10.62), with here and there an allegorical castle (10.128). The praise of poverty and the warnings against wealth are done in exclusively rural and agricultural

imagery (12.143, 178–91, 218–33), as is the vision in the Mirror of Middle-
Earth (13.131). The ideal of poverty is found among the Desert Fathers,
dwelling in woods and wildernesses (17.11, 28), and the Tree of Charity is
planted in a garden (18.5). What is striking is how commercial activities
that were problematic realities in the *Visio* have now become the vehicles
of metaphor. The carding and combing of wool, one of the unskilled and
most tedious and poorly paid operations in cloth-making, becomes Dame
Study's image for how learning nowadays must be dressed up in the apparatus of profit (in modern terms, demonstrate how it is cost-effective) and
"be cardet with coueytise, as clotheres kemben here wolle" (11.15). The
taking in of clothes for washing, as a real part-time job for women burdened with children (9.73, 80), is a mere trace of memory in the "lauen-
drie" (16.330) where Charity takes in the dirty washing of sin and makes it
whiter than snow in accordance with the text, "Lavabis me, et super nivem
dealbabor" (16.332a, Psalm 50:9). There is a wonderful example of this use
of metaphor in B 15.450–57 (part of a long passage omitted in C), where
the act of christening is compared to cloth-processing:

> Clooth that cometh fro the wevyng is noght comly to were
> Tyl it be fulled under foot or in fullyng stokkes,
> Wasshen wel with water and with taseles cracched,
> Ytouked and yteynted and under taillours hande.
> And so it fareth by a barn that born is of wombe:
> Til it be cristned in Cristes name and confermed of the bisshop,
> It is hethene as to heveneward, and helplees to the soule.
>   (B 15.450–57)

The metaphor is prompted by the happy pun of "fullynge" (B 15.449),
baptism, and "fulling" (thickening or felting the cloth in cloth-making by
beating or compressing it), and is accompanied by a display of technical
detail such as has not been seen since the *Visio*, all of it now separated from
its uncomfortable reality. This sense of detachment is almost explicit in the
lavacrum-lex-dei to which sinful man is taken by the Good Samaritan to be
cured (19.71). It is an outlying farmhouse or grange, we are told, "syxe myle
or seuene bisyde þe newe marcat" (19.72), as if to symbolize how far remote
the life of the Christian must be detached, at least for a therapeutic time,
from the busy world of getting and spending, the "new" world of the *Visio*.
    In the last two passus of the poem, there is some return to the lit-
eral world of fourteenth-century England, and of London, in the vision

of the establishment of the Christian community as Christ's Church, and
of the threat to this community from the forces of Antichrist. In describing the establishment of the Church, Langland extends the mediation of
the Holy Spirit to cover not only discipleship but also the work of all men,
religious and secular. In a characteristic enumeration of trades and professions (21.229–49), he returns to the world of the Prologue to the *Visio*,
echoing its language in a significantly altered way:

> Som men he ȝaf wyt with wordes to shewe,
> To wynne with treuthe þat the world asketh,
> As prechours and prestes and prentises of lawe. (21.229–31)

Sanction is given to those who earn their living by buying and selling
(235) as well as to agricultural and other laborers, and all crafts are urged
to love one another, so that "no boest ne debaet be among hem alle" (251).
Some crafts are "clenner" than others (252), but all come of the gift of
Grace ("Diuisiones graciarum sunt," 21.228a, 1 Cor. 12:4) and there must
be no jealous backbiting, speaking ill, or envy between them.

In this manner, Langland deals with or sets aside the critical conflicts
being fought out among the London craft guilds, which were the source
of much of the turbulence of London in his time.[32] The conflicts were part
of the essentially monopolistic, protectionist, and competitive function of
the craft guilds, and they were inevitable in the emergent urban economy.
But they are loathsome to Langland, and his attempt is always to create
an imagined ideal community in which the conflicts between craft guilds,
between masters and journeymen, between the aldermen and the com-
monalty, between London and foreign workers, are resolved, cloaked, or
forgotten.[33] "Kynde Wytt and þe comune," we were told, in a passage directly anticipating, in the secular sphere, the one in Passus 21, "contreued
alle craftes" (Prol. 144), and Piers Plowman, in preparing the way for the
ideal community, had "caste on hym his clothes of alle kyn craftes" (8.58)
and will work for "alle kyne crafty men þat conne lyue in treuthe" (8.69),
with the exceptions already noted.

The crafts are thus legitimated, and Craft appointed as their steward
(21.256): to think of him as a kind of Trades Union Congress general secretary may have a poignant appropriateness. There follows the ploughing
scene that symbolizes the work of the church, and the establishment of
the barn of Unity where the harvest is stored; the barn later turns into

a castle with barred gates and a porter (22.298, 329). Pride threatens to sabotage the work of Piers in the field, and also to cause such confusion that merchants will not know whether their winning is lawful or usurious (21.350–51). A brewer responds to Conscience's exhortations with a commercial cynicism and references to his practice of adulterating ale (21.398) that remind us of the London world of the *Visio* (e.g., 6.226), and there are occasions in the last passus when we are back in the corrupt London of the courts of law, at Westminster (22.133) and the Arches (22.136). But for the most part these are scattered references: the backcloth is not London, but a variety of predominantly rural allegorical tableaux.

In this rapid survey of the poem, I have talked about London as the center and symbol of the world of money and commerce: this world was of course not confined to London nor exclusively to large urban centers, but since it is London that acts as the focus for Langland's own description of the commercial world, it seems legitimate to speak of it so. His own experience was the basis for his practice. He states that he lived in London, on Cornhill, and implies that he came there as an unbeneficed cleric when he completed his university education.[34] Unbeneficed clerks greatly outnumbered those with benefices (in London in 1379 there were 647 unbeneficed chaplains and 94 clerks in an area with 110 parishes), and they tended to settle in cities, especially London, where there were laymen with enough money to pay for prayers and other services. Some would be chantry-priests, but only the very wealthy could endow a chantry, and wills make it clear that people of quite modest means would make provision for masses and prayers to be said for their souls after death and assumed that mass-priests could be readily recruited for this purpose.[35] If Langland belonged to this group (he may have been in minor orders only, and much less well established), he was in appropriate company: "There were many mass-priests, and this numerous, mobile, and hard-to-discipline group must have been not only a matter of concern to the ecclesiastical authorities but also a prominent feature of London life at the time."[36]

Langland's work as a kind of clerical odd-job man, saying prayers for and perhaps with those who could not afford anyone better, took him all over London and also out into the country, as he says (5.44). Whether any of the geographical references to places near London should be taken to allude to places he knew well from personal experience is doubtful: hungry hounds of Hertfordshire (6.413) and beadles of Buckinghamshire (B 2.110) derive their geographical origin most probably from the needs of alliteration; but the change of the latter in C to "Bannebury sokene" (2.111) is oddly specific, and Skeat suggests that there may be a personal reference (note to C 3.111).

Other changes between the different versions of the poem are suggestive of changes in the poet's circumstances. There is no mention in A of Envy's account of his career as a "brokour of bakbytynge" (6.95, B 5.129) among London merchants and Skeat has the idea (note to C 7.96) that the author was not much acquainted with London in 1362, having only recently arrived there. This is not convincing, since the following confession of Covetousness, which is packed with detailed London allusion, is fully represented in A. On the other hand, there are some slight indications that rural life still has a stronger hold in A than in B. The preparations for the marriage of Meed in A involve the setting up of a pavilion on a mountain side (A 2.40), where all around are fields full of folk, as in the Prologue; there is nothing of this in B or C. The list of guests at the wedding in A includes no specifically London groups, where B and C are very detailed (C 2.60–61); A, meanwhile, has a reference to "laboureris of þropis" (A 2.45) among Meed's entourage which is dropped in B and C, presumably when Langland discovered that farm laborers were mere beginners in avarice in comparison with Londoners. It must be recalled that the Prologue in A has none of the elaborate Westminster material introduced in B. In its very abbreviated version of the *Vita*, A seems to hold longer to the optimistic *Visio* view that "alle kyne crafty men þat cunne here foode wynne" (A 11.185) have a place in the good Christian society: they are defined by Clergy as part of Dowel and "taillours and souteris" (A 11.184) are mentioned as well as tillers of the soil. This view is abandoned earlier in B and C, though it returns in metamorphosed form late in the poem.

It seems to me quite likely that Langland left London before he began the version known as C. The evidence is partly external: it is now well established that, whereas manuscripts of A and B come from a wide range of dialect areas, including London, nearly all manuscripts of C derive from the southwest Midlands, in fact from an area close to the Malverns.[37] Other evidence is more speculative. The absence, for instance, of any mention of the Peasants' Revolt of 1381 in the C-text of Piers Plowman has always been a puzzle to commentators, especially since the circumstances from which the Revolt sprang are so fully displayed in the Ploughing of the Half-Acre. The answer may well be that Langland left London before the rebels arrived, or that he left in haste in the aftermath of the Revolt, when the author of the poem that had been so inflammatorily used and alluded to by the spokesmen for the Revolt may have believed himself to be about to become extremely unpopular with the authorities.[38] Other evidence is internal and quite flimsy: is the fact that "a rakiere of Chepe" in A and B (B 5.315) becomes "a rakeare and his knaue" in C (6.371) and "Godefray of Garlekhithe" in B (B 5.317) becomes "Godefray þe garlek-monger" in C (6.373) a sign that Langland is no longer in London and less interested in specific London allusion?

Generally, Langland's view of the city is a traditional one: it is the place of iniquity, the modern Babylon.[39] When Will describes his sojourn in "the lond of longyng" (11.170) where he is ravished by Fortune, he may be describing the condition of longing for carnal things; but this land is also the *regio dissimilitudinis*, the land of unlikeness of which Augustine speaks (*Confessions*, vii.10), into which the soul strays away from God. This in turn was often associated with the *terra longinqua*, the far-off land ("this fer contre" which is "the lif of man in synne," as a Wycliffite writer calls it) into which the prodigal son goes away from his father.[40] The "lond of longyng," in allusion to this, may mean "the land of being-distant (from God," and, coincidentally, London. The only "good" city is the heavenly Jerusalem, at which Langland's poem never really arrives.

Langland's observation of the operation of money and commerce in London is close, detailed, and appalled, but it becomes no part of the essential structure of his thinking. He uses commercial imagery in much of his analysis of the religious life, as James Simpson has pointed out in an important essay,[41] but it seems to me that this does not signal acceptance of the world of money and profit and new forms of economic relationship but is a characteristic appropriation of its language for the purposes of spiritual paradox.[42] The figurative references to traditional social and economic relationships, on the other hand, seem to embody ingrained attitudes: Langland really thinks it means something to say that all men will become gentle through the redemption (12.109) and that the Jews became churls, and cannot own land, because of their rejection of Christ (20.108, 21.34); and he is content, it seems, to accept that no churl may "chartre make ne his chatel sulle/Withouten leue of þe lord" (12.60) in his pursuit of the analogy of churl/sinner. Generally, Langland's allegory remains rooted in the traditional world of agricultural labor, the countryside, pilgrimages, and castles: London, with all its ambiguities and challenges to traditional moral arbitration, is what he must address, but the old rural world is what he falls back on. His idea of community is likewise tied to traditional feudal kinds of relationship, and he makes no decisive use of possibly respectable

kinds of commercial relationship, such as apprenticeship.⁴³ Apprentices are
occasionally neutral figures (3.279), sometimes simply trainees in commercial malpractice (2.224, 6.208, 279); with *Activa Vita* (the Haukyn of B)
the term is deeply ambiguous (15.195).

The social mobility which is part of the developing commercial world
is constantly deplored by Langland: he sees only a wicked subversion of

Langland wishes to avert his eyes from the conflict of class and economic interests which is the reality of commercial life in London, and to
reinscribe an idealized community in which the crafts live harmoniously
together and in which the hierarchical order of mayors and other officials
acts to impose traditional restraints upon trade. Conflicts created by and
within the system, that is, are simplified into offenses against it, though at
the same time Langland recognizes fully that some of the worst offenses
against the system are committed by those charged with the responsibility of administering economic justice within it, such as mayors (3.122).
Mayors are allegorically idealized as the mediators of the law of love, imposing their "mercement" (1.158) upon man for his misdeeds; but Piers's
son is instructed to do what they say, not what they do (8.89–91).

The social mobility which is part of the developing commercial world
is constantly deplored by Langland: he sees only a wicked subversion of
social hierarchy in which usurers and "regraters" (3.113) bribe their way
into the freedom of the city of London, in which knights, under pres-
sure from money lenders and mortgage holders, become like apprentices
to mercers and drapers (6.25), in which shoemakers buy knighthoods, and
bondmen's sons and bastards become high-ranking church officials (5.70–
72). Money buys everything, and even replaces compatibility of birth and
natural affection in marriage-making (10.258). Yet money and wealth cannot be condemned absolutely ("Reddite Cesari . . . ," 1.48), much as the
young Langland, with that Franciscan or primitive Benedictine streak in
him, might have wished it. Scripture in A and B has an enthusiastic recommendation of Paul's words about the rich: "Poul preveth it impossible
riche men to have hevene" (B 10.333). The C-reviser omits this, perhaps recalling that this is not at all what Paul said (he spoke thus, or similarly, of
those who desire riches, 1 Tim.6:9, not of those who are rich, 1 Tim.6:17),
and also seems to attribute to the unreliable Rechelesnesse the assertion
that it is ploughmen and land-tilling people whose prayers are most worthy
and who will win salvation (11.295). The speaker at the beginning of C 13,
meanwhile, whether Rechelesnesse or the dreamer, confirms that rich men
have a legitimate place in society and can get to heaven (13.25), provided
they give to the poor a kind of toll (13.72). The specifics of this, as we have
remarked before, are left notably vague.

I have spoken of Langland as an independent observer, seeing what he wished to see, and choosing to avert his eyes. I am aware that many modern literary and cultural historians would prefer to speak less of the poet's choices and more of the networks of ideological constraints and determinants within which such "choices" are constructed. The constraints are there, of course, but individual thinking people can come to terms with or negotiate them in various ways. Chaucer and the poet of *Wynnere and Wastoure* are different from Langland and Gower. For Skeat, "London is the origin of the poem, and the true key to the understanding of it." For Langland, I would suggest, it is also the problem of the poem, and one to which he found no solution.

Notes

1. I should like to thank David Aers, Anna Baldwin, Kathryn Kerby-Fulton, James Simpson, Paul Strohm, and David Wallace, who have all looked at drafts of this essay at various stages, and given me many valuable comments and suggestions for improvement.

2. Walter W. Skeat, ed.,*The Vision of William concerning Piers the Plowman, in Three Parallel Texts*, 2 vols. (London: Oxford University Press, 1886), 3. I have had this edition constantly beside me in working on this paper, but the editions I quote from are as follows: George Kane, ed., *Piers Plowman: The A Version* (London: Athlone Press, 1960); A. V. C. Schmidt, ed., *The Vision of Piers Plowman: A Critical Edition of the B-Text* (London: J. M. Dent, 1978); Derek Pearsall, ed. *Piers Plowman, by William Langland: An Edition of the C-Text* (Berkeley and Los Angeles: University of California Press, 1978). All references are to the C-text unless A or B is specified.

3. A "feld" may be simply a large open piece of land and area of activity, as with a field of battle. There are scriptural suggestions, too: "The field is the world," says Christ, interpreting the parable of the tares (Matt. 13:38).

4. See J. A. W. Bennett, ed., *Piers Plowman, Prologue and Passus I–VII of the B Text* (Oxford: Clarendon Press, 1972), 101, n. to Prol. 161. A Writ to the Sheriff of London to restrict the distribution of liveries by great men to their retinues is recorded in Reginald R. Sharpe, ed., *Calendar of Letter-books, Preserved among the Archives of the Corporation of the City of London: Letter-Book H, circa A.D. 1375–1399* (London: John Edward Francis, 1907), 353. For some of the abuses associated with "livery and maintenance," see Anna P. Baldwin, *The Theme of Government in Piers Plowman* (Cambridge: D. S. Brewer, 1981), 25–49; Paul Strohm, "Appendix 2: The Literature of Livery," in *Hochon's Arrow: The Social Imagination of Fourteenth-Century Texts* (Princeton, N.J.: Princeton University Press, 1992), 179–95.

5. For the careful protocol associated with these occasions, see *Liber albus: The White Book of the City of London*, ed. Henry Thomas Riley (London: Richard Griffin & Co., 1861), 45–50. Bennett considers that the mayor's role as mediator

"was to be strikingly illustrated by the events of 1381, when William of Walworth, mayor of London, acted as intermediary between king and commons" (Bennett, *Piers Plowman, Prologue and Passus I-VII of the B Text*, 115), but I hope that Langland would not have agreed.

6. See Gwyn Williams, *Medieval London: From Commune to Capital* (London: Athlone Press, 1963), 29, 83.

7. John A. Yunck, *The Lineage of Lady Meed: The Development of Mediaeval Venality Satire*, Publications in Mediaeval Studies 17 (South Bend, Ind.: University of Notre Dame Press, 1963), 298. Yunck considers that the older clerical satirists may have had less urban material to work with, but in any case were generally less outraged by small-scale urban corruption than by the sale of the gifts of God.

8. For London regulations concerning the prevention and control of fire, which was an ever-present hazard in the city, see *Liber albus: The White Book of the City of London*, 288–89; also Henry Thomas Riley, ed., *Memorials of London and London Life in the XIIIth, XIVth, and XVth Centuries, 1276–1419* (London: Longmans, Green, 1885), 46–47. Riley's *Memorials* contains a selection of fully translated items from the Letter-Books of the City of London, which are elsewhere fully summarized and excerpted, also in English, in Sharpe, *Calendar of Letter-books, Preserved among the Archives of the Corporation of the City of London: Letter-Book H, circa A.D. 1375–1399*.

9. Baldwin, *The Theme of Government in Piers Plowman*, 31, gives examples from the London records of these practices, including one instance in 1378 in which Mayor Nicholas Brembre sold the freedom of the city to an alien; she suggests that this "may have been the very case which prompted Langland's allusion."

10. Caroline M. Barron emphasizes this contrast in her essay, "William Langland: A London Poet," in *Chaucer's England: Literature in Historical Context*, ed. Barbara A. Hanawalt (Minneapolis: University of Minnesota Press, 1992), 91–109 (see esp. 94–95).

11. For the "law merchant," see A. H. Thomas, ed., *Calendar of Plea and Memoranda Rolls, Preserved among the Archives of the Corporation of the City of London at the Guildhall, A.D. 1381–1412* (Cambridge: Cambridge University Press, 1983), vii–xli.

12. We have had many warnings against the dangers of oversimplifying the relationship of poet and dreamer, e.g., Kane, *The Autobiographical Fallacy in Chaucer and Langland Studies*, The Chambers Memorial Lecture, 1965 (London: H. K. Lewis, 1965); David Mills, "The Role of the Dreamer in *Piers Plowman*," in *Piers Plowman: Critical Approaches*, ed. S. S. Hussey (London: Methuen, 1969), 180–212; John M. Bowers, *The Crisis of Will in Piers Plowman* (Washington, D.C.: Catholic University of America Press, 1986); David A. Lawton, "The Subject of Piers Plowman," *Yearbook of Langland Studies* 1 (1987): 1–30. For an example of the dangers, see Allan H. Bright, *New Light on "Piers Plowman"* (London: Oxford University Press, 1928); and for a witness to the desire still to authenticate the "autobiographical" references, see Lawrence M. Clopper, "The Life of the Dreamer, the Dreams of the Wanderer in Piers Plowman," *Studies in Philology* 86 (1989): 261–85. In the early history of the study of the poem, particularly in relation to the multiple-authorship controversy, there was much discussion of the veracity of Langland's "autobiographical" references: see the listings in Derek Pearsall, *An Annotated*

Critical Bibliography of Langland (Hemel Hempstead: Harvester Wheatsheaf, 1990), 45–64. There is a particularly subtle exploration of the poem's representation of the experience of the self in Anne Middleton, "Narration and the Invention of Experience: Episodic Form in *Piers Plowman*," in *The Wisdom of Poetry: Essays in Early English Literature in Honor of Morton W. Bloomfield*, ed. Larry D. Benson and Siegfried Wenzel (Kalamazoo, Mich.: Medieval Institute Publications, 1982), 91–122; see also Anne Middleton, "William Langland's 'Kynde Name': Authorial Signature and Social Identity in Late Fourteenth-Century England," in *Literary Practice and Social Change in Britain, 1380–1530*, ed. Lee Patterson (Berkeley and Los Angeles: University of California Press, 1990), 15–82. "What is always at issue," she says in the first essay, "is the value, autonomy, and cultural authority of personal history as a genre, and the status of a serious fictive work centered upon it" (103). A distinction that she makes between "the experience of the self as a historical integer" and "as the locus of a spiritually receptive eye" (105) needs to be reexamined in the light of a recent essay by Kathryn Kerby-Fulton, " 'Who Has Written This Book?': Visionary Autobiography in Langland's C-Text," in *The Medieval Mystical Tradition in England*, ed. Marion Glasscoe, Exeter Symposium, vol. 5 (Cambridge: D. S. Brewer, 1992), 101–16. She stresses that specific authentic autobiographical detail was considered necessary as "a reliable marker of actual experienced vision" (106) and, citing Denise Despres, *Ghostly Sights: Visual Meditation in Late-Medieval Narrative* (Norman, Okla.: Pilgrim Press, 1989), 122, that the Apologia was probably written "to buttress a growing sense of spiritual autobiography" (110). A persuasive essay by John A. Burron, "Langland *nel mezzo del cammin*," in *Medieval Studies for J. A. W. Bennett, aetatis suae LXX*, ed. P. L. Heyworth (Oxford: Clarendon Press, 1981), 21–41, argues that, in references such as that of Imaginatif to his forty-five-year acquaintance with Will (B 12.3), Langland is talking about himself.

13. Middleton, "Narration and the Invention of Experience: Episodic Form in *Piers Plowman*," 100–101.

14. For this word "makynges" (cf. "y made of tho men," C 5.5), see B 12.16, which is the hint from which Langland conjured the new "autobiographical" passage in C.

15. See *London Lickpenny*, 85–88. "Then Into Cornhyll anon I yode,/where was mvtch stolen gere amonge, / I saw where honge myne owne hoode,/that I had lost amonge the thronge"; in Rossell Hope Robbins, ed., *Historical Poems of the XIVth and XVth Centuries* (New York: Columbia University Press, 1959), 133; also *Liber albus: The White Book of the City of London*, 624–25 (where the dealers in cast-off clothes are called "fripperers"). There is "an heep" of "vphalderes" in Glutton's tavern (6.374).

16. See Riley, *Memorials of London and London Life in the XIIIth, XIVth, and XVth Centuries, 1276–1419*, 339 (dated 1369) and 532 (1393).

17. The word "opelond" means "in the country as opposed to the town" and more specifically, from a London point of view, "outside London," as in *Liber albus: The White Book of the City of London*, 602. Huntington Library MS HM 137, the MS used by Skeat as his base manuscript for C, has an interesting scribal variant in this line, "opelond] on londene," which shows a recognition on the part of the scribe of the poet's embarrassment at the potentially disreputable and predatory nature (living on London) of his occupation. His visiting, "now with hym,

now with here" (5.51), is uncomfortably like that of the friar of Chaucer's *Summoner's Tale*, going on his rounds. Langland is conscious, too, of how close his life is to that of the "lewede ermytes" (5.4) among whom he lives; the Letter-Book for 1412 records the punishment in the pillory of a shuttlemaker who pretended to be a hermit and went about saying he had been on pilgrimages, feigning sanctity of life and begging money under false pretenses (Riley, *Memorials of London and London Life in the XIIIth, XIVth, and XVth centuries, 1276–1419*, 584).

18. This is the suggestion first made by Middleton, "Narration and the Invention of Experience: Episodic Form in *Piers Plowman*," 91–122, in relation to the Second Statute of Laborers in 1388, and further explored by Lawrence M. Clopper, "Need Men and Women Labor? Langland's Wanderer and the Labor Ordinances," in *Chaucer's England: Literature in Historical Context*, ed. Barbara A. Hanawalt (Minneapolis: University of Minnesota Press, 1992), 110–29. See also Middleton's essay in the present volume.

19. For changes in the circumstances of poor people in the fourteenth century, and changes in attitudes to poverty, see Derek Pearsall, "Poverty and Poor People in *Piers Plowman*," in *Medieval English Studies Presented to George Kane*, ed. Edward Donald Kennedy, Ronald Waldron, and Joseph S. Wittig (Woodbridge: D. S. Brewer, 1988), 167–86, and the further references cited there.

20. London, in *Wynnere and Wastoure*, a poem probably of the 1360s, is certainly the place of conspicuous consumption, "þer moste waste es of wele"; Stephanie Trigg, ed., *Wynnere and Wastoure*, EETS 297 (1990), l. 473. The king encourages Waster to live in Cheapside and to order great feasts in Bread Street (480) and the Poultry (490) at the expense of out-of-town visitors. He also explains how he needs Winner, in the person of wine merchants and wool merchants, to go on trading and winning in London so that they may finance his wars.

21. See, e.g., Toulmin Smith and Lucy Toulmin Smith, eds., *English Gilds*, EETS, o.s. 40 (1870), 366–67; Ephraim Lipson, *The Economic History of England*, Vol. 1, *The Middle Ages* (London, 1959), 298–99; *Liber albus: The White Book of the City of London*, 233, 290, 504–8, 607–19. The *Liber albus*, as always, gives the impression that the municipal authority has every possible commercial activity regulated to a nicety for the common good, and of course is so designed.

22. For *femmes soles*, that is, women (whether married or not) allowed to trade independently in their own name, see Kay E. Lacey, "Women and Work in Fourteenth- and Fifteenth-Century London," in *Women and Work in Pre-Industrial England*, ed. Lindsey Charles and Lorna Duffin (London: Croom Helm, 1985), see esp. 41, 536; also *Liber albus: The White Book of the City of London*, 181.

23. *Liber albus: The White Book of the City of London*, 313, 609.

24. David Aers, *Community, Gender, and Individual Identity: English Writing, 1360–1430* (London: Routledge, 1988), 39.

25. Thomas, *Calendar of Plea and Memoranda Rolls, Preserved among the Archives of the Corporation of the City of London at the Guildhall, A.D. 1381–1412*, lxiv.

26. See G. R. Owst, *Literature and Pulpit in Medieval England* (Cambridge: Cambridge University Press, 1933), 371.

27. Honorius is cited by R. H. Tawney, *Religion and the Rise of Capitalism* (Harmondsworth: Penguin, 1928), 33.

28. Ibid., 45. See, further, Lester K. Little, *Religious Poverty and the Profit Economy in Medieval Europe* (Ithaca, N.Y.: Cornell University Press, 1978), 178–79. According to canon law, a merchant who makes money is bound to give what is superfluous to his needs to those who are needy; what he keeps more than he needs is theft. See Brian Tierney, *Medieval Poor Law: A Sketch of Canonical Theory and Its Application in England* (Berkeley and Los Angeles: University of California Press, 1959), 367. On the other hand, all the authorities make it clear that there is no scholastic opposition to profit as such: see J. T. Noonan, *The Scholastic Analysis of Usury* (Cambridge, Mass.: Harvard University Press, 1957), 180–90.

29. See Smith and Smith, *English Gilds*, 143, 194, 231, 249.

30. The simple and legally actionable version of this practice, that is, buying up goods wholesale before they came to market, is called "forestalling" (see 4.59), and receives detailed attention in the city and guild ordinances: see Smith and Smith, *English Gilds*, 343, 353, 381; *Liber albus: The White Book of the City of London*, 172, 230, 236, 239, 326, 396, 601–7, 622–24; Lipson, *The Economic History of England*, Vol. 1, *The Middle Ages*, 300. The practice of "regraterye" was particularly associated with "brokeres" (2.60); see *Liber albus: The White Book of the City of London*, 235. It hardly seems necessary to point out that these are not "criminal" practices, nor are they necessarily against the public interest; they are activities on the part of small entrepreneurs (non-guild and alien) which interfere with the attempt of the city and guild authorities to control the market.

31. With equal blandness, Chaucer speaks, in the *General Prologue*, I.282, of the dignity with which the pilgrim Merchant manages his "bargaynes" and his "chevyssaunce"; Geoffrey Chaucer, *The Riverside Chaucer*, ed. Larry Benson (Boston: Houghton Mifflin, 1987). The latter, as described in Thomas, *Calendar of Plea and Memoranda Rolls, Preserved among the Archives of the Corporation of the City of London at the Guildhall, A.D. 1381–1412*, was in practice "an attempt to evade the ecclesiastical laws against usury, by cloaking the transaction under the guise of legitimate bargain and sale" (25). In the *Liber albus*, it is regarded as little more than a euphemism for the practice of usury (319). An essay by Kenneth S. Cahn, "Chaucer, Merchants, and the Foreign Exchange: An Introduction to Medieval Finance," *Studies in the Age of Chaucer* (1980): 81–119, argues earnestly that Chaucer's Merchant had done nothing illegal, but that is not quite the point.

32. The classic study of this subject is Ruth Bird, *The Turbulent London of Richard II* (London: Longmans, Green, 1949). There is a brisker treatment in the useful general book by A. R. Myers, *London in the Age of Chaucer* (Norman: University of Oklahoma Press, 1972), 85–115. It is a conflict to which Chaucer makes only cautious, allusive, and enigmatic reference: his guildsmen, for instance, are all from small and unimportant guilds not involved in the struggles for power. See Ernest P. Kuhl, "Chaucer's Burgesses," *Transactions of the Wisconsin Academy of Sciences, Arts, and Letters* 18, no. 2 (1916): 652–76. Kuhl's arguments are qualified, but not substantially challenged, by Peter Goodall, "Chaucer's 'Burgesses' and the Aldermen of London," *Medium Ævum* 50 (1981): 284–92. For a lively account of London as a place of social conflict and disorder (and a contrast with the urban community of Boccaccio's Florence), see David Wallace, "Chaucer and the Absent City," in *Chaucer's England: Literature in Historical Context*, ed. Barbara A. Hanawalt (Min-

neapolis: University of Minnesota Press, 1992), 59–90. Chaucer's London, he says, can perhaps "only be imagined as a discourse of fragments, discontinuities, and contradictions" (82). Paul Strohm, "Politics and Poetics: Usk and Chaucer in the 1380s," in *Literary Practice and Social Change in Britain, 1380–1530*, ed. Lee Patterson (Berkeley and Los Angeles: University of California Press, 1990), 83–112, gives an account of the grim fate of one who had a small part in this dangerous discourse.

33. James Simpson, "'After Craftes Conseil Clotheth Yow and Fede': Langland and London City Politics," in *England in the Fourteenth Century: Proceedings of the 1991 Harlaxton Symposium*, ed. Nicholas Rogers (Stamford, England: Paul Watkins, 1993), 109–27, sees this passage likewise as "a statement within the fraught and often violent context of London city politics" (111), and he gives an excellent account of that context, but he views the passage more positively, within a theological as well as a political context, as a serious attempt to find a realistic solution to interguild strife, perhaps on the model of the parish fraternity or guild. (I am very grateful to Mr. Simpson for letting me see a copy of his essay in advance of publication.)

34. See 5.35–52, and the note to 5.36 in Pearsall's edition; also the discussion of this passage in Skeat, *The Vision of William concerning Piers the Plowman, in Three Parallel Texts*, xxvii–xxxviii; E. Talbot Donaldson, *Piers Plowman: The C-text and Its Poet* (New Haven, Conn.: Yale University Press, 1949), 199–226; George Kane, *Piers Plowman: The Evidence for Authorship* (London: Athlone Press, 1965), 25–35.

35. See A. K. McHardy, "Ecclesiastics and Economics: Poor Priests, Prosperous Laymen and Proud Prelates in the Reign of Richard II," *Studies in Church History* 24 (1987): 131–32.

36. A. K. McHardy, *The Church in London 1375–1392* (London: London Historical Society, 1977), xv. For hints that Langland, in addition to being a kind of para-ecclesiastical worker, may also have been a professional free-lance part-time scribe, see A 8.43 (not in BC), C 13.118, B 14.191 (not in C), C 19.15, and the notes in Skeat and Pearsall. According to McHardy, "Ecclesiastics and Economics: Poor Priests, Prosperous Laymen and Proud Prelates in the Reign of Richard II," 136, one of the occupations of the unbeneficed was in providing secretarial services.

37. See M. L. Samuels, "Langland's Dialect," *Medium Ævum* 54 (1985): 232–47.

38. The "Letters of John Ball," with their allusions to *Piers Plowman*, are conveniently available in R. B. Dobson, *The Peasants' Revolt of 1381*, 2d ed. (London: Macmillan, 1983), 380–83. For an excellent recent discussion of the letters, and a complete text, see Richard Firth Green, "John Ball's Letters: Literary History and Historical Literature," in *Chaucer's England: Literature in Historical Context*, ed. Barbara A. Hanawalt (Minneapolis: University of Minnesota Press, 1992), 154–75.

39. See Jacques Le Goff, "The Town as an Agent of Civilisation," in *The Fontana Economic History of Europe: The Middle Ages*, ed. Carlo M. Cipolla (Glasgow: Collins/Fontana Books, 1972), 72–73, for some brief exposition of the traditional view. The author of *Wynnere and Wastoure* alludes to this view in describing the apprehension of a "westren wy" (7) that (like Wordsworth's *Michael*) he will never see his son again if he sends him "southewarde," that is, to London.

40. Anne Hudson and Pamela Gradon, eds., *English Wycliffite Sermons* (Oxford: Clarendon Press, 1983–90), 3.103, Sermon 158, ll.50–51. For discussion of this

passage, see Joseph S. Wittig, *"Piers Plowman* B IX–XII: Elements in the Design of the Inward Journey," *Traditio* 28 (1972): 232–34.

41. See James Simpson, "Spirituality and Economics in Passus 1–7 of the B Text," *Yearbook of Langland Studies* 1 (1987): 83–103, and compare the similar argument, in a different context, of James Simpson, "Spiritual and Earthly Nobility in *Piers Plowman,*" *Neuphilologische Mitteilungen* 86 (1985): 467–81.

42. This vocabulary of spiritual paradox is best exemplified in Paul's appropriation of the term "fools" for those who are true in the faith (e.g., 1 Cor. 4:10). Langland uses the word similarly in 22.61, and makes extensive use of a whole range of pejorative terms ("lollares," "boys," "bourdyors") for the purposes of paradox in 9.105–27. See Derek Pearsall, " 'Lunatyk Lollares' in *Piers Plowman,*" in *Religion in the Poetry and Drama of the Late Middle Ages in England*, ed. Piero Boitani and Anna Torti (Cambridge: D. S. Brewer, 1988), 163–78; and notes to 9.105, 136, in Pearsall's edition of the C-text.

43. For an account of the system of apprenticeship in London, see Thomas, *Calendar of Plea and Memoranda Rolls, Preserved among the Archives of the Corporation of the City of London at the Guildhall, A.D. 1381–1412*, xxx–xlvii.

5

Acts of Vagrancy: The C Version "Autobiography" and the Statute of 1388

Anne Middleton

Non licet vobis legem voluntati, sed voluntatem coniungere legi. C 9.212

Redde rationem villicacionis tue. C 9.274; Luke 16:2

Preface: Reading Literature and Reading Law

THIS ESSAY BEGINS WITH A "factual" claim: that the waking interlude between the first and second visions of the C version (C 5.1–104), often called the poet's *apologia* or "autobiography," takes its premises and development as a narrative event from the provisions of the second Statute of Laborers—more accurately and centrally a statute concerning vagrancy—enacted by the Cambridge Parliament of September 1388. The statute, I shall demonstrate, provides the most immediate and pervasive "pre-text" for the encounter of Will with Reason and Conscience, and supplies a narrative matrix and occasion upon which the poet reframes, at a complex new discursive juncture, several of the disparate questions of social ethics and spiritual value surrounding the receipt of alms, the meaning of labor, the practice of begging, and the enterprise of "making" that have arisen throughout the poem in all its forms, and with heightened urgency in the C version.

Yet beyond the density of its reference to contemporary events and discourses, its complex political and ecclesiastical intertextuality, perhaps the most profound and significant aspect of this new episode is its complex *internal* intertextuality—its self-referential function within the poem, and its reflection upon the situation of the poet and his work within a specific moment and situation in literary as well as social history. Indeed, its most complex reflection on the poem's cultural moment lies in the revision it enables in the internal dynamics of the long poem. It has long been claimed that this episode reflects upon the moral and representative status of the poetic subject, Will, and the enterprise of vernacular "making." I propose to add to these interpretive conjectures the materials to show that it does so with extraordinary depth and cultural specificity, and with full and specifically literary self-awareness at a particularly fraught juncture in the history of vernacular writing.

I shall also argue that this waking interlude is the last major revision Langland made in his poem, and that it serves to organize, formally and thematically, many of the distinctive concerns of the C-revision. Offering a retrospective account of the "maker's" anomalous enterprise, in form of a fictive narrative of the inception of the long work years earlier, in the poet's youth, it provides a reflection on the peculiar institution of vernacular fiction, early in a decade that proved to have been one of its most intensely formative periods in English—largely because of the complex intersection of political and cultural pressures of precisely the kind this episode indirectly represents.

Beyond the demonstration of a close and detailed intertextual relation between Langland's "apologia" and the 1388 statute, this essay proposes a way in which literary work *as such* can through its formal and generic as well as referential properties illuminate and enrich—and in which a close examination of its distinctive textual and formal history can disclose—a different kind of understanding of the work's political moment and cultural milieu from those afforded by other kinds of documents available to historical inquiry. In other words, I want to propose that specifically literary self-awareness offers a distinctive kind of social intervention, through which other kinds become the more richly legible. A poem can anatomize and demystify, as well as participate in, the social mythologies and ideological constructions in which political and ethical imperatives are invariably framed, and which provide the conditions and much of the language with which poets imaginatively "play"—as the late fourteenth century's most talented writers invariably term the strangely underauthorized interventions made by their "works"—and it can do both things with the same repertory of gestures.

Of late there has been a great variety of deeply informed and nuanced rereadings of long-canonized "literary" texts of this era—a categorical label that necessarily begs some questions while provoking others—in their several relations to events and writings previously seen as relatively inert "context" or "background." Though these studies have rightly and eloquently repudiated the subordination implied by these terms, and the privileging of "literary" endeavor as a self-evident category of value or cultural experience, in demonstrative logic they have proceeded mostly (though by no means exclusively) from sociopolitical discourses to literary texts, rather than in the other direction. Though their ultimate burden of interest usually lies with the poets and their works which these circumstances richly gloss, the relations between literary texts and the complexities of their cultural moments and discursive contexts often remain elusive, and lead to a somewhat generic conclusion—that poets and their inventions are everywhere embedded in the perspectives and terms their situations afford, and nowhere exempt from or capable of transcending the blindnesses, prejudices, and ideological and economic investments of these, and that poems and their authors, like other texts and actions, are made in languages and conditions "not of their own choosing"; all are alike efforts both to live and to revise the world, and no privilege or exemption attaches to "artistic" insight, in quality or kind. Nor would I argue otherwise: I am gratefully aware of my debt to very many of these, acknowledged below, and aware too that the present essay proceeds expositorily in much the same fashion: from a legal text to political moment, at a moment of desublimation of many diverse ideological forces, to an interpretation of a poem. Yet in doing so I wish at least to shift the accent a bit; I intend here a more specific suggestion about the blindnesses and insights to which their discursive situations subject poets.

My expository order here is not meant to imply a critical subordination of either side of the discarded binarism of "text" and "context" to the other, nor on the other hand to minimize distinctions between kinds of textual intervention in the socially "real" and imaginable. It is, on the contrary, to propose that every ideological construction is capable of being systematically and consciously critiqued, even as another construct— perhaps equally powerful yet serving different ends and priorities—is reinforced, or set in its place, precisely because the pressures on the one and on the other are equally urgent, but scarcely ever commensurable. Critical, in all senses of the term, in the present densely analyzed example, is the radically eccentric purpose to which the poet bends the text and occasion he appropriates—and what he thereby renders visible, both about the statute and its moment and about his own poem in the course of its cultural life, and of his own career. His idiosyncratic use of the Statute to defend what it prohibited thus becomes a key episode in the nascent life of what would come to be designated "literary" composition as a kind of imaginative intervention in social actuality. Neither intervention is more complex than the other; they cannot be placed on a scale of lesser or greater "disenchantment" with the social mythologies by which each is deeply marked. In this encounter, for example, Langland appears to be making a deft, if wittily indirect, plea for renewed or altered patronage with the same highminded rhetoric he uses to abhor social parasitism and misplaced benefit; he at once participates in and unsparingly analyzes the flood of hypocrisy that both his own act and the statute instantiate. But this very dislocation, the act of complex citational capture of one discourse by another, nevertheless—the poet claims, and I agree—makes a difference in the world.

✳   ✳   ✳

Fictively staged as an incipient prosecution under the 1388 statute, Will's waking encounter, "in a hote hervest," is represented as having befallen him in his youth, in London, immediately following the end of his first vision, the dream of Lady Meed at court. At the end of that vision—and only in the C version—the King appoints his advisers Reason and Conscience to the two chief judicial offices of the realm ("cheef chaunceller" and "kynges justice," respectively). The end of the first vision and the inception of the second is in every version a critical formal and ethical juncture in Langland's poetic venture. Formally, in the sequential unfolding of his fiction, it is the point at which his dream-vision veers significantly away from all of its proximate formal and generic models, by the simple act of reiteration: a second vision of the same dream-scene, the field of folk, immediately follows the close of the first. It provides a re-visionary return to the poem's primal scene, this time following its implications to a new ethical site, beyond *la cour et la ville* to the site of agrarian production, a move from questions of governance to those of sustenance which in turn reinvoke matters of governance from a different perspective and rationale. This simple replication of the initial dream scenario, the Field of Folk, thereby calls into question the implicit claims of affective and ethical comprehensiveness, of an interpretable plenitude, conventionally claimed for visionary displays in literary fiction, which are invariably single dreams, however multiple or complex the scenes and events they present may be.[1] In this first waking moment, a brief gap or hinge in what proves to be an opening poetic diptych, Langland's poem issues its first significant signal that it intends to stretch its chief fictive premise and enterprise, the literary dream-vision, to conceptual and critical tasks unprecedented in his vernacular.

Ethically the moment is equally critical. Each of the first two visions presents a fully articulated logic out of which a community may be constructed—and displays that totalizing internal logic as almost unstoppable, all the way to the commune's undoing by the very principles that generated it. It is precisely because each vision (the first presenting the moral and salvational economies of honor, the second those of labor) seems in itself comprehensive, while in their political premises or spiritual preoccupations they scarcely coincide at any point, that Langland can project beyond them a still more searching examination of human needs and powers, extending a thoroughgoing reconstruction of salvation history into the space they define together, but neither encompasses alone—a space at once conceptually universal and historically concrete. The complementary pair of visions gives the poem an extraordinary depth of field, the product of a binocular view of the field of the world's work. The waking interlude between these two dreams—the moment at which the poem first announces its anomalous structure, and begins to manifest as such its method for achieving its extraordinary conceptual richness—is thus the formally logical site for declaring the anomalous cognitive and social ambitions of this work. Langland could make that declaration fully explicit only in retrospect, and in a fashion profoundly embedded in the historical specificities of this moment of simultaneous hindsight and foresight.

Both the visionary antecedent of this waking episode (the anatomy of reward and its proper recipients in the first vision) and its consequent episode (a reflection on labor and those who truly perform it, and the introduction of Piers as leader, in the poem's second vision), gain ethical complexity and political resonance when considered—as the C 5 addition requires—in relation to the 1388 Statute and its circumstances. By inserting an explicit critique and rationale of the poetic subject's activities and manner of life into the gap between these two visionary anatomies of reward and labor, the C 5 addition implicitly offers an account of the literary enterprise, of "making" itself, its standing as work and the kind of reward it might merit. It thereby offers a revised account of the literary form of the long versions, and makes explicit far-reaching discursive connections across the length of the poem that have heretofore remained largely inaccessible when this waking encounter is regarded (as it has been by most analysts thus far) as underwritten chiefly by the regimens of penance, and the confession and expiation of sins—or when, alternatively or in addition, it is read as a prosecution under the labor ordinance of 1349 (made statutory in 1351), as has more recently been proposed.[2]

Seen from the perspective I propose here, the episode becomes the closest counterpart Langland offers to Chaucer's Retractions: both assess the moral fruits and chaff of a life's work in writing, and hence implicitly constitute a vernacular poet's "career" as an ethical unit—with the important difference that the poet of the C version *apologia* manages thereby to regret everything but retract nothing. In a more profound and thoroughgoing way than Chaucer's, Langland's retrospective reconstruction and assessment of his literary enterprise calls into question, through fictive displacement, what Chaucer's, a few years later, would merely assume: that the poet's life work is simply the sum, or array, of his works. With this added waking episode, Langland also brings to the foreground an anomaly that had not ceased to trouble the poem and its society in the 1370s and 1380s: the continued incommensurabilities between conceptions of social and spiritual identity as performed and as textualized—and hence the anomalous standing of vernacular "literature" itself.[3]

The dense intertextual and discursive relationship between statute and poem gives the "autobiographical" aspect of this encounter, as a representation of the poetic persona and project, a quite different character as a literary gesture and discursive "statement" from any heretofore attributed to it. In most accounts of this episode to date, the scene acquires its meaning by immediately dissolving a literal into a spiritual confrontation; the legal vehicle or figuration of the event is in itself of little interest, and is presumed to be a relatively stable referent, a solid contemporary actuality of legal precept and practice that the poet turns to figurative purposes of his own, which in turn become the primary focus of critical interest. Yet the legislation itself, as text or as act, is far from transparent, and from some perspectives may be regarded as no less an imaginative and imaginary venture than the poem that adapts it to its own ends.[4] Therefore, while this essay begins with a fairly conventional demonstration of a textual "source" and a cultural "context" for the C 5 addition, it concludes by suggesting that the syntax of relationship between them—indeed, between any historical "document" and a cultural "monument" for which it provides what has traditionally been designated a source or referent—is more complex and less determinate than that, and points to a need for different models of the relations between literary history and history of institutions or events than either Old or New History has proposed.[5]

Insofar as this is in the first instance, however, an argument about relations in time and space between two texts, it entails as consequences several others of a kind ordinarily considered "factual," and hence in principle falsifiable by other evidence. These are chronological corollaries of the initial claim, the most minimal of these being that the reviser who produced the C version in the form we have must have lived at least through the final months of 1388—and probably, as I shall argue, for a year or two beyond that.[6] Another implication of the relationship I propose between poem and statute—less inevitable, perhaps, but I think also demonstrable from textual evidence as well as the logic of verbal and thematic relations between this passage and other substantial C-additions on related themes of vagrancy, idleness, and licit and illicit receipt of alms—is that the passage postdates in the sequence of revisions all other large-scale additions to C. It presupposes, and disposes into more manifest formal and gestural relations, three substantial additions to the C-text: the additions to the Pardon (C 9.71–281), concerning honest and fraudulent beggars; a new account of patient poverty (just under a hundred lines) at the end of C 12 (153–247) that in C launches the articulation of Rechelessnesse as a temporary alter ego of the dreamer; and the exemplary *distinctio* between the merchant and the messenger that concludes Rechelessnesse's speech, beginning C 13 (32–127) with almost a hundred new lines augmenting an existing B passage condemning venal and ignorant priests. The relative lateness of the C 5 waking episode in relation to other major C revisions has been proposed before, but the present account offers further support, albeit of a different kind, for that view, for which since Donaldson and Day there have also emerged additional grounds, in the form of further discussion of textual and semantic relationships, and evidence concerning manuscript production and dissemination.[7] In other words, the insertion of the waking episode between the first and second vision of the C version can also be shown on this evidence to be the last thing the poet did to his poem.[8] Fictively representing the beginning of the poem as a continuous and sustained project rather than an occasional or topical "making," imagined within the fictive narrative as launched at a moment in the poet's youth when habit (and *habitus*) were first challenged, then transformed into vocation rather than renounced, this new waking episode positioned early in the poem stands paradoxically within its production history as the poet's last word.

But like other purported last words, what it gains in weight and portentousness by this monumentalizing retrospective view, it tends to lose in contextual specificity and force. One must read its explicit claims of constancy of purpose and enterprise "against the grain"—an exercise for which the poet supplies within it plentiful material and encouragement. The immediate situational anachronisms and political densities of the several discourses he invokes in this passage remain manifest, indeed glaring, in it, and give the encounter a deep, overdetermined, and paradoxical clarity. The conjunction of poem and statute in this scene gives to both the poetic *apologia* and the statutory act a historical depth of field that neither possesses without the other, for each, within its generic resources, exemplifies a quixotic effort to give permanent and irrevocable textual stability and fixity—and thereby perpetual accountability before the law—to social identity, at the end of a decade in which this very project had been both extended and questioned as never before in English public life, by acts of civil rebellion and religious dissent. Langland's episode both implies and demands of its readers a heightened awareness of these paradoxes of both the legal initiative and his own.

Both fictive episode and legislative act attest to heightened cultural doubts about the very possibility of legible "intente" in human affairs, about the continuous narrative intelligibility of either social or personal *telos*—and hence of unitary models of both individual probity and social totality—at precisely the historical juncture when both were being asserted in a variety of increasingly sophisticated narrative forms. Both texts, in other words, envision the prospect of fully accountable, narratable, legible, exemplary—in a word, representative—identity on a scale, and with a specificity, not heretofore projected within their respective performative modes. Both imagine a stable published identity as guaranteed by textual mediation; yet both implicitly concede the defeat of this project by the very terms and methods in which it is to be asserted. Reduced to its most schematic form, the episode deploys the terms of the Statute to give literal narrative form to the maxim—invoked explicitly in C 9—that *non licet vobis legem voluntati, sed voluntatem coniungere legi* (it is not for you to will the law into being, but rather to conjoin your will to the law): the Dreamer Will is enjoined by Reason and Conscience to conform his apparently unregulated will to the law, and the applicable statutory as well as ecclesiastical law is invoked with a specificity and thoroughness unprecedented at any earlier stage of composition. Yet the imperative to fix one's identity into the permanence of a textually stabilized first intention decomposes as it is asserted: the poetic "work" remains episodic, even if cumulative and reiterative in its affective force, as at the end of this encounter a second vision succeeds the first, to establish the oscillating form through which Will's "work" attains whatever constancy and integrity of purpose it achieves. Likewise, the statutory initiative against vagrancy was not only unenforced, but virtually unenforceable—as even far more technologically advanced societies have discovered in their efforts to document migrant populations and thereby control the vagrant and ambitious will.

If the 1388 legislation serves as a contextualizing gloss on the fictive encounter, disclosing the political circumstances within which Will's elusive identity articulated an urgent public as well as personal issue, the imagined poetic encounter, *mutatis mutandis*, likewise glosses the parliamentary initiative. Langland's episode displays, as no petitionary or statutory language can, a sense of the multiple and inchoate social fears and spiritual mandates from which this unprecedented and overdetermined legislative measure arose. It suggests that the vagrancy law of 1388 (and for that matter most of the rest of the enactments of the Cambridge Parliament) was a bold act of projective imagination rather than an achievable regulation. The Statute may thus itself be regarded as a product of a cultural imaginary, a fantasy of the power and authority of the administrative state to secure both legible individual identity and a stable social totality—a fantasy that was as seductively unreal as any of Langland's, and far less benign. Literary episode and parliamentary act thus hold each other in momentary equipoise, each enabling a deeper reading of the other. In order to grasp the historical and formal significance of this ultimate move in the C revision, it will be necessary to situate both the Statute and the C-addition within the several discourses and immediate contexts that informed each—for neither simply stabilizes the other, and both register conflicts that were not brought to rest by the act to which each attests.

I. Visionary Legislation: The 1388 Statute, Its Contexts and Its Voices

So manie hedes as there were, so manie wittes; so manie statute makers, so manie mindes.
Egerton, *Discourse on the Understanding of Statutes*[9]

In exploring the relation of Langland's literary act to an act of Parliament, we must perforce proceed almost immediately from a narrow focus on each text itself to progressively wider views, first to the immediate political circumstances of each initiative and the various antecedents and models of the 1388 legislation, then to the discourses in which each participates and which each further inflects. Yet the statutory text of the 1388 labor regulations that I wish to juxtapose to Langland's poetic one is in its own right remarkable for the sheer detail and specificity with which its reach and enforcement are concretely imagined, and it occupies a large fraction of the total record of the Cambridge Parliament's enactments.[10] Surprisingly large, one might say, since there is evidence that the labor measure did not in fact absorb a comparably large share of the assembly's deliberation and energies. The expansiveness of the labor regulation in the Cambridge Statute is rather an index of its innovation, and it is precisely where it is most innovative—that is, where it departs most sharply from any previously existing law, custom, or administrative practice—that it is most massively incorporated by Langland into his fiction.

The 1388 measure begins (c.3) by reaffirming, and asserting its continuities with, "all the statutes of artificers, laborers, servants and victuallers" of both Richard II's reign and that of Edward III, the most important of which was the 1349 Ordinance of Laborers. But it departs immediately and decisively from any statutory precedent in three of its seven headings (it occupies c.3–9 of the enrolled Statute of Cambridge) in ways that are reflected in specific features of Will's encounter with Reason and Conscience. These are the three provisions that shape the basic terms and plot of Langland's fictive dialogue; in the order in which the poet deploys them—which corresponds to that of the Statute—they specify:

1. the liability of all "artificers and craftsmen as well as servants and apprentices, who are not of great account and of whose craft or mistery men have no great need in time of harvest" to "be forced to serve in harvest at cutting, gathering and bringing in the corn" (c.3);

2. that "he or she who is employed in labouring at the plough and cart or other labor or service of husbandry until they be of the age of twelve years shall remain thenceforward at that labor without being put to any mistery or craft," and all covenants or bonds of apprenticeship made for any such person shall be invalid (c.5);

3. that "every man who goes begging and is able to serve or labor," excepting "people of religion and hermits approved," is liable to forced labor under the first provision, while "beggars unable to serve" must "remain in the cities and towns where they are dwelling at the time of the proclamation of this Statute, and that if the people of the said cities or towns will not or cannot suffice to find

[provide for] them, the said beggars withdraw to the other towns within the hundred, rape, or wapentake, or to the towns where they were born, within forty days after the said proclamation be made, and dwell there continually for their lives" (c.7).

As these measures suggest, and the remainder confirm, the 1388 legislation emphasizes the control, enforcement, and punishment of mobility as such, in the social as well as spatial sense, in a manner entirely foreign to any previous national regulation of labor and wages. Underwriting all clauses of this legislation—now tellingly self-described not only as *les ordinances des servantz et laborers* (like previous measures), but also of *mendinantz et vagerantz* (c.9)—and serving as the primary technology of control is an elaborate system of "internal passports": letters patent, sealed with a king's seal to be devised for the purpose, authorizing the comings and goings of workers traveling beyond their local residence and terms of service (c.3), and of pilgrims begging during their journey as well as clerks of the university who beg (c.7); "people of religion and hermits approved" must have "letters testimonial of their ordinaries" to travel beyond their regular ambits (c.7). Those returning from abroad claiming to have been imprisoned there must likewise bear a testimonial letter, either "of the captains where they have dwelt, or of the mayors and bailiffs where they make their landing," indicating where they have been and their destination within the realm (c.8). "Servants who ride or go on the business of their lords or masters," however, are "not intended . . . to be comprehended within this ordinance during the time of the same business" (c.3)—a provision absent from the commons petition as represented in the Monk of Westminster's text, but included in the statute as enrolled. Likewise added to the statute, though not present in the petition, is a reassurance that, in prohibiting the bearing of weapons by agrarian or craft workers in peacetime and authorizing the justices of the peace to levy fines for violations, "it is not the King's intent that prejudice be done to the franchises of lords touching the forfeitures due them" (c.6). Moreover, the statute specifies, though the petition does not mention, the construction of stocks in every town "as is ordained in the Statutes aforesaid" (c.3), for the punishment of these offenses.

The differences between the statute as enrolled and the petition as recorded in the Westminster Chronicle are minor in substance, but in language and emphasis they attest to a significant distinction between the interests at work in framing these measures, and those that it was politically necessary to address in order to enact them into law. The slight differences in tone and focus between the two textual forms of the enactment, however, help to clarify Langland's interest in the measure, and also suggest the institutional position and social allegiances he articulates, as well as the dense interpenetration of diverse ethical discourses to which he gives complex voice with the new fictive act of self-disclosure of C 5.

The 1388 measures concerning labor and vagrancy lack any prefatory rationale at all. In this they differ markedly from their professed antecedent, the 1349 Ordinance, which began by specifying "the grave disadvantages which might arise from the dearth especially of tillers and workmen" as the reason for imposing limits on wages in both agrarian and craft occupations and for requiring landless laborers without other prior contracts to serve in agrarian toil as offered. The lack of such a preamble might at first seem surprising, since the measures proposed in 1388 are still more innovative in their time, and far more sweeping in the range of social surveillance they envision, than those of 1349 were in their immediate context. Indeed, the virtually universal control of mobility proposed in 1388 is more pervasive and minutely imagined than that of any kind of legislation, except perhaps fiscal measures, entertained by any parliament to date. It is certain that nothing resembling the "internal passports" device had ever been used on anything like the scale proposed here—and the petition was if anything even more fussily detailed about the creation of the seals, authority over them, charges to be levied for sealing, and so forth, than the statute as enacted.

Virtually all historians who have discussed the 1388 vagrancy measure have remarked on the breathtaking thoroughness with which it projects surveillance and control, and they have registered with expressions of dismay and distaste their sense that the measure is not merely unprecedented but premonitory—of a fundamentally different relation of the pragmatic to the normative in sociopolitical thought and imagination, and an early sign of the formation of an idea of the state as such, as an entity with intrinsic and supervening interests somehow in excess of those of the communities and individuals that constitute it.[11] It is the comparatively sudden and full—and seemingly unprepared—emergence in the text of this statute of a new attitude concerning social regulation itself that for these historians prompts surprise, and one of the purposes of this essay is to attempt to account for this new manifestation, and its imaginative uses.

Yet despite the many unprecedented features of the 1388 legislation, there are three reasons why the absence of a separate prefatory rationale for the labor and vagrancy measure is understandable in its immediate political context. First, as the administrative details of the petition clearly show, this initiative came from, and served the interests of, those who by now had a generation's experience in enforcing the earlier law, and in the interim a series of commons petitions and local measures had supplied the rationales and precedents, left unstated in 1388, for proposals now conceived chiefly as matters for administrative implementation.[12] From the perspective of those who framed these measures, the question underlying them was no longer why or whether vagrancy control was warranted, or what behaviors were to be regulated, but merely how it was to be done. Once the need and presuppositions of regulation were conceded—as apparently they were by the occasion and circumstances—the legislation that followed took the form of a kind of fantasia of the administrative unconscious.

Second, its purpose is in any case implicit, in a more diffuse form, in the full list of items before this parliament. To the extent that it took written form at all on this occasion, the rationale of the vagrancy measure was effectively furnished by the first and most controverted item of business undertaken when the assembly began: the proposal to abolish liveries and maintenance (of which the petitionary record of the Cambridge Parliament provides the first explicit definition to reflect the capacious vernacular understanding of this practice). The overarching theme of the Cambridge Parliament, manifest in nearly every agenda item in one form or another, seems to have been the curtailment of what were perceived as status offenses, the suppression of various excesses attributed to newly asserted group and communal identities and affiliations.[13] The principles by which livery and maintenance were linked, by those who proposed these measures, with vagrancy and parasitism on public charity, as they evidently were in the acts of the Cambridge Parliament (and, as we shall see, also in the several plaints and petitions that led to them), is not at first glance obvious, since these are not only are practices of quite different classes but would appear to cause quite different kinds of apprehension and irritation in otherwise divergent groups. The underlying parallel between them, however, seems rather to be broadly structural and discursive, matters of ideological association rather than of immediate sectarian political and economic interests: both are manifestations of the fearsome possibilities latent in extremely mobile allegiances and "bought" men—of bonds that transparently do not outlast the immediate cash nexus that sustains them.[14] It is nothing less than the fluidity of social identities, and the construction of new affinities beyond the reach of some forms of customary restraint, that these measures as a group attempt to arrest and reverse—in the event not only unsuccessfully, but to some of their addressees, almost unintelligibly.

Third, the political circumstances of this parliament created a brief and unstable alignment of forces and interests that were usually engaged in uneasy competition and negotiation; it was this reconfiguration, however fleeting, that allowed the articulation of the desires expressed here in such sweeping and uncompromising form. The Cambridge Parliament followed by only four months the Merciless Parliament, in which the Appellants had last exercised their brief ascendancy over Richard and the favorites they had sought to purge; within seven months they would once again lose their advantage, largely for lack of both strategic political acumen and decisive accomplishments manifested in the Cambridge Parliament. If they were to demonstrate that the good of the realm, in the name of which they had asserted their political centrality, was anything more than a rhetorical cover for magnate faction, Richard's opponents would have to address a diversity of commons' political anxieties of more than a decade's standing concerning perceived social faction (and fraction) in general, perceptions of threatened social disorder that had thus far failed to find legislative expression commensurate with the mobile and wide range of fears that prompted them.[15] The Cambridge Parliament thus in effect marked a moment of desublimation of ideological pressures that had been building for a generation, and thus displays in unusually full and schematic form the defining features of markedly contrasting discourses for characterizing the ills and the good of the realm, as well as implicitly divergent notions of the purview of government itself. The entire array of measures proposed to the Cambridge Parliament, and the actions taken, document a standoff between these, a discursive gap into which the Appellants were to fall in the following year.

As proposed—that is, in the form recorded by the Monk of Westminster—the labor and vagrancy measures devote a proportionately greater share of their specification to the bureaucratic details of the creation and custody of new seals for the "internal passports," and to the ultimate use of the fines levied to cover the jurisdiction's fiscal debt to the Crown, than does the statute.[16] The version enacted, by contrast, takes more care than the petition to specify that lords' legal prerogatives will not thereby be compromised, that lords pay a share of the enforcing officers' wages equal to their share of fines collected, and that various kinds of double jurisdictional allegiance—such as the appointment of a steward of a lord to a commission of the peace—be prevented (c.10). Where the petition is preoccupied with the imprisonment of offenders, and heavy fines for gaolers releasing such prisoners, the Statute emphasizes the use of public stocks for punishment, as well as the answerability of the local enforcing officials—mayors, bailiffs, stewards, constables and gaolers—to the King's Council for any plaint lodged against them in their execution of their charge (c.10).[17] In short, the measures enacted clearly reflect the inherently unstable compromises with magnate interests—and an admixture of magnate styles of social sanction—that would be required to make these initiatives of the commons' administrative mentality into applicable law. This new discursive compound proved to have an unusually brief half-life in implementation, yet a remarkably durable imaginative appeal, whose full power was not to be realized for over a century.

Before turning to the heterogeneity of these measures as enacted, we must examine the mentality and values implicit in them as proposed. The 1388 petition understands vagrancy—much as it views the other social ills to which it proposes remediation—as a social threat not merely in practical or economic terms, but as what one might call an ontological and epistomological problem, as a kind of solecism in social semantics and grammar that threatens the universal and common intelligibility of personal design and social telos. To the disturbing performative indeterminacy of vagrant populations, the countermeasure proposed is similarly a universal legal mechanism: that of documentary fixity and accountability, a project of textualizing and authorizing identity. In this respect, the legislation of the Cambridge Parliament offers an unprecedented early vision of the reach of the administrative state, even though in the immediate future the idea remained largely visionary rather than applied.

As I use the term here, the administrative state is a mode of governance deploying uniform methods of accounting, certification, and regularity of procedure, rather than spectacle, ritual, and public exemplification, as the preferred and fundamental means of inviting social trust and securing social compliance. Virtually every measure of this parliament proposes documentary accountability as a universal device restraining the threatening migration of groups and their members outside the boundaries of proper roles and relationships that had putatively, in some more traditional condition of the community, gone largely without saying. Yet the very act of attempting to secure them by this omnibus means irreversibly changes their political form—and also quietly accepts without comment, as *fait accompli*, much of what the 1349 measure had resisted. The regulatory mechanism of "internal passports" was to be realized uniformly throughout the realm across the boundaries of local jurisdictions of enforcement, while operating so as to confer fiscal benefit on these localities in return for, and in direct proportion to, its active enforcement. The petition bespeaks in every detail the administrative mind at work, secure in its social premises, even (or perhaps especially) where these are internally conflicted. In effect, a market in labor in place of fixed terms of service, whether agrarian or craft, has in this proposal been quietly and fully introjected, while status instability and fluidity, its social accompaniment, has not—and it is the latter that is most fundamentally the focus of the 1388 labor and vagrancy regulation as proposed, as it is the dominant theme running through all of the topics considered by the 1388 parliament.

Two other notable measures proposed to the Cambridge Parliament— the abolition of liveries, and the abolition of "gilds and fraternities and their common chests"—likewise proposed status control through positive and universalizing legislation, and restraint of social mobility by administrative procedure. Both proposals, unlike those on labor and vagrancy, failed of enactment—an implicit index of the seated interests, present in this or any parliament, certain to resist such efforts, and further highlighting the absence of any representation there of the potential victims of the anti-vagrancy measures, who were almost by definition the unenfranchised. Both of these attempts are, however, telling, and the terms in which they were proposed help to define the mentality from which the anti-vagrancy measures also issued, just as the terms in which they were modified in parliament also indicate the alignment of discursive forces that were also implicit in the adoption of vagrancy controls.

As might have been anticipated, the proposal to abolish liveries—the first matter to be taken up when parliament convened on September 9— was heatedly resisted by the lords.[18] The commons' opening salvo, protesting the "badges issued by the lords" as conducing to what amounted to class arrogance against the "rights of the middle and other classes," met with the lords' protest of the overgeneral nature of the complaint (*generalitatem hujus querimonie elidere cupientes*), while the latter also invited the commons to "hand over to them those offenders who did such things, who would be so punished that their collegues would be scared off similar behavior." The differing identifications of the problem, and the contrasting styles of remedy proposed, are revealing. The lords insist on their prerogative to discipline others of their own class, and propose selective and exemplary public display of correction as deterrence, while the commons insist on universal legal abolition, by positive parliamentary action, of the forms of display and signs of association that symbolically sustain the abuses complained of. Ritual spectacle versus universal prohibition, the egregious versus the uniform, display versus erasure, the performed versus the documentary, define the opposed discursive poles and stylistic repertoires of reform for these two counterposed forces. As we shall see, these two styles of representation are also very much at issue for Langland in his use of the statute.

The commons, however, remained adamant, insisting on the elimination of badges and liveries altogether rather than the conspicuous selective punishment of those who abused these associational forms. In this impasse the king himself intervened, "out of a desire for domestic tranquillity," offering "for the sake of peace and in order to set an example to others to discard his own badges"—an offer "which gave the utmost satisfaction to the commons," according to the Monk of Westminster. When the lords still refused, the king proposed the compromise that carried the day. Showing the same tactical flair that he had displayed in 1381 at Mile End for staging his mediatory initiatives at dramatic junctures, Richard's intervention was calculated to impress upon the assembly that it was the king himself, not the Appellants, who could best gratify and harmonize the conflicting demands of the disparate groups among his subjects, and his initiative paid off: Richard reassumed his full powers the following spring. The lords were allowed to keep their badges until the next parliament, to which the matter was carried over, "in the hope that in the meantime amendment will be effected by him and the lords of his council, without prejudice to the dignity of the king and of the lords and of all other estates of the parliament."[19]

Commons' proposal to dissolve guilds and their properties bespeaks a similar stylistic standoff, though with far less perspicuous motives and outcome. As proposed, the measure seems at first to be aimed chiefly at appropriating the wealth of the guilds, and it specifies that the confiscated "goods and chattels" are to be "laid out upon the war at the discretion of the lords of parliament." As an act of political calculation on the part of commons, this appears shrewd, for it presumes that the lords will be eager to approve raising funds for the war from some other source than their own land revenues. Yet the commons appear to have additional motives for wishing to dissolve guilds, animated by the same suspicion they attached to liveries: the guilds too, it seems, are social sites of potentially untrustworthy forms of association, which, like liveries, are enacted in public rituals of solidarity and exemplification. The proposal continues, in the characteristic mixture of piety and censoriousness that marks the language of the petition throughout, to except from such confiscation those guild commitments to "chantries ordained in ancient time for the souls of their founders and others acquired in mortmain by royal license and other things ordained to the honour of Holy Church and increase of divine service," but subtracting from their allowed activities and properties "livery, confederacy, maintenance, or riots in hindrance of the law." While this proposal never became law, it did issue, shortly following the end of the Cambridge Parliament, in an inquiry into the "constitution, property, finances, and objects of all gilds and fraternities."[20] Like the measure against liveries, this one is most fundamentally about forms of representing—and enforcing—community.

All of these measures proposed to the Cambridge Parliament betray a common image of the community, and what might be called a common discursive style, in envisioning the amelioration of its ills. While the two measures concerning livery and guilds may indeed have been strategically framed for the Cambridge Parliament in the most extreme and absolute terms possible, in the hope of gaining lesser concessions, their resemblance to the labor and vagrancy measures remains significant.[21] Like most discursive styles, this one had emerged into the fullness and consistency of statement it had attained in 1388 from long and overdetermined development of at least a generation's duration. By extending our perspective to a longer view than that of the political circumstances surrounding the brief ascendancy of the Appellants, we may discern in greater historical depth the subtext of the statute—its pervasive, yet largely implicit, anxiety about violations of social boundaries and status and the proper means of curtailing such vagrancies—in the making. A dense and heterogeneous assemblage of legal precedents, some of them very old, interspersed with recently coined and highly partisan vernacular ethical and political terminologies for contemporary behaviors, produced the volatile discourse surrounding work and vagrancy that is largely presumed rather than asserted by the 1388 petition and statute. These form, in effect, the unwritten but understood preamble to the measures enacted at Cambridge. In tracing the disparate antecedents and models for the components of this remarkable measure, we must return once again to the 1349 labor regulations, which provided the slight but significant revision of then-prevailing terms and legal assumptions upon which the 1388 measure would base its far more radical departure in principles and premises.

In general, the 1349 Ordinance had emphasized restoration of the economic status quo before the plague; it addressed the social and political arrangements that supported this pre-plague community only peripherally and largely implicitly, proposing merely to shore up rather than revise traditional lord–servant relations. It devoted most of its attention and explicit positive regulation as written, and certainly most of its enforcement by the justices, to wage and price offenses. It had fixed penalties for both givers and takers of excessive wages in the craft and agricultural occupations, the measure of excess being the customary rate in the twentieth year of Edward III's reign (i.e., 1347). Victuallers' prices were likewise, though more vaguely, controlled; there the measure of excess was "moderate profit" for the seller and the price current "in neighboring places."[22] The 1388 Statute, by contrast, not only shifts its main regulatory attention sharply away from prices and wages to social mobility and vagrancy, but also in the process silently and completely abandons retrospective comparison for its economic norms, making no reference to pre-plague standards, either for prices and wages or as a reference point for proper terms of land service or employment practices. On the contrary, the 1388 measure acknowledges explicitly that "the wages of the said laborers and servants have not been put in certainty before these times" (c.4)—that is, there are no customary "correct" rates; there are now simply legally fixed ones. In the following year, the discretionary power of the justices to determine rates "according to the dearth of victuals" was made statutory.[23] This positive rather than restorative conception of "standard" rates of wages and prices is consistent with an often-remarked tendency, first manifested fitfully in the latter half of the fourteenth century, toward the view that law and government have an active rather than custodial role in identifying and solving perceived social problems—and that the state in which this power resides is personified in acts of parliament and decisions of justices rather than in the will or edicts of the monarch.[24] In this respect the language of the 1388 labor measure contrasts sharply with that of its 1349 predecessor in suggesting that the state so conceived is—as it came to be seen in the Tudor period—the primary source of meliorative policy, rather than the guardian of customary and largely static social arrangements.[25]

The Ordinance of 1349 had also envisioned, though with less clear legal devices and more doubtful success, the restoration of normative pre-plague social and political relations between workers and employers. Its innovations were largely inadvertent, and lay in its redeployment of a tissue of older and local precedents in new jurisdictions above the level of manorial justice. It aimed to merely to correct an implicit "abnormality," perceived as temporary and easily remediable, that is not openly identified as such by the Ordinance at all: a mobile labor force traveling to seek employment at better wage rates than terms of annual service provided. Indeed, we may find the most important implications of the 1349 Ordinance, and the platform it offered for the more flamboyant positive corrective measures proposed by its 1388 successor, in what it does not say explicitly about the state of affairs that called it into being. If statutes may be said to have an audience, an implied "you" that is categorically assigned specific remediation and rights, one whose rhetorical and actual position in the world corresponds to the perception and explanations of imputed wrongs that are implicit in the law, then the audience of the 1349 Ordinance consists solely of employers and prospective employers, and the purported "dearth of labor" as a commodity is the single inconvenience afflicting this group that underwrites the diverse provisions of the law. The subjects thus commodified are not addressed at all, and they are not penalized until or unless they refuse proffered employment. Vagrancy and idleness figure explicitly in the 1349 law solely as epiphenomena of the mobility of laborers, and the vagrant is no more than a temporary aspect of the mobile worker. Vagrancy is not yet a covert guise, or a political code word, for violence and sedition—as it had become by 1388.

Three clauses of the 1349 Ordinance did, however, provide sanctions directly against what would come to be called the able-bodied unemployed; these would later become the focus and chief subjects of the 1388 measure. The first of these three provisions, which Putnam calls the "contract clause," penalized with prison anyone ("reaper, mower, or other servant, of whatsoever rank or condition he be") who departs from employment before the end of the term of service agreed upon; an employer who employs such a fugitive is likewise subject to imprisonment. In effect, this provision merely reinforced at a national level existing local and manorial provisions for retaining and returning land laborers; its chief innovation lay in extending this contractual understanding to other (unspecified) "ranks and conditions" of workers—though in this extension also lay its most chequered history of enforcement.[26]

A second provision, the "enforced labor" clause, as Putnam calls it, specified that an unemployed person, "servile or free," is bound by law to "serve him who shall require him" at the specified customary rate, but his offense against the Ordinance was not in his wandering or unemployment per se, but came at the moment when he refused proffered work at the rate set into law by the ordinance. Only when a wandering worker in search of day labor refused service—to be offered, it should be noted, with "regard to his rank"—was he culpable under the law; his offense under the 1349 Ordinance was not seen as intrinsic to his status or his way of life. Moreover, this clause applied to a defined spectrum of persons in the 1349 Ordinance: "able-bodied and under the age of sixty years, not living by trade nor exercising a certain craft, nor having of his own whereof he shall be able to live, or land of his own, in the tilling whereof he shall be able to occupy himself, and not serving another man"—that is, solely agrarian landless laborers or those whose holdings were insufficient to support them without wage labor—and it acknowledged the prior rights of lords, against other prospective employers, to retain in their service their own bondmen and tenants of their lands.

Both the enforced-labor and the contract clauses of the 1349 Ordinance claim to offer no more than an added enforcement of lord-servant bonds already sanctioned by common law, now written into national legislation. Yet however backward-looking these measures were in general intent, the very existence of a new level of legal sanction suggests that the traditional measures for returning laborers bound in terms of annual service to their lords were no longer considered to be fully effective, as the problem was now perceived to transcend local jurisdictions. As Putnam has copiously shown, the enforced-labor clause of the Ordinance was more difficult to prosecute successfully than the wage and price standards, or even the contract clause, precisely because its application necessarily invoked questions of the status or rank of the putative wage worker: whoever possessed sufficient land or other income, or a trade or craft, was exempt. The far more sweeping and stringent enforced-labor clause of 1388, which encompassed all trades- and craftspersons whose work was deemed (by the enforcing agency) unnecessary "in time of harvest," is aimed at closing precisely this apparent gap or escape provision in its earlier counterpart.[27] As we shall see, it is the 1388 version of the "enforced-labor" clause that is applied first by Reason and Conscience to the questionable identity of Will.

A third clause of the 1349 ordinance attempting to regulate the lives of the wandering unemployed or occasionally employed is indirect: it forbids the giving of alms to "sturdy beggars" who are physically able to work. This prohibition brings into positive secular law a matter that had also been articulated in canon law dealing with almsgiving, although it invokes very different reasoning from that urged by the canonists.[28] Significantly, the Ordinance provided a separate prefatory rationale for this clause, as if in recognition that the measure concerning alms raised an issue distinct from that of the rest of its provisions, and different in kind—one that had traditionally been a matter for the church's moral authority:

... because many sturdy beggars, so long as they can live by begging for alms, refuse to labour, living in idleness and sin and sometimes by thefts and other crimes, no man, under the aforesaid penalty of imprisonment, shall presume under colour of pity or alms to give anything to such as shall be able profitably to labour, or to cherish them in their sloth, so that they may be compelled to labour for the necessaries of life.[29]

This is the earliest shadowy appearance in national legislation of a category that was to have an enduring existence in political action and ideology, and virtually displaced high prices and wages as the focus of the 1388 Statute: the manner of living of those who in the intervening four decades took on a variety of more pejorative names and threatening identities—*mendinantz* and *vagerantz*, but also *stafstrikers, faitours*, and, by the 1380s, *lolleres*. Though each term had a somewhat different shade of meaning, all of them, together and almost interchangeably, had become by 1388 a scarcely differentiated political *bête noire*. Especially in view of the legislative and polemical afterlife of this provision, three features of the 1349 clause prohibiting almsgiving to "sturdy beggars" merit notice here. First, it imagines some able-bodied beggars as refusing to work out of slothful habit or nature, but this is seen as an individual failing, not an attribute of any specific group identifiable as such or self-identified in any other way. Second, it supposes that such persons may engage in petty crime for their livelihood, and imposes labor as a corrective; it does not imagine groups or confederations of such persons against the law. Third, and by far the most important, it directs penalties solely to the giver, rather than the beggar, of alms.[30]

The inclusion of idle and begging vagrants in legislation nominally concerned with labor and wages was in 1349 visibly anomalous, and acknowledged as such by the framers of the Ordinance, while in 1388 it would become the primary emphasis of the second labor statute, requiring no special justification, or even very precise definition of the seemingly highly miscellaneous category of offenders against whom it was directed. The intervening forty years between the two labor measures saw the full-blown development of a complex ideological invention, the pejorative figure of the alms-seeking able-bodied vagrant. Yet in tracing the rapid rise of this figure to contentious eminence in the 1370s and 1380s, one should notice some slightly earlier and subtler discursive changes, on which this ideological construction of vagrancy in turn depends, and for which the 1349 measure provided substantial conceptual groundwork. Both logically and chronologically antecedent to the invention of the idle vagrant was the appearance and ideological deployment, chiefly in the 1350s and 1360s, of his complementary opposite, the "worker" as both an object of national political interest and intervention, and as the national "good subject." This discursive invention was in every way a less spectacular development than that of his notorious opposite, the "sturdy beggar"; it seems to have occurred without notable skirmish, and almost beyond conscious awareness, in fourteenth-century English usage, and is also much more easily taken for granted without critical reflection by modern scholars. Yet a subtle shift of terms and assumptions, in which work rather than "estate" designated the most fundamental term for the participation of individuals and groups in the totality of the human community, was one that the 1349 Ordinance, despite its purportedly merely restorative aims, did much to promote, and it directly enabled the creation of the fraudulent nonworker as a kind of back-formation of its own largely implicit and inadvertent political logic.

Even excepting for the moment its legally anomalous clause concerning almsgiving to the able-bodied unemployed, the whole panoply of regulation of laborers in the 1349 Ordinance subtly and irreversibly redefined the political and social relations they proposed to restore. Its chief positive enforcement innovation, beyond the always-quixotic effort to control wages and prices by fiat, was the attempt to regulate from a single national platform both agricultural labor relations, heretofore the task of manorial custom and village bye-laws, and craft labor, which had been the subject of several earlier municipal measures—as for example, the building trades.[31] In the defense of traditional labor relations, it began to envision, if not a national standard for prices and wages, at least the possibility of uniform national structures of legal constraint—and hence to imagine a single overarching rationale, an implicit new ontology of the state itself, nominally justifying all of these at once under a single principle. It was paradoxically in the professed conservativism with which it claimed to shore up traditional and local economic and political relations that it displayed its most significant conceptual revision of these. In the practice of enforcement, even though nowhere explicitly acknowledged in its wording, the Ordinance had the effect of implicitly positing a contractual relationship between agrarian lord and servant, as between craft or trade employer and employee; the customary annual term of rural labor service was in effect quietly subsumed in a new form even as it was reaffirmed. Thus, while it contained nothing professedly innovative—no acknowledgment by either its framers or judicial enforcers of a fundamental change in policy or social models—inferentially the 1349 legislation newly assigned to the purview of the king's justice, and not merely to the village or the manor an interest in seeing to it that wanderers were employed. This inference, and this view of the national interest, become explicit and primary in the Statute of 1388.

As the 1349 measure implicitly articulates the nation or state, not simply lords or employers, as the entity whose "good" it promotes, so the logical complement of this totalizing national interest is its "good subject"—the worker who, whatever his vocation or condition, is engaged in some form of activity for the good of the entire community. Encompassing secular and spiritual "good" within one broad and complex continuum, it envisions clerical vocations and their spiritual imperatives within the same single rationale for social differentiation as applied to lay occupations: the sustenance of the entire community.[32] In the years between the two labor measures, the imperative of socially useful occupation gradually came to assume many of the discursive functions formerly allotted to "estate" (conceived as a functionally differentiated system of privileges and prerogatives), and the nation or realm came to encompass in its legal purview matters of social morality formerly dealt with at the level of local jurisdictions and ecclesiastical exhortation.[33] In the process, the very notion of status prerogative—and hence of mutually supportive functional identities and "ways of life" regulated by purportedly divine sanctions—begins to dissolve, as the primary representative relationship in the community becomes the one binding the individual directly to the reason of the state, and to its image as a totality, chiefly through the category of "work."

The 1349 Ordinance inadvertently facilitated this shift in the terms by which social order and social membership were imagined.[34] The change in imaginative framework was evident chiefly in the way in which the first two of the three positive measures concerning those considered potentially employable, the "contract" and "enforced-labor" clauses, defined the implicit objects and objectives of its enforcement—the worker and the national state as interdependent constructs. As we shall see, the 1388 statute provides an explicit new ontology for this "good subject," as it also brings into full view its opposite, the "bad subject" upon which the law must invoke universal identification and sanctions. Forming the other half of the binary conceptual structure of the 1388 statute, and of the waking interrogation of Will in C 5, the constitution of the good subject as worker *tout simple* rather than specifically someone's bondsman or employee, or someone of a specific estate, is latent in the definitions and assumptions of the 1349 measure, and becomes explicit in both a revised ontology of the agrarian laborer and the greatly extended application of the enforced-labor clause in 1388.

In turning now to the discursive formation that was the obverse of both old "bondman" and new "worker," the begging vagrant, we encounter a surplus of determining forces. The transition from wage inflation, the focus of anxiety in 1349, to vagrancy—itself, as we have seen, a term largely metonymic for social mobility more generally—as the focus of "moral panic" and parliamentary concern in 1388 was neither sudden nor simple, and the several separate fronts on which the latter Statute proposed prosecution each acknowledge their own constitutive genealogies. Perhaps the clearest traceable path of antecedent legal texts and models to bridge the gap between the 1349 measure and its 1388 successor is the one that leads directly to the second of the three provisions of the Cambridge Statute explicitly invoked by Langland in the C 5 addition: the prohibition of those born to land service and so occupied until the age of 12 from entering a "mistery or craft" thereafter (c.5). From the perspective of legal history, this may be seen as merely a conceptual expansion of the ancient fugitive-laborer provisions of manorial custom—and thereby also a radical enlargement of the "contract" provision of the 1349 ordinance—but now extended to prosecution on a new front and in new jurisdictions so far as to change the nature of the object of regulation. The 1388 Statute, by invalidating other, later occupational "contracts" for anyone deemed an agrarian worker by birth, gives to the identity of the agrarian laborer a more explicit and encompassing ontology. The bond to agrarian toil is now defined as an identity distinct from villein status, with its defining legal tie to the land itself (a legal category nowhere mentioned by either the petition or the Statute of 1388), and is constituted instead by habitual or customary occupation from early youth rather than by hereditary legal condition. The 1388 Statute in effect asserts that free agrarian workers are now to incur the same legal disabilities as villeins in relation to future employment beyond the cultivation of the land.

There is no clear precedent for this new account of the agrarian worker's perpetual fixity of identity as established by childhood employment, independently of heritable legal condition, though there are in the years surrounding the 1388 Statute at least two other notable efforts to enforce specifically villein legal disabilities, in each case by closing access to a new adult occupation beyond agriculture. A London ordinance of July 18, 1387, provides that "henceforth no foreigner should be enrolled as an apprentice nor received into the city's liberty by the way of apprenticeship, unless he first swears that he is a free man (*liber homo*) and not a bondsman (*nativus*)."[35] In 1391, a parliamentary petition asks that "no bondsman or villein should henceforth place his children in schools in order to advance them into the clergy."[36] While each of these, like the 1388 measure, aims at controlling social mobility and the extension of the franchise, only the Cambridge Statute so clearly and decisively registers in its language the later medieval expansion of the definition of the rural peasant beyond the traditional category of the bondsman, to encompass all country dwellers who cultivated the soil.[37] This revised account of agrarian worker identity as fixed by childhood occupation, and the equally unprecedented parliamentary provision for the forcible draft of harvest laborers from beyond the category of those born to, or long employed in, agrarian pursuits, are both profound innovations of the 1388 Statute. Unlike those we have examined heretofore, however, they inhere chiefly in its buried logical premises rather than in any noteworthy new enforcement measures. Both conceptual developments, as we shall see, are also evident in Langland's representation of Will as worker in the C 5 addition, as well as implicit in his placement and figurative framing of the new waking episode.

In these paired definitions of the worker as "good subject," and of the political community as a whole, rather than a master, employer, or patron as the entity with an ultimate supervening interest in exacting and enforcing labor, the 1388 Statute records the fundamental reframing of the "problem" of the mobile laborer in the nearly forty years since the first labor measure. Excessive wage costs in both rural and urban occupations now yield to a perceived stark contrast between rural field and village as places where there were until lately stable and intelligible forms of "work"—even though these would now be enforced in royal rather than manorial courts—and the city and metropolis, where human desire, skill, and intent are asserted in threateningly unclassifiable new ways.

In this reconfiguration, the rural stands for stable and proper identities, the city for the irregular and improvisatory, the former providing a "then" and "there" in terms of which a corrupt "here and now" must be measured and found perpetually wanting. As we shall see, Langland will freight this binarism still more heavily, by mapping onto it his own double representation of the community in terms of two rival philosophical metaphors for the economy of salvation. On the one hand, salvation is seen as earned by deserving through good works, a process staged allegorically in the form of largely rural and small craft work, as in the second vision;

on the other, salvation is seen, not as a definite quid pro quo, but rather as a divine courtesy or favor extended to humankind by grace, attained through a radical, and radically uncertain, wager of faith, and an admission of radical dependency. The latter process, with all its risks and attendant anxieties, is imagined in the poem in the form of royal and magnate gift— a kind of sublimely generous divine largesse or patronage—which nevertheless resembles too closely various forms of morally problematic and extravagant metropolitan enterprise, as in the Meed episode in the first vision. The metropolis becomes for Langland not only what it implicitly was for the framers of the 1388 Statute, the place of opportunistic redefinition of self and community, but also, paradoxically, the site of an unearned plenitude of reward through spiritual venture and trust bordering on folly, asserted in the teeth of traditional prudence, temperance, and reasonable needs. It is for these reasons both thematically and structurally significant that Langland inserts the C 5 waking encounter between these two figurations of the economy of salvation, thus in effect anatomizing Will's work as an anomalous combination of labor and risk venture.

By assimilating the whole range of useful activities to the generic category of "work," and rendering the entire political community as its beneficiary, the 1388 Statute discloses a further consequence of its own logic: that while the occupations of the countryside are broadly exchangeable by individual fortune and election for those of the town or the gown, at the command of need they are also all in principle once again reducible to the universal imperative of the harvest.[38] The 1388 harvest provision defines all other crafts of the realm as in effect superstructures erected on an agrarian base, and renders obligation to that base as, at least in theory, never fully abrogated by another subsequent occupation.[39] The cultivation of the land thus becomes the original and therefore "true" occupation of humankind, with an inalienable prior claim forever upon its subjects. By this figurative logic, which renders the sustenance of the human material and social body paramount, need comes to be defined (as it was by the canonists) as the primal condition of humanity in history, one whose claims can never be transcended or renounced in life on earth—not even, in time of declared communal need, by an appeal to the spiritual imperative of Mary's "better part," as against that of her dutiful sister Martha.

The ethical and political consequences, both individual and communal, of this postulate—which projects a standoff between the claims of the state and those of the gospels upon the inalienable obligations of the individual human subject—are put directly at stake in Will's final waking encounter with Need, which forces the matter to the point of moral crisis. In the C version the poet underscores, through a newly created structural symmetry, the mutual implications of these two linked moral problematics of humankind in historical existence: the rival claims of spiritual vocation and Christian community. Will's waking encounter with Need, which befalls him in old age and occurs between the two last dreams of the long poem, acquires in the C-revision its formal counterpart and chiastic structural match: Will's C 5 waking encounter with Reason and Conscience, which befalls him in youth and is placed between the poem's first two visions. The new "autobiographical" episode in C is thus positioned as an individual apocalyptic confrontation, in time of harvest, that structurally forecasts the ultimate universal gathering-in of the entirety of the folk— structurally casting Will's work, its ambiguities and its moral responsibilities, as representative, metonymic, of those of the commune.

The obverse ideological postulate of the 1388 Statute, the incipiently criminal vagrant as the polar opposite of the community's representative "good subject," is likewise a hybrid construction, an uneasy ideological amalgam emerging in the period of nearly forty years between the first and second labor statutes. It has two key components, historically unrelated antecedents which are explicitly merged and subsumed, for the first time in parliamentary legislation, in the Cambridge Statute. One is the association of vagrancy with seditious violence, the other the suspicion of false professions of indigence by claimants of alms and charity—that is, the cultural reconstruction of the begging poor in negative rather than idealizing terms. The social character of the vagrant given the appearance of ideological stability by the 1388 Statute thus encompasses both of the twin dangers to the polity identified in late medieval political thought: force and fraud. In some respects it is highly artificial even to distinguish between these two aspects of the new account of vagrancy: especially in political discourse of the later fourteenth century the two are usually found together, as warp and weft of a single tissue of fear and blame. Yet they are at least heuristically separable; each strand has its own social genealogy and legal antecedents, and each has figured recently in critical studies of the discursive matrix within which Langland's accounts of these suspect groups, their activities and their representative value, may be understood. By tracing the threads of this fabric, we can more fully understand Langland's complex strategic motives in representing the poetic persona under the "shroudes" it afforded.

In understanding how the 1388 measure rather than its 1349 predecessor came to furnish the narrative material for the C 5 waking encounter, one must trace the genealogy of the shadow-subject of "labor" legislation created in the intervening generation: no longer the wage-demanding worker, but the putatively seditious or parasitic nonworker. If the 1349 Ordinance was a response to the plague and its economic effects, the 1388 Statute was a reaction to the Peasants' Revolt, its purported social causes and political effects, and both the language of the Statute and Langland's deployment of it in staging Will's apologia for "making" clearly register these motives. The formation of the begging vagrant as an ideological construct was recorded with notable clarity and fullness in commons petitions around the time of the Good Parliament of 1376—another politically pivotal moment, like the autumn of 1388, in which contested group interests and fears in the process of rapid and volatile realignment were briefly desublimated.

The incipiently rebellious and possibly even seditious character of mobile "labourers, artificers, and other servants," rather than their exorbitant wage demands per se, is the central rationale of a 1376 commons petition to the Good Parliament, which notes that the 1349 Ordinance has been ineffective at restraining workers' demands, largely because it fails to restrain their mobility. While professedly a request for additional measures to secure the enforcement of the 1349 legislation, the 1376 petition tellingly and fundamentally redefines the problem.[40] In effect, the 1376 petition, with its full social analysis of the cause and cure of a vagrant work force, may be regarded as the absent explanatory preface to the 1388 labor and vagrancy measures, for each of the new remedies it proposes—notably the prosecution of false takers of charity, as well as the restraint of the mobility of alms-seekers and mobile workers—is adopted by the Cambridge Parliament. The 1376 petition demands that stocks be constructed in every village to punish runaway servants and "stafstrikers"—the term in English appears both in the petition (otherwise in French) and in Langland's usage (C 9.159, "over-land strikares"). When such fugitives are apprehended, the petition demands, they should be held until "by oath or by compulsion" they give name, place of origin, and the name of the master they have deserted. Moreover, these are to be kept in stocks or in gaol until "they show themselves willing to submit and return to their own areas and serve their neighbors" according to the provisions of the labor ordinance.[41] In the same petition commons also urges the prohibition of alsmgiving to these "faitoures mendinantz" and beggars, and recommends that no one be allowed to give a strange fugitive a job, under penalty of a heavy fine. It demands that no laborers be taken into craft apprenticeship as long as the place in which they live has need of labor to maintain the cultivation of the soil. Though none of these proposed measures becomes law in 1376, every one of them is adopted into law by the 1388 Statute—a clear sign that the political forces that came into brief alignment in 1376, and first provided an extensively articulated and internally consistent voice, vision, and stage for the commons, were later, if only briefly, able to regroup and propound this agenda when unstable political leadership and rapid realignment of political constituencies again offered an opportunity to assert it.

Although they depart markedly from earlier parliamentary efforts to regulate the labor force, most of the commons' proposals of 1376 have broad and often ancient precedents in local jurisdictions; what is strikingly new in 1376 is not the restraints themselves, but the redefined legal interests they serve, and the nascent redefinitions of the polity and the economy they indicate. Originally part of the armature of provisions for returning fugitive bondsmen to the lords legally responsible for them, these measures now replace the lord-employer with the state itself as not only the enforcer but the beneficiary of the worker's labor obligation. As in the old fugitive laws, a wanderer when apprehended should not be released until he is cleared of "robbery or other felony," of which he is apparently to be considered automatically suspect. The prohibition against harboring a fugitive had existed since before the Conquest; this, along with the laws that forbade the harboring of a guest for more than three nights without his lord's recommendation, or dismissing such a man from one's custody before he is cleared of every charge for which he has been cited, was reaffirmed by William the Conquerer. The Assizes of Clarendon (1166) and Northampton (1176) instructed judges to enforce prohibitions on the harboring of strange guests.[42] The earlier, more strictly manorial, version of this provision exists because a lord who harbors or engages a man is himself legally responsible for the latter's conduct under his hospitality or service, and for administering justice.

The Commons' implicit revision of this measure in the 1376 petition substitutes for the master's responsibilities those of the apprehending bailiff or justice in the name of the law of the realm. Largely missing from the Commons' petitions, and from the 1388 Statute which adopts their proposals, is the primary sense that the master's rights as lord-landowner are the end or raison d'être of these ancient measures. Instead, the vagrant detained under the Statute is now seen as in effect everybody's "man"; commons gives no attention to restoring him to his lord, or using this customary practice to maintain customary rights. Instead it is the purpose of both

petition and statute to get the wanderer to work at something for the public good, "commun profit." This tendency to regard the apprehended wanderer as not only the state's problem, but also the state's servant rather than
his original master's, makes virtually its first appearance in law in the Ricardian statute. It becomes completely explicit by the time of Edward VI,
whose harsh enactments against vagabonds (1547) are in legal spirit its direct descendants. In the Tudor law, the runaway is not only to be branded
as such with a mark on the forehead, when he is returned to his birthplace is

to be nourished and kepte of the same Citie, Towne or Village in chaynes either at
the Comen workes in amending highe waies or other Comen worke, or from man
to man in order til theie which may beare be equally charged, *to be slave to the Cor-
poracon of the Citie or to the inhabitants of the Towne or Village*. (emphasis mine).[43]

The role of the lord-landowner in the old fugitive-servant laws is here
taken by the commonwealth, the political form of the social collectivity
itself. The commons petition of 1376 can therefore be seen as a proposal to
use some very ancient measures to enforce some new conceptions of the
individual's relation as worker to the state, and as an example illustrating a
newly political awareness of the wanderer as a national problem, for royal
rather than manorial or village justice. Moreover, it is now a problem of
public order, not merely of wage and price controls.

The tonal similarity between the commons' request in 1376 and the
1388 Statute is as striking as the measures proposed, and their suggested
use. The community is twice impoverished by the state of affairs it describes, the commons petition asserts: not only by workers' refusal to work
on the specified terms—or at all—but also by the practical impossibility of
collecting the fines set for violations.[44] Commons argues that it is not only
for the "great profit and ease" of the "commune" that "beggeres" should
be apprehended, but also for the *bone salvation de la Pees*, and a "sovereign
remedy and chastisement" of their "malice and riot." In sharp contrast to
the language of 1349, that of 1376 speaks of vagrants in the aggregate, as a
class large enough to impose its will on those who attempt to enforce the
earlier Ordinance's terms of employment. It is their intimidating mass as
well as their mobility that now prevents implementation of the terms of
1349, with the result that penalties and fines cannot in practice be applied
to offenders,

for they are taken into service immediately in new places, at such dear wages that
example and encouragement is afforded to all servants to depart into fresh places,

and go from master to master as soon as they are displeased about any matter. For fear of such flights, the commons now dare not challenge or offend their servants, but give them whatever they wish to ask. (Dobson, 73)

No longer regarded as incipient or temporarily delinquent workers in a state of disruptive transition, likely as individuals to turn to theft when unmoored from the constraints of their usual social ambit, wanderers as imagined by the 1376 petition are apparently believed to evade the law primarily for the sake of expressing defiance per se, and hence asserting their collective coercive power, rather than for personal or familial economic self-improvement. Commons' general analysis of the problem of a mobile work force includes a strong and pervasive presumption of guilt—if not of offense against the labor laws, then of other crimes which are by now far more vividly imagined. Guided not merely by "malice and riot"—violence here imagined as a coercive means of gaining a livelihood—some choose fraud rather than force, that of feigning neediness as "mendicant beggars" in order to avoid labor of any kind. It is here that idleness as a legal offense rather than merely a human condition or estate makes its first significant appearance in national regulation; it was to have a rich and varied imaginative career.

By the following year, anxiety about domestic disorder has become fear of treason. In 1377, at the first parliament of Richard's reign, the commons again protests the rebelliousness of villeins who refuse to do their customary services.[45] As once in the preceding petition, they are now repeatedly called "rebels" rather than "felons," and treated as an identifiable group or social category with well-formed interests and purposes of its own. The making and motives of a wanderer are now further elaborated into a full-blown imaginary narrative of conspiracy. Those who flee their customary places of service now not only have a common condition, lending itself to a general description that identifies them as a class, and a passive or latent inclination to violence when challenged, but also have taken on active conspiratorial designs and the resources—not only financial but legal and documentary—to sustain them. It is feared that "unless a speedy remedy is applied" either war will arise within the realm or "the villeins and tenants will, to avenge themselves on their lords, adhere to foreign enemies in the event of sudden invasion." Commons explicitly fears the importation of the Jacquerie (1358), because of the "confederation of villeins against their lords." Those who depart their agrarian occupations not only leave "the corn unharvested . . . to the serious damage of all the commons" as well as the "destruction of [lords'] inheritances and estates," but are considered inclined to treasonous political leanings, and they are thought to have amassed large sums of money for their purposes, as well as access to legal instruments for pursuing their cause. Again "the King and council of Parliament" are placatory, and a commission of inquiry is appointed to look into the matter of "rebeales" among the refractory villeins. The use of Domesday Book presentations as bases for claims of freedom is disallowed, but nothing specific is done about the claims of sedition.[46]

The 1388 Statute was, it appears, exactly the legislation that both the 1376 and 1377 petitions demanded, but had failed to obtain until after the 1381 rebellion, which had served to confirm many of the commons' perceptions of the inclination and capacity for systematic violence and seditious confederation behind the facade of free and mobile labor. The social analyses in the petitions of 1376 and 1377 help to explain, for example, as nothing in its 1349 antecedent does, the presence in the 1388 "labor" statute of a clause explicitly mandating the disarmament of those to whom its controls apply: "No servant of husbandry or labourer or servant of an artificer or victualler [may] carry henceforth baslard, dagger or sword, on pain of forfeiture of the same, except in time of war for defense of the realm, and then by survey of the arrayers for the time being" (c.6).[47] The revolt of 1381 was clearly a pivotal moment in the passage of the commons' imagination of social ills from generalized anxiety in the 1370s to an operative structure of legal sanctions in the Cambridge Statute.

But if the events of 1381 served dramatically to corroborate one half of the new myth of the vagrant—the concerted and intimidating force latent in the populace of mobile lay workers—the other half of this myth, the suspicion of fraud in these wanderers, had a more diffuse and overdetermined history. As the petition of 1376 shows, the belief that destitution was widely and falsely claimed as a cover for idleness underlay the provisions of the 1388 statute to place unauthorized wanderers in gaol or the stocks, and to return them to their home parishes, there to receive such charity as they could legitimately claim, in a neighborhood where the false pretenses under which they were presumed to act would be known and their falsity exposed. It was the threat of fraud rather than force in the vagrant that made this figure in all senses a critical representative, a kind of metonymy, of the deepest contraditions of later fourteenth-century political, ecclesiological, and ethical as well as economic discourses.

This second half of the myth pursues, in the form of an imaginary narrative, the "problem" of social mobility as a threat to a fundamental enabling myth of community itself, the key premise by which it sublimated social conflict: the organic and manifest intelligibility of both individual identity and the form of the social order as an integrated whole. The anonymity of the stranger, the permutability of social identity, the potential for dissimulation, and as a consequence the dissolution of "estates" proprieties and the collapse of "real" differentiation into a plangent rhetorical cacophony of professions of need—in short, the replacement of visible "real" structure and intent with universal hypocrisy—all these are seen to follow from the failure of local jurisdictions to control and restrain within local boundaries the laborer in search of better conditions; they are, in short, heralds and indices of the failure of the "organic" figuration of society itself.[48] The obverse aspect of the defiance and seditious inclinations of "sturdy beggars" and "stafstrikers" was the feigned abjection of "faitours mendinantz," fraudulent seekers after alms whose numbers were believed to include not only able-bodied layfolk who purportedly chose to live by this means without laboring at all, but also a motley assortment of pretenders to religious vocation and enterprise, from cynical friars to hermits "unholy of werkes" to palmers, pilgrims, pardoners, and other *operarii* and con artists of the spirit. If the threat of force from a heterogeneous mass of vagrants inspired commons' fear, the fraud imputed to them justified not merely commons' indignation, but a soberer concern, less easily put to rest: that these wanderers, by preying upon the sympathies of the individual and the charitable motives and resources of the community, violated a far more fundamental trust than the physical security of body and property.

Fraudulent begging mocked a key moral axiom and, even more centrally, a constitutive imaginative and cognitive practice, of the community: its capacity, inculcated by the church and depended upon by the secular powers, locally and nationally, to discern in unaccommodated human form the image of divinity, and by its charitable response, according to the Gospel principle articulated in the Acts of Mercy ("insofar as you have done thus to the least of these my brethen you have done so unto me"), to honor its creator, and acquire a blessing. To the extent that the fraudulent claimant of alms was successful, his fictive profession of *indigentia* harmed the entire community by falsely appropriating its resources, taking from the *potentes* by deception, and from the *impotentes*, the genuinely poor— especially those who simply could not live on what they could earn under adverse economic conditions but who were ashamed to proclaim their condition rather than struggle quietly and "show the fair outward"—by robbing them of the alms they needed to get by. Fraudulent claims of need, even if no more than a pervasive suspicion activated at the moment any person or group asserted a claim on others' goods, in effect appropriated the community's discursive capital, corroding the shared premise of mutuality in charity, by which the community both ameliorated on discrete occasions, and continued to justify in principle, the unequal distribution of goods according to "estate."

Fraudulent appeals to need thus implicitly called into question the benign fiction by which society professed to sustain itself as a community: its sense of its own self-transparency and moral legibility as an organic whole, within which the allocation of economic goods and social prerogatives was rationalized in terms of the functional differentiation of interdependent groups—as Langland puts the case, "euery man helpe ooþer for hennes shul we alle" (B 11.211; C 12.118). In principle, a claim of "need" might be considered at least a momentary social solvent, an appeal to the requirement of social mutuality that recalls the giver's ultimate commonality of human estate with the importuning recipient and reduces social distinction to a universal "liminal" condition. It also evokes a key philosophical and theological postulate: the presumed primal state of humankind categorically considered in its radical insufficiency to itself to effect its own restoration of its image-likeness to the divine. To assert such an appeal falsely is thus to disrupt key origin myths of the social contract, and also to turn to personal advantage a resonant memorial image of the divine likeness in human form, in a manner almost sacrilegious. Yet in practice, as medieval terminology makes clear, the fundamental antonym to *pauper* is not *dives* but *potens*; the ritual adversion to "need" in sociopolitical discourse, and the sanctioned forms of social response to it, tended in fact to patrol and maintain rather than dissolve the social boundaries that secured the distribution of economic and symbolic goods, and of social power.[49] A false assertion of need both depends on and parodies social good faith, mocking the truth of social appearances that are held to represent a deeper and common truth behind the vicissitudes and diversities of fortune. With such fraud, an individual's "estate," and hence his or her implicit entitlements, became radically unknowable, and thus returned in farcical form, as counters in a debased game, a fictive simulacrum of society's "real" but vanished structure—in short, as a trade in its representations. This is the extended logic according to which an inquiry into an offense against the most recent labor legislation can become in Langland's hands a platform for reconceiving in terms of work the value of making fictions.

None of this is to say that commons' imagination of vagrants was a factually accurate account of the diverse motives and conditions of actual alms-seekers and beggars in the later fourteenth century. It seems rather to have been an ideologically interested narrative by-product—durable precisely because it served so many discursive purposes at once—functioning both to explain and to mask the various economic dislocations of the period, some of them the demographic consequences of the plague, some the results of landowners' responses to the "price scissors" whose bite had been increasing since the 1320s.[50] It does, however, suggest why this half of the later fourteenth-century myth of the vagrant, the perceived pervasiveness of "faitours mendinantz" in the society, was from the outset a highly overdetermined discourse, ramifying simultaneously and unpredictably throughout ecclesiological, theological, and moral as well as parliamentary thought and vocabulary.

It also begins to indicate why the longer term consequences of the idea of "faitours mendinantz" for both political and religious thought were profound: it is a key construction in the change from "estate" to "work" as the main term of social identity and membership in a community—and in the ultimate simultaneous devaluation of *otium* as a class prerogative of both the propertied and learned. Unlike belief in the violence and conspiratorial capacities of vagrants as "masterless men," which seems to have been confined in England to the applied secular political discourses of the period, the heterogeneous image of those called "faitours"—and, virtually uniquely by Langland, "lolleres"—was from its first appearance a "crossover" discourse, at once secular and religious in source and continued utility, and fed throughout its history by several tributaries.

It acknowledges several genealogical forebears: controversies over "novel" religious orders and rules, never silent since the twelfth century, and much increased in volume by the foundation of the orders of friars; polemics over property and poverty generated by conflicts both between and within religious orders; satires surrounding the irregular behaviors of ruled religious of every order, especially the "gyrovagus," who wandered beyond both rule and fixed geographical place; ecclesiastical condemnation of unsanctioned or eccentric individual religious callings, especially hermits; the later medieval development of allegedly "mercenary" forms of religious occupation, such as chantry appointments and various forms of paid "piecework" by unbeneficed clergy, including the employment of clerics in civil posts requiring documentary literacy, from copyists to chancellors; the proliferation of forms of literate occupation that seemed to "sell" God-given wisdom, knowledge, or verbal skill, as for example by university teachers or lawyers. All these practices, and the increasingly elaborated polemics surrounding them, contributed as much to the complex condemnation of idleness and charges of fraudulent claims to entitlements and prerogatives as did the enactment of sanctions against idleness by landowners in their own interests in the local and national apparatus of government. In other words, the nascent "work ethic" and increased blaming of indigence widely remarked in the later middle ages was not simply generated by the assertion of "secular" economic interests and political ideologies with an insistence that gradually overwhelmed earlier "religious" ideals of virtuous poverty, in both its elected form as a clerical ideal and in its lay form as the patient suffering of an involuntary condition. It was from the beginning a conflict not only between but within secular and ecclesiastical discourses, and the question of the "productivity" or "idleness" of various mediatory and symbolic activities was at all points a weapon in these contests.

Fortunately for Langland scholars, it is no longer necessary to trace *ab ovo* the several antecedents of the complex discourse of "faitours mendinantz," or demonstrate their general pertinence to the poem; we will advert to several such studies below. What has not yet been sufficiently explored, however, is the formal, generic, and performative as well as thematic or ideational importance of these for the poem, and especially why and how they are not merely invoked as terms of value but turned to self-referential uses by the poet, as part of an effort to define the distinctive and anomalous status of his literary and his spiritual enterprise. Yet paradoxically it is here that the compound legal and discursive genesis of the Cambridge Statute concerning labor and vagrancy is most instructive. For Langland deploys the Statute in his fiction in such a way as both to exploit and to dismantle its monologic facade.

The 1388 Statute is the first parliamentary enactment fully to incorporate into its prohibitions and enforcement mechanisms the imputation of both force and fraud to the vagrant. The profound heterogeneity of the concerns that led to it, and of the enforcement components from which it was assembled, were rhetorically well submerged in the comprehensive provisions of the Cambridge Statute, especially by the device of the "internal passport" as universal textual warrant of social identity. As we have seen, however, the apparently monologic authority and broad synthetic imagination from which the Statute seems to speak was born not of overwhelming consensus but of precisely the opposite: a brief moment of intersection among divergent interests, and strategic efforts to forge political alliances between forces inherently at odds. It was only when both king and Appellants, in the effort to consolidate their respective positions in the wake of the Merciless Parliament, were forced to vie for the support of the commons that parliament would appear to endorse, in a comprehensive program of national legal sanctions, the gentry's diverse fears and hybrid ideological analysis of the ills that afflicted the realm. These evanescent political circumstances alone gave to the enactments of the Cambridge Parliament an appearance of wide and solid consensus that its constituent discourses did not in fact possess. Yet at this brief and critical moment in 1388, the composite narrative etiology of the suspect vagrant inscribed in the several clauses of the Statute had acquired a kind of rough dynamic stability, sufficient at least to obviate the need for prefatory rationales in the text of the enactment. All that was required by the Cambridge Parliament was the enactment of the legal protocols that would translate diverse suspicions and fears into the single-minded policing mechanisms and juridical instruments of prosecution. It is that seemingly unified and monologic legal authority that Langland adapts to his own dialogic purposes.

In a final *mise-en-abŷme* of the poem's thematic concerns with social as well as eschatological "treuthe," and with the recurrent question of whether salvation history most resembles the economy of earned recompense and "right," or that of gift and grace, privilege and "honor," Langland stages his ultimate representation of the art of representation itself, of "making," as an incipient prosecution under the 1388 Statute, on grounds of idleness. The waking interlude exhaustively applies to Will's condition every possible pertinent clause of the Cambridge Statute, and thereby not only reactivates the multiplicity of discourses that had led to its formation, but evokes the specific political and cultural moment in which both the acts of the Cambridge Parliament and the C-revision were articulated. Only the 1388 Statute, and nothing before it, assembles the entire array of authorities both lay and ecclesiastical, and of enforcement protocols and social mythologies that are brought into play in the fictive staging of the C 5 apologia. Langland captures—and anatomizes—late medieval "visionary legislation" at its most grandiose and homiletic, and applies to it a kind of homeopathic cure. If the Cambridge Parliament gave to the several disparate voices, interests, and enforcement protocols that it incorporated the only brief monologic textual form and performative mode they were to attain in the fourteenth century, Langland's imaginative recasting of them exposes once more the diversity of voices with which they speak, and sets them in dialogue. It is to the form of that intertextual engagement in C 5.1–104 that we now turn.

II. Arrested Development: The C 5 Waking Interlude and the Defense of Idleness

> To dig I am unable, to beg I am ashamed.
> Luke 16:3

> When you are arrested, do not worry about what you are to say; when the time comes, the words you need will be given you; for it is not you who will be speaking: it will be the spirit of your Father speaking in you.
> Matthew 10:19–20

The C 5 waking interlude is one of the most densely overdetermined and intertextually saturated passages in any version of the poem. On the framework of an interrogation under the Cambridge Statute, Langland builds an episode that reorients the poetic persona and the architecture of the poem around the question of social productivity and idleness—and away from two other ideal images already deeply inscribed in the poem's episodic structure: of poverty as an image of human dependency and purity; and of "estate" as a category of communal participation. Although its wit is richly self-contained and topically complex, the effects of this new encounter also extend both locally and throughout the poem, drawing into unprecedently sharp focus the problematic relation between the social and rhetorical identity of the "maker" and the representative claims of the poem. The reframing of the persona of the maker under interrogation offers a revised account of both poetic structure and of the nature and place of literary production and knowledge in human affairs, and its relation to the economy and history of salvation. For the first time in any version of the poem, Langland stops apologizing for being a vernacular maker, in the very act of depicting a concession of the almost-indefensible character of the enterprise.

To enter fully into the impacted wit of the episode, it will be useful to distinguish three separate dimensions of its operation: the intertextual, the mimetic, and the structural. The heuristic separation of these aspects is of course at all points highly artificial, since each supports the others, but the strategic isolation of each for expository purposes has two further critical advantages. First, it displays to analysis a more pervasive feature of Langland's poetic technique: the literary strategies of this episode present in highly concentrated form an instance of one of his most deeply characteristic procedures at work, the elevation of a seemingly fortuitous or peripheral preoccupation into a conscious principle of form. Second, it allows us to grasp the historical as well as individual poetic resonance of this fictive act of self-justification.

MAKING THE LAWS: THE INTERTEXTUALITIES OF REGULATION

In the preceding section we noted the three clauses of the 1388 Statute— all of them new to national labor legislation with the Cambridge Parliament—that form the explicit premises for Reason's "arating" of Will. We must now examine more closely the way the Statute informs not only the fictive occasion and the course of Reason's interrogation but also Will's replies, which are otherwise seemingly inapposite at several points. But while the Statute defines one intertextual matrix of the episode, Langland also from the outset introduces into Will's responses in this scene a scriptural matrix for self-representation, a subtextual as well as intertextual reference point, that has an effect throughout the passage much like the explicit "*contra*, quod I" of so many of Will's encounters with authority—yet considerably more complexity than this open verbal announcement of formal debate. Will's scriptural self-presentation becomes a kind of counterpoint and countertext to the Statute, serving as the unspoken ground of his paradoxical self-assurance, and enabling his simultaneous compliance with and defiance of the terms of value so massively articulated by the parliamentary measure under which he is initially apprehended. The scene is suspended between statute and gospel authority as between two magnetic poles of authority; in the course of the episode we watch these begin to pull the "maker's" enterprise into a new and precarious stability and legitimacy. We can best pursue the effects of this contraposition of the parliamentary and scriptural construction of individual probity by following the dialogic process by which they exert their claims on Will.

The season and place of the encounter immediately ground the application of the draft-labor clause of the Statute: it befalls Will "in a hote hervest," when, as we have seen, those "of no great account" not otherwise visibly occupied about activities needful to the community are liable

to "be forced to serve at cutting, gathering and bringing in the corn." To
the eye of Reason as enforcer of the Statute, Will's signal characteristic,
which initially attracts suspicion, is his idleness, his lack of any discernible occupation. His residence in Cornhill, a district that was a site of the
stocks used to punish offenders against the London ordinance that, as we
have seen, was in part the prototype of the Cambridge Statute, gives an
added pointedness to Reason's inquiry about Will's occupation. The list of
useful tasks that Reason rehearses as possible occupations for Will belong
chiefly to the grain harvest (C 5.13-17) and exemplify the modeling of the
totality and mutuality of the "comune" upon the figure of the agrarian village that we have noted as an implicit, and implicitly nostalgic, political
image in the Statute. Those few tasks not directly applied to bringing in the
grain and securing it against thieves are in effect other "support services"
for an agrarian village: "service" or song in a parish church (12), making
shoes or clothes for workers, keeping sheep or geese, hedging and harrow-
ing of fields (18–19) — these stand metonymically for "eny other kynes craft
þat to þe comune nedeth," by which Will might reciprocally benefit those
"þat byleve the fynden." Will's urban habitation affords him no protection
from the draft-labor clause of the 1388 Statute, for unlike its 1349 counterpart, the later measure has no regard for rank, envisioning the draft not
only of migrant agrarian workers but even of those "of whose craft or mistery men have no great need in time of harvest"; the provision in principle
dissolves the distinction between town and country labor, and hence the
traditional liberating exemption of *Stadtluft*. The fundamental premise is
clear: legitimate activity, urban or rural, is to be judged by the same uniform standard and must discernibly deliver social value. Reason speaks on
behalf of the entire political community in imposing this standard; he acts,
in other words, not for the municipality but the realm.

Will's response seems at first an appeal to physical incapacity as a
ground for exemption:

> Y am to wayke to worche with sykel or with sythe
> And to long, lef me, lowe to stoupe,
> To wurche as a werkeman eny while to duyren. (23–25)

At one level this remark functions as a self-referential "signature," adverting to other representations of the distinctive bodily appearance of the
poetic persona as exceptionally tall or "long."[51] It thus activates the strategically enigmatic relation between the historical and fictive identities of

the poet, drawing the question of the maker's enterprise and the probity of his occupation into the field of reference of all that follows. Yet because it invokes a bodily notation of the poet already established in earlier versions and other (mostly narratively "later") episodes in the poem, its referential reach extends beyond the immediate fictive occasion and violates its boundaries. Adverting to, and depending referentially upon, the previously written and disseminated status of the poem—as that known body of life and work to which this intervention is said to be prior, the originary moment that will ultimately explain what follows (and is already written and known), this episode declares a metapoetic purpose, announcing its status as a kind of commentary on what is compositionally past, yet still lies in the narrative and authorially biographical "future," the ensuing sequence of dream visions that constitute the work we are reading. For insofar as it is cast within the provisions and assumptions of the 1388 Statute, which exempted the physically handicapped from the universal imperative to labor, it is more than faintly ridiculous—and knowingly, hilariously so: the inconvenience of tall stature for stoop-labor is not likely to have convinced an enforcer of any version of the labor laws to exempt a healthy, strong, and youthful man (lines 6, 11) from the imperative to work, and hence to allow his implicit claim upon public benefit or charity. The reference of Will's reply is pointedly and wryly in excess of the occasion, speaking around the boundaries of the fictive prosecution to another kind of performative occasion and mode. As one sign of this referential excess, it introduces one of the main Gospel subtexts of the episode, and of the "maker's" revised self-representation in C.

Will's plea is reminiscent of the rationalization of the Dishonest Steward of the parable (Luke 16:2ff). Commanded to render his accounts (*redde rationem villicationis tue*), the steward faces the certain consequences of his maladroit management of his lord's property, and, in expectation of his dismissal, considers his options for a "liflode" in future. In his own eyes a man of letters, not a manual laborer, he anticipates status degradation after his dismissal by his lord: *fodere non valeo, mendicare erubesco*, "to dig I am unable, to beg I am ashamed" (Luke 16:3). Instead of either of these unthinkable alternatives, he resolves upon a course of chicanery in accounting in favor of his lord's debtors, in an effort to secure them as new patrons in the future:

I know what I must do, to make sure that, when I have to leave, there will be people to give me house and home. (Luke 16:3-4)

Will's response invokes in a few allusive strokes a scenario of desperate itinerant currying of favor and hoped-for patronage, as parabolic sanction for his own insistence, soon to be stated explicitly, that he not suffer the indignity of manual rather than literate work. And like the Steward of the parable, Will at the end of this waking episode receives that sanction, in the form of a similarly absurd and unlooked-for reprieve.

The parable of the Dishonest Steward was one of the most difficult and vexing to medieval commentators, for in the master's commendation of the steward's "wise" or "astute" strategem it was hard to avoid the implication that chicanery itself, the making of an untruthful record, was being rewarded. As a teaching of Jesus offered in the hearing of the Pharisees, it seems to have derived its point from this context of its utterance: by averting the expected absolute denigration of money, and by turning an instance of worldly prudence to a paradoxical figuration of the route to heavenly reward, it renders an anological relation where an absolute distinction was anticipated, complicating the way in which the anecdote has meaning. The parable was evidently as difficult, either to use or to dismiss outright, for medieval glossators as for the Pharisees: the one kernel of edification that could be securely derived from the enigmatic anecdote was the counsel to deploy worldly wealth (the problematic "mammon of unrighteousness") for the purchase of "an eternal home" (Luke 16:9). This was commonly read by medieval interpreters as a counsel to bestow wealth in charity and works of mercy, and (by extension) upon ritually poor religious for intercessory prayers for heavenly favor.[52]

While the Latin text of *fodere non valeo* is not cited in any of the three generally received versions of the poem, it does occur in the "Z-text" in a thematically similar context.[53] In a passage that seems to show some admixture of influence from its counterpart passage in both the B and C traditions, "Robert the robbere on *reddite* locut," and acknowledges his dilemma: he has not wherewith to restore what he owes as restitution for his thefts, an act that is the precondition of his obtaining mercy.[54] In the Z-manuscript only, he laments further that he cannot by his labors make up the sum, "For *fodere non valeo*, so feble ar my bones" (Z 5.142). The C 5 passage (and, as glossators painstakingly insisted, the parable) does not concern primarily restitution of ill-gotten gains for the sake of divine forgiveness, but rather the broader imperative of social mutuality that demands that all labor in some vocation as the condition by which God's creatures use worldly goods to acquire merit in their maker's sight, but the verbal prompt for both concerns is similar: the imperative, *redde/reddite*, to render an account of one's actions.[55] The Z passage, like the C 5 addition, also involves a questionable claim of physical incapacity for work, made by someone who is to all appearances perfectly able to labor; the robber and the loller, as we have seen, share a type-cast role in the political ideology of vagrancy, as the idle who prefer force or fraud to "leel labor," of which both are physically capable. The lord's imperative to the steward, *redde rationem villicationis tue*, was the topic of a famous 1388 sermon and of many of the C additions.[56] The steward's excuse, *fodere non valeo*, had long and strong associations with clerical privilege, invoking the traditional identity by which the *litteratus* was indistinguishable from someone of divine profession—and hence had a rich tradition of use, often ironic, in clerical apologiae.[57]

But if Will invokes here the first of the key counterpoised Gospel subtexts that inform his self-presentation here and sporadically throughout the poem, Reason shows no sign of engaging his reply directly, either as literal claim of incapacity or as a figuration of clerical identity—at least not yet. Setting aside for the moment the issue of whether Will's stature counts as a physical disability, he puts the question Will seems already to have anticipated in a more direct and uncompromising form—for by this point both are operating quite clearly within the discourse and protocols of the Cambridge Statute, and each anticipates the other in exploring its applicability to Will's case. Reason follows the enforcement conditions of the 1388 measure to the letter, methodically listing the two remaining allowable circumstances that would exempt a layman from the terms of its application: has Will either sufficient land to live by without wage labor, or an inheritance that confers an equivalent level of support (26)? Lacking either of these, only one other exception could legitimately exempt Will from toil—the one Will has already implicitly introduced:

Or [art thow] broke, so may be, in body or in membre
Or ymaymed throw som myshap, whereby thow myhte be excused?
(33–34).

Will answers directly neither question about his inheritance or income, however, venturing instead as an exempting condition still another factor, his (clerical) education. In effect, he here makes the claim that *fodere non valeo* makes for the steward: he is by upbringing and status—in effect, by prior customary occupation—rather than by income level or physical condition, unfit for manual labor. His response seems at first so wide of the point that it is momentarily comically ambiguous whether he means to cast his schooling as a kind of inheritance or as a "myshap" that has maimed him. Couched in the form of a condensed life-narrative, his reply implicitly defines his status as constituted less by formal profession than by education, as a "vocation of desire."[58] Yet by framing his claim to the status of *literatus* in terms of education from early childhood rather than ordination or rule, he cannily and preemptively addresses the one remaining circumstance by which the Statute could force his degradation (as Will sees it) to agrarian rather than urban or literate labors: since his schooling began in youth, he was never engaged in "service of husbandry" before the age of twelve—a childhood condition which could, under the statute (c.5), invalidate whatever occupation he now claims against Reason's implicit efforts to draft him into harvest work.

Having made a spurious claim that his stature and "weakness" is an exempting disability, he now argues that his youthful schooling and the "long clothes" to which it still entitles him are an exempting privilege.[59] The labor and vocation in which he is entitled to gain his "lyflode" are, implicitly, those of a cleric, and for good measure Will cites St. Paul, *in eadem vocacione in qua vocati estis* (1 Cor. 7:20). The Pauline axiom belongs to the apostle's summary discussion of Christian vocation and spiritual condition under a pagan political regime; the cited text pertains specifically to the *servus*, the slave or servant, and the relation between his legal status and his identity before God:

Were you a slave when you were called? Do not let that trouble you; but if a chance of liberty should come, take it. For the man who as a slave received the call to be a Christian is the Lord's freedman, and, equally, the free man who received the call is a slave in the service of Christ. You were bought at a price; do not become the slaves of men. (1 Cor. 7:20–23)

Langland uses the same Latin axiom in the A-version of Wit's account of Dowel (A 10.110). Wit adduces it, along with more of its Pauline context concerning the proprieties of lay marriage and celibacy, as an adage counseling stability of vocation and estate, and directs it especially against *gyrovague* religious,

> be romberis þat rennen aboute
> Fro religioun to religioun, reccheles ben þei euere. (A 10.105–6)

In C 5, the apostle's axiom is positioned to yield more of its contextual wit, since the incipient prosecution of Reason entails the issue of whether

Will is by upbringing, if not by legal status, an agrarian "servant" who can be returned under the Statute to his primal condition.[60] In its structural role as a new proem to the poem's second vision, the C 5 waking dialogue further exploits the wit of this claim, for the status degradation from cleric to agrarian laborer that Will here attempts to forestall is in effect enacted and wholly transformed in the ensuing dream of the lay worker Piers as Truth's spokesman and loyal servant. Piers's "liflode" in effect transcends the claims here debated, namely that "truth" can be served in verbal labor only by those of clerical status. The new C 5 episode thus proleptically and explicitly reorients the poem away from the argument that the proprieties of verbal intervention may be exemplified and policed solely by ordained clerics, declaring outright the anomalous scope of the poem's address and discursive ambitions by placing it among the useful crafts of the field, which is where, the waking episode implicitly claims, it rightly belongs.

Following the Pauline citation, Will's life-narrative exceeds the scope of Reason's pointed question, but continues in its preemptive relation to the Statute, as he now implicitly acknowledges the more conventional medieval application of the Pauline text, as illustrated by its use in the A-version citation of it, to those religious wanderers who stray from their social estate and chosen vocation, "In ensaumple þat suche shulde not renne aboute" (A 10.110). Having in his own eyes successfully established that he is not subject to the legal requirement of manual labor, Will must now claim, against all appearances, that he is not a vagrant. Turning his life-narrative from his past clerical education and habit to his present *habitus*, Will now adds—seemingly gratuitously, as well as paradoxically—"*And so y leue yn London and opelond bothe*" (44; emphasis mine). Just as Will's rehearsal of his childhood education has at first seemed oblique to Reason's question about his inheritance or disability, so now his reference to his double, or itinerant, habitation, both in London and "opelond," seems both excessive to the occasion and pointless to the legal issue of whether he is an "idle man" under the Statute. Yet in fact it addresses precisely the latter point, by anticipating its penalty: "beggars unable to serve" must "remain in the cities and towns where they are dwelling at the time of the proclamation of this Statute," or, "if the people of the said cities or towns will not or cannot suffice to find [provide for] them," they must "withdraw to the other towns within the hundred, rape, or wapentake, or to the towns where they were born, within forty days after the said proclamation be made, and dwell there continually for their lives" (c.7). Will's reply thus appears to be an effort to defeat the statute's most fundamental premise: that everyone ultimately belongs to a single local habitation, presumptively identified with a native place, which serves both as a fixed workplace with a primary claim upon his or her labors, and as the venue charged with the support of its disabled indigents. Ecclesiastical charity administration, like the parliamentary labor laws, is enlisted by the Cambridge Statute in the state's interest in stabilizing wanderers both able-bodied and "maimed." By claiming that his regular "place" is not single but multiple, Will in the first instance attempts to defeat the determination of a proper "place" to which he can be committed if found indigent. Yet with the same gesture—"*and so*"— he also claims the deeper legitimacy of his apparently irregular and vagrant existence: Paul's injunction is taken by Will specifically to *authorize*, not to condemn, the "vocation" and manner of living he now confesses.[61]

To this point, it should be noted, Reason has not recognized Will as a cleric of any kind: the questions posed thus far have been aimed solely at establishing the lay category applicable to Will's conduct and condition— is he a laborer, able-bodied or disabled, or the possessor of sufficient landed or inherited income for his "lyflode"? To be sure, the first of the agrarian labors Reason offers for Will's acceptance—"Can thow seruen . . . or syngen in a churche?"—includes the possibility that Will holds at least minor orders, but Reason does not further assume that whatever "churche"-service Will might perform exempts him from the purview of the Statute and the moral authority Reason articulates in upholding it.[62] As a consequence, neither does Reason "arate" Will up to this point specifically as a religious wanderer from a rule or vocation, a *gyrovagus*, although much of Will's self-description and self-explanation invites precisely this identification. It is solely Will's apparent idleness that attracts Reason's censure and incipient prosecution:

> . . . For an ydel man þow semest,
> A spendour þat spene mot or a spille-tyme,
> Or beggest thy bylyue aboute at men hacches
> Or faytest vppon Frydayes or feste-dayes in churches,
> The which is lollarne lyf, þat lytel is preysed
> There ryhtfulnesse rewardeth ryht as men deserueth:
> *Reddit unicuique iuxta opera sua.* (27–32)[63]

Reason here names Will's manner of living with exactly the term Will himself has used to describe his visible *habitus* in the opening lines of the episode: he lives in Cornhill "yclothed as a lollere," although "lytel ylet by . . . Amonges lollares of Londone and lewede eremytes" for having "made of tho men as resoun me tauhte" (2–5).[64] Reason thus takes Will for what he appears to be, a fraudulent idler who begs rather than works for his "lyflode," while Will both invites and evades a double association: on the one hand he dwells among his neighbor "lollares," whose manner of living is apparently identical with his, though it is ridiculed in Will's "makings" of them; on the other, while reason is claimed by Will as the tutelary spirit of those "makings," as an interrogatory figure Reason does not in any way acknowledge Will's professed discipleship to his lore.

Will's defensive "autobiography" now turns to *apologia*, as he describes (45–52) and defends in categorical terms (53–69) his manner of living. He is an itinerant performer of prayers—in effect a clerical pieceworker—of no fixed abode, who does not accumulate what he gains in payment for his services. For this activity he explicitly claims the cleric's civil privilege of exemption not only from manual labor but also from military service[65]—and at last answers, figuratively and wittily, Reason's long-evaded question of his inheritance, with another scriptural support: *Dominus pars hereditatis mee* (Ps. 15:5). This Latin tag could serve as the "neck-verse," by which a cleric could plead benefit of clergy by reading a passage from the Psalms in Latin, and it is adduced in that function elsewhere in the poem:

> *Dominus pars hereditatis mee* is a murye verset
> That haþ take fro Tybourne twenty stronge þeues,
> Ther lewed þeues ben lolled vp; loke how þei be saued!
>   (B 12.189–90; cf C 14.128–30)[66]

This verse was also used in the tonsuring of clerics, giving it a double declarative force in this context in proclaiming Will's clerical self-identification.[67]

CITATION AS MIMESIS

Will's peroration in his own defense now turns from a specific self-justification to categorical self-righteousness (63–81), and an increasingly unmoored sense of injured merit. In the process, Langland's citational and allusive strategy takes on added mimetic complexity. Will's discourse in the latter half of the episode is intelligible not simply as argument, but as a kind of argument that belongs to a recognizable generic voice or position—or to several at once. As Will goes momentarily on the offensive, Langland prompts us, by several signals, to become aware not simply of the authoritative ground of Will's citations, but of the investments and self-identification implicit in them, to turn our attention more fully to the enigmatic person who wields these claims in his own defense, and to the mimetic techniques that align his voice and professional identity with those of culturally authorized speakers. From this point the episode turns from incipient prosecution under the Statutes against idleness and vagrancy to a more fundamental and more indeterminable question; as Harry Bailly puts it to "Chaucer": "what man artow?" Will's specifically literary affinities with other notable plaintiffs, in contemporary life and in art, becomes increasingly audible as his own discourse becomes more plaintive.

No longer content to rest his case on the binary differentiation of social functions between those "crouned" (in this context, tonsured) and the laity, Will now proceeds to differentiate among the hereditary states of the laity: free birth in wedlock is a proper condition of entry to the clergy, to be firmly distinguished from both low birth and illegitimacy, which should not only disqualify one from a clerical vocation but also doom those in these conditions to serving "lordes kyn." Nowadays it is all otherwise, Will recklessly continues:

> Ac sythe bondemen barnes haen be mad bisshopes
> And barnes bastardus haen be erchedekenes
> And soutares and here sones for suluer han be knyhtes
> And lordes sones here laboreres and leyde here rentes to wedde . . . .
> And monkes and moniales, þat mendenantes sholde fynde,
> Imade here kyn knyhtes and knyhtes-fees ypurchased,
> Popes and patrones pore gentel blood refused
> And taken Symondes sones seyntwarie to kepe,
> Lyf-holynesse and loue hath be longe hennes,
> And wol, til hit be wered out, or oþerwise ychaunged. (70–81)

Most commentators have recognized in this little harangue a characteristically Langlandian move and voice, a miniature run of "evil-times complaint." Fewer have noticed that it also associates the utterance and the speaker specifically with *gyrovague* satire, especially its technique of castigating the vices and sociopolitical perversions of clergy and court through the voice and rhetorical posture of one deeply implicated in them—and hence a voice that in effect positions both itself and its audience rhetorically within the slippery and treacherous moral and semantic universe it represents.[68] But none to my knowledge has considered it necessary to account for the specific performative force of this tirade as it operates within the fictive episode and literary act, and its specific effect at this point within the dialogue. Most often these remarks have been examined for clues to the persona's, and possibly the poet's, identity: for example, does this harping upon bastards, which similarly (and with equally tenuous local motivation) obsesses Wit in the third vision, indicate something of the poet's own raw animus and resentment toward this condition, either as himself a bastard or as someone supplanted in his inheritance or thwarted in his ambitions by a person of such estate?[69] While the desire to determine the historical address and tonality of these remarks and gestures is not altogether off the mark, it can be pursued only through, not around, the fictive vehicle, mode, and occasion, in which it scatters very complex—and high-comic—effects. I propose that this passage functions mimetically in several ways at once, and serves to focus and identify the mimetic energies at play throughout the episode. It also, as I shall ultimately propose, serves to identify more clearly the rhetorical position, strategies, and function of the persona throughout the poem and thereby renders this episode a sign of poetic closure for the project.

In the first instance, as I have indicated, this is a genre performance, a brief miming of a satiric tirade against the dissolution of "traditional" status differentiation, and hence of semantic stability itself, by flattery, favor, patronage, and cash—the classic topics, and in the classic voice and rhetorical mode, of goliardic art. As Mann notes, it activates the fundamental comic indeterminacy of the relation between satiric object and satiric subject: the speaker of such satire discloses his implication in the pleasures, temptations, and intrigues—and above all his mastery of the learned textual citations under which all of these are justified—of the world against which he rails, and nowhere to more hilarious effect than when he professes to be scandalized by modern dissolution of those traditional proprieties in which he himself has a manifest, mercenary, and duplicitous stake. Will's brief run in this mode serves as an intensely realized evocation of this genre-voice, and as a reminder that it everywhere pervades the poem we have been reading, albeit to far more unpredictable and indeterminate effects.

Its effects here are more volatile, however, than those of goliardic satire, precisely because its mixed linguistic strategy is of a different order than that of verse made solely by and for the clerically learned. The poem we are reading is not, after all, a Latin mimesis of the comic clash between certain citational techniques and paradigmatic habits of thought of Latin clerical culture, and hence a satire on the self-interested clerical economic and political arrangements these buttress, but rather a linguistically hybrid poem, thought and experienced in Latin and English at once, and responsive to the resources and registers of both literary languages by turns if not simultaneously—and it is precisely the hybrid and divided character of the poem's literary commitments that is now centrally at issue.[70] If the poetic voice here briefly resembles that of a recognizable form of clerical satire, he also mimes a less ironic speaker, that of evil-times complaint, a more firmly vernacular mode, and thus this voice also demands to be taken "straight," as an outraged castigator of contemporary ills, in a voice of almost prophetic sincerity and urgency.[71] It is both ethically essential and on this occasion almost impossible rhetorically to distinguish these very different generic voices and motives, roughly identifiable as the learned and the vernacular, and as a reply it puts Reason in the same untenable position as the audience of the episode. On the one hand, the complaint, insofar as it is addressed to Reason, functions as a kind of *captatio benevolentiae*: with it Will attempts to proclaim his professed affinity with Reason by identifying, more in sorrow than in anger—and knowingly, as to a fellow *litteratus*—the clergy's laxity and its governors' negligence, to "ma[k]e of tho men *as Resoun me tauhte*," and thereby gain approval for his perspicacity and virtuous intent. On the other, however, he risks condemnation out of his own mouth, as a pretender to a vocation for which he has no sanction.

Yet even with this comic attempt at the rhetorical disabling of Will's prosecution, Langland has not exhausted the immediate situational possibilities of vocal and social mimesis. In this brief and self-conscious genre performance, Langland also ventriloquizes, through the instrument of Will, a mode of popular vernacular critical discourse with which the poem was widely associated by its most politically suspect audience. This was figured most clearly by John Ball in the letters of 1381, but by 1388 also included Wycliffite (and other) forms of vernacular anticlericalism, and claimed that the perceived decline of both clerical and magnate leadership from their supposed primal authority and virtue heralded the dissolution of exemplarity itself in contemporary life as a moral guide and beacon to the ordinary layman.[72] It is possible that Will's specific obsession with bastardy and marital virtue, the platform from which he launches the rest of his harangue, is meant as a travesty of John Ball's peculiar teaching (according to Walsingham's report) that "no one was fit for the kingdom of heaven who was born out of wedlock"—an idiosyncratic tenet that may be traceable to Ball's reading of Wit's equally rambling moral teaching in Langland's third vision; certainly much of Walsingham's account of Ball's teachings corresponds, topic for topic, to the incipiently heterodox features of Will's self-justification in this passage.[73] Possibly Will's harangue about modern clerical negligence and vice in C 5 was intended by Langland to fix more explicitly than he had in earlier versions the association of anticlerical invective with a speaker more patently unreliable and limited by his own compromised interests in such matters than, for example, Wit had earlier been perceived to be. But even if Will's tirade against clerical misconduct here does not refer beyond the poem itself, its effect in this episode is to associate this kind of invective with a speaker whose own probity and purity of motive concerning clerical attainments and ambitions is itself here pointedly, and *generically*, under suspicion.

Insofar as any discernible argument about Will's own conduct and status lurks in his scattershot complaint, its claim seems to be that since "lyf-holynesse and loue" has vanished from both lay and ecclesiastical governing classes, and the governed lack exemplary guidance, those who aspire to virtue have no recourse except to their own consciences. By this reasoning, lords' and the clergy's abdication of their responsibility to exemplify virtue to the lesser mortals who depend on them in Will's view actually justifies and authorizes his own idiosyncratic self-determination of what constitutes rectitude:

> *Forthy* rebuke me ryhte naughte, Resoun, y ʒow praye,
> For in my consience y knowe what Crist wolde y wrouhte (82–83;
> emphasis mine).

It is that claim—a position that in these circumstances is self-interested and self-justifying to the core, yet nevertheless transforms the legal and political discourses that elicited it—that, like the Dishonest Steward's stratagem, effects Will's paradoxical, even absurd, reprieve at the end of this encounter.

Finally, the passage works at a level of mimesis that returns the satiric point of the harangue to the immediate action at hand, Will's condition as it subjects him to incipient prosecution under the 1388 statute. Will's professed outrage at the deplorable modern fluidity of social estate, and the venality with which vocations and titles are acquired and shed nowadays, mimes the reasoning of the commons that underwrote the creation of the Cambridge statute in the first place. It allies his bluster with the statute's most fundamental proposition: that differentiated identities need to be secured by hedges and buttresses of positive legal prohibition, and the boundaries of social aspiration and social self-coinage policed. The itinerant idler, "maker," and spiritual piece-worker Will thus takes it upon himself to bemoan precisely the fluidity of social and economic conditions that are the basis of his own precarious livelihood. He thereby travesties the self-righteousness of commons' attempts to control not only status mobility but representation itself, through the universal stabilizing mechanism of textual certification of identity and intent. In effect conceding that no other sign but a written document is any longer effective in representing and securing social differentiation, since public self-representation has turned universally duplicitous, the 1388 measure acknowledges the defeat of its own ideological project by the very mechanism of its enforcement. The sense of injured merit ("pore gentil blod refused") that pervades Will's harangue echoes and broadly parodies the commons' plaints and petitions that had invoked the law under which he now faces prosecution.

As an incipient prosecution under the 1388 statute, this interrogation is driving toward the imposition on Will of a textually fixed determination and stability of his social identity—and all parties to the encounter, including Langland's immediate audience, know it. Yet as the self-appointed embodiment of the elusive, multiform, and carnivalesque voice of both prophetic and satiric imperatives to "arate dedly sinne"— imperatives that change their form of realization with the historical circumstances into which they are inserted—Will can scarcely comply in the fashion the law requires. The pursuit of the fictive legal action all the way to its full prosecution is soon deflected by rival and incontrovertible scriptural discourses, and the interrogation never reaches the point of imposing penalties or documentary enforcement. It issues instead in a paradoxical reprieve, which releases Will into a form of penitential rectification that is quickly transformed into the dreaming and "making" of *the rest of Langland's poem*.

Thus part of the wit in using the fiction of an incipient prosecution under this statute as the narrative matrix of the scene is to bring to the foreground a recurrent modal ambivalence of Langland's own poetic enterprise: its dual representation of "voice" and identity as at once textually mediated and disseminated—"published," and hence out of reach of its "maker's" subsequent recall—and as socially performed and passionately remembered, as utterance continuously in dialogue with, and reinterpreted through, historical exigency. From the perspective of this incipient prosecution, the dream that follows, calling into the poem Piers the Plowman as vernacular leader, and Will's "making" of these events, also in effect produces the "document" that certifies the virtuous intent of Will's work—the poem we are reading, whose chief formal anomaly in relation to other visionary poems is pointedly marked as such by this interrogation of Will's anomalous status, and the questionable value of his "makings." From the point early in the waking interlude in which Will acknowledges that his "makings" of his Cornhill neighbors are ill-received by their subjects, to his final abashed capitulation to a cold-eyed demolition of his claims by Conscience, the entity under whose tutelage he finally claims to act, the scene focuses intensely on the paradoxical double existence of Will: as himself a memorial image, and as "maker" of memorable texts; as a person spoken and spoken of, and also as the disembodied producer of writings that purport to act at a distance from that to which they refer. Will, whose satiric "makings" morally indict others, is here shown as never outside the ethical reach of his own writings, or exempt from the indictment of positive law.

Will finally rests his case, and his integrity as a "laborer," with the irreproachable (if here enigmatic) claim that prayer and penance is the "labor" God most loves—a claim he supports by the maxim that man does not live by bread alone (83–88).[74] The continuing prosecution is now taken up by Conscience, who like Reason is in effect called into action by Will himself: just as he had claimed that his earlier "makings" of his fellow-lollers are prompted by "reson," he now defends the spiritual integrity of his itinerant calling as revealed to him and supported by conscience:

Forthy rebuke me ryhte nauhte, Resoun, y зou praye,
For in my consience y knowe what Crist wolde y wrouhte.
Preyeres of a parfit man and penaunce discret
Is the leuest labour þat oure lord pleseth. (82–85)

Conscience seems as unmoved by this general or axiomatic cover for Will's conduct as Reason had been by his claim to a legitimate place within the world's reasonable division of occupational labors, and he now enters the dialogue to press further the question of Will's professed clerical identity and spiritual condition. "By crist, y can nat se this lyeth," Conscience trenchantly observes, but begging as a religious practice, and a broader exemption from worldly toil, must be authorized by specific religious sanction ("obediencer to prior or to mynistre"); it is not a vocation of unlicensed

individual desire alone.[75] In the face of this exposure of the pure idiosyn-
crasy of his vocation, Will's defense, insofar as it pertains to his past and
present conduct (all that the Statute can address), seems suddenly to collapse:

"That is soth," y seyde, "and so y beknowe
That y haue ytynt tyme and tyme myspened." (92–93)

Conceding his idleness and waste of time to date—and hence admitting
that his habit does in fact reflect his *habitus*—he now wagers all on his
future amendment, in a turn to more "profitable" enterprise hereafter, and
again adduces scriptural sanction.

Will's ultimate defense is drawn from the parables of the kingdom:
that of the treasure hidden in a field (Matthew 13:44), which a man sold
all he had to purchase, and that of the woman who found a coin (Luke
15:10)—which as Pearsall notes prefaces, and in effect thematically introduces, that of the prodigal son and his celebrated return. Both depict the
ultimate wisdom, the higher folly, of forms of conduct that to the eye of
worldly prudence defy reason, dignity, self-interest, and common sense
(the latter modern phrase a rough counterpart to "inwit" as Will uses it
in this scene). By these analogies, Will's enterprise hereafter is defined as a
piece of counterintuitive vernacular wisdom in the guise of folly, an absurd
wager of faith, in worldly terms at best a risk-fraught venture of no certain returns. But if the continued slipperiness of Will's definition of his
vocation by this point shows an unsurprising persistence in the wily and
evasive Will, his interlocutors' acceptance of his resolve is nothing short
of astounding, when considered within the discursive terms that initially
defined the moral and legal parameters of the encounter. As Reason and
Conscience urge him "to bigynne / The lyif þat is louable and leele to
thy soule," Will proceeds to "þe kyrke" where, knocking his breast in self-
accusation and "wepyng and waylyng" before the cross, he falls asleep, to
dream once again of the field of folk, the second vision of the poem. In
this vision, Reason, now vested as a pope, preaches a sermon enjoining all
to universal repentance, including a newly added pointed exhortation to
"wynne here sustinaunce/ Thorw som trewe trauail and no tyme spille"
(C 5.126–27; cf. A, B 5.24–25). The moral if not the strict legal terms of the
Statute continue to inform Reason's imperatives to the folk, yet no justice
in England would have released Will on his own recognizance and estimate
as these interlocutors have. Within the figurative terms of the fiction—

and only there—Will has boldly met the standards defining "leel labor" imposed by the most comprehensive and censorious legislation against idleness ever promulgated in England, thus giving a kind of legitimacy to Will's venture, whatever it may be.[76] It remains to define that occupation, and to understand the implications of this waking encounter for the form and genre of the poem.

As Will enters with this sanction upon the "lyif þat is louable," it at first seems to be merely a continuation of the one he had ultimately professed and with which he had rested his defense: prayer and penance (84), spiritual labor as a higher and deeper calling than earthly toil. This crisis over vocation induced by the interrogation of Reason and Conscience, and Will's resolution in response to it, thus anticipate in narrative order—though in compositional order they recall—the crisis of identity, and the narrative impasse, generated by the Priest's intervention in Piers's ministry of truth, in the second vision. In A and B Piers resolves that crisis in a similar way, by renouncing his worldly occupation—to sustain the nurture and survival of the community (its "byleue") and to mediate to it the terms of divine justice—in favor of penitential personal enactment of the common faith; that is, by exchanging political for sacramental representation. Significantly, the Piers of the C version remains in his occupation, much as Will in effect remains in his at the end of this waking interlude, while this encounter mysteriously exculpates his enigmatic form of living of the imputation of idleness and time-wasting. No longer answerable simply for his discrete activities but rather for the motives and purposes for which he performs them, Will's moral burden of proof has shifted, with his interlocutors' reprieve, from his occupation or vocation to his life and work—just as in A and B Piers's occupation underwent a kind of *Aufhebung*, precisely by being "taken personally." Yet Will's habit and habits, here those of a suspect and vagrant idler, proclaim a continuity that survives his vow to change his life, as Piers's *habitus* as a lay vernacular worker and leader survives his challenge by the priest and endures and deepens for the rest of the poem. In effect, the C 5 episode becomes the displaced form of Piers's tearing of the Pardon sent from Truth that is cancelled from C—and like that disturbingly enigmatic act, Will's ambiguous reprieve from charges of vagrancy and idleness radiates its implications throughout the work.

Will's release from civil penalty does not cause him to divest himself of either habitation or habits: in the act of rectification he once again enters the unwilled world of vision. Formally, as we shall see, this move announces a continuity of literary intention of the poem in all its versions at precisely the point in the unfolding of the poem that in fact marks its remarkable formal departure from its models. But intertextually, the principle of this paradoxical constancy and continuity amid new beginnings resides once again in adversion to Scripture, and intensifies still further the wit of Will's incipient prosecution under the statute. The "lyflode" Will professes to Reason and Conscience from the outset, not simply the penitential one he has formally begun at their behest, is an enigmatic embodiment of an apostolic vocation. To the eye of worldly rationality and prudence, it remains just as preposterous and suspect as its scriptural prototype, everywhere courting arrest—just as Jesus anticipated.

In protesting to Reason and Conscience that his begging entails no accumulation but enacts a subsistence-level mode of "winning," and that he dwells "now with hym, now with here," Will's itinerant occupation as he describes it in C 5 (45–52) appears to be an effort to enact Jesus's charge to the apostles, in a form that conflates the versions of Matthew and Luke:

The crop is heavy, but labourers are scarce; you must therefore beg the owner to send labourers to harvest his crop. Be on your way. And look, I am sending you like lambs among wolves. Carry no purse nor pack, and travel barefoot. Enchange no greetings on the road (*salutaveritis neminem per viam*; KJ, "salute no man by the way"). . . . Stay in . . . one house, sharing their food and drink, for the worker earns his pay. Do not move from house to house. (Luke 10:2–11; the calling of the seventy-two)

You received without cost; give without charge. Provide no gold, silver, nor copper to fill your purse, no pack for the road, no second coat, no shoes, no stick; the worker earns his keep. . . . Look, I send you out like sheep among wolves; be wary as serpents, innocent as doves. And be on your guard, for men will hand you over to their courts, they will flog you in the synagogues, and you will be brought before governors and kings, for my sake, to testify before them and the heathen. But when you are arrested, do not worry about what you are to say; when the time comes, the words you need will be given you; for it is not you who will be speaking; it will be the Spirit of your Father speaking in you. . . . So do not be afraid of them. There is nothing covered up that will not be uncovered, nothing hidden that will not be made known. What I say to you in the dark, you must repeat in broad daylight. . . . To receive you is to receive me, and to receive me is to receive the One who sent me. Whoever receives a prophet as a prophet will be given a prophet's reward, and whoever receives a good man because he is a good man will be given a good man's reward. (Matthew 10:5–42, the calling of the twelve)

These subtexts, invoked in a more sustained and detailed fashion in C 5 than in any previous single place or version of the poem, concentrate and force into systematic articulation and judgment the implications of Will's intermittent and scattered self-characterization throughout earlier forms of the work. By this standard, Will remains far from a "parfit man," but the lineaments of his literary as well as spiritual aspirations are at last clear.

From its figuration of the apostolic calling as harvest labor to its acknowledged threat of misprision and civil prosecution, and from the claim that its message is a disclosure of the "dark" of divine truths to its representation as a kind of higher folly, the gospel subtext of the episode functions as both intensification and countertext of the Statute, and retroactively sanctions several aspects of Will's intermittent insouciance throughout the poem. It offers, for example, a gloss upon a waking interval in B between the end of the vision of Activa Vita and that of Anima/Liberum Arbitrium:

> And so my wit weex and wanyed til I a fool weere.
> And some lakkede my lif—allowed it fewe—
> And lete me for a lorel and looþ to reuerencen
> Lordes or ladies or any lif ellis,
> As persons in pelure wiþ pendaunt3 of siluer;
> To sergeaunt3 ne to swiche seide no3t ones,
> "God loke yow, lordes," ne louted faire,
> That folk helden me a fool; and in þat folie I raued . . . B 15.3–10

Such conduct not only mimes the licensed foolery of the professional jester, here of the kind ironically claimed by St. Paul, but also willfully enacts the injunction *salutaveritis neminem per viam*, "salute no man by the way"—here as sanctioned defiance rather than as fearless obliviousness of earthly authority. On the other hand, against the charge to the apostles in Luke, Will does "move from house to house"—"now with hym, now with here," and at Clergy's banquet, we find he openly resents those who dine on more delicate fare than he and Patience have at their "side table." Will is accosted as a *gyrovague*, and to a large degree he is never throughout the poem free from either the suspicions his vagrancy arouses or from the fraught awareness that these suspicions are in large part warranted. It seems there is no resolution to the enigma such folly presents; it must by judged by its works, and Will's chief work remains the ambiguous project of visionary spectatorship and "making" into which he has been released by the authorities with this reprieve.

There is fortunately no need to rehearse in detail here the apostolic and even prophetic dimensions of Will's vocation as delineated here; the admirable recent work of Kerby-Fulton, Scase, and Hanna provides a richly detailed account of the several ecclesiastical and scriptural intertexts of this encounter, and opens the tonal and moral complexities of Will's mimesis of both satiric and homiletic righteous indignation. As all of these suggest, Will's vocation and literary identity is not an uncertainty (suspect "faitour" or professed prophet) to be decided and resolved into unitary meaning simply by recourse to historical "information" about antecedent texts and beliefs, but an ethically and affectively productive enigma. Yet it remains to ask why Langland gathers and concentrates such effects—effects which we are by now well justified in regarding as poetically and ethically self-reflexive—*in this place*, and *in this manner*, and *at this historical juncture*, in the C-revision—and why he does so by bringing these important spiritual and ecclesiastical themes into focus through a fictive scrutiny under the terms of the recent parliamentary vagrancy statute. Why *here*, in a new episode inserted between the first two visions, rather than at any of the several preexisting narrative junctures, most of them in the midsection of the poem devoted to the steps in Will's own quest to know Dowel, that might seem ready-made for such a self-reflexive inquiry—and in which Langland had already, in the B-version, made more limited gestures of a similar kind?[77] And why *now*, and only now—at the end of a decade that had seen the association of the term "loller" with Wycliffite dissent (1382), as well as the appropriation of his fictive hero Piers by the forces of political rebellion in 1381 that were among the implicit targets of the 1388 Statute—does Langland here associate the "maker" with "lollers" specifically, whether this term denotes delinquent clerics, quasi-heretics, mere layabouts, or potentially felonious as well as idle workers more broadly considered? What are the specific literary and historical implications of this move, at this point in the formal and chronological development of Langland's project? To answer both questions, we must return briefly to the moment in both literary and social history reflected fictively in this staged encounter "in a hote hervest."

NARRATIVE INTERVENTION: SYNCHRONIC AND DIACHRONIC FORM

Presuming for the moment the poet's desire to provide somewhere in the revised long version of the poem a representation of the "maker's" perspective on his life and work, meant as a form of self-declaration about his enterprise designed to affect others' understanding of it, what is the significance of placing the new waking episode between the first two visions? The question has two kinds of answers, and they are interdependent.

One concerns the synchronic or strictly formal dimension of the C-revision, the recast internal relations among key parts and major narrative blocs of the poem that this small but powerful addition radiates throughout the long version in its last revised form. To be sure, no one is likely to be fully convincing who would argue that Langland is, like Dante, the kind of poet who dwells expansively or securely within abstract symmetries of literary form, or invites his readers to live in expectation of them. At no point in any version of his poem does this writer invoke a principle of imitative form (beyond that of pilgrimage, itself a fitfully invoked figure) to account for the narrative shape of his "makings," or suggest that any of the large referents of the poem, the most pervasive being salvation history, provide comprehensive structuring analogies for the poem as a whole. Even though there are haunting periodic resonances of this kind between the universal narrative figured in its scriptural citation and mimesis and the impulsive and recursive adventures of "myselue in a mirrour" that offer fitful and fragmentary analogues of it, no amount of abstract formal analysis is likely to persuade a reader of *Piers Plowman* that its episodic encounters are developed from the first within a clear mental "foreconceit" of architectonic structure, or that Langland is the poetic equivalent of the sculptor who can diagram and measure his way to the figure he makes. Langland's discursive materials and his handling of them nevertheless allow us to ascribe to him a recognition and deep understanding of an emergent form in the work, and a capacity to emphasize it by every means possible once it has come to light in realization over the long period of its composition and revision.

In this way Langland more closely resembles the sculptor who professes to "find" the figure in the block of marble, and having done so, manages to make its viewers share his conviction that every speechless lump of stone likewise encloses a figure of equally profound and hard-won beauty. There is no inert matter so intractable, no encounter so fortuitous, as to be fully impervious to such a gaze thereafter. To note this is to begin to understand the basis of the poem's remarkably broad and rapid cultural assimilation: it had given its users a powerful cognitive instrument by which to take their own sightings and soundings within vernacular spiritual culture. Indeed, it is in large part due to the spectacular success of the poet's seemingly more diffident and accretive approach to narrative development—an approach that in effect makes his audience into independent actors/auctors of his poem—that Langland's strictly formal options for revision are so limited. Hence the other kind of answer to the question of "why here?" speaks to the diachronic form of the poem's existence in its world, and to its double life, not merely as a circulated text but as a sustained cultural performance of vernacular literary "work."

With the C 5 addition, as with other C-additions and major moves of material to other parts of his poem, Langland intervenes formally and thematically in a work that already has a public existence and reputation, and a life in copying and circulation, of which the main outlines are probably largely beyond alteration in reception either through retraction or by subtle and minute recastings. In making this or any alteration meant to have an effect on the reception and understanding of the long version of his poem, Langland could not pretend to start from a clean slate, as if its previously circulated form(s) still had the status of private papers. Except within certain limits—limits which the C 5 addition finds a way to acknowledge gracefully and turn to advantage—the poem was in some sense no longer, in any sense that a writer in the age of fully developed intellectual-property law could understand, his. This unalterable fact of prior reputation and circulation will not, of course, preclude authorial attempts to make closely worked and subtle local revisions in the act of rewriting, or in (what the C-revision may have been) preparing something more like an "authorized" release of a work that had, perhaps in less sanctioned forms, entered public awareness and memory. Indeed as any reviser of a context-bound or limited-circulation text for more general and distant reception can attest, this kind of prior reception may even help the writer to notice places where inadvertent mistakes in understanding can occur, and painstaking clarification is in order. But such revision is a manifestation of writerly conscience, a reflex or habit inseparable from the act of primary writing; it blends almost seamlessly into the even smaller-scale practice of correcting (or accepting) yet more minute perceived defects in wording, a level at which the author's and his scribes' behavior are in some instances nearly indistinguishable, and the results have virtually indifferent effects, as many scholars of Langland's poem have noted.[78]

The large scale C-revisions are, in these circumstances, best understood not as analogous to proof correction, editing, or revising an edition—all activities that presuppose mechanical reproduction—but rather as interventions marking the *work* (the sustained enterprise, not the text) as existentially Langland's. They declare it to be the production of a single individual, and of a particular kind, an emanation of a continuous and serious intent, however diverse and dispersed its textual realization, a work whose integrity is not embodied solely or primarily in textual detail, but is co-extensive with that of a life, at once a labor and vocation and a manner of living that has little precedent in its literary culture. What required adjustment therefore—indeed virtually all that could effectively be adjusted—was an articulation of that "intente" as continuous and integral, a statement about its maker's ethics and position as author, not about intellectual property or textual propriety. It is with these general caveats, and a sense of the practical and historical circumstances in which the C-revision was made, that one may approach a formal and historical account of the placement and character of the C 5 *apologia*.

By placing a waking encounter between the first two dream-visions, Langland further underscores the latent similarities, a pattern of cyclical return, of theme and form that joins the beginning to the end of the poem, markedly enhancing a broad chiastic symmetry between the two opening visions and the two post-Resurrection visions that conclude both long forms of the poem, and remain unrevised in the C-version. These broad echoing effects—the resemblances by which the final two visions take on the character of a reprise, in a universal register, of the concerns of the more topically satirical first two—have often been remarked. Several critics have noted the thematic focus in the first and last visions on the venality and avarice that corrodes the political and ecclesiastical community, for example, as well as the fact that only in the second and the penultimate visions is Piers as plowman a sustained narrative presence, acting on the field of the world as worker, leader, and spokesman of a community, and not simply as an elusive and largely remembered spiritual image, or as the human guise of the redeeming Christ (the roles in which, one might add, he figures in the next-innermost chiastically paired visions—Will's long intellectual quest for Dowel, which is as it were "fulfilled" in Christ's chivalric adventure into Jerusalem to save humankind, as the figure of perfect charity that Will has long sought).

The aura of apocalyptic harvest that surrounds the second instauration of Piers's plowing and the building of the barn echoes and complements the plowing and sowing of the second vision as nominal preface to pilgrimage, just as the "wasters'" rebellion that had fractured the folks' concerted labors on the half-acre is echoed in the penultimate passus by the nearly universal rhetorical subversion of moral categories—the specious claim of the cover of cardinal virtues by kings and lords for their individual advantage. Lady Meed's "ravishing" attractions are echoed by the corrosive vitality of Antichrist's forces: both are surrounded by an obsequious retinue and pompous ceremony, exerting suasive shows of power to which only fools are immune. And both first and last, Will stands in an oblique

and complex ethical relation to each pair of complementary analytic scenarios, of which he is largely a visionary spectator, albeit an enigmatically
implicated one. Between each pair of visions in the C-version, both his
stake in these displays and his putative immunity from their implications,
as well as his vocation of representing them, receive searching critical examination.

Will's represented position and identity at the beginning and end of
the long versions of the poem provides a similarly symmetrical pair of
perspectives, framing its fictive duration as the dreamer's lifetime. In the
final vision, as the world is besieged by the universal ravages of mortality,
heralding the approaching end of the saeculum itself, Will is among those
over whose heads callous Age drives, rendering him bald; his protest at this
indignity invites Age's further revenge, in the form of toothlessness and
impotence. Correspondingly, the opening vision presents itself to Will as
a "wonder," appearing suddenly to fill the eager view of the conventionally
youthful and receptive dreamer, who begins his worldly wanderings in a
rural pleasaunce in the conventional May morning, garbed enigmatically as
an unholy hermit. In character with the adventurer's inchoate and latently
amorous longings, the apparition of the predatory Lady Meed and her
metropolitan rout "ravishes" his heart with its opulent attractions, as the
old dreamer's visionary sight finds nothing but universal infirmity, and his
body acknowledges the extinction of sexual desire and generative powers,
while a demonically potent Life and his progeny enlist in Antichrist's rout.
And as if to reinforce this impression of biographical comprehensiveness
at mid-poem, Will's fall into the enchantments of the Land of Longing
arouses his explicit fear of coming to a bad end without realizing his spiritual rectification.

The only other waking interval of a scope and pivotal narrative function in the poem comparable to the C 5 encounter—and similarly marking
a problematic relation between poetic subject and poetic object—occurs
between the final two visions of the poem. This is Will's meeting with
Need, who appears in the opening lines of the final passus, upon Will's
awaking from the vision of the building of the Barn of Unity—a common
effort that, like the plowing of the half-acre, meets with defiance from some
who "wol nat be yruled." Need greets Will insultingly, calling him "faitour" (essentially the same suspicion with which Reason and Conscience
accost him) for failing to provide for himself. Since "nede ne hath no lawe,"
Need invites Will to satisfy his urgent noonday hunger by taking what he
requires to live, and to explain this act to any who might question it as ex-

emplifying the *spiritus temperancie*, thereby emulating those he has just seen and heard in the final moments of the preceding vision invoking the other cardinal virtues to justify their views of the perquisites to which their positions entitle them. By virtue of its insertion between the first two visions, the C 5 episode becomes the C version's formally symmetrical match to the previously written but narratively later Need episode, which has long posed to readers an ethical and representational enigma remarkably similar to that posed by the C 5 encounter.

Interpreters have debated whether Need's sudden appearance to a hungry Will at midday represents an especially dangerous last temptation to willful self-deception, in encouraging the subject to represent his cupidity, even to himself, under a vocabulary of probity (it does, after all, immediately preface Will's final dream of Antichrist), or whether on the other hand it reasserts—tragically here, against the more powerful and worldly forces of Antichrist—a last glimpse of the fragile and elusive ideal, fitfully imagined throughout the poem and as often lost again, of holy simplicity and sufficiency. Need's speech explicitly admits both possibilities. In the same ways, and invoking many of the same cultural and discursive materials, critics have likewise disagreed whether Will's self-representation to Reason and Conscience in C 5 articulates and rationalizes a *sui generis* visionary vocation, or rather displays the gyrovague's and goliard's inevitably parasitic and mimetic collaboration in the moral duplicity upon which their spiritual and literary occupations depend. The poem gives substantial episodic and formal warrant to both alternatives in each instance— and that, I believe, is precisely the point of Langland's symmetrical disposition of them in the C version.

Although for each of these episodes, considered within its local narrative circumstances, I would slightly favor the former over the latter interpretative possibility, as offering a somewhat more nuanced account of immediate ideational effects, the far more important point for our purposes is that both episodes gain their most powerful implications for poetic design from being strategically placed, formally linked, and ultimately irresolvable enigmas. Both singly and together, they yield to no final or decisive determination, not only by appeal to cognate contemporary discourses, but even by reference to other sites in the poem at which these themes have sporadically been broached. In this symmetrical relation, the C 5 addition assigns not only to itself but also to its formal counterpart, the Need episode, a role in declaring the intentional form of the poem as realized. To be sure, Need does not raise the question of Will's occupation, but rather charges him with a profound cultural and moral incompetence, while the insidious form of his argument places Will in a moral double bind. He berates Will for failing to act on the rational moral axiom (which is in itself sound canon law, though Need does not say so, appealing instead to the classical four cardinal virtues for sanction) that in dire and extreme need, one may take what one does not possess to preserve life. There is no shame in this, Need continues somewhat paradoxically, for not only philosophers of old but Christ himself willingly became needy, forsaking earthly possessions for the sake of moral and spiritual discipline.

If poverty is not shameful, it is also in Need's account a wholly ambivalent sign, denoting both spiritual self-discipline and a kind of cultural fecklessness, a contemptible incapacity for both material and argumentative self-help. While Need confines his attentions to Will's form of living and its ethical armature, it is in the B version the wholly separate task of Ymaginatif, about midway through the poem, to question Will's chosen work as an otiose use of both time and wits: the health of one's own soul might better be improved by saying one's psalter than by "making," and for the edification of others there are in any case already "bokes ynow." The C 5 waking episode in effect absorbs these two separate interrogations, of form of living and of occupation or vocation, into one, leaving to the Need episode, unchanged in C, the formal task of marking at the end of the poem the continued double significance of Will's lifelong, and seemingly willful, vocational marginality, his inexplicable and provocative difference from others, his seeming lack of full cultural conviction when all around him on the field in its last days can engage enthusiastically in irreproachable moral reasoning, without unbecoming ambivalence.

By its placement in the narrative sequence, the C 5 episode thus goes considerably further in its metacritical and organizing power than the two separate B version challenges together. Presented as if in biographical hindsight, as an encounter that occurred in the dreamer's youth, when Will's life and livelihood were both still so inchoate and haphazard that his clerical schooling, and the "long clothes" to which it entitled him, still constituted for him the chief definitive constant of his identity, his worklife to date is represented at the end of the first vision as having been punctuated by merely occasional "making," his life thus far to all appearances devoid of both event and notable conviction. As a consequence of this interrogation, the Will of the C version undertakes with the sanction of Reason and Conscience "the lyif þat is louable and leele to thy soule." He does so by falling, amid an act of penitential rectification, into the dream that produces the advent of Piers on the field—the vision that it has since become Will's vocation to pursue and recreate, and Langland's literary career to expound. In this way the episode retrospectively asserts the poem's immanent and intentional design, rather than its episodically fortuitous and merely additive character, as a long-term and large-scale *literary* enterprise. In the process this declaration also has the effect of rendering explicit and problematic the poem's double social and cognitive "mode of existence" in its historical world—as a fixed textual object (in fact a series of them), which may in theory be assimilated by the mind as a whole, and contemplated and reflectively elaborated as a single intent and narrative, yet produced and disseminated as a continuing and never-ending reiteration, a kind of liturgical performance, of an act from which the actor is, in the nature of the case, never fully free, a work of which the maker can never take his leave, as a book he can never close. It is at this metacritical level that the C 5 addition gains its most profound formal and historical effects.

In making these claims of large-scale formal design for the C-version I am acutely conscious of the risk of misrepresentation. By speaking of a loosely chiastic structure as the realized form of the long versions, intensified by his C-revisions, I do not mean to claim that Langland's enterprise had from its inception, *as the C 5 addition narratively pretends it did*, a clearly articulated immanent structural or architectural principle—a claim for which there is little evidence, and against which there is a great deal. But that the *emergent* form of the long versions tended toward realization in broad symmetries of the sort described here is an effect already latent in its chief discursive materials, which consist of the broad figural-historical resonances of salvation history and a rich store of capacious analogical relations linking the believer and the objects of his faith, Old and New Testament event, and other binary relations (a binarism realized all the way down and through to the verse form), rather than in the "foreconceit" of an architectonic narrative form of the sort proposed, and everywhere visibly realized, by Dante, for example. Though Langland's actual production and development of his poem seems to have been largely additive, generated continually anew out of local oppositional encounters, the form as achieved by this means nevertheless lent itself to retrospective claims of sustained and single intention—as, in other words, a continuous "work" that has in effect become a "life" rather than an assemblage of "makings."[79]

The C 5 *apologia* is positioned to assert such a claim. Following the first dream, which could have stood alone as a satire in the general mode of *Wynnere and Wastour*—and may well have been initially conceived in

that way—this waking episode announces the first, and by far the most influential, of the many unprecedented literary moves the poem will make
before its narrative reaches, fictively years later, the last days of the saeculum, to close even its final vision with a false cadence, a recursive or open
prospect of the renewed search for its most memorable and elusive imaginative object, and its most culturally powerful invention, Piers the Plowman. At this thematic juncture, Reason's "arating" of Will proleptically
parallels Reason's general sermon and call of the entire folk to repentance
in the opening moments of the second vision, just as Will's resolution to
"bigynne a tyme / That alle tymes of my tyme to profit shal turne" heralds
the ambiguities of the Sins's confessional "unmaking" of themselves (in C
alone, a complete array of all seven). Likewise Conscience's share in the interrogation forecasts the more distant prospect of his ultimate hailing of
the whole folk to build and fortify themselves within the Barn of Unity.

In the wider dynamic of the narrative, emphasizing the suture of
metropolitan and agrarian scenes at the point where the first dream of the
folk yields to a re-vision of a place that is both opposite and the same, the
C 5 *apologia* also asserts a mysterious and special relation of the "maker"
to Piers himself. It projects the urban "loller" suddenly into the prospect
of agrarian work at bringing in the harvest (and in the process heralds the
distant future of Will, who at the world's final harvest will once again be
caught unprepared either to provide or account for himself, as Need will
pointedly remind him). The encounter displaces onto the "maker's" own
fictive biography the sharp rupture between past and future, required by
personal and communal *renovatio*, that in A and B had been enacted by
Piers's tearing of the pardon, and thus obviates Piers's consequent disavowal of his "byleue," in favor of the dreamer's own resolve to unmake
his past and present, and to remake his life in a new image—which proves,
however, to be fully continuous with the vocation he professed to his interrogators, as Piers's likewise remains constant in the face of the priest's
challenge, its representative powers only intensified throughout the poem.
The symmetrical relation of the C 5 encounter to the Need episode also
recalls the fact that the noon meal was the harvest workers' due from the
lord, and it is the recurrently hungry Will's lack of a place to dine, and by
implication a clear and secure workplace (possibly to be read as the poet's
indirectly stated plea for more stable patronage), that subjects him to the
wandering improvidence and anxiety in which he encounters Need's reasoning, thus supplying the circumstances that make this figure's blandish-
ments dangerously likely to be persuasive.

The generic and performative implications of the C 5 episode's insertion between the first two dreams are, however, still more powerful than its thematic and narrative functions in asserting the "maker's" existential identity with his life-work. The episode implicitly brackets within its dual temporal reference the poet's career, the entire duration of the production of his work, representing it both narratively, in the retrospection of memory, and as it were dramatically, from the point of view of Will in his unformed youth, when his "makings" were still regarded—not only by his audience but even by Will himself—as sporadic utterance, loose ends not yet discernibly woven into the single fabric of a sustained project.[80] It explains the strange persistence of Will's enigmatic *habitus* across the purported prosecutorial and life-defining rupture of the waking interrogation —his continuation of his itinerant and irregular form of living and the unclassifiable and enigmatic insouciance in the face of apparent resourcelessness that makes his conduct a matter of suspicion and contempt from first to last—as somehow necessary to his "work." The episode thus redefines realized form as if it had all along been immanent form, the only possible form, a "life-work." The encounter with Reason and Conscience (those two root principles of all English legal and juridical theory, and hence the roots of legitimacy itself) projects into the "maker's" early years both the primary confrontation with his powers and talents that formed and articulated the first intention of the work, as well as the sense of sanction for it that purportedly *allowed* the generation of what became the poem. With this patently fictive and after-the-fact tale of its beginning, Langland *in effect declares his work finished—as finished as it will ever be* (though that to which it refers cannot, in the nature of the case, be complete).[81]

To do so, the poet had to set into dissonance the most basic diachronic facts of the poem's production as they were already known to his primary audience—to use the weight of that prior knowledge on his own behalf, as it were—in order to claim synchronically its intentional integrity, and thereby both to reclaim and shape, in the only manner now available to him, the cumulative cultural significance of the dispersed forms of his own previous production. Inventing this story of the "remembered" inception of the poet's work as serious endeavor, its distinction from Will's occasional "makings," Langland creates, as the pseudo-historical framework and occasion of his first acknowledgment of the dreamer-poet's vocation at a time in his now-distant past, an incipient prosecution under a parliamentary measure recently enacted, and possibly not yet even instituted. With this bold counterfactual and openly anachronistic move, he effects still another strategic displacement, more striking and more significant for the poem's social history, than the anachronism of the "recalled" prosecution of Will in his youth as "an idle man." With this displacement, Langland substitutes a fictively manageable threat of secular prosecution for another that his work seemed far more likely to incur in the late 1380s: ecclesiastical suspicion of it as unauthorized vernacular theology. Langland frames the interrogation of the irregularities of Will's life and work within the secular vagrancy statutes rather than dramatize the possibility that the Cornhill "loller" is a self-proclaimed religious teacher or preacher.

By means of this newly invented imaginary encounter Langland attempted specifically to recapture his own wandering discourses of "lolleres," to resubordinate this volatile and ambiguous term of art and contest in the 1380s and 1390s—one which Langland had introduced into strategic use in the poem only with the C-revision—to the uses to which he put it in the C version, and in particular to wrest it away from its growing, and increasingly exclusive, association with heresy. As Wendy Scase has shown, Langland's idiosyncratic C-usage of the term did not ultimately prevail, but the attempt to deploy it as an integral part of his final addition to the C-revision—to integrate it into what became a literary *apologia* while pointedly eschewing retraction—illustrates how much was culturally at stake for Langland in this period in differentiating his enterprise from heterodoxy, and how much more difficult this task had now become. It was only by the most transparently fictive device he had yet deployed that he could define, against worsening odds, the integrity and continuity of motives of England's most ambitious and complex instance to date of vernacular theology in a vernacular literary mode. This poem, he implicitly argues in the C 5 fictive "autobiography," was not what led him into a "loller's" life, and a "loller's" insouciance, but what led him beyond it, to the other side. All along his "makings" were real work, not the absence of it. But now they have ceased to be his.

It is beyond the already vast scope of this essay to rehearse, at the length it warrants, the evidence that inclines me to accept a modified form of Scase's suggestion that the "makings" of "lolleres," to which Will refers in the opening lines of the C 5 waking episode, may be some form of the passages on this topic that Langland inserted into Piers's pardon in the C-revision—additions that also, in substantially variant form, appear in other places in the poem in two anomalous manuscripts.[82] It is, however, pertinent to our consideration of the C 5 addition, and in particular its use of the 1388 statute, to examine briefly the substantive rather than textual reasons for inferring that the C 5 *apologia* was the last large-scale addition Langland made to the C version—and especially later than, and putting paid to, the apparently provocative C 9 discourse of "lollers."[83] These involve considerations that link our two initial questions about the C 5 addition—why here? and why now?—both to each other and to the third we have just broached: why is the fictive vehicle for this *apologia* the 1388 vagrancy statute? If Will's irregular and anomalous vocation is at issue, why *isn't* this interrogation focused more closely from the start on his visible estate and condition, signaled by his "long clothes" as well as by the "abite of an eremyte" in which he ventures into his first vision—that is, his apparent identity as a cleric *manque* rather than simply an idle laborer? Why invoke Reason and Conscience to enforce a labor-and-vagrancy statute if they can't see what is before their eyes?

III. Conclusion: Reclaiming and Renouncing Will's Work

Thy pardon moste y rede. C 9.282

To this point we have considered the question of the poetic placement of this confrontational encounter ("why here?") in terms of both abstract chiastic design, with its capacity to reinforce significance by sheer symmetry and repetition, and its internal narrative and metacritical effects: the poet draws explicit and conscious attention to the sustained literary and social anomaly of his poetic project at that point in the unfolding of the poem where it both decisively departs from its single-dream literary prototype and introduces its most culturally powerful invention, Piers. We have also examined the relation of this addition to the successive stages of poetic production and revision ("why now?") in largely internal formal and self-referential terms: the episode gathers and turns upon the "maker" himself all the centrifugal forces of a complex contemporary social and spiritual discourse involving poverty, labor, begging, idleness, clerical *otium*, clerical fraud, and clerical moral authority that Langland has dispersed and combined in various ways throughout both long versions, and intensified by revisions and additions at several points in the C-narrative. In this way, the C 5 waking episode and its placement may be seen as preemptive—anticipating in narrative sequence, and fictively authorizing, the poem's unusual

procedures, and rationalizing the poet's questionable standing throughout as a self-appointed and precariously positioned imaginative visionary
of the truths of the faith.

The use of the 1388 Statute as a vehicle for this purpose might seem
in some respects almost unproblematic, even inevitable. It is likewise, as
we have seen, a very heterogeneous measure, nominally about labor but
in fact outlawing vagrancy rather than regulating wages and contractual
work arrangements, and proposing to control "wandering" by means of
unprecedented documentary certification. It is heterogeneous, too, in the
interests it bespeaks: it addresses the gentry's inchoate fears of "crime," and
of large-scale and elusive shifts in social identity and communal form, with
measures far more pervasive—if also almost entirely phantasmal—than this
group's direct economic and legal stakes as employers and consumers, and
their possession of political means, in limiting workers' wages and mobility. Yet the deeper cultural significance of Langland's use of the 1388
labor legislation in a fictive and retrospective *apologia* for his work may lie
more tellingly in what the statute does *not* attempt to do, in its historically significant silence rather than in the wide and diffuse regulatory ambitions that differentiate it from its 1349 prototype. Despite its wide social
reach, especially in its provision for "internal passports" which clerics as
well as layfolk were to obtain, each from the appropriate agency, to authorize their itineraries, the 1388 vagrancy measure does not concern itself in
any substantive way with either irregular clerical vocations or anomalous
lay religious callings and other vernacular forms of spiritual profession and
theological reflection.

From a strictly legal and juridical perspective this is of course no more
than to be expected; as we have seen, ecclesiastical self-regulation was
always an entirely separate matter of law and jurisdiction, though often,
as in the several issues of the circular *Effrenata*, it developed parallel and
complementary measures. In practice, the justices enforcing the labor laws
were reluctant to countenance the extension of their purview to the activities of stipendiary clerics considered as waged or salaried "workers,"
since as they noted, matters of personal conscience and discretion and of
spiritual preparation were involved in a cleric's performance or nonper-
formance of his several duties.[84] Moreover, as the justices also noted, it
was the prerogative of the church, not of the king and council, to regulate
both its own officers and the laity in matters of faith and morals. But for
the purposes of our inquiry that is precisely the point: at the end of the
1380s the fantastic legal matrix of the Cambridge vagrancy statute, with its

prospect of universal documentary "passports" to certify the purposes of one's apparently extra-vagant itineraries in the land, offered Langland far wider latitude as an imaginary scenario, and more apposite and capacious literary and cultural terms, within which to construct a positive justification of Will's anomalous enterprise—and by extension a legitimation of philosophically serious vernacular imaginative literature generally—than any form of ecclesiastical scrutiny that this decade (or for that matter the next three decades) could possibly have afforded.

If, as we have already observed, no actual justice in the land would have accepted Will's ultimate appeal to his own conscience at the end of this episode—to say nothing of his invocation of scriptural parables as the sanction for his enigmatic and self-defined customary "work"—as grounds for releasing a lay worker from the obligation to undertake secular employment, especially harvest work, under the 1388 Statute, it is still more certain that by the end of the 1380s no bishop could have been as disinterested and agnostic as Reason and Conscience in the face of Will's unshakeable, albeit unauthorized, conviction that his manner of living and of work constituted some kind of legitimate spiritual vocation. In other words, of the two possible courts of appeal for fictively staging a defense of a legitimate, serious, and theologically adventurous vernacular poetics in the 1380s, Langland chose the secular venue in strategic preference to the ecclesiastical one, as by far the more promising for fantastic projection, and by far the more likely to concede its authority to a claim of scripturally informed vernacular conscience and calling—in short, more likely to accept, even if only by default, the verbal, citational, and sartorial trappings of *clergie* at face value.

It is time to put my claim more plainly and assertively. Langland uses the Statute as a screen, in both current senses of the term: on the one hand, as a bright and highly visible *surface on which to project* an argument he wished to make about his literary enterprise; on the other, as a *means of concealment*, to mask from view or inference another, quite different and equally possible, argument or claim that could also, he feared, be made about his work—one which he expended considerable inventive energy, and in the event apparently succeeded, in keeping from view. In effect, Langland calls down upon his persona the threat and mechanisms for prosecuting the vagrancy of idle laborers, elaborating these in detailed close-focus, in order to divert attention from the possible imputation to it of a kind of vagrancy that had far more swift, dire, and certain consequences: doctrinal, theological, and intellectual error, and pretensions of clerical authority. Will's sudden—even eager—capitulation to the dicta of

these imaginary king's officers, unconcerned with such bishops' prerogatives beyond their mild penultimate demurrer about Will's apparent lack of
"parfitnesse" in engaging in forms of begging outside obedience to "prior
or mynistre," strategically masks a graver and more fundamental anomaly
of this work: its enigmatic truth-claims, and its indefinable character as a
socially intelligible form of clerical utterance, in relation to the authorized
instructive discourses of the church, which it everywhere mimes and incorporates.

    The argument Langland projects with this secular interrogation is that
Will's enterprise, and hence the poet's, was not "idle" talk, fable, or fantasy,
but in some socially significant and spiritually valuable sense "real work"—
a positive claim of some historical importance in an era, and within a social
imaginary, that had, as we have seen, increasingly tended to replace the
terminology of "estate" proprieties and prerogatives with the obligation
to work in some manner to the common good. Moreover, we recall, this
was by now a "crossover" discourse: clerical and lay vagrancy were both,
and almost interchangeably, culpable evasions of social duty, in a polity
in which membership was increasingly signified by a single standard. Perhaps the most crucial consequence of this historical shift in underlying
models of community is its virtual ideological abandonment of the notion
of *otium*, a withdrawal of sanction from this condition not only as a functional subdivision of the community, and as an aspect of the social and
moral health of the individual, but also as a role identified with the preserve of an "estate" within the whole—that of the "lered," and specifically
the clergy. Hereafter the activities and privileges of *literati* will increasingly
have to be justified in social theory in some version of the laity's political
terms—as simply another form of "work" for the community's good, not
as "louable" exemption from, or obverse of, the laborious, as embodying
the contemplative, speculative, or reflective "sabbath" of soul and society.
The excuse of the Dishonest Steward, *fodere non valeo*, has been put on
notice by the end of the fourteenth century, its philosophical lease as an
argument about the individual in the polity decidedly limited—where, as
scholars in the arts and humanities have observed, it precariously remains.

    The argument Langland masked with the one he offered, however,
turned upon "lollers," and the semantic contest over the referents of that
term that seems to have been in its most volatile phase during the fairly
brief period of time during which the C version assumed the form in which
it was disseminated. "Loller" was likewise a "crossover" pejorative term—
one that could be applied to both lay and clerical derelictions; what was at

issue was the kind of dereliction or malfeasance to which the noun referred. Wendy Scase has discussed two rival senses of the word current—and, she argues, actively in contest with each other—in the 1380s. Its use as interchangeable with, and ultimately replaced by, "lollard," to denote a follower (lay or clerical, learned or "lewed") of Wyclif's heresy, coexisted with the sense that Langland, prominently in the C-version, gave to the word: "the gyrovagues of the late fourteenth-century church in England"—a definition that, she shows, was largely driven out by the former one, which became the most general usage of the word by early in the fifteenth century.

Langland presents the fullest description of this group in C 9.188–218, part of the C-addition to the pardon, and offers an etymology of the term (213–18). And not only an etymology: he prefaces it with a social etiology of their false professions: these "lollares, lache-draweres, lewed ermytes" were once "werkmen, webbes and taylours, and carteres knaues" as well as "clerkes withouten grace," who noticed that they were living less well with "long labour and litte wynnyng" than those who "faytede in frere clothinge" and had "fat chekes." Making a reasonable inference from these facts, these laymen in effect invoked the Dishonest Steward's plea, exempting themselves from manual toil for the sake of a softer living, hoping to be taken for members of "som ordre—or elles a profete." The chain of social logic is worth noting: the example of unobservant and ill-living but presumably legitimately ordained religious prompts layfolk to counterfeit them, imitating their deeds and miming their discourse in hope to be taken for adherents of their "ordres," for the sake of profit as prophets. Clerical *otium*, in short, has become a game any number can play, and it is mostly a confidence game.

Scase's carefully argued discussion succeeds, I think, in showing not only that Langland introduced the "gyrovague" sense of the noun into English (the continental term "lollard," she notes, already denoted a gyrovague, or extraregular, religious), but that he did so quite purposefully and self-consciously, with his explicit and painstaking definition of the term in C 9.213–18. That definition—which as she persuasively claims has generally been mispunctuated so as to obscure its assertive logic—invokes an analogy to create a purported etymology of the term, thus providing for the noun a domestic lexical pedigree in English, a derivation that the term cannot be shown to have. Just as the "Engelische of oure eldres" speaks of the lame, or those whose legs are out of joint, saying of them that in their (abnormal, unintentionally ungainly) motions they "loll," Langland explains, so false "eremytes lollen aȝen þe byleue and þe lawe of holy churche." This derivation of the English noun from the English verb is ingenious—and as we shall see, strategically so—but implausible, and shown to be so by Langland's own uses of the verb in all versions of the poem.[85]

As Scase shows, there is in fact before the *Piers Plowman* examples no attestation in English of the noun "loller"—either in the sense "idler" that has been presumed to exist in English before this date, or in either of the two still more pejorative contested senses of this period that she discusses. Scase suggests that what this C 9 passage actually offers is not a historical etymology, or even a false etymology of the meaning of the noun current in the late fourteenth century, but rather a brilliant metaphorical substitution that is original with Langland, and deeply inbuilt into the moral and social logic of the C-additions to his own poem: gyrovague "lollers" are those who by their feigning usurp the place of the lame, the halt, and the blind as legitimate claimants of alms, and thus defraud the needy; moreover, they most often do so by feigning lameness or injury, walking in a stooped fashion. Langland's etymology is invented in the service of a social etiology of false religious.[86] It appears that the backformation "loller," with the imputed historical meaning "idler" and the special imputation of fraudulent or wilful idleness, from the Middle English verb "lollen," is a fanciful etymologizing of a noun that had entered the language on its own from continental usage in about this period, and that Langland was a key agent and sponsor of that domesticating fiction. Why?

Scase's account of the competition over this noun in the later fourteenth century leaves out of account another, more capacious and fluid, sense that occupies much broader and less charted ground between these contested definitions—which were both, it should be noted, in English still largely stipulative and self-conscious in the late fourteenth century. This is the broad lay sense of the term, fully naturalized into English and available in ordinary vernacular use at least by the 1390s, yet it implied neither of the two senses that Scase documents as in contest in the late 1380s. This third sense of the noun, which may have coexisted with the two contested senses, certainly survived Langland's, and continued to compete in ordinary usage with the specific pejorative sense "Wycliffite" well into the fifteenth century; it appears to me to have been part of the semantic terrain out of which the contested uses were precipitated in the brief period of their active cultural competition. It too is pejorative, but it is a broad social slur about the decorum of religious practice and discourse, not about doctrinal postulates or about mendicant hypocrisy. When Harry Bailly "smells a loller" in the Parson's antiludic protestations he is not imputing indigence, fraudulent or otherwise, to this cleric, or ascribing to him either begging under false pretenses or pretended holiness as a cover for general cynicism. Nor is he discerning in this visibly hard-working and dedicated parish priest any doctrinal error, dissenting views of the institutional church, or critical anticlericalism (any of which could be imputed to Wycliffite thought). On the contrary, the Parson specifically and significantly is said by Chaucer, and evidently perceived by his fellow pilgrims, not to do any of the things the cynical, venal, lazy, or heretical members of his vocation might do: for example, leave his parish in the care of a substitute to "sing for silver" in London—to take but one of many possibilities open to a less conscientious member of his vocation, mentioned by Chaucer as it had been by Langland before him. Yet the Parson's conduct, opinions, and values do not include the slightest odor of Wycliffite taint. As has been widely noted, the Parson is not merely an ideal but a fantasmal antitype to the charges against the church wielded by both Wycliffite and broader anticlerical controversy. His "character," as reported by "Chaucer," makes him indeed a discursive product and literary invention born of late fourteenth century controversy over both doctrinal dissent and anticlerical critique, but he is not himself in any sense a practitioner of either. What, then, for Harry, is a "loller"?

Harry's perception of the Parson as "loller" is prompted not by suspicious scrutiny of his character, conduct, and speech, but is an almost instinctual and instant social response to the Parson's emphatically expressed distaste for the innkeeper's colorful and indecorous outburst of oaths by God's body. In short, what is at issue is a conflict in social decorum: Harry somewhat ostentatiously exhibits, as he has often done before, a form of colloquial "manly" behavior that is still recognizable as such a signal today, even if no more widely approved now than it was then as a conversational register that is appropriate in all companies. The Parson's response to it, in turn, signals to Harry that the cleric is one of those familiar types who always intrude religious discourse where it does not belong, as into secular "felweshipe" outside of church, holy days, and other occasions and places not specifically marked as "religious."

For such as Harry—as for those who a decade or two later similarly regarded Margery Kempe's blissful accounts of heaven at the dinner table, or her cryings and "holy conversation" that might erupt into nearly any ordinary form of social interaction—to be a "loller" seems to have been no more nor less than to be a particular kind of social irritant, an offender against the unwritten decorum that "religion" is a marked discourse, appropriate for occasions so designated, and not at other times. For Harry as for Margery's traveling companions and the civil authorities (significantly key officers of the church do not generally ascribe heresy to Margery, though some clerics of less secure position find it an embarrassment to be associated with her), a "loller" is no more than someone practicing (to adapt Mary Douglas's useful formulation to our purposes) "religion out of place." It has little to do with doctrinal conformity, or with prohibited devotional practices or proscribed forms of skepticism or critique of church institutions, but simply registers the deeply held perception that the "loller" has in some way violated or revised the boundaries, the conventional and wholly unstated social "rules" concerning what is, and is not, "religious," in such a way as to introduce a small and irritating crisis in social decorum, specifically through activating one's awareness of, and sense of guilt, about what commonly goes without saying. Society's accused hypocrites are often those whose perceived or imputed hypocrisy consists in no more than bringing to consciousness and crisis the "normal vices" of their society, those that the good subjects of the social contract would prefer to continue not to notice.

All of this is exactly what we should expect in fully vernacular and common usage by the 1390s if the noun entered English (without reference to the English verb), bringing with it its full range of association, from the continent—where it encompassed not merely fraudulent religious, but putatively sanctimonious practitioners of the *devotio moderna* (those "prayer-mumblers") who could easily be lumped with them. To an ordinary nonsympathetic observer of both phenomena, both kinds of assertive claims of religious sentiment and symbology upon common and secular social space are offensive. To such a view both are merely variant forms of the same religious hypocrisy: the one consciously and fraudulently, the other in a kind of wilful or obtuse, though not necessarily scheming, violation of "community standards" of religious expression. In effect, a conventionally minded laity experiences both as merely different kinds of confidence tricks, manipulating the observer through his or her own largely unarticulated sense of the truths and exemplars of their faith, and the principles of social trust. The annoyance aroused by both phenomena concerns, in short, these figures' selective (and in the case of the gyrovague's fraud, schemingly self-interested) desublimations of religious categories of thought; their reference to religious obligation consists of acts of social disruption that force religious language into social notice, and hence into situations requiring open and conscious choice, rather than the "normal," implicitly and widely agreed-upon and unconscious small acts of failure to live up to the strenuous absolutes of the faith—such as Harry Bailly's (in his view innocuous enough) "manly" tavern speech-idiom.

The late fourteenth-century contest over this term—marked most tellingly by the array of competing etymologies which not only modern scholars but late medieval "native speakers" of this discourse advance to account for the term—was of course a linguistic displacement of a genuine and fundamental social contest. Prayer-mumbling, lameness of gait, languishing, tares or weeds (*lollium*)—all of these purported etymologies were, like Langland's, useful and suitably overdetermined origin myths consciously applied to assert intellectual control over a perceived disruption or pervasive malaise, to which the accusations of "loller" in any of its senses testified.[87] To define the threshold for the application of the term "loller" as the perception of "religion out of place," as intruding improperly into "secular" social space, is of course itself to beg the question by entering the controversy. From the perspective of many forms of loosely linked and difficult-to-classify late medieval forms of lay pious observance and of spiritual renewal, as well as sui generis eremitic "vocations," there could be no such thing as fully "secular space"; countering the perceived cultural claim that there was seems to have been the entire point of their various endeavors, from condemnation of the ludic (and worse) aspects of pilgrimage, to diatribes against outrageous fashion.

The "moral panic" over unauthorized wandering by laborers as free agents, as well as over liveries and the unexplicit resources and purposes of guilds that we have seen in the acts of the Cambridge Parliament, may be regarded from this vantage point as still further ramifications of the same sense of dangerously fluid and "permutable" boundaries of social forms and cultural sanctions—as remedies against, and instances of, what I have called the general desublimation of social anxiety concerning permutability of identities and relations. The largely lay forms of religious vocation asserted in the later middle ages involve the effort to reverse such fluidity, yet they replace the possibility of return to earlier static paradigms by a new discursive strategy (most often in *Piers Plowman* studies labeled "Franciscan," but by this period both wider than and different from that important initiative in lay and urban ministry): to reinfuse the ordinary with sanctity, and reawaken a sense of the eschatological integrity and total form of the entire *saeculum*, by asserting the claims of "religion" in everyday life. Much like the quixotic efforts of the Cambridge Parliament, these newer invocations of "religion" paradoxically concede the irreversibility of the "permutability" they deplore by the very cultural technologies they invoke against it. To both, the most fundamental cultural threat is not simply the irruption into normal hypocrisy of "religion" out of place but the positive claim that attends it—that vocation is in *cor hominis*—taken to its logical and literal conclusion.

What has this to do with Langland's concerted invocation of "lollers," the contested term and the equally contested social fact, in the newly controverted senses in his two large-scale additions to the C-version—and in particular his application of this controverted term to the fictive representation of the visionary poet in C 5? What strategy is implied by these moves? The question is urgent precisely because it seems such a counterintuitive gesture, if Langland's purpose was, as Scase's analysis implies, simply intended to hold some tenable ground for the continued use of the term "loller" in the face of the imminent capture of the term solely by anti-Wycliffite polemic. Though she does not explicitly say so, her explanation for Langland's pervasive use of the noun *only after* the 1382 condemnation of Wyclif's Oxford adherents—to whom this term had been applied as early as 1382, and therefore *only after* there existed explicit support in secular administration for suppression of heresy—seems to be that his purpose in using the term, and specifically in stipulatively defining it as he did, was thereby to preserve the continued possibility of anticlerical critique apart from the imputation of Wycliffite sympathies to its speaker.[88] That might indeed explain the painstaking network of distinctions in the C 9 addition, if that were all there were to explain—though it would still leave unanswered a broader question of the prudence of this move: the need for light to find the source of a gas leak still does not recommend the lighting of a match. But it could scarcely account for the C 5 waking episode, which links this volatile term to the poetic persona himself.

With the further—and, as I hope I have now demonstrated, later—C 5 association of the poetic persona, both by habit and the explicit suspicion of the King's officers, with the "lollers" so painstakingly distinguished in the C 9 Pardon, Langland demands that we find this explanation insufficient. It should now be clear that Langland invokes this charge upon Will as Cornhill loller at the end of the 1380s as a way of both defusing and relocating a potentially dangerous claim that could be made with increased plausibility against the poem, especially in view of the reception it had already received in both the rebel letters of 1381 and in pro-Wycliffite expression with which its key figure, Piers as lay teacher of truth, bore some noticeable affinities: that the poem was an egregious instance of "religion out of place," and its author a "loller" in the broad common sense of the term that Harry Bailly invokes against the Parson, and the town council of Leicester marshals against Margery—an incipient sower of discord, set loose in the house of social fiction. In short, Langland offers with this episode a *mise en abŷme* of the gravest charge that can be made against his poem, both as literature and as vernacular theology or "holy conversation," and gives back a defense of its legitimacy as both.

The implicit double charge is itself a double bind: as literature—that is, as a form of vernacular discourse marked as such in this case by the nugatory beginning, unbounded speculative frame, truth-claims assigned to the realm of the hypothetical, and adventurous and episodic narrative development of the dream-vision—the poem is captured only minutes into its court-satirical opening panorama by a demanding and complex moral and eschatological, and explicitly religious, discourse—that of Holichurch. This preemptive interpretative intervention, much like the Parson's into Harry's festive pilgrimage tavern talk, in fact makes such recurrent intrusion of the *magisterium* the very heart of its matter, the principle of its continued and fertile narrative generation. As vernacular theology, however, the poem does not discernibly submit itself to any canons of instructive order and comprehensiveness, or indeed doctrinal firmness of outline, being guided by Will's vagrant quest for the one thing needful to his salvation. With the C 5 apologia, Langland stages the double claim that his work is vernacular theology, and that it is literature—and also that it is a serious and sustained effort at both, not merely a self-promoting or occasional ploy. Will is neither a sower of faction by fiction, nor one whose sporadic amateur avocation is "making"; neither does he claim clerical literacy and vocation for gain. Claimed retrospectively as single and continuous enterprise, the principle of constancy in Will's identity, the poem is both life and work. Yet neither first nor last is it a "book," a unitary and enduring record of "truth," for which its maker could be held liable outside the time and situation of its making.

While in the B-version Ymaginatif had mildly reproved Will for his "makings" not merely because they occupied time better spent in prayer and psalms, but because they were in any case superfluous amid "bokes ynow" to "telle men what Dowel is," by the time the C-revision attained the form in which it was disseminated, vernacular books of religion were regarded by the church as far less benign superfluities. After both the 1381 rebellion and the 1382 condemnation of Wyclif's teachings, and nearly a decade of archiepiscopal proceedings against lay as well as university heretics, vernacular religious *texts*—not only the scriptures in the vernacular but other writings on faith and religious experience outside explicit clerical authorization for instructive and meditative purposes—were dangerous to possess, and surely still more dangerous to produce and disseminate. It may be for this reason that the C 5 *apologia* is so evasive about the specifically *textual* status of Will's "makings," instead defending his enterprise not as scribally reproduced product (in the manner of Chaucer in "Adam Scriveyn"), but as activity or performance for his own and the general good, almost a sui generis lay liturgy—that is, as legitimate *work*, to which his itinerant and suspect *way of living* is paradoxically not only appropriate, but in fact necessary. Langland seems to have chosen to rest his ultimate defense of his makings on the enigmatic status of a way of life, and the social and cognitive legitimacy of his "work," rather than on the integrity and generic stability of his texts, as the vehicle by which his "intent" was likeliest to be fully intelligible, and to pass sympathetic muster in its, and his, reckoning by its ultimate judge(s).

Epilogue: Text, Vision, Book: The Work of Literature

As poetic *apologia*, the C 5 waking episode is remarkably—indeed, as we can now infer, strategically—diffident about the ontological, material, and social status of the poem *as text*, as a written object or document rather than as an almost-continuous act of hard-won insight and perpetual recomposition of "intent." Textual scholars of the poem have begun to acknowledge that such diffidence seems in fact to have been characteristic of Langland's relation to the material realization and embodiment of his poem throughout his work on it—as manifested in, and inferrable from, the surviving testimony concerning the state of his fair copies of it, and his intervention in its scribal production and supervision of its dissemination—and to recognize that such diffidence or disregard is not at all incompatible with his discernible and often minute care for poetic craft and intellectual precision. It is, however, the cultural and historical determinants and significance of these attitudes or habits, rather than their implications for the reconstruction of Langland's texts, that require our attention here.

Significantly, Langland's work, the long poem we read, is never internally designated as a "book"—the aspect under which Chaucer could in retrospect commend his conditionally completed verse creation into the world for "amendment" and judgment ("goo litel book"). Though in the later reaches of the long versions the dreamer says that upon waking he "wroot as me mette," he never identifies those writings with the poem we are reading. This dissociation of Will's writings and makings from the "work" he defends in C 5 seems absolute; paradoxically, it seems to be a condition of the integrity of his "work," or the defensibility of the project, that it never be fully identifiable or coexistent with any form of its (merely) textual incarnation. Insofar as Will's enterprise is called "making(s)," it is always so designated at the moment of being called into question or disavowed, as it is by Ymaginatif in the B-version or by the waking Will in C 5—as, so to speak, a faintly embarrassing surviving residue of an act that is removed in time from the present, devalued, misclassified, or all three. Will's "work" seems always to have been produced in some other condition or state of life than the one in effect at the moment of its acknowledgment or recollection—to be not accidentally or incidentally but fundamentally, as a condition of its being, *anti-textual*, continuously performed and perpetually renewed, as penitence is, not "made." The ethical problem for "Langland," and the task for this *apologia*, lies in owning up to his *work*, while acknowledging that he has never in any sense owned his "makings," and has no real desire to do so. What he has published—that into which he inserts this last profession of intent—is a life and a work, not a text.

But if his "makings" are largely objects of distrust and disavowal, it is quite otherwise with Will's visions: none of his interlocutors, however hostile or rebarbative, ever suggests that they come of demonic promptings, biological disorder, unchecked "fantasye," or any of the other myriad forces by which dreams may issue out of the ivory gate and insinuate themselves into human awareness. And for all the goliardic affinities of his art—including his knowing satiric aside that in some cases he "dare not" expound the meaning of what he saw, or that if "lewed men" could expound it they would find its purport not entirely to their liking—Will does not at any point espouse Pertelote's hermeneutic of suspicion to question the ontological status of his visions, nor does Langland invoke it upon his dreamer in the form of challenges from any of his informants. On the other hand, he does not assert, implicitly or explicitly, any special positive ontological claims for these visions. If Will never fears the devil's hand in them, he also never claims divine agency for them; they are, rather, "sightes" of the kind available throughout history to "kynde-witted men" as the form in which the acutely perspicuous apprehend the concentrated distillate of their experience, and such "sightes" must be supported and informed by "clergie," an outcome of systematic "techyng," to accord with truth. But as Ymaginatif continues, "grace is a gyfte of god"; prophets and apostles have it, and Will is still searching for it at the end of the poem.

The discourse of continuous prophetic revelation—of which, as Kathryn Kerby-Fulton has shown, Langland is well aware, and to which in some ways he provocatively alludes—is nevertheless not, I think, one to which he directly annexes his own poetic enterprise, except by analogy, as a strategy for his own quite different ends. (Indeed, I take it to be the reflexive purpose of the Ymaginatif episode to underscore the distinction between what one must by default call literary prophecy and those latter-day reformist texts which properly invite ecclesiastical scrutiny of the most searching and profound political earnestness.) Reformist apocalyptic utterance stands rather in the same provocative relation to Will's life and work as does the goliardic voice and posture—and that, I think, is the point of these haunting resemblances: they define and exacerbate rather than resolve the extreme anomaly under which this literary work labors from first to last. The poem stages from the outset the quixotic cultural quest for a vocation and mission for serious and searching vernacular philosophic fiction as the only (and at that barely) "lowable" form that vernacular theology can take beyond the *magisterium*. The last act of the drama of producing such an impossible thing is the one that pretends to be its first: the sanctioning of this project at its moment of inception as a vocation, as a first intention, years ago—though it is now in fact as achieved as it will ever be—by Reason and Conscience.

In this respect, the worldly "mode of being" of the poet's "makings" as he represents his own case, and hence his sense of social or cognitive precariousness in the enterprise of vernacular literature, is defined in diametrically opposed ways by Langland and Chaucer. "Chaucer" is self-represented to us as someone for whom books are solid, august, enduring, consoling, a refuge from the contemporary and the merely spectacular, while all claims to visionary apprehension of truth, classical or scriptural, are almost invariably attended by doubts that range from earnest philosophical skepticism to temporizing learned or pseudo-learned classification to playful mockery. "Langland" depicts his poetic persona in just the opposite dilemma: as a visionary who vividly and almost effortlessly apprehends the truths of the faith in action in contemporary life, and can find scriptural dicta as well as those of the "poetes" confirmed plainly and copiously in every encounter, whose struggle with the meaning and social status of this talent and enterprise begins with its exposure to the waking world, and who has no place, no social or textual genre, in which to frame or disseminate those truths without fundamental risk. For Langland, moreover, that risk is not merely of casual distortion in transmission, indignities of the kind that befall texts in documentary reproduction conducted at one social remove from the author—"mismetering," generic miscategorization, or sheer moral obtuseness, of the kind to which Adam Scriveyn, the God of Love, or the Man of Law subject "Chaucer" in reception. The hazards of "Langland's" makings have immediate contemporary social consequences —dangers seemingly far more urgent and pressing, if less clearly named, than the spiritual risk of inadvertently misguiding readers that Chaucer forestalls with his Retractions (a prospect that seems oddly untroubling to Langland). In the 1380s, Langland's entire enterprise looks altogether too much like the vernacular theologizing and unauthorized teaching of Scripture against which the ecclesiastical authorities directed not only heightened suspicion, but active and vigorous prosecution. Its continued unclassifiability, mordantly marked by its repeated preemptive strikes against pretensions that might be imputed to it, remained the paradoxical guarantor of its cultural survival, and the exemption of its maker from suspicion of spiritual failings far worse, and far more eminently prosecutable, than idleness and wasting time.

Nor was this inbuilt sense of the cultural danger of "theology out of place" a belated recognition on Langland's part, arising along with the heightened risk of prosecution in the 1380s; on the contrary, it seems to be in several ways the founding condition of the poem in all its forms, fictively incorporated into its allegorical action from the first, and indeed anticipating many of what would later become key points of contention within the church about lay piety and religious observance and its relation to clerical example, both moral and discursive. Dame Study's contempt for both Will's pretensions to intellectual progress in knowledge of Dowel and for contemporary dinner table theological speculation, Scripture's and Anima's scorn for Will's display of his own gestures toward participation in the discourse of university theology, the cultivation of skill at academic "redeles" rather than "holy conversation" at the banquet for the Doctour of Divinity are all of a piece, and entirely continuous with all critiques throughout the poem, from nearly all of his instructors, of Will's virtually indefensible way of spending his time. These are the circumstances in which "Langland's" diffidence about the *textual* minutiae of his makings, and his evasiveness about fixity of social place or occupation, brought into concentrated fictive realization late in the C-revision, must be historically understood.

It is within these immediate historical pressures, experienced by the "maker" as pressures to define one's intent vis à vis the vernacular promulgation of scriptural text and interpretation, that we may at last return to the concentrated wit in Langland's appropriation of the recent vagrancy statute. There are in its several immediate sociopolitical contexts numerous ironies in the effort of Reason and Conscience to prosecute an apparently idle man in "long clothes"—not for his otiose and superfluous "makings" (which weigh far more heavily on Will's conscience than they do on the more businesslike concerns of his interrogators), still less as one of the clerical "faitours mendinantz," pretenders to religious vocation who have become both the target of popular suspicions and an excuse for growing anticlericalism, but rather for failing to take sufficiently seriously the universal obligation to labor in some manner for the sustenance of humankind. If the best outcome Will might hope for from this incipient draft into agrarian labor—indeed the one that in the event he is granted—amounts under the statute to a release back into his occupation, now pronounced "louable," then in effect Will "continues" from this point in the poem with his internal passport in hand. No such document is issued, of course; the implication of this intensely realized figuration seems to be that the authorizing document is none other than that which he has already made (of) himself—the work that is already "out there" in the world, everywhere and nowhere in particular, certainly not on the maker's person, and certainly not as a fixed text for whose discrete propositions he might be called to less fictive account. Will no longer has any need to carry this "passport"; his letter is already "patent" in the world in which Piers is a well-known figure—and has already registered his maker's anxious view of legally performative and actionable texts by tearing his pardon in half.

It is in this profoundly witty sense that Will's interrogation by Reason and Conscience, and his release into the "louable" life of which the laborious outcome is the poem we are reading—and which, this encounter reminds us, we have in some sense already read, since as the primary audience of this work we can no longer remember a time in which we did not know and desire Piers—may be said to displace and replace, in the larger dynamic of the "work," Piers's tearing of the pardon, now cancelled in C. With this last fictive supplementation of his work, Langland declares the sense in which his book is one of those that, as Boke announces in the Crucifixion passus, will be destroyed in the moment in which that which it declares and attests is realized—as the purely provisional performative character of all books and texts is made good in the user's action, while the text is rendered otiose. With his last fictive act of vagrancy, "Langland" is realized within the poem as a worker without papers, as Reason and Conscience in effect release him on his own recognizance, to "continue," like Rechelesnesse's messenger—or the lords' messengers exempted by the statute—without them. The social imaginary of his documentary society and the surplus literacy of the cleric *manqué* have colluded in a kind of implosion of the literary work as text. In its place appears the cultural work of literature.

Notes

1. For an argument that at the inception of Langland's poetic project the dream-vision functioned as the sign of literary fiction, see my essay, "The Audience and Public of Piers Plowman," in *Middle English Alliterative Poetry*, ed. David Lawton (Cambridge: D. S. Brewer, 1982), 114–15.

2. Lawrence M. Clopper, "Need Men and Women Labor? Langland's Wanderer and the Labor Ordinances," in *Chaucer's England: Literature in Historical Context*, ed. Barbara A. Hanawalt (Minneapolis: University of Minnesota Press, 1992), 110–29, argues that the C 5 episode draws on the 1349 labor ordinance and a 1359 London ordinance, but makes no claims concerning the 1388 measure. Anna P. Baldwin, *The Theme of Government in Piers Plowman* (Cambridge: D. S. Brewer, 1981), 59, 101, notes resemblances between arguments of the poem and the 1388 Statute, but makes no explicit inference about a relationship or its implications for the dating of the versions.

3. Critics have recently begun to articulate a more precise assessment of the impact of political, social, and ecclesiastical dissidence at the end of the fourteenth century, not simply in discrete reference by individual writers, but in creating a climate in which "literature" as such would, as it were in self-defense amid more noticeable pressures to textualize conformity, begin to claim a cultural space in some degree exempt from direct doctrinal, material, or historical truth-claims, a realm of the indeterminately speculative—a space of "play," yet of more than nugatory value. For authors of vernacular theology, vernacular political critique, or vernacular fiction these cultural pressures, focused on the question of social control and authorization of the command of textual competence, markedly intensified from 1381 on, and had similar effects; we will return briefly in conclusion to their mark on Langland's work. For an exemplary recent demonstration that Julian of Norwich was in effect negotiating these same perilous tracts at about the same time as Langland and Chaucer, see Nicholas Watson, "The Composition of Julian of Norwich's *Revelation of Love*," *Speculum* 68 (1993): 637–83.

4. David Aers, *Community, Gender, and Individual Identity: English Writing, 1360–1430* (London: Routledge, 1988), 20–72, offers a searching and complex examination of workers and "wasters" in Langland's poem and identifies these topics

as contested ideological projections of the period rather than fixed tenets of universal cultural opinion against which to fix the poet's attitudes and the meaning of his poem. In Aers's view, Langland adopted some of the ideological discourses by which his society blamed the economic victims of its practices for their own condition, but Aers sees these as having entered the poem as a kind of involuntary cultural tropism in which the poet caught himself and, realizing their unacceptable moral consequences, retreated into a principled, if perhaps no longer fully tenable, neo-Franciscan affirmation of the "rights" of the poor to the means of subsistence. In this account, the poet is enmeshed in ethical difficulties he shares with the surrounding culture, and strives valiantly if ultimately unsuccessfully to resolve; Aers does not seem to regard Langland's evocation of these anomalies as accessible to the kind of critical mimesis I shall propose here, or as an aspect of his specifically literary realization of his project, or as a complex figuration of authorial self-reflexivity. I agree with Aers that the poet does not resolve into an ethically consistent or politically tenable position the conflicting attitudes toward workers and wasters that his poem activates; my emphasis here, however, is on the internal work these evocations perform for poem and poet, and only by these means in and for their society.

　　5. Allen J. Frantzen, "Documents and Monuments: Difference and Interdisciplinarity in the Study of Medieval Culture," in *Speaking Two Languages: Traditional Disciplines and Contemporary Theory in Medieval Studies*, ed. Allen J. Frantzen (Albany: State University of New York Press, 1991), 1–24, 225–32, invokes Foucault's distinction between these terms in an admirable account of the past and of a desirable future of medieval studies. I do not here use either term in Foucault's sense, which seems to me exactly to reverse their conventional and applied scholarly meanings (as is very often the case in his work, and in that of other later twentieth-century theorists; Barthes, for example, uses "text" in a sense that cannot possibly refer to the object of "textual criticism").

　　6. It follows in turn from this claim that the John But who wrote of "Will"'s death in a conclusion he added to the A version cannot have been the king's messenger of that name whose death is registered by several documents as having occurred no later than April 1387 or, if he was, he wrote from conjecture or by inference from the long form(s) of the poem, rather than from knowledge of the poet's identity or the circumstances of production of the poem. I have argued elsewhere for the latter explanation of the A 12 ending; I would now, on further consideration of the wording of that ending, as well as on the basis of information not known to me at the time of that writing, argue that the John But of A 12 was not the king's messenger of Edith Rickert's conjecture. See my essay, "Making a Good End: John But as a Reader of *Piers Plowman*," in *Medieval English Studies Presented to George Kane*, ed. Edward Donald Kennedy, Ronald Waldron, and Joseph S. Wittig (Woodbridge: D. S. Brewer, 1988), 243–66. For information on the messenger John But's will and family connections with Gloucester, of which I was unaware when I wrote on the A 12 ending, see Caroline M. Barron, "William Langland: A London Poet," in *Chaucer's England: Literature in Historical Context*, ed. Barbara A. Hanawalt (Minneapolis: University of Minnesota Press, 1992), esp. 102–3. For more records concerning John But and discussion of the date of the poet's death, see Ralph Hanna III, *William Langland* (Aldershot: Variorum, 1993), 8–9, 28–29.

7. E. Talbot Donaldson, *Piers Plowman: The C-Text and Its Poet* (New Haven, Conn.: Yale University Press, 1949), 26–28, discusses the order of the C-revision, supporting with different and fuller arguments the view of Mabel Day that the C 5 "autobiography" and the C 9 additions to Piers's pardon were the two latest additions to the poem. A more detailed account of the sequence of the changes in C must await the publication of the Athlone C version, and I do not further discuss these below. I do, however, accept Donaldson's view of the relative lateness of these two passages, confining my attentions here only to the argument that the C 5 waking episode also postdates and refers to the C 9 additions. Ralph Hanna, "On the Versions of *Piers Plowman*," in *Pursuing History: Middle English Manuscripts and Their Texts* (Stanford, Calif.: Stanford University Press, 1996), 203–43, offers a conspectus and new hypothesis about the production and dissemination of the poem.

8. There is a further corollary to these claims, geographical rather than chronological. It follows from this sequence and its implications for dating the last stages of the C-revision, including the dependence of the ultimate one, the C 5 waking episode, on a Statute not promulgated in the commissions to the Justices of the Peace until 1390—that the C-reviser may well have derived his acquaintance with the Statute's provisions from metropolitan circles and circumstances, most probably those surrounding Chancery, through which the parliamentary enactments had to pass at several points as texts. If, as has been shown, the C-version was circulated initially from the Malvern region, this does not necessarily imply that the poet was himself at the end of the 1380s, or at the end of his life, located there or, if so, wholly removed from London affairs; the C 5 *apologia* is in fact staged to reemphasize the poem's character as a metropolitan production, from first (in the fictive time of the dreamer's youth) to last (the documentary time of the C 5 insertion), and in pointed contrast to both court (the imaginary site of the first vision) and countryside (the imaginary site of the second), between which it forms a pivot. We shall explore below the double time specification of the *apologia*, as situated imaginatively both in the poet's past—the time of inception of this poem as a project—and the present of fictive recollection and writing, as well as the significance of the placement of the episode in the poem. For a conjecture from textual evidence that broadly supports the present account of the C 5 episode—one that revises previous views concerning the circulation of the poem, see Robert Adams, "Editing *Piers Plowman* B: The Imperative of an Intermittently Critical Edition," *Studies in Bibliography* 45 (1992): 62–63. For evidence that C also entered dissemination early in London, see Ralph Hanna III, "Studies in the Manuscripts of *Piers Plowman*," *Yearbook of Langland Studies* 7 (1993): 12.

9. Cited by Helen M. Cam, "The Legislators of Medieval England," in *Law-Finders and Law-Makers in Medieval England: Collected Studies in Legal and Constitutional History* (London: Merlin Press, 1962), 156.

10. The roll for the Cambridge Parliament of 1388 has been lost; the enrolled Statute of Cambridge survives, as does an account of the parliament and a copy of the statute in Knighton's Chronicle, and another account in the Chronicle of the Monk of Westminster, which includes the text of the otherwise lost commons petitions to the parliament. J. A. Tuck, "The Cambridge Parliament, 1388," *English Historical Review* 84 (1969): 225–43; for the text of the Monk of Westminster's ac-

count, see L. C. Hector and Barbara Harvey, eds., *The Westminster Chronicle, 1381–1394* (Oxford: Clarendon Press, 1966), 355–69. The pertinent labor and vagrancy sections of the statute appear as Appendix 6 (pp. 31–32) in Hanna, *William Langland*, from the text in *Statutes of the Realm* 2. 56–59; the translations I quote in the essay are from the reprinting of the statute in English in A. E. Bland, P. A. Brown, and R. H. Tawney, eds., *English Economic History: Selected Documents*, 2d ed. (London: G. Bell, 1915), 171–76.

11. See T. F. Tout, *Chapters in the Administrative History of Mediaeval England: The Wardrobe, the Chamber, and the Small Seals*, Vol. 3 (Manchester: Mancester University Press, 1928), 440, on the "reactionary and repressive attitude" of the 1388 Statute; also A. L. Beier, "Vagrants and the Social Order in Elizabethan England," *Past and Present* 64 (1974): 3–29. May McKisack, *The Fourteenth Century, 1307–1399* (Oxford: Clarendon Press, 1959), 339, notes the unprecedentedly censorious designs of the 1388 statute, and in a note to their reprinting of it, Bland, Brown, and Tawney state (171) that it is "the basis of all subsequent Vagrancy and Poor Law legislation."

12. See Cam, "The Legislators of Medieval England," 135, 142, on the role of the justices on framing legislation; on preambles to statutes, see 143.

13. Paul Strohm has observed the loose association of kinds of "new associative practices" with each other in the discourse of this period and in the several measures of the Cambridge Parliament; see "The Textual Environment of Chaucer's 'Lak of Stedfastnesse,' " in Paul Strohm, *Hochon's Arrow: The Social Imagination of Fourteenth-Century Texts* (Princeton, N.J.: Princeton University Press, 1992), 57–74, esp. 57–65, and also in that volume Appendix B, "The Literature of Livery," 179–85.

14. It is in this light that another late fourteenth-century political sentiment, the increased suspicion of minstrels and entertainers, takes on a new aspect. Minstrels share the suspect characteristics of both groups whose alleged excesses the Cambridge Parliament sought to curtail, resembling paid retainers, day laborers, and fraudulent claimants of alms all at once: they propagate their employers' interests (and thus serve their own) while capitalizing on traditional forms of respect and assent accorded the maker of aesthetically powerfully occasions and objects of communal delectation. Minstrels are, in short, "bought" men, who mask the interestedness of their performances by broad allusion to, and exploitation of, professedly "traditional" social forms, bonds, and atavistic sentiments. The forms of mutual allegiance and communal self-help exemplified by guilds incur suspicion for similar reasons: they in effect construct and maintain their own communities through common discipline and ritual, instantiating (however innocuously in their own estimation), the constructed rather than "organic" character of all community affiliations. In effect, then, all these suspect groups have in common the property of quite self-consciously and self-interestedly deploying culturally powerful representations to coerce traditional moral and emotional sanctions to serve their immediate interests: they are in effect all knowingly and purposefully making and participating in social fictions as such.

15. The concerns of this parliament are throughout those of the commons, and show themes that were to become prominent once again as Henry of Lan-

caster came to power a little over a decade later: a notion of communal participation based in a nascent notion of "citizen" membership in a political community rather than subject status; a sense of national goals shared by the gentry, the urban burgesses, and the minor nobility; and the inability of the great magnates to form a secure alliance or coalition with them in these issues. On the conflict over liveries and maintenance, see Tuck, "The Cambridge Parliament, 1388," 236, 240; also both R. L. Storey, "Liveries and Commissions of the Peace, 1388–90," in *The Reign of Richard II: Essays in Honour of May McKisack*, ed. F. R. H. DuBoulay and Caroline M. Barron (London: Athlone Press, 1971), 140, and Caroline M. Barron, "The Quarrel of Richard II with London, 1392–7," in *The Reign of Richard II: Essays in Honour of May McKisack*, ed. F. R. H. DuBoulay and Caroline M. Barron (London: Athlone Press, 1971), 173–201. On magnate relations with the minor nobility, gentry, and burgesses, see Kenneth Bruce McFarlane, *Lancastrian Kings and Lollard Knights* (Oxford: Oxford University Press, 1972), 76–77.

16. See Monk of Westminster, 361, second paragraph, describing the seal—a detail not in the statute—and 363: "all the fines and amercements made before the said justices shall be levied by the sheriff and delivered to two persons, chosen by the county before the said justices, for the sustaining of the war and for the upkeep of the county where they are levied." The proceeds from fines under the earlier labor statutes were applied against the lay subsidies of their jurisdiction; this specification in the 1388 petition thus means to insure that the new regulations were similarly "revenue-enhancing" for the jurisdictions charged with their enforcement; see L. R. Poos, "The Social Context of Statute of Labourers Enforcement," *Law and History Review* 1 (1983): 37–42. Also relevant to the effort of the present essay to identify the interests served by this legislation—and to infer the poet's imaginative stake in adapting it to the uses of his fiction—is Poos's conclusion (57): "The immediate impetus behind the Statute of Labourers' creation undoubtedly stemmed from the aristocracy and gentry's concern to counter the increasingly high cost and problematic availability of labour which threatened to overturn their economic regime, a concern whose persistence is reflected in successive reenactments of the labour legislation during the later fourteenth and early fifteenth centuries. . . . But by effectively co-opting elements within rural communities into the machinery for the labour laws' enforcement, as had been accomplished at a very early date for English criminal law in general, proceedings under the Statute betray a much more complex web of interests, shared by medieval villagers themselves, in controlling labour resources, and any consideration of the Statute of Labourers must embrace their participation in the legal sanctions regulating those interests."

17. On the political give-and-take of this parliament generally, and its role in effecting Richard II's reassertion of his powers, see Tuck, "The Cambridge Parliament, 1388," 225–43.

18. The Monk of Westminster's account trenchantly records the conflicting rhetorics of class and prerogative at work in the dispute; see 354–59.

19. It is far from incidental that in the course of proposing the abolition of maintenance, commons was also forced to define what it understood by the term "because there are different opinions about the cases in which maintenance ought or ought not to be adjudged." The definition it provides is lengthy, and unprece-

dentedly broad. Barbara Harvey notes that "maintenance, in the strict sense, was the supporting of another's plea without an arrangement to share the profits," while the petition uses the term "to cover also the offences of champerty (supporting a plea in consideration of a share in the profits) and conspiracy to abuse legal procedure and frustrate the course of justice," and that "all three had been statutory offenses since 1293" (Hector and Harvey, *The Westminster Chronicle, 1381–1394*, 358–59). Beyond this it should be added that the petition extends the term to forms of collective activity that it might be difficult to prosecute even as conspiracy, e.g., "when any gather together in great routs and multitudes of people in excess of their degree and condition (*outre leur degre et estat*) in fairs, markets, sessions of justices, courts, lovedays, and elsewhere and maintain and support false provisors or others in their churches or prebends with great power, to the disturbance of the law or to the intimidation of the people." See Tuck, "The Cambridge Parliament, 1388," 234–35, on the dispute, and later outcomes, concerning the restriction of livery; also Strohm, *Hochon's Arrow*, 57–74, 179–85.

20. Tuck, "The Cambridge Parliament, 1388," 237–38. Tuck notes that nothing was ever done with the information collected, and that in the absence of any explanation for the measure in the writ ordering the inquiry, the masters and wardens of many guilds were understandably puzzled about the purposes of the inquiry, and responded in a variety of ways, including prostestations of innocence of any illegal intentions or activities, or disloyalty to the king. Tuck notes that such responses were especially frequent from the eastern counties, the main center of the 1381 revolt, where fear of sedition, the scarcely concealed subtext of the parliamentary petition, was inferred, though absent from the writ. Caroline M. Barron, "The London Middle English Guild Certificates of 1388–9," *Nottingham Medieval Studies* 39 (1995): 108–18, discusses the shared language and the sociopolitical position of those who made returns in London.

21. Tuck offers this interpretation of the absoluteness and universality with which commons' demands were framed. While this may be true from the short-range immediate political perspective of the participants in the assembly, in longer retrospect the text of the labor and vagrancy proposal, and its enactment almost without revision, admits of a more ominous reading. All of these measures—the one on labor and vagrancy that was adopted as well as the two on livery and on guilds that failed of enactment—implicitly assert a "state" or encompassing common interest, as over against those of lordly prerogative, ecclesiastical privilege, or individual conscience, in matters formerly regulated in a variety of different and less comprehensive jurisdictions. It should not be overlooked that the most important legal principle involved in the 1388 petition to abolish livery was not the definition of the crime, but in effect a jurisdictional mandate, which was addressed only indirectly by the protesting lords: that "justices of the peace and assize should have power to investigate and try cases of maintenance, bribery, or other means of corrupting juries," Tuck, "Cambridge Parliament," 234; that is, they object to the prospect that the ancient prerogatives of the lords should be subject to determination in local courts. Similarly, as we shall see below, ecclesiastical charity administration is implicitly ceded to, or at least shared with, a "state" interest in crime and public order as the regulatory principle of almsgiving, as individual employers' interests

in obtaining workers on mutually acceptable terms is implicitly ceded to the state's authority to command enforced labor and selectively punish alms-seekers.

22. *Statutes of the Realm* (London: HMSO, 1810), 1. 307; the English translation from which I quote appears in Bland, Brown, and Tawney, *English Economic History: Selected Documents*, 164–67. On enforcement, see Bertha Haven Putnam, *The Enforcement of the Statutes of Labourers during the First Decade after the Black Death, 1349–59* (New York: Columbia University Press, 1908). It is noteworthy that terms for specifying price standards, which also include allowance for the cost of transporting victuals, have a general resemblance to canon law determinants of the "just price," heretofore the only systematic thinking on the topic available for adaptation; see Odd Langholm, *Economics in the Medieval Schools* (Leiden: Brill, 1992), passim.

23. 13 Richard II. c. 8. Nora Kenyon has suggested that the unaccustomed delay in enforcing the 1388 statute (it was not included in the Commissions of the Peace until June 1390) was due to Parliament's slow recognition that there was in practice no enforceable national standard for these wages—that a highly elastic labor market was still in the process of becoming stabilized. An inquiry into prices and wages in Essex, held before the justices of the King's Bench in 1389, seems to acknowledge this; see Nora Kenyon, "Labor Conditions in Essex in the Reign of Richard II," *Economic History Review* 4 (1932): 429–60.

24. It is this attitude whose durability and force Richard badly miscalculated from the time he assumed his majority. The Lancastrian monarchy, by contrast, shrewdly grasped and exploited this sentiment, and the strategic alignment of *mediocres* that could sustain it. That this reconfiguration was visible and accessible to theoretical as well as applied general description in this period is attested by Sir John Fortescue, and its constituents were well in place for at least a century before that; see E. F. Jacob, "Sir John Fortescue and the Law of Nature," *Bulletin of the John Rylands Library* 18 (1934): 359–76. While it is broadly true that "medieval governments had no social policy in our understanding of the term," there are in the latter half of the fourteenth century sporadic ventures into what I have called in this essay "visionary legislation"—parliamentary initiatives, usually drawn in sweeping and virtually unenforceable terms, indicating "moral panic" about large perceived dislocations in social and economic regularities and attempting to control them by a variety of universal calibrations—of wages, prices, degrees of luxury of attire, and the like. Such "visionary legislation" is usually marked by a censorious preface and firm and ambitious social goals, accompanied by a far less steady grasp of what prosecution and enforcement measures could actually achieve, through the operation of existing policing measures and common-law procedures. Some of these measures, notably the labor and vagrancy legislation of 1388, served as patterns of later and more widely implemented measures, especially of the Tudor period. Sumptuary laws—the first of which was enacted in 1363 and repealed the following year—also instantiate this "moral panic"; see Christopher Dyer, *Standards of Living in the Later Middle Ages* (Cambridge: Cambridge University Press, 1989): on "social policy" (251), on the "moral panic" of the later fourteenth century and its legislative and other expression (88, 105, 238, 252), and on the sumptuary law of 1363 and its repeal (88).

25. Eileen Power and M. M. Postan, eds., *Studies in English Trade in the Fifteenth Century* (London: Routledge, 1933), 102–3; Arthur B. Ferguson, *The Articulate Citizen in the English Renaissance* (Durham, N.C.: Duke University Press, 1965).

26. Bertha Haven Putnam, "Maximum-Wage Laws for Priests After the Black Death, 1348–1381," *American Historical Review* 21 (1915): 12–32, discusses attempts to enforce this clause upon clerics, especially those engaged in what amounted to clerical "piece-work" such as the singing of masses or prayers—efforts that at least attest to the perception in this period that certain clerical occupations could be described in terms of quantifiable tasks, like other production or service crafts. In her book *The Enforcement of the Statutes of Labourers* (n. 22 above), 188–89 and Appendix, 432–33, Putnam cites a case of 1376, invoking the law on a chaplain retained to sing the divine service, who in the view of his employer failed to provide all that he had contracted for. While the case is determined on jurisdictional grounds, in favor of the legal responsibility of the chaplain's ordinary rather than the royal courts, the arguments also offer interesting substantive reasoning against the applicability of the law to chaplains: such service is not quantifiable like other labors, for it both requires spiritual preparation, and might also entail other duties, performed at the discretion of the chaplain, and as occasion requires; he "might be at one time disposed to sing and at another not."

27. The corresponding weakness in the 1388 version of the enforced-labor clause, however—the mark by which it displays its even more visionary character as legislation—is its harvest-time applicability, which presents another kind of problem to enforcement in the proposed venues. In its broad outlines, the measure is not without precedent: village by-laws had included measures providing for the employment of poor villagers at harvest, and determined their rates of pay; see Dyer, *Standards of Living in the Later Middle Ages*, 144. These by-laws may have been the distant model for the 1388 provision for a forced draft of laborers in time of harvest from a pool of workers beyond those customarily so employed, but the extension of the parliamentary provision beyond the village to a far broader jurisdiction substantively changed the feasibility of its enforcement. Seasonal necessity, however urgent, was of short duration, and after it had passed the effort became moot; the antecedent 1349 draft-labor measure, which specifically does not apply to craft workers or tradespeople, would then become the only one that could, in practice, be invoked successfully, and even then it could only be effective in returning the agrarian laborer to his original lord or employer, or forcing the worker offered employment to work at the locally customary rate; it could not successfully serve as a specifically harvest provision. Hence the enforced-labor clause of the 1349 Ordinance remains in application a kind of visionary addendum, little used, but an indication of the latent ambitions of the enactment to involve royal rather than manorial or village justice in regulating the freedom of able-bodied laborers, and a germ and augury of the more far-reaching designs of the 1388 Statute to extend the mandate to labor still more widely through the fabric of society—indeed, to assimilate all activity in the world to conceptualization as "work."

28. Brian Tierney, *Medieval Poor Law: A Sketch of Canonical Theory and Its Application in England* (Berkeley and Los Angeles: University of California Press, 1959), offers a comprehensive survey of the canonists' reasoning and its relations to secular governments' treatment of poor relief and vagrancy. Over several cen-

turies there had also been debate among the moral authorities of the church about these matters, especially concerning the conditions under which aid to those who importuned it might morally be withheld; Brian Tierney, "The Decretists and the Deserving Poor," *Comparative Studies in Society and History* 1 (1959): 360–73 offers a useful brief summary of this discussion. To note the underlying contrasts in moral reasoning between the canonists on the one hand and, on the other, the increasing—and increasingly assertive—national legislation on the topic of vagrant beggars is not to say that either of these authorities felt itself to be in open conflict with the other, or competing in either moral principle or practical jurisdiction. The 1388 statute presupposes the continued existence of the ecclesiastical charity apparatus to provide for those truly unable to labor, and in 1391 a statute was enacted that used the authority of the secular government to secure enforcement of existing ecclesiastical law to distribute an annual sum to "poor parishioners" (15 Richard II, c. 6); Tierney, *Medieval Poor Law: A Sketch of Canonical Theory and its Application in England*, 129. Yet although the canonists disapprove of vagrancy and idleness in broad terms, ecclesiastical legislation and justice continues well into the fifteenth century to ignore the category of mobile and able-bodied unemployed as the growing social and ethical problem it was perceived to be, on the evidence of municipal and ecclesiastical regulation. William Lyndwood's *Provinciale* (1443), a collection of the canons of English provincial councils in the manner of the *Decretals*, with extensive interpretive commentary, attempts to define "extreme need," but as Tierney observes (124) "one would never gather from reading Lyndwood's glosses that there was an acute problem of vagabondage in the England of his day." Royal and parliamentary views of vagrant beggars, and those of ecclesiastical administration, were like the blind men's view of the elephant: they approached the same phenomena with different preconceptions, from different directions, and with different ideological and practical objectives—and therefore each described a different creature.

29. The 1349 Ordinance to this point was directed not only by writs to the sheriffs, but also by royal letter to the bishops, asking them to cause it to be proclaimed throughout dioceses, and also to constrain the wages of chaplains and other stipendiary clerics, compelling them "under penalty of suspension and interdict, to serve for the accustomed salary, as is expedient." The result was the circular *Effrenata*, issued by Simon Islip as Archbishop of Canterbury in 1350 and again in 1362; Archbishop Sudbury reissued it again in 1378. See Putnam, "Maximum-Wage Laws for Priests After the Black Death, 1348–1381," 18–27.

30. Presumably the nonlaboring recipient of alms might also be subject to draft labor, or to imprisonment for leaving a contracted term of service—and hence punishable under one of the other two clauses enforceable upon the able-bodied unemployed. But such a person would be prosecuted for not working, not for other crimes imputed to him, including begging under false pretenses or any other alleged deceptive practice, or for attitudes or designs attributed to him. Insofar as the penalty, and the "address" of this clause, is directed to the prospective almsgiver, it also in effect encourages contractual rather than open-ended "gift" relations between payer and recipient of any form of benefit, and thus might even be seen as a measure drawn very broadly against gangs, retainers, and other confederations of "honor" and patronage, such as those promoted by Lady Meed.

31. Putnam, *The Enforcement of the Statutes of Labourers During the First Decade After the Black Death, 1349-59*, 155-56, cites a twelfth-century regulation *de conditione operariorum*, drawn up by members of the trades and approved by London authorities, as well as several subsequent examples in London records.

32. It is by no means incidental to our concern that this ontology of the commune—that it is generated out of humanity's efforts to organize itself according to reason and nature to provide for its own material and spiritual sustenance—forms the basis for Langland's second vision. It is thus counterposed to the chief competing ontology of the human community—that it is an order of honor, rather than nature, devolved in the image of the heavenly hierarchy—the philosophical basis for the first vision, expounded by Holichurche. I shall develop this analysis elsewhere.

33. For an apposite discussion of "estate" as "the public aspect of individual property" and an account of its social operation that helps to clarify why display and spectacle were increasingly integral to this conceptual framework, see Howard Kaminsky, "Estate, Nobility, and the Exhibition of Estate in the Later Middle Ages," *Speculum* 68 (1993): 684-709.

34. This new formation is also implicit in the playful binary analysis of the king's "good subjects" under the banners of Wynnere and Wastour. This poem, datable, I think, to very shortly after 1352-53, shows that this reconfigured account of social membership was recognized as such—as an ideological discourse—early in its political genesis, and in circles closely intersecting those from which the 1349 ordinance and its enforcement had emanated. See Stephanie Trigg, ed., *Wynnere and Wastoure*, EETS 297 (Oxford, 1990), 37, n. 317; for the evidence on the date of the poem that I find persuasive, see Juliet Vale, *Edward III and Chivalry* (Woodbridge: Boydell and Brewer, 1982), 73-74. Jill Mann's analysis, in *Chaucer and Medieval Estates Satire* (Cambridge: Cambridge University Press, 1973), of the way in which the category of "estate" largely yields to that of work or occupation as a ground of social and moral differentiation, and of individual self-awareness and self-definition in the General Prologue to the *Canterbury Tales* also documents this shift of terms and perspectives.

35. *Liber albus* in *Munimenta Gildhallae Londoniensis*, ed. Thomas Riley, Rolls Series, vol. 1 (London: Longman, Brown 1859), 453; English translation in R. B. Dobson, *The Peasants' Revolt of 1381*, 2d ed. (London: Macmillan, 1983), 345. It is conceivable that this London measure furnished a model for the proposal to the Cambridge Parliament of the clause invalidating apprenticeship agreements for those who have spent their youth in land service; the distinctiveness of the parliamentary measure, however, is its definition of this category as distinct from, and more inclusive than, villein legal status.

36. This is part of a two-point proposal made "to protect the honour of all free men (*frankes*) of the kingdom"; it also asks that bondsmen of ecclesiastical estates be prohibited from purchasing lands or tenements in fee, since "such purchases pass for all time from the hands of temporal lords to those of spiritual lords, to the great destruction of the lay fee of this kingdom"; *Rotuli parliamentorum* (London: HMSO, 1783), 3:294; English translation appears in Dobson, 346. The purpose of the latter is to maintain the extent of lay (and hence taxable) domains, while not diluting the franchise; that of the former is less clear, but it appears aimed

at stemming the diminution of villein ranks and decreasing routes of upward social mobility for those of villein status, since clerical estate was yet another means of attaining civil freedom. (The king refused both measures.) Skeat, following the suggestion of Jusserand, believed that this 1391 petition was the specific referent of C 5.63, where "Will says that no clerk ought to receive the tonsure unless he be the son of a free man"; see Walter W. Skeat, ed., *The Vision of William concerning Piers the Plowman, in Three Parallel Texts* (London: Oxford University Press, 1886), 2:xxxv. I argue below that the logic of the passage is rather more duplicitous than that: Will appears not only to scorn the acceptance of bondsmens' sons into the clergy, but also to claim for himself an exemption from the labor statutes on grounds of clerical status. When Reason and Conscience inquire concerning his fitness for agrarian labor and note that the only circumstances that could exempt him from the harvest imperative would be either physical disability or sufficient land income to live on, Will's response, scarcely intelligible without reference to the 1388 statute, is to cite his early schooling—as if it were an equivalent form of exemption to those offered by his interlocutors. It is noteworthy that this sense of "free" (legally and civilly enfranchised) predominates numerically in C-version usage (C Pro. 73; C 3.108, III, 114; C 20.106 = B 18.103; C 21.33 = B 19.33; C 21.39 = B 19.39; C 21.59 = B 19.59; C 22.146 = B 20.146) over the senses that occur in the B-version: "liberal in bestowing benefits" (B 10.75, B 15.150, and B 15.151); "noble, magnanimous" (which cannot be firmly distinguished from the preceding; e.g., B 2.77), "(physically) unencumbered" (B 17.148 = C 19.122), or the equivalent of *liberum*, as in *liberum arbitrium*, "free will" (B 8.53, B 16.223; cf. C 10.51 [also "free wit"]), or (a sense unique to C) "available without cost or expense" (C 9.57). The sense "enfranchised," as, for example, by clerical orders, as well as ennobled or elevated, seems intended in Holichurche's introduction of herself to Will in a phrase unique to C: "'Holy churche y am,' quod she, 'þou oughtest me to knowe; / Y undirfenge þe formeste and fre man the made'" (C 1.72–3; cf. A 1.74, B 1.76). It is also in C alone that Holichurche is said to address Will "by name" (cf. "faire" in A and B), and also in the next line speaks the name "Wille," rather than "sone" as in A and B (C 1.4–5). As in the C 5 waking encounter, the C-version of the initial exchange between Will and Holichurche encompasses Will's civil as well as spiritual identity.

37. Christopher Dyer, "Piers Plowman and Plowmen: A Historical Perspective," *Yearbook of Langland Studies* 8 (1994): 155–76, discusses the ambiguities surrounding the term and the social category of "plowman," which could denote "either a full-time farm servant with the duty of plowing, or a self-sufficient peasant owning and using his own plow" (158), and observes that after "briefly invoking the image of the loyal farm servant in Piers Plowman's first appearance, Langland makes his principal vehicle for social and moral comment a peasant" (162). He discusses (161–62) the range of available terminology: "The more legalistic terms *villein* and *naif* were in decline in the late fourteenth century, and in the long term the words 'bond' or 'bondsman' (also meaning unfree) were going through a transition, until 'husbandman' came to imply in the fifteenth century a substantial peasant, without carrying any stigma of servile status." He adds that the assessors of the poll taxes of 1379 and 1380 had difficulty in finding a suitable vocabulary to describe peasants (a term scarcely used in England), and "perhaps realising the

growing irrelevance of legal distinctions, especially in the context of taxes which were related to wealth, they borrowed the classical word *agricola*. Often they called the main body of peasants *cultores* or cultivators, which could well be translated as plowmen. Besides the *cultores* were the smallholders, called labourers (*laboratores*), and other types of wage earners, servants called *famuli* or *servientes*." The semantic picture is further complicated by interlingual and cross-cultural differences in terms: the French *laboureur* denoted "a peasant with his own plough, as distinct from the smallholder who works with his hands, the *manoeuvrier*, a word which could confusingly be translated into English as 'labourer.'" The 1388 Statute forbidding "mistery or craft" employment of those engaged in agriculture until the age of 12 designates those to whom it applies as *celuy or celle qe use de laborer a la charue et charette ou autre labour ou service de husbandrie*; it is very clearly not about enforcing villein disabilities.

38. This point is concisely reflected in the 1388 Statute's significant erasure of virtually all of the important circumscriptions of the applicability of the 1349 "forced-labor" clause. The earlier measure, as we have seen, pertained only to those "not living by trade or exercising a certain craft," as well as lacking sufficient land for self-support and currently not in service to anyone, while the later one undertook to draft laborers, at least in harvest time, even from the ranks of craftspersons whose productive activities were not especially needful during the harvest. The virtual unenforceability of this provision should not obscure the important conceptual change it reflects: that occupations themselves were "permutable," at least temporarily, at the mandate of general community need—to be determined, of course, by the enforcing agency. (In structure, the provision broadly resembles the conception of "critical occupation" in wartime, invoked in the United States during the Second World War to exempt from the military draft those employed in industrial production occupations deemed essential to the war effort—with the difference that in the latter case the notion served to define the reach of the exemption rather than the draft.) An equally significant omission in the 1388 version of the harvest-time forced-labor clause was the 1349 provision that proffered employment was to be "in a suitable service, regard being had to his rank." Although the 1388 measure claimed to extend rather than replace previous labor laws, this omission likewise reflects the theoretical effacement of structural and legal distinction between the occupations of country and town, and implies that "rank" itself has begun to dissolve in the official imagination of the populace as a differentiated but mobile work force. Hence, in its most innovative provisions, the 1388 Statute has already largely conceded the immutable actuality of the social mobility it proposes to control.

39. It is probably for this reason that the 1388 enactment completely abandons the notable thematic interest of the 1349 ordinance in the contractual character of labor relations, whether within or beyond agrarian activity. Society is now seen as constituted by permutable rather than fixed specific work arrangements, though membership in it entails a supervening general obligation to work.

40. *Rotuli parliamentorum*, 2:340–41; English translation in Dobson, *The Peasants' Revolt of 1381*, 72–74.

41. Clopper, "Need Men and Women Labor? Langland's Wanderer and the Labor Ordinances" notes (119) that the City of London had earlier (1359) ordained

the use of stocks to punish those able-bodied who refused to work. The same ordinance notes that many of these from diverse counties converge on London as "mendynauns pur avoir lour ese et repos," depriving the legitimate poor of alms, and therefore requires that they void the city within a specified period of days or face being put in the "seps [stocks] sur Cornhill" by the constable and beadle of each ward; Clopper considers these London provisions and those of the 1349 Ordinance to be the immediate referents of the C 5 waking encounter, and sees Reason and Conscience as acting in the capacity of constable and beadle. He does not consider the 1388 statute in this connection, possibly because the received view has been that Langland was dead by then—a view that in turn depends chiefly on accepting both the identification of the "John But" who wrote a conclusion to the A version as the king's messenger of that name whose death is recorded in 1387, and the premise that in reporting the poet's death But spoke from knowledge (rather than, for example, inference from the long versions to which he refers, at the end of which Will is represented as old and infirm and desiring to die). For a different view of But's testimony, see my essay, "Making a Good End: John But as a Reader of Piers Plowman"; also Hanna, *William Langland*, and Hanna, "On the Versions of *Piers Plowman*." In the C-version alone, Reason and Conscience have been appointed by the king at the end of the vision of Meed, within ten lines of the waking encounter, as "cheef chaunceller" and "a kynges iustice," respectively. It appears that Langland wishes to suggest that the legal authority under which Will is asked to account for himself is the highest and most encompassing in the realm. (This is not to say that such supreme officials would in fact have heard offenses against the labor statutes; it is, however, to say that the law in question is that of the kingdom itself, not simply that of London, however metonymic the metropolis may be in other respects.)

42. C. J. Ribton-Turner, *Vagrants and Vagrancy* (London, 1887).

43. 1 Edward VI. c. 3. See Beier, "Vagrants and the Social Order in Elizabethan England," 3–29. The marking of the vagrant's face renders his status an essential and ineradicable aspect of his identity; it cannot be effaced by any change in his fortune. It is in effect another form of the same function, the stabilizing of his identity through an inscription, a document, that is assigned in 1388 to the "internal passports"; the more intimate and indelible inscription is now the body itself.

44. A great deal of the diverse agenda of the Good Parliament is underwritten by a concern for the state of the royal finances, especially for the conduct of the French war; see George Holmes, *The Good Parliament* (Oxford: Oxford University Press, 1975), 63, 161. Fines collected under the labor laws were to be applied to paying the lay subsidies of the jurisdiction in which they were collected; the locality thus has an immediate and practical interest in their enforcement; see also n. 16 above.

45. *Rotuli parliamentorum*, 3:21–22; English translation in Dobson, *The Peasants' Revolt of 1381*, 76–78.

46. Rodney Hilton, *Bond Men Made Free: Medieval Peasant Movements and the English Rising of 1381* (London: Temple Smith, 1973), 158 and n.; Margaret Aston, "Lollardy and Sedition," *Past and Present* 17 (1960): 1–44. On the increase in expressed fear of social upheaval and crime throughout the fourteenth century,

the "changing social threshold for the perception of violence and toleration of disorder," and the concomitant sense that the old means of control were no longer effective, see Richard W. Kaeuper, "Law and Order in Fourteenth Century England: The Evidence of Special Commissions of Oyer and Terminer," *Speculum* 54 (1988): 736–37; also Kaeuper, *War, Justice, and Public Order: England and France in the Later Middle Ages* (Oxford: Clarendon Press, 1988). The 1377 petition dwells prominently on the use of Domesday Book as a source for tenant claims of ancient rights; see Dobson, 76, especially his note on the text of the petition, indicating that exemplifications from Domesday Book were in use for at least a century before 1381 as a means for peasants to secure legally the withdrawal of villein customs and services from their lords. Equally noteworthy for our purposes is the 1376 petition's firm conviction that those who seek to make such representations are well provided with "counsellors, procurers, maintainers and abettors" for this purpose. This group of refractory agrarian workers is, in short, perceived to be capable of acting collectively to secure its economic aims; see Simon A. C. Penn and Christopher Dyer, "Wages and Earnings in Late Medieval England: Evidence from the Enforcement of the Labour Laws," *Economic History Review* 2d ser. 43 (1990): 365. They were also seen as having access to the legal knowledge, instruments, and know-how to make good their claims by the required documentary means. On the validity of this belief, see Steven Justice, *Writing and Rebellion: England in 1381* (Berkeley and Los Angeles: University of California Press, 1994).

47. Unexplained goings-about by workers are imagined by the 1388 statute in revealing vividness, extending to the possibility that their games and recreations may quickly turn to rebellion and violence—as indeed in 1381 the Corpus Christi feast and midsummer bonfire festivities had rapidly been annexed to the expressive vocabulary and power of the revolt (see Justice, *Writing and Rebellion: England in 1381*, ch. 4): "Servants and labourers shall have bows and arrows and use them on Sundays and feast days, and entirely forsake games of ball as well hand as foot and the other games called quoits, dice, casting the stone, skittles and other such unsuitable games" (c. 6).

48. The interdependence of these perceptions of social fracture and permutable social identity is discussed in more detail in my essay, "William Langland's 'Kynde Name': Authorial Signature and Social Identity in Late Fourteenth-Century England," in *Literary Practice and Social Change in Britain, 1380–1530*, ed. Lee Patterson (Berkeley and Los Angeles: University of California Press, 1990), 15–82. For a vivid example of the kind of imposture that was apparently considered all too easy to bring off, see the account of the arrest in London in 1380 of two men, one from Somerset and one from York, who pretended to be mutes whose tongues had been cut out by robbers who had also deprived them of all their goods. Brought before the mayor, aldermen, and sheriffs, they were found to be "stout enough to work for their food and raiment, and had their tongues to talk with"; they were exhibited in the pillory with the instruments of their imposture ("tongues" made out of leather, which they had displayed in sign of their misfortune and disability) "to the end that other persons might beware of such and the like evil intent, falsity, and deceit." See Henry Thomas Riley, ed., *Memorials of London and London Life*

in the XIIIth, XIVth, and XVth Centuries, 1276–1419 (London: Longmans, Green, 1885), 445–56.

49. On the increasingly fictive deployment of a discourse of ideal "lives" and an appropriation by secular political apologetics of the claim of radical "need," see Anne Middleton, "Langland's Lives: Reflections on Late-Medieval Religious and Literary Vocabulary," in *The Idea of Medieval Literature: New Essays on Chaucer and Medieval Culture in Honor of Donald R. Howard*, ed. James M. Dean and Christian K. Zacher (Newark: University of Delaware Press, 1992), 227–42.

50. See Dyer, *Standards of Living in the Later Middle Ages*, 101–3, 238–39.

51. For discussion and a list of poetic signatures that incorporate reference to Will's long and lean stature, see my essay, "William Langland's 'Kynde Name': Authorial Signature and Social Identity in Late Fourteenth-Century England," 15–82.

52. The *Glossa Ordinaria* on the parable offers a succinct example (PL 113, col. 314): in this "similitude" the steward is commended "not because he acted fraudulently against God, but because he conducted himself prudently." Hugh of St. Cher and Nicholas of Lyra make the interpretive hazards of the parable progressively more explicit, cautioning that the steward's conduct is not in all its features an imitable example of conduct, and emphasizing that the presence of the Pharisees at the rehearsal of the parable is a factor in its interpretation. Hugh expands "prudence" as "providence," explaining that it consists in the distribution of alms to the indigent; of "the mammon of iniquity" verse, he adds, "This part subverts some people toward perdition, namely, those who poorly understand it"; Hugh of St. Cher, *Opera omnia* (Venice, 1754), 6. f. 226v. Expanding upon the Gloss's term, Nicholas somewhat plaintively explains the necessarily enigmatic aspect of a parable—"Parabola enim similitudo est. Similitudo autem non semper currit quattuor pedibus immo si teneret in omnibus iam non esset similitudo sed magis identitas" ["For a parable is a similitude. A similitude however does not always 'run on all fours,' for if it corresponded in all features (to the thing expounded) it would not be similitude but identity"]; Nicholas of Lyra, *Postilla super Epistolas et Evangelia quadragesimalia* (Venice, 1494).

53. A. G. Rigg and Charlotte Brewer, eds., *Piers Plowman: The Z Version* (Toronto: Pontifical Institute of Mediaeval Studies, 1983).

54. On this passage, and the vexed history and interpretation of the text at this point, see Ralph Hanna III, "Robert the Ruyflare and His Companions," in *Literature and Religion in the Later Middle Ages: Philological Essays in Honor of Siegfried Wenzel*, ed. Richard G. Newhauser and John A. Alford (Binghamton, N.Y.: Medieval and Renaissance Texts and Studies, 1995), 81–96.

55. It is not surprising that for Robert the Robber, the lord's command to "render accounts" implies a requirement that he repay his ill-gotten gains, and prompts his use of the Dishonest Steward's reply as a protestation of his lack of the means to do so, for the gospel passage almost invariably prompts the commentators' distinction on just this point. Later medieval glossators were at pains to make clear that the "mammon of unrighteousness" through which the steward in the parable rectified his situation referred not to the restoration of ill-gotten gains, which

according to Augustine and all subsequent moral and canon law had to be repaid to the injured party (an act which belonged to restitution, not charity), but rather to worldly goods generally, *divites huius mundi*, which ought to be dispended in charity rather than hoarded; see both Hugh of St. Cher and Nicholas of Lyra, loc. cit. (note 52 above).

56. Thomas Wimbledon of Merton's *sermo ad status* on this text has long been assigned to the year 1388, but the occasion on which it was preached is unknown. See Thomas Wimbledon, *Wimbledon's Sermon Redde rationem villicationis tue: A Middle English Sermon of the Fourteenth Century*, ed. Ione Kemp Knight (Pittsburgh: Duquesne University Press, 1967). In view of its complex thematic resonance with the topics of the Cambridge Parliament, one might surmise that it was composed specifically in anticipation of that parliament, and with reference to its agendas. The text is the gospel lection for the Wednesday after the Sunday after Trinity (i.e., the Wednesday six days after Corpus Christi Day), which in 1388 fell on June 3. On that day the king renewed his coronation oath in the presence of the assembled estates, and on the following day the long Merciless Parliament finally adjourned (Hector and Harvey, *Westminster Chronicle*, 294, 306, 342). The chronicler notes that a "solemn mass and sermon" preceded the king's oath-taking, and Harvey notes (343) that Robert Braybrooke, bishop of London, celebrated Mass on that occasion, and that thirteen bishops were present. By then the Cambridge Parliament was already being planned: though the king spent the remainder of June and much of July in the pleasures of the chase, he held a council at Oxford on July 27 where it was determined that the next parliament would be held at Cambridge on September 9. Tuck, "The Cambridge Parliament, 1388," 231, adds, citing Higden, that at the July council it was also agreed that "the convocation of Canterbury should meet on the same date at Great St. Mary's, and the convocation of York at York 'or elsewhere'"; in the event, the convocation of Canterbury adjourned to London, and that of the northern province was postponed to January 24, 1389. The first order of business at the Cambridge Parliament was the direction of four new bishops to their sees (all assumed their temporalities within the month of September), acting upon papal provisions proclaimed the preceding April 3 (see Hector and Harvey, *Westminster Chronicle*, 334, 354, and notes). Almost any of these occasions, from June 3 through the opening of the Cambridge Parliament, could have furnished the highly visible platform from which Wimbledon's *Redde rationem* sermon was preached, concerned as all of them were with one form or another of the three questions into which Wimbledon subdivided the commandment to render accounts: "how hast þou entred; . . . how hast þou reulid; . . . how hast þou lyuyd"; Wimbledon, *Wimbledon's Sermon Redde rationem villicationis tue: A Middle English Sermon of the Fourteenth Century*, 70. Especially pertinent to Langland's use of the parable in the C 5 episode is Wimbledon's application of these questions to clerics, beginning with its pointed reference to ecclesiastical patronage: "Why also setten men here sones oþer here cosynus to scole? Wheþer for to gete hem grete auauncementis oþer to make hem þe betere to knowen how þey shulden serue God?" (72). Whether the sermon was designed specifically in reference to the Cambridge Parliament, as Brinton's convocation sermon containing the fable of the rats and mice

was in 1376, is beyond conjecture here; like the earlier sermon, however, it resonates with those C-revision additions discussed here, as the rat-parliament fable similarly resonates with his additions to the coronation scene in the B-version, though the question of "source" and direction of verbal indebtedness, if any, is probably indeterminable.

57. In many instances this phrase serves as a witty learned shorthand for the profession of the cleric as nonmanual "laborer," and thus efficiently evokes—sometimes with mordant irony—the banner under which clerical self-justification could easily become self-righteous, the mask under which it could conceal, even from itself, mere idleness, and claim a pseudo-independent dependency. Abelard, in *Historia calamitatum*—I cite the translation of Abelard, *The Story of Abelard's Adversities*, trans. J. T. Muckle (Toronto: Pontifical Institute of Mediaeval Studies, 1964), 59–60—invokes it in describing his founding of the Paraclete, in the face of the detraction of his enemies, who are depicted as baffled that in his degradation he is still surrounded by his students, "who have at hand in the cities everything they need, [yet] despise the comfort of city life and flock to a solitude with its poverty, and of their own accord become wretched." It is thus in status degradation like that of the steward that Abelard invokes the steward's excuse: "at that time unbearable poverty compelled me to run a school since *to dig I was not able, and to beg I was ashamed.* And so having recourse to the profession I knew, I was driven to work with my voice instead of my hands." Jill Mann, "Satiric Subject and Satiric Object in Goliardic Literature," *Mittellateinisches Jahrbuch* 15 (1980): 63–86, cites the Archpoet's satiric invocation of the "wisdom of the children of this world" in his miming of the steward's voice (in the poem *Archicancellarius, vir discrete mentis*), and the comically compromised and paradoxical nature of the claims to mental independence he asserts with this gesture (*fodere non debeo quia sum scolaris*). Even if Langland did not know Abelard's work, he was, as Mann notes, familiar with goliardic verse and the complexities of goliardic personae. And he would have recognized another echo of the steward closer to home, and in a context much like that he invokes in this episode. In a letter of 1391 reminding his diocesan bishops of the circular *Effrenata* (an injunction against clerical avarice promulgated by the Archbishop of Canterbury in 1350, as a clerical parallel to the 1349 Ordinance of Laborers, and reissued with elaboration in 1362 and 1378), Archbishop Courtenay speaks of greedy pluralists, those who buy and sell benefices ("choppe churches," *vulgariter nuncupatim*) as those who profess themselves, by virtue of their clerical training, "unable to dig" and by hoarding benefices and stipendiary appointments leave none for other clerics, forcing the latter into unfitting beggary. The letter was directed particularly against the abuse of stipendiary clerical positions in London, and like Langland's C 5 episode, invokes in this connection the verse used in the ordination of clerics that also became a "neck-verse," "The lord is a portion of my inheritance" (Ps. 15:5; cf. C 5.60). *Effrenata*, and the increasingly heated rhetoric of its three fourteenth-century promulgations, is discussed in Putnam, "Maximum-Wage Laws for Priests After the Black Death, 1348–1381," 25–26. For Courtenay's letter, and the texts of the three versions of *Effrenata*, see David Wilkins, ed., *Concilia Magnae Brittaniae et Hiberniae* (London, 1737), 3:215–17; also 1–2, 29, 50–61, 135. For

a translation of the letter and a discussion of its circumstances, see Joseph Dahmus, *William Courtenay, Archbishop of Canterbury 1381–1396* (University Park: Pennsylvania State University Press, 1966), 214–17, 261–65.

58. On the eremitic life as a "vocation of desire," see Ralph Hanna III, "'Meddling with Makings' and Will's Work," in *Late-Medieval Religious Texts and Their Transmission: Essays in Honour of A. I. Doyle*, ed. A. J. Minnis (Woodbridge: D. S. Brewer, 1994), 85–94.

59. Putnam, *The Enforcement of the Statutes of Labourers during the First Decade after the Black Death, 1349–59*, 71, notes sporadic efforts to prosecute chaplains and stipendiary clerics under the contract clause of the 1349 Ordinance; by later in the fourteenth century, "while quarter sessions were enforcing the wages and price clauses against what are technically called the labouring classes, the upper courts were upholding an extension of the contract clause so wide as to make it apply to all who were working for salaries, an extension undoubtedly never contemplated by the framers of the ordinance." She cites a King's Bench case of 1377 against a chaplain, in which it was ultimately decided that, although his terms of employment were in effect a contract of service, he was not "bound by the statute as other people are" because his service, unlike that of a "laborer or artificer," did not consist in any set array of daily tasks, but varied according to the dictates of conscience as well as diverse duties of an unpredictable character, such as visiting the sick, performing last rites, and the like; see her Appendix, 433.

60. As noted, the 1388 Statute is the first to dissolve the distinction between bond and free agrarian workers and extend its application to the latter as well as to the enforcement of villein legal disabilities. An interesting, if ultimately unsuccessful, effort to prosecute *gyrovague* religious under the labor ordinances occurred in Hertfordshire in 1356. A vicar and a hermit were indicted before the justices of laborers for having "scorned and poured contempt day after day on the king's statute and ordinance of labourers . . . and proclaimed that all who made the same, support or agree to them and execute them or maintain them . . . are excommunicate." The hermit in question is said to be "a common malefactor, wandering about with [the vicar] night and day, at various times and places. Dressed in various changes of garments of various kinds, changed every day, he wanders about, goes into hiding and dodges here and there on the king's highways as well as in other places, public and private, *carrying a long, thick stick*, waylaying the king's justices . . . and savagely threatening their ministers and even themselves with death and mutilation and arson and other hideous and unspeakable evils" (emphasis mine). The accused were, as Sayles describes it, "found guilty of denouncing the statutes and trapesing round the countryside, but of nothing else." The vicar was allowed to make fine, but the hermit was outlawed four years later. See G. O Sayles, ed., *Select Cases in the Court of King's Bench*, vols. 6, 7, Pubications of the Selden Society (London: Quaritch, 1965, 1971), 108–11. This case provides an episode in the early history of the surly "stafstriker" and his vagrant profession as warranting legal redress.

61. The dual habitual "place" claimed by Will here—"in Londone and uppe lond boþe"—also has some applicability to Langland's career, so far as one can judge from the combination of the poet's dialect, internal reference, and the com-

plex history of manuscript dissemination; see below, and Hanna, "On the Versions of *Piers Plowman*," 203–43.

62. "Seruen" in this context is at best ambiguous, and is not usually used by Langland to denote the conduct of the Mass, but rather to denote appointed or contracted work obligation of any kind, from appointment as chancellor to agrarian wage service. Those who "singen" in a church need be no more than choristers, not necessarily ordained priests; on the status of choristers, and the education and role of the "song-school," see the forthcoming University of California, Berkeley, doctoral dissertation of Katherine Zieman. On attempts to prosecute stipendiary clerics under the labor statutes, especially those engaged in occasional prayer service, and hence broadly analogous to lay day laborers or piece-workers, see Putnam, *The Enforcement of the Statutes of Labourers during the First Decade after the Black Death, 1349–59*, 27–29.

63. Here again, the Latin tag concords on the thematic term *redde*, sustaining both the parable intertext of the Dishonest Steward called to account (*redde rationem villicationis tue*), introduced into the episode by the manner of Will's first response, and the larger ultimate apocalyptic sorting of the community evoked by the harvest-time occasion. It also thereby evokes the many resonances of this episode with both the final visions of the earthly field and the other anticipations of divine judgment invoked by the imperative *redde/reddite* throughout the poem; see below.

64. On the use of the term "loller" in the poem, almost exclusively in the C version, see Wendy Scase, *Piers Plowman and the New Anticlericalism* (Cambridge: Cambridge University Press, 1989), 149–60.

65. As does the Archpoet, in his invocation of *fodere non valeo* (see note 57 above).

66. Ymaginatif, who speaks these lines to Will/Rechelesnesse, uses them in recounting the salvation of the thief on the cross, noting that "thogh the theef hadde heuene he hadde noen hey blisse" (C 14.135) and among the blessed at the lord's feast he must in consequence sit, not on the dais or even at a side table, "bote as a beggar bordles be mysulue on þe grounde" (140). His point is that "he þat is ones a thef is eueremore in daunger," and that works are therefore not inconsequential in the economy of salvation. Once again, the C 5 representation of Will draws upon a rich associative matrix of biblical texts already established in the poem, consistently associated by Langland with the rendering of accounts of one's deeds, particularly by those of low or indeterminate social status, morally suspect lives or criminal conduct—Robert the Robber, the thief on the cross, the servant called to Christ.

67. See John A. Alford, *Piers Plowman: A Guide to the Quotations* (Binghamton: State University of New York Press, 1992), 80, and references.

68. Mann, "Satiric Subject and Satiric Object in Goliardic Literature," 63–86, observes the fondness of goliardic satirists for the "problem parables," among them that of the Dishonest Steward, as sites for fictive positions and voices. Her analysis is especially suggestive on the indeterminately fictive character of the speaker of such tirades in the poem, especially in her emphasis on the goliard as, in Langland's phrase, "a glotoun of wordes"—someone in love with and enmeshed in language itself as his distinctive medium of self-definition. Scase, *Piers Plowman and the New*

Anticlericalism, 125–37, discusses at length the relation of this episode to anteced-ent traditions of anticlerical satire. Her account of the complex intertextualities and genre-resonance of this episode is indispensable, and a salutary critical corrective to the search for directly "autobiographical" information in it. She does not, however, discuss the structural and immediate historical purpose of Langland's introduction of this episode into the C-version, which is my chief concern here.

69. Though mediated by a complex mimesis of interested satiric diatribe, Will's remarks on reduced standards for entry into the clergy, and his pointed charge that this is a new as well as deplorable development, are not solely self-justifying fantasy, but refer to relatively recent changes. In an effort to replenish the ranks of the clery diminished by the 1349 plague, conditions for admission to the clergy were revised to allow some previously excluded to undertake holy orders; see Putnam, "Maximum-Wage Laws for Priests after the Black Death, 1348–1381," 13.

70. As Scase notes, *Piers Plowman and the New Anticlericalism*, the vernacu-larity of Will's "makings," and that of Langland's literary enterprise, greatly com-plicates the poem's relation to anticlerical satire. "To articulate a relationship with, and difference from, the clerical literary tradition was therefore to articulate the relationship between the poet and the cleric. But the antireligious rendition only allowed the poet to say who, in generic terms, he used to be and therefore who he was not now. . . . The poet could not yet say who, in literary terms, he was to be-come" (173).

71. See Daniel Embree, "*Richard the Redeless* and *Mum and the Sothsegger*: A Case of Mistaken Identity," *Notes & Queries* n.s. 22 (1975): 4–12; Daniel Embree, *The Sothsegger at Court* (Ph.D. diss., University of California, 1981).

72. On the many ideational and political instabilities of "complaint" literature in relation to the themes of the 1381 revolt and religious dissidence, see Richard Firth Green, "John Ball's Letters: Literary History and Historical Literature," in *Chaucer's England: Literature in Historical Context*, ed. Barbara A. Hanawalt (Min-neapolis: University of Minnesota Press, 1992), 189, 193. Scase, *Piers Plowman and the New Anticlericalism*, 144–49, 161–73, discusses the multiform character of late medieval anticlericalism as a political and ideational force distinct from Lollard critique, and Kathryn Kerby-Fulton, *Reformist Apocalypticism and Piers Plowman* (Cambridge: Cambridge University Press, 1990), 172–86, emphasizes that criticism of the clergy and of church institutions extended in the English fourteenth century well beyond Wycliffite discourse. On complaint as a mode of courtly discourse, specifically for covert and indirect political criticism, see Lee Patterson, "Writing Amorous Wrongs: Chaucer and the Order of Complaint," in *The Idea of Medi-eval Literature: New Essays on Chaucer and Medieval Culture in Honor of Donald R. Howard*, ed. James M. Dean and Christian K. Zacher (Newark: University of Delaware Press, 1992), 55–71; Lee Patterson, "Court Politics and the Invention of Literature," in *Culture and History, 1350–1600*, ed. David Aers (London: Harvester Wheatsheaf, 1992), 7–41.

73. For a discussion of the relation of Ball's teachings to Langland's poem, see Justice, *Writing and Rebellion: England in 1381*, 102–39, especially, on bastardy, 106–17.

74. John A. Burrow notes the momentary pun on "soil" (*solum*) created by

Langland's separation of the adjective *solo* from its noun *pane* ("bread alone") in his disposition of this Latin citation; Burrow, *Langland's Fictions* (Oxford: Clarendon Press, 1993), 104.

75. On the strength of the adversative conjunction *ac* that follows it, Ralph Hanna (in a recent communication in typescript) has proposed the reading of "lyeth" as "misrepresents," "tells an untruth" rather than "applies (to your condition)," the sense in which Derek Pearsall (in his edition of the C-version) understands the verb here, a common legal usage of the word. Hanna's argument is that if the verb is to be construed as meaning "applies," one would expect the following remarks to be introduced with "for" or another conjunction denoting a causative or explanatory rather than oppositional relation to the preceding clause. For the suggestion that the inquiry of Reason and Conscience is to be understood within the terms of *probatio*, the formal protocols for ascertaining the authenticity of a spiritual vocation or distinctive spiritual experience or vision, see Kathryn Kerby-Fulton, " 'Who has Written this Book?': Visionary Autobiography in Langland's C-Text," in *The Medieval Mystical Tradition in England*, ed. Marion Glasscoe, Exeter Symposium, vol. 5 (Cambridge: D. S. Brewer, 1992), 101–16.

76. It should not in the least give us pause that at the end of their interrogation of Will the function of Reason and Conscience in effect fuses their role at the end of the first dream, as the king's chief counsellors—and in C as "chief chancellor and chief justice"—with the preaching function proper to high ecclesiastical office that initiates the second; Will's waking encounter serves as the suture between these two guises of Reason and Conscience, as at once political and spiritual guides. It is indeed precisely in the name of the good civil and moral order of the land that both clerical and royal legislation about wages, labor, economic excess, and idleness coincided virtually seamlessly in this period. As Putnam, "Maximum-Wage Laws for Priests after the Black Death, 1348–1381," 29, notes, while the courts attempted to uphold the distinction between the jurisdictions of church and state concerning clerical remuneration, the commons by the later fourteenth century held that stipendiary clerics' wages were matters of contract, and that all contract belonged to the royal courts. The point for our purposes is not to determine whether, as I have attempted to demonstrate above, the most fundamental fictive terms of the C 5 episode are given by the 1388 Statute *rather than* (as been argued heretofore) those of ecclesiastical or scriptural injunction or moral theology, but rather to indicate how fully these discourses had interpenetrated by the time this episode was written—and hence the density of the superimposed vocabularies within which the scene acquires its rich significance for the poem. It is my argument here that the formal and ethical richness of the episode, whether considered as *probatio, sui generis* confession, authorial apologia, or an combination of these genres, is deepened by the historical specificities, and the political-juridical genres, including the Statute and its surrounding political discourses, within which it is staged, and that its larger formal implications are discernible chiefly in these terms.

77. For example, Anima's critique in B 15 of Will's use of his time in "meddling with makings" when he might instead say his Psalter—especially when there are "bokes ynow" already with aspirations to inculcate "dowel." For an argument that the poet's several self-naming and self-referring moments form a "signature

system" that operates diacritically across the narrative, see Middleton, "William Langland's 'Kynde Name': Authorial Signature and Social Identity in Late Fourteenth-Century England," 15–82.

78. Adams, "Editing Piers Plowman B: The Imperative of an Intermittently Critical Edition," 31–68.

79. See Anne Middleton, "Narration and the Invention of Experience: Episodic Form in *Piers Plowman*," in *The Wisdom of Poetry: Essays in Early English Literature in Honor of Morton W. Bloomfield*, ed. Larry D. Benson and Siegfried Wenzel (Kalamazoo, Mich.: Medieval Institute Publications, 1982), 91–122.

80. It might be noted that this dual positional and temporal perspective on the encounter resembles the artful deployment of double rhetorical ordering, the "natural" order of chronology and the "artificial" order of rhetorical selection and heightening allowed by argumentatively informed hindsight, so often admired in *Sir Gawain and the Green Knight*; see, for example, Larry D. Benson, *Art and Tradition in Sir Gawain and the Green Knight* (New Brunswick, N.J.: Rutgers University Press, 1965).

81. I intend the further implication of this claim, namely, that I am not fully convinced by any evidence or arguments thus far published that the C-revision was halted, discernibly short of realization of the poet's intended scope, by death, or by other disruption that requires the hypothesis of an executor to account for the state of the C-version as disseminated. I must, of course, suspend judgment until the Athlone C-version appears; in the meantime, it must be noted that all hypotheses about the process of revision and new production at all stages imply a poet who, while indeed careful of both craft and conceptual precision, as the Athlone editors rightly insist, is also not at any stage of his work either in secure control of the production of copies, or in possession of the full array of his working papers—a state of affairs that seemingly does not change greatly over the entire span of years during which the poem was being produced. Ralph Hanna's discussion, "On the Versions of *Piers Plowman*," in *Pursuing History* is especially valuable.

82. HM 114 (sigil Ht of the B-version), a heterogeneous text that conflates all three circulated forms of the poem in a way peculiar to itself, inserts its quite corrupt form of the C 9 materials on true and false hermits, "lunatik lolleres," and the deserving recipients of charity into the B-version text of the revolt of the "wasters" on Piers's field. "Ilchester" (sigil I of the C-version), University of London Library S.L. V. 88, a C-version for most of its length, begins with an A-Prologue that incorporates the same passages of C 9 that occur in Ht—in a form likewise corrupt, but corrupt in a way that suggests its descent from a form something like that of the Ht-text of these lines—into the array of folk on the field, among the false religious. See Wendy Scase, "Two *Piers Plowman* C-text Interpolations: Evidence for a Second Textual Tradition," *Notes & Queries* 232 (1987): 456–63.

83. The major C-additions pertaining to this topic include the following: C 12.153–247, a passage on patient poverty, replacing a much briefer one in B on forsaking possessions for the sake of "perfection," and uttered by Rechelessenesse soon after this figure is in C distinguished from the dreamer-persona as a kind of speaking alter ego; C 13.32–127, a new *distinctio* on poverty, which closes Rechelessenesse's discourse, figuratively comparing the patient poor to the messenger

traveling through the world unencumbered by anything but "hus mouthe ful of songes," and contrasting the joy and ease of his worldly journey with the burdened travel of the merchant; and C 9.70–161 and 188–281, two entirely new C-passages bridged by a passage (162–187) on beggars, thoroughly rewritten to replace 17 lines on similar matters in B and A. The C 9 additions form a long and virtually free-standing *distinctio* on true and false beggars and hermits, and turn prominently on a new and painstakingly defined use of the term "loller." With the C 5 waking *apologia*, these additions have been since Donaldson chief exhibits in scholars' discussions of the poet's interest in poverty, begging, and social parasitism as linked phenomena, troublesome to both social harmony and moral philosophy; they have also been the focus of intense critical speculation on Langland's reasons for increasing and focusing his attentions to these matters in the C-version specifically, and in a few long passages chiefly. While it is beyond the scope of this essay to rehearse either Donaldson's well-known discussions, or Scase's detailed account of the C 9 passages, a curious common feature of all of these additions *except* that in C 5 warrants mention: their very close similarity in length. The C 12 "patient poverty" addition is 95 lines, the C 13 poverty passage on messengers and merchants is 96, and the two free-standing C additions in Passus 9 are 92 and 94 lines, respectively. Each of them could have been contained on a single bifolium ruled for at least 24 lines per page, written for insertion into the poet's working revision copy. It may be significant that both Ht and I use only the two separate blocks of entirely new material of C 9, omitting the 26-line bridge between them that rewrites an AB passage. (With the bridge, the entire continuous C 9 addition would require two bifolia ruled for no more than 27 lines per page.) If Scase is correct in thinking that the makings of "lollers" referred to in C 5 are some form of the C 9 addition on this topic that entered circulation before the latter was firmly fixed into Piers's pardon and joined by the bridging material that refers to the pardon episode as its context, then possibly the variant placement of the two separate "loller" passages in Ht and I indicates scribal access to, and alternative dissemination of, the two bifolium inserts in the 24-line page format that, with the bridge, became the addition to the pardon. Such a hypothesis still assigns to scribal activity, rather than authorial "draft," the markedly variant state of both the Ht and I forms of these passages, while possibly explaining how the poet could refer in the new C 5 episode to Will's "makings of lollers" as having some form of prior circulation or reputation (and moreover in London specifically), distinct from reference to this topic in the C-version itself—since, as Scase has shown, with one exception in the B-version (a single instance of the term "loller" in B 15), Langland's use of the term is confined solely to the C-version, and is confined almost entirely to the C 5 and C 9 additions. Unlike all of the foregoing large-scale C-additions, the C 5 waking episode is 108 lines in all, including its four-line bridge to preexisting B material at the beginning of the second vision, suggesting its insertion on a bifolium ruled for at least 27 lines per page—the format, incidentally, of two of the earliest C-version manuscripts, both products of the London book trade. See Hanna, "Studies in the Manuscripts of *Piers Plowman*," 12.

84. Possibly it is more than coincidence that the extensively reasoned case against a chaplain, hired by the plaintiff (a parson) as seneschal but also to "be his

parochial chaplain at certain times," reported by Putnam, *The Enforcement of the Statutes of Labourers during the First Decade after the Black Death, 1349-59*, Appendix, 432–33, came to the justices in 1376, the year of the petition to the Good Parliament requesting measures against "stafstrikers" and others who wandered beyond their determined labors and vocations that, as noted above, served as de facto preamble or prologue to the 1388 measure. It may also be significant that in the case above it was Walter Clopton as KB Justice who introduced the crucial distinction that determined Justice Belknap of the Common Bench to decide this case against the jurisdiction of the king's courts: the defendant was not hired as a "parson singulier" — i.e., for the sole purpose of singing the divine service — but as "chaplein parochial," a role that included visiting the sick and other "service necessaries" which are not at all times the same. Clopton was at the time of the Cambridge Parliament not only Chief Justice of King's Bench but its sole sitting justice from his appointment on January 31, 1388 (succeeding Tresilian, condemned in his absence by the Merciless Parliament and executed in February 1388) for the next 18 months; see G. O. Sayles, ed., *Select Cases in the Court of King's Bench*, vol. 7, xi. Whether Clopton is to be understood as the contemporary referent or counterpart of the "cheef justice" appointed by the king at the end of the first vision in C is a question that in turn raises the larger critical issue of how or whether in general Langland encodes contemporary personages in his allegorical scenarios, and is beyond the scope of this essay.

85. Langland uses the English verb in several places in B (and A), and retains these uses in C (e.g., A 5.110, B 5.191 = C 6.199, "lik a leþeren purs lolled hise chekes"; B 12.191 = C 14.130, "Ther [i.e., Tybourn] lewed þeues ben lolled up"; B 16.269 = 18.285, "Lollynge in my lappe til swich a lord us fecche") to mean "lie slackly or helplessly, hang"; it never has the slightest pejorative or moral overtone of idleness of any kind, still less wilful or fraudulent idleness. On the contrary, all uses of the verb emphasize the lack of choice or agency, moral or physical, in one who "lolls." This is also its meaning in the one remaining occurrence outside the C 9 passage, the one instance of the verb in a context in the poem that involves the least hint of a moral distinction: B 12.213 = C 14.152, "wel losely he lolleþ þere by þe lawe of holy chirche." The referent is Trajan, who is saved but has been assigned an otherworld place "in the lowest of heuene": like the "lazar" in "Abrahames lappe" he "lies" or languishes where divine dispensation has put him. In purporting to derive the English noun for a gyrovague religious or wilful nonworker from the English verb, Langland performs a crucial sleight-of-hand: one who lies helplessly because he is in fact unable to help himself becomes one who wilfully chooses to feign helplessness. This most unwilling act of lying helplessly becomes in Langland's derivation not only a willed but also a fraudulent act.

86. Though I agree that the etymology is Langland's invention, he may have confected it as an Anglicized calque of a commonplace exegetical interpretation of Ps. 17:46: "filii alieni mentiti sunt mihi, filii alieni inveterati sunt, et claudicaverunt a semitis suis." It is attested by Bernard of Clairvaux; see *Sermo* 80:3, Bernard of Clairvaux, *Opera omnia*, ed. Jean Leclercq, C. H. Talbot, and H. M. Rochais (Rome, 1957), 2:279; for a translation, see Bernard of Clairvaux, *Works*, ed. Killian Walsh and Irene Edmonds (Kalamazoo: Medieval Institute Publications, 1981), 149: "When the soul has 'lost its uprightness,' 'man passes an an image,' but he

limps, as it were on one foot, and has become an estranged son." Of someone like this, it can, I think, be said, "The estranged sons have lied to me; they have become weak, and have limped away from the path." The Psalm verse presented difficulties of both translation and interpretation to Christian exegetes; Jerome's translation *iuxta hebraeos* renders it *filii alieni defluent et contrahentur in angustiis suis*, and says nothing of limping, which appears to be an approximation of a word in the Hebrew that means "trembling." The interlinear Gloss on *claudicaverunt* cites Augustine, *Enarrationes*, to the effect that the lame-footed alien sons are those who cling to the Old Testament, and turn away from the New. Cassiodorus, following Augustine, says that the Jews, by following in the flesh the precepts of the Old Testament, became lame in half of their minds. (I am grateful to Willis Johnson for information about the Hebrew text, and help with early translations and the Gloss, and to Shanna Byrne for further information on the glossators of this passage, to which I will return on another occasion.)

87. Even Chaucer's "Lollius," the purported antecedent "author" of the story of *Troilus*, participates in this wider cultural ferment. To be sure, this fiction can be mediately attributed to the well-known misconstrued line of Horace—but what made it, as an authorial name taking the place of the never-named actual author Boccaccio, *ben trovato* to Chaucer?

88. Less than a week after the Blackfriars Council condemned Wyclif's teaching and adherents, parliament enacted a statute which in effect directed the chancellor to authorize the sheriffs to arrest any such preachers; see Dahmus, *William Courtenay, Archbishop of Canterbury 1381–1396*, 83.

Bibliography

Abelard. *Historia calamitatum.* Ed. J. Monfrin. Paris: Vrin, 1967.
———. *The Story of Abelard's Adversities.* Trans. J. T. Muckle. Toronto: Pontifcal Institute of Mediaeval Studies, 1964.
Adams, Robert. "Editing *Piers Plowman* B: The Imperative of an Intermittently Critical Edition." *Studies in Bibliography* 45 (1992): 31–68.
———. "Langland's *Ordinatio: The Visio and Vita* Once More." *Yearbook of Langland studies* 8 (1994): 51–84.
———. "The Nature of Need in *Piers Plowman* XX." *Traditio* 34 (1978): 273–301.
———. "The Reliability of the Rubrics in the B Text of *Piers Plowman.*" *Medium Ævum* 54 (1985): 208–31.
Aelred of Rievaulx. *De institutione inclusarum.* Paris: Cerf, 1961.
Aers, David. *Community, Gender, and Individual Identity: English Writing, 1360–1430.* London: Routledge, 1988.
Alford, John A. *Piers Plowman: A Glossary of Legal Diction.* Cambridge: D. S. Brewer, 1988.
———. *Piers Plowman: A Guide to the Quotations.* Binghamton: State University of New York Press, 1992.
Allen, Hope Emily. *Writings Ascribed to Richard Rolle Hermit of Hampole and Materials for His Biography.* MLA Monograph 3d Ser. New York: D. C. Heath, 1927.
Aquinas, Thomas. *Contra impugnantes dei cultum et religionem.* Ed. Dominican brothers. Rome: Sancta Sabina, 1970.
———. *Summa theologiae.* Ed. Blackfriars Brothers. Cambridge: Blackfriars, 1964–1976.
Aston, Margaret. "Lollardy and Sedition." *Past and Present* 17 (1960): 1–44.
Baker, J. H. *An Introduction to English Legal History.* 3d ed. London: Butterworth's, 1990.
Baldwin, Anna P. *The Theme of Government in Piers Plowman.* Cambridge: D. S. Brewer, 1981.
Bale, John. *Scriptorvm illustrium maioris Brytannie quam nunc Angliam & Scotiam uocant.* Basel: Ionnem Oporinum, 1557?
Baluze, Etiénne. *Vitae paparum Avenionensium.* Ed. G. Mollat. Paris: Librairie Letouzey and Son, 1914–1927.
Barney, Stephen. "The Plowshare of the Tongue: The Progress of a Symbol from the Bible to *Piers Plowman.*" *Mediaeval Studies* 35 (1973): 261–93.
Barr, Helen, ed. *The Piers Plowman Tradition.* London: Dent, 1993.
Barron, Caroline M. "The London Middle English Guild Certificates of 1388–9." *Nottingham Medieval Studies* 39 (1995): 103–18.

————. "The Quarrel of Richard II with London, 1392–7." In *The Reign of Richard II: Essays in Honour of May McKisack*, ed. F. R. H. DuBoulay and Caroline M. Barron, 173–201. London: Athlone Press, 1971.

————. "William Langland: A London Poet." In *Chaucer's England: Literature in Historical Context*, ed. Barbara A. Hanawalt, 91–109. Minneapolis: University of Minnesota Press, 1992.

Bazire, Joyce, ed. *The Metrical Life of St. Robert of Knaresborough. EETS* o.s., 228.

Beier, A. L. "Vagrants and the Social Order in Elizabethan England." *Past and Present* 64 (1974): 3–29.

Bennett, H. S. "The Production and Dissemination of Vernacular Manuscripts in the Fifteenth Century." *The Library* 5th ser. 27 (1947): 167–78.

————. *Six Medieval Men and Women*. New York: Atheneum, 1960.

Bennett, J. A. W., ed. *Piers Plowman, Prologue and Passus I–VII of the B Text*. Oxford: Clarendon Press, 1972.

Benson, C. David and Barry Windeatt. "The MS Glosses to Chaucer's *Troilus and Criseyde*." *Chaucer Review* 25 (1990): 33–53.

Benson, Larry D. *Art and Tradition in Sir Gawain and the Green Knight*. New Brunswick, N.J.: Rutgers University Press, 1965.

Bernard of Clairvaux. "Epistola contra vitam heremiticam." In *Etudes sur saint Bernard et le texte de ses écrits*, ed. Jean Leclercq, 138–39. Rome: Curia Generalis Ordinis Cisterciensis, 1953.

————. *Opera omnia*. Ed. Jean LeClerq, C. H. Talbot, and H. M. Rochais. Rome, 1957.

————. *Works*. Ed. Killian Walsh and Irene Edmonds. Kalamazoo, Mich.: Medieval Institute, 1981.

Bihl, Michael. "Statuta generali ordinis edita in capitulo generali an. 1354 Assisii celebrato." *Archivum Franciscanum Historicum* 35 (1936): 35–112, 177–253.

Bird, Ruth. *The Turbulent London of Richard II*. London: Longmans, Green, 1949.

Bland, A. E., P. A. Brown, and R. H. Tawney, eds. *English Economic History: Selected Documents*. 2d ed. London: G. Bell, 1915.

Bliss, A. J., ed. *Sir Orfeo*. 2d ed. London: Oxford University Press, 1966.

Bloomfield, Morton W. *Piers Plowman as a Fourteenth-Century Apocalypse*. New Brunswick, N.J.: Rutgers University Press, 1962.

Bloomfield, Morton W., and Marjorie Reeves. "The Penetration of Joachism into Northern Europe." *Speculum* 29 (1954): 772–93.

Boffey, Julia and John J. Thompson. "Anthologies and Miscellanies: Production and Choice of Texts." In *Book Production and Publishing in Britain 1375–1475*, ed. Jeremy Griffiths and Derek Pearsall, 279–315. Cambridge: Cambridge University Press, 1989.

Bolotinus Paganus. "La poème de Payen Bolotin contre les faux ermites." Ed. Jean Le Clerq. *Revue Bénédictine* 58 (1958): 52–86.

Bonaventure. *Collationes in Hexaëmeron*. Florence: College of St. Bonaventure, 1934.

————. *Opera omnia*. Ed. Quaracchi fathers. Quaracchi: College of St. Bonaventure, 1882–1902.

The Book of Privy Counsel. In *The Cloud of Unknowing*, edited by Phyllis Hodgson. London: Oxford University Press, 1944.

Bougerol, Jacques-Guy. *Lexique Saint Bonaventure.* Paris: Editions Franciscaines, 1969.

Bowers, John M. *The Crisis of Will in Piers Plowman.* Washington, D.C.: Catholic University of America Press, 1986.

———. "*Piers Plowman* and the Police: Notes toward a History of the Wycliffite Langland." *Yearbook of Langland Studies* 6 (1992): 1–50.

Boyd, Beverly. "The Infamous B-Text of the *Canterbury Tales.*" *Manuscripta* 34 (1990).

Brentano, Robert. "Autobiography and Memory: Some Late Medieval Examples." Plenary Address, Medieval Academy of America. Boston, March 31, 1994.

Breviarium ad usum insignis Ecclesie Eboracensis. Surtees Society 71. Durham: Andrews, 1880.

Brewer, Charlotte and A. G. Rigg. *Piers Plowman: A Facsimile of the Z-Text in Bodleian Library, Oxford, MS Bodley 851.* Woodbridge: Boydell and Brewer, 1994.

Brieger, P. "Pictorial Commentaries to the *Commedia.*" In *Illuminated MSS of the Divine Comedy*, ed. P. Brieger, Millard Meiss, and C. S. Singleton, 1:88–89. Princeton, N.J.: Princeton University Press, 1969.

Bright, Allan H. *New Light on Piers Plowman.* London: Oxford University Press, 1928.

Brooks, St. John. "The *Piers Plowman* Manuscripts in Trinity College, Dublin." *The Library* 5th ser. 6 (1951): 141–53.

Brown, Cynthia J. "Text, Image, and Authorial Self-consciousness in Late-Medieval Paris." In *Printing the Written Word: The Social History of Books, circa 1450–1520*, ed. Sandra Hindman, 103–42. Ithaca, N.Y.: Cornell University Press, 1991.

Browne, Sir Thomas. *Religio medici.* Ed. James Winny. Cambridge: Cambridge University Press, 1963.

Bruns, Gerald L. "The Originality of Texts in a Manuscript Culture." *Comparative Literature* 32 (1980): 113–129.

Bullock-Davies, Constance. *Menstrellorum multitudo: Minstrels at a Royal Feast.* Cardiff: University of Wales Press, 1978.

Burdach, Konrad. *Der Dichter des Ackermann aus Böhmen und seine Zeit.* Vol. 32. Berlin: Weidmannsche Buchhandlung, 1932.

Burr, David. *Olivi and Franciscan Poverty: The Origins of the usus pauper Controversy.* Philadelphia: University of Pennsylvania Press, 1989.

Burron, John A. "Langland nel mezzo del cammin." In *Medieval Studies for J. A. W. Bennett, aetatis suae LXX*, ed. P. L. Heyworth, 21–41. Oxford: Clarendon Press, 1981.

Burrow, John A. "Autobiographical Poetry in the Middle Ages: The Case of Thomas Hoccleve." *Proceedings of the British Academy* 68 (1982): 389–412.

———. *Essays on Medieval Literature.* Oxford: Clarendon Press, 1984.

———. *Langland's Fictions.* Oxford: Clarendon Press, 1993.

———. *Medieval Writers and Their Work: Middle English Literature and Its Background, 1100–1500.* Oxford: Oxford University Press, 1982.

———. *Thomas Hoccleve.* Ed. M. C. Seymour. Authors of the Middle Ages 4. Aldershot (Hants): Variorum, 1994.

Cahn, Kenneth S. "Chaucer, Merchants, and the Foreign Exchange: An Introduction to Medieval Finance." *Studies in the Age of Chaucer* (1980): 81–119.

Cam, Helen M. "The Legislators of Medieval England." In *Law-finders and Law-makers in Medieval England: Collected Studies in Legal and Constitutional History*. London: Merlin Press, 1962.

Carr, Aidan, O. F. M. Conv."Poverty in Perfection According to St. Bonaventure." *Franciscan Studies* 7 (1947): 313–23, 415–25.

Casale, Ubertino da. "Responsio [ed. Franz Ehrle]." *Archiv für Litteratur- und Kirchengeschichte des Mittelalters* 3 (1887): 51–89.

———. "Rotulus [ed. Franz Ehrle]." *Archiv für Litteratur- und Kirchengeschichte des Mittelalters* 3 (1887): 93–137.

Cassian. *Conferences*. Trans. Colm Luibheid. New York: Paulist Press, 1985.

Catto, Jeremy I. "An Alleged Great Council of 1374." *English Historical Review* 82 (1967): 764–71.

Chambers, R. W. and Marjorie Daunt, eds. *A Book of London English*. Oxford: Oxford University Press, 1931.

Chaucer, Geoffrey. *The Riverside Chaucer*. Ed. Larry Benson. Boston: Houghton Mifflin, 1987.

Chaytor, H. J. *From Script to Print: An Introduction to Medieval Vernacular Literature*. London: Sidgwick and Jackson, 1966.

Chenu, M.-D. "Auctor, actor, autor." *Archivum Latinitatis Medii Aevi (Bulletin du Cange)* 3 (1927): 81–86.

———. *La théologie au douzième siècle*. Paris: Vrin, 1957.

Chiappini, P. Anicetus. "Communitatis responsio 'Religiosi viri' ad rotulum fr. Ubertini de Casali." *Archivum Franciscanum Historicum* 7–8 (1914–1915): 654–75 [7], 56–80 [8].

Christianson, C. Paul. "A Community of Book Artisans in Chaucer's London." *Viator* 20 (1989): 207–18.

Clanvowe, E. John. *The Works of Sir John Clanvowe*. Ed. V. J. Scattergood. Cambridge: D. S. Brewer, 1975.

Clareno, Angelo. *Expositio regulae fratrum minorum*. Ed. Livario Oliger. Quaracchi: College of St. Bonaventur, 1912.

Clay, Rotha Mary. "Further Studies on Medieval Recluses." *Journal of the British Archaeological Association* 3d ser. 16 (1953): 74–87.

———. *Hermits and Anchorites of Medieval England*. London: Methuen, 1914.

Clopper, Lawrence M. "Langland's Franciscanism." *Chaucer Review* 25 (1990): 54–75.

———. "The Life of the Dreamer, the Dreams of the Wanderer in *Piers Plowman*." *Studies in Philology* 86 (1989): 261–85.

———. "Need Men and Women Labor? Langland's Wanderer and the Labor Ordinances." In *Chaucer's England: Literature in Historical Context*, ed. Barbara A. Hanawalt, 110–29. Minneapolis: University of Minnesota Press, 1992.

———. "*Patience*: Meditations on a Whale and a Woodbine." *Mediaevalia* 14 (1988 for 1981): 157–77.

———. "*Songes of Rechelesnesse*": *Langland and the Franciscans*. Ann Arbor: University of Michigan Press, forthcoming.

The Cloud of Unknowing. Ed. Phyllis Hodgson. EETS o.s. 218. London: Oxford University Press, 1944.

Coleman, Janet. "FitzRalph's Antimendicant 'Proposicio' (1350) and the Politics of the Papal Court at Avignon." *Journal of Ecclesiastical History* 35 (1984): 376–90.

Congar, Yves. "Aspectes ecclésiologiques de la querelle entre mendiants et séculiers dan la seconde moitié du XIIIe siècle et le début du XIVe." *Archives d'Histoire Doctrinale et Littéraire du Moyen Âge* 28 (1961): 35–151.

Cooper, Helen. "Langland's and Chaucer's Prologues." *Yearbook of Langland Studies* 1 (1987): 71–81.

Coulton, G. C. *Medieval Panorama.* New York: Collins, 1961.

Courtenay, William J. *Schools and Scholars in Fourteenth-Century England.* Princeton, N.J.: Princeton University Press, 1987.

Creytons, Raymond, O.P. "Les Constitutions des Frères Prêcheurs dans la rédaction de s. Raymond de Peñafort (1241)." *Archivum Fratrum Predicatorum* 18 (1948): 5–68.

Crompton, James. "Leicestershire Lollards." *Transactions of the Leicestershire Archaeological and Historical Society* 44 (1968–1969): 11–44.

Curtius, Ernst Robert. *European Literature in the Latin Middle Ages.* Trans. Willard R. Trask. Princeton, N.J.: Princeton University Press, 1953.

Dahmus, Joseph. *William Courtenay, Archbishop of Canterbury 1381–1396.* University Park: Pennsylvania State University Press, 1966.

Davis, Charles T. "Le pape Jean XXII et les spirituels: Ubertin de Casale." In *Franciscains d'Oc: Les spirituels ca. 1380–1324,* ed. Edouard Privat, 263–283. Toulouse: Centre d'Etudes Historiques de Fanjeaux, 1975.

Davis, Virginia. "The Rule of St. Paul, the First Hermit, in Late Medieval England." *Studies in Church History* 22 (1985): 203–14.

Dawson, James Doyne. "Richard FitzRalph and the Fourteenth-Century Poverty Controversies." *Journal of Ecclesiastical History* 34 (1983): 315–44.

de Hamel, Christopher. *A History of Illuminated Manuscripts.* Oxford: Phaidon, 1986.

De Looze, Lawrence. "Signing Off in the Middle Ages: Medieval Textuality and Strategies of Authorial Self-Naming." In *Vox intexta: Orality and Textuality in the Middle Ages,* ed. A. N. Doane and Carol Braun Pasternak. Madison: University of Wisconsin Press, 1991.

Delorme, F. M. "Trois chapitres de Jean Peckam pour la défense des ordres mendiants." *Studi Francescani* 29 (1932): 47–62, 164–93.

Despres, Denise. "Ecstatic Reading and Missionary Mysticism: *The Orcherd of Syon.*" In *Prophets Abroad: The Reception of Continental Holy Women in Late-Medieval England,* ed. Rosalynn Voaden. Woodbridge: Brewer, 1996.

———. *Ghostly Sights: Visual Meditation in Late-Medieval Narrative.* Norman, Okla.: Pilgrim Press, 1989.

Dickens, Bruce and R. M. Wilson, eds. *Early Middle English Texts.* London: Bowes and Bowes, 1951.

Dobson, R. B. *The Peasants' Revolt of 1381.* 2d ed. London: Macmillan, 1983.

Donaldson, E. Talbot. *Piers Plowman: The C-text and Its Poet*. New Haven, Conn.: Yale University Press, 1949.

Douie, Decima L. "Three Treatises on Evangelical Poverty by Fr. Richard Conyngton, Fr. Walter Chatton, and an Anonymous from MS. V III 18 in Bishop Cosin's Library, Durham." *Archivum Franciscanum Historicum* 24 (1931): 341–69; 25 (1932): 36–58, 210–40.

Doyle, A. I. "The Manuscripts." In *Middle English Alliterative Poetry and Its Literary Background*, ed. David Lawton, 88–100. Cambridge: D. S. Brewer, 1982.

———. "More Light on John Shirley." *Medium Ævum* 30 (1961): 93–101.

———. "Publication by Members of the Religious Orders." In *Book Production and Publishing in Britain 1375–1475*, ed. Jeremy Griffiths and Derek Pearsall, 109–23. Cambridge: Cambridge University Press, 1989.

———. "Remarks on Surviving MSS of *Piers Plowman*." In *Medieval English Religious and Ethical Literature: Essays in Honour of G. H. Russell*, ed. G. Kratzmann and James Simpson. Cambridge: D. S. Brewer, 1986.

———. "The Work of a Late Fifteenth-Century English Scribe, William Ebesham." *Bulletin of the John Rylands Library* 39 (1957): 298–325.

Doyle, A. I. and M. B. Parkes. "The Production of Copies of the *Canterbury Tales* and the *Confessio amantis* in the Early Fifteenth Century." In *Medieval Scribes, Manuscripts and Libraries: Essays Presented to N. R. Ker*, ed. M. B. Parkes and Andrew G. Watson, 163–210. London: Scolar Press, 1978.

Doyle, Eric, O. F. M. "William Woodford's 'De dominio civili clericorum' against John Wyclif." *Archivum Franciscanum Historicum* 66 (1973): 49–109.

Drogin, Marc. *Anathema: Medieval Scribes and the History of Book Curses*. Totowa, N.J.: Allanheld and Schram, 1983.

Dyer, Christopher. "Piers Plowman and Plowmen: A Historical Perspective." *Yearbook of Langland Studies* 8 (1994): 155–76.

———. *Standards of Living in the Later Middle Ages*. Cambridge: Cambridge University Press, 1989.

A. S. G. Edwards. "John Shirley and the Emulation of Courtly Culture." In *The Court and Cultural Diversity*, ed. John J. Thompson. Cambridge: Boydell and Brewer, forthcoming.

Edwards, A. S. G. and Derek Pearsall. "The Manuscripts of the Major English Poetic Texts." In *Book Production and Publishing in Britain 1375–1475*, ed. Jeremy Griffiths and Derek Pearsall, 257–78. Cambridge: Cambridge University Press, 1989.

Eisenstein, Elizabeth. *The Printing Press as an Agent of Change*. Cambridge: Cambridge University Press, 1979.

Embree, Daniel "*Richard the Redeless* and *Mum and the Sothsegger*: A Case of Mistaken Identity." *Notes & Queries* n.s. 22 (1975): 4–12.

———. "The Sothsegger at Court." Ph.D. diss., University of California, 1981.

The Episcopal Register of Robert Rede, Ordinis Praedicatorum, Lord Bishop of Chichester, 1397–1415. Ed. Cecil Dudes. Sussex Record Society. London: Mitchell, Hughes, and Clark, 1908.

Ferguson, A. B. *The Articulate Citizen in the English Renaissance*. Durham, N.C.: Duke University Press, 1965.

Fisher, John H. "*Piers Plowman* and the Chancery Tradition." In *Medieval English Studies Presented to George Kane*, ed. Edward Donald Kennedy, Ronald Waldron, and Joseph S. Wittig, 267–78. Woodbridge: D. S. Brewer, 1988.

FitzRalph, Richard. *Defensio curatorum*. Ed. Melchior Goldast. Hanover: Conrad Biermann, 1614.

———. *Proposicio: Unusquisque*. Ed. L. L. Hamerich. Copenhagen: Levin and Munksgaard, 1938.

Fleming, John V. "The 'Collations' of William of Saint-Amour against S. Thomas." *Recherches de Théologie Ancienne et Médiévale* 32 (1965): 132–38.

Foucault, Michel. *The History of Sexuality*: Vol. 1. *An Introduction*. Translated by Robert Hurley. New York: Pantheon, 1978.

Fowler, David. "Editorial 'Jamming': Two New Editions of *Piers Plowman*." *Review* 2 (1980): 211–69.

Frank, Robert Worth. "The 'Hungry Gap,' Crop Failure, and Famine: the Fourteenth-Century Agricultural Crisis and *Piers Plowman*." *Yearbook of Langland Studies* 4 (1990): 87–104.

———. *Piers Plowman and the Scheme of Salvation*. New Haven, Conn.: Yale University Press, 1957.

Frantzen, Allen J. "Documents and Monuments: Difference and Interdisciplinarity in the Study of Medieval Culture." In *Speaking Two Languages: Traditional Disciplines and Contemporary Theory in Medieval Studies*, ed. Allen J. Frantzen, 1–24, 225–32. Albany: State University of New York Press, 1991.

Friedman, Albert B. and Norman T. Harrington, eds. *Ywain and Gawain*. EETS o.s. 254, 1964.

Frye, Northrop. "The Structure of Imagery in *The Faerie Queene*." In *Fables of Identity: Studies in Poetic Mythology*, 69–87. New York: Harcourt Brace Jovanovich, 1963.

Galbraith, G. R. *The Constitution of the Dominican Order, 1216 to 1360*. Manchester: Manchester University Press, 1925.

Galloway, Andrew. "The Rhetoric of Riddling in Late-Medieval England: The 'Oxford' Riddles." *Speculum* 70 (1995): 68–105.

Giraldus Cambrensis. *The Autobiography of Giraldus Cambrensis*. Trans. H. E. Butler. London: Jonathan Cape, 1937.

Godden, Malcolm. *The Making of Piers Plowman*. London: Longman, 1990.

———. "Plowman and Hermits in Langland's *Piers Plowman*." *Review of English Studies* 35 (1984): 129–63.

Goldschmidt, E. P. *Medieval Texts and Their First Appearance in Print*. London: Oxford University Press, 1943.

Goodall, Peter. "Chaucer's 'Burgesses' and the Aldermen of London." *Medium Ævum* 50 (1981): 284–92.

Gougaud, Louis. *Ermits et reclus: études sur d'anciennes formes de vie religieuse*. Liguge: Abbaye Saint-Martin, 1928.

Gower, John *English Works of John Gower*. Ed. G. C. Macaulay. London: Oxford University Press, 1900–1901.

Gradon, Pamela. "Langland and the Ideology of Dissent." *Proceedings of the British Academy* 66 (1980): 179–205.

Green, Richard Firth. "John Ball's Letters: Literary History and Historical Literature." In *Chaucer's England: Literature in Historical Context*, ed. Barbara A. Hanawalt, 154–75. Minneapolis: University of Minnesota Press, 1992.

———. *Poets and Princepleasers: Literature and the English Court in the Later Middle Ages*. Toronto: Toronto University Press, 1980.

Greenblatt, Stephen. "Murdering Peasants: Status, Genre and the Representation of Rebellion." In *Representing the English Renaissance*, ed. Stephen Greenblatt. Berkeley and Los Angeles: University of California Press, 1988.

Griffiths, Jeremy and Derek Pearsall, eds. *Book Production and Publishing in Britain, 1375–1475*. Cambridge: Cambridge University Press, 1989.

Grindley, Carl. "From Creation to Desecration: The Marginal Annotations of *Piers Plowman* C Text HM 143." Master's thesis, University of Victoria, 1992.

Guibert of Nogent. *Self and Society in Medieval France: The Memoirs of Abbot Guibert of Nogent*. Trans. John F. Benton. New York: Harper, 1970.

Gwynn, Aubrey. *The English Austin Friars in the Age of Wyclif*. London: Oxford University Press, 1940.

Habig, Marion A., ed. *St. Francis of Assisi: Writings and Early Biographies*. 4th ed. Chicago: Franciscan Herald Press, 1983.

Hammond, E. P. *English Verse Between Chaucer and Surrey*. New York: Octagon, 1965.

Hanna, Ralph III. "'Meddling with Makings' and Will's Work." In *Late-Medieval Religious Texts and Their Transmission: Essays in Honour of A. I. Doyle*, ed. A. J. Minnis, 85–94. Woodbridge: D. S. Brewer, 1994.

———. "On the Versions of *Piers Plowman*." In *Pursuing History: Middle English Manuscripts and Their Texts*, 203–43. Stanford, Calif.: Stanford University Press, 1996.

———. "Robert the Ruyflare and His Companions." In *Literature and Religion in the Later Middle Ages: Philological Essays in Honor of Siegfried Wenzel*, ed. Richard G. Newhauser and John A. Alford, 81–96. Binghamton, N.Y.: Medieval and Renaissance Texts and Studies, 1995.

———. "Sir Thomas Berkeley and His Patronage." *Speculum* 64 (1989): 878–916.

———. "Studies in the Manuscripts of *Piers Plowman*." *Yearbook of Langland Studies* 7 (1993): 1–25.

———. *William Langland*. Aldershot: Variorum, 1993.

Harris, Kate. "Patrons, Buyers and Owners: The Evidence for Ownership, and the Role of Book Owners in Book Production and the Book Trade." In *Book Production and Publishing in Britain 1375–1475*, ed. Jeremy Griffiths and Derek Pearsall. Cambridge: Cambridge University Press, 1989.

Harwood, Britton J. and Ruth F. Smith. "Inwit and the Castle of *Caro* in *Piers Plowman*." *Neuphilologische Mitteilungen* 71 (1970): 648–54.

Hector, L. C. and Barbara Harvey, eds. *The Westminster Chronicle, 1381–1394*. Oxford: Clarendon Press, 1966.

Heysse, P. Albanus. "Fr. Richardi de Conington, O. F. M. Tractatus de paupertate Fratrum Minorum et abbreviatura inde a communitate extracta." *Archivum Franciscanum Historicum* 23 (1930): 57–105, 340–60.

Hilton, Rodney. *Bond Men Made Free: Medieval Peasant Movements and the English Rising of 1381*. London: Temple Smith, 1973.

Hilton, Walter. *Walter Hilton's Latin Writings*. Ed. John P. Clark and Cheryl Taylor. Analecta Cartusiana 124. Salzburg: Institut für Englische Sprache und Literatur, 1987.

Hinnebusch, William A., O. P. *The History of the Dominican Order*. 2 vols. New York: Alba House, 1966–1973.

Hoccleve, Thomas. "Regement of Princes," in *Hoccleve's Works*, ed. F. J. Furnivall. London: Kegan Paul, 1897.

———. *Selected Poems*. Ed. Bernard O'Donoghue. Manchester: Carcanet, 1982.

Holmes, George. *The Good Parliament*. Oxford: Oxford University Press, 1975.

Holub, Robert C. *Reception Theory: A Critical Introduction*. New York: Methuen, 1984.

Holzknecht, Karl J. *Literary Patronage in the Middle Ages*. New York: Octagon, 1966.

"How a Holy Hermit Prayed a Sinful Woman Pray to God for Him [IMEV 971]." In *The Minor Poems of the Vernon Manuscript, Part I*, ed. C. Horstmann. EETS o.s. 98, London: Oxford University Press, 1892.

Hudson, Anne. "Lollard Book Production." In *Book Production and Publishing in Britain 1375–1475*, ed. Jeremy Griffiths and Derek Pearsall, 125–52. Cambridge: Cambridge University Press, 1989.

———. *Lollards and Their Books*. London: Hambledon Press, 1985.

———. "*Piers Plowman* and the Peasants' Revolt: A Problem Revisited." *Yearbook of Langland Studies* 8 (1994): 85–106.

———. *The Premature Reformation: Wycliffite Texts and Lollard History*. Oxford: Clarendon Press, 1988.

Hudson, Anne and Pamela Gradon, eds. *English Wycliffite Sermons*. Oxford: Clarendon Press, 1983–90.

Hugh of Digne. *Hugh of Digne's Rule Commentary*. Rome: College of St. Bonaventure, 1979.

Hugh of St.-Cher. *Opera omnia*. 8 vols. Venice, 1754.

Hughes, Jonathan. *Pastors and Visionaries: Religion and Secular Life in Late Medieval Yorkshire*. Woodbridge, Suffolk: Boydell Press, 1988.

———. "Vers la société de l'écriture." *Poétique* 50 (1982): 155–72.

Humphreys, K. W. "The Library of John Erghome and Personal Libraries of Fourteenth-Century England." In *A Medieval Miscellany in Honour of Prof. John le Patourel*, ed. R. L. Thomson, 106–23. Leeds: Leeds Philosophical and Literary Society, 1982.

Iser, Wolfgang. *The Implied Reader: Patterns of Communication in Prose Fiction from Bunyan to Beckett*. Baltimore: Johns Hopkins University Press, 1974.

Jacob, E. F. "Sir John Fortescue and the Law of Nature." *Bulletin of the John Rylands Library* 18 (1934): 359–76.

Jauss, Hans Robert. *Toward an Aesthetic of Reception*. Trans. Timothy Bahti. Brighton: Harvester, 1982.

Jefferson, Judith A. "The Hoccleve Holographs and Hoccleve's Metrical Practice." In *Manuscripts and Texts*, ed. Derek Pearsall, 95–109. Cambridge: D. S. Brewer, 1985.

Jusserand, J. J. *Piers Plowman, A Contribution to the History of English Mysticism.* London: T. Fisher Unwin, 1894.

Justice, Steven. *Writing and Rebellion: England in 1381.* Berkeley and Los Angeles: University of California Press, 1994.

Justinian. *Institutes*, IV, tit. iv, ed. J. A. C. Thomas. Amsterdam: North Holland, 1975.

Kaeuper, Richard W. "Law and Order in Fourteenth Century England: The Evidence of Special Commissions of Oyer and Terminer." *Speculum* 54 (1988): 736–37.

———. *War, Justice, and Public Order: England and France in the Later Middle Ages.* Oxford: Clarendon Press, 1988.

Kaluza, Max, ed. "The Eremyte and the Outelawe." *Englische Studien* 14 (1890): 171–77.

Kaminsky, Howard. "Estate, Nobility, and the Exhibition of Estate in the Later Middle Ages." *Speculum* 68 (1993): 684–709.

Kane, George. *The Autobiographical Fallacy in Chaucer and Langland Studies.* London: H. K. Lewis, 1965.

———, ed. *Piers Plowman: The A Version.* London: Athlone Press, 1988.

———. *Piers Plowman: The Evidence for Authorship.* London: Athlone Press, 1965.

———. "Some Fourteenth-Century Political Poems." In *Medieval English Religious and Ethical Literature: Essays in Honour of G. H. Russell*, ed. Gregory Kratzman and James Simpson, 82–91. Cambridge: D. S. Brewer, 1986.

———. "The Text." In *A Companion to Piers Plowman*, ed. John A. Alford, 175–200. Berkeley and Los Angeles: University of California Press, 1988.

Kane, George and E. Talbot Donaldson, eds. *Piers Plowman: The B Version.* London: Athlone Press, 1988.

Kaulbach, Ernest. "*Piers Plowman* B.IX: Further Refinements of Inwitt." In *Linguistic and Literary Studies in Honor of Archibald A. Hill*, ed. Mohammed Ali Jazayery, Edgar C. Polome, and Werner Winter, 103–10. The Hague: Mouton, 1979.

Kempe, Margery. *The Book of Margery Kempe.* Ed. Sanford Brown Mecch and Hope Emily Allen. London: Oxford University Press, 1940.

Kenyon, Nora. "Labor Conditions in Essex in the Reign of Richard II." *Economic History Review* 4 (1932): 429–60.

Kerby-Fulton, Kathryn. "*Piers Plowman.*" In *The Cambridge History of Medieval English Literature 1066-1547*, ed. David Wallace. Cambridge: Cambridge University Press, forthcoming.

———. *Reformist Apocalypticism and Piers Plowman.* Cambridge: Cambridge University Press, 1990.

———. "A Return to 'the First Dawn of Justice': Hildegard's Visions of Clerical Reform and the Eremitical Life." *American Benedictine Review* 40 (1989): 383–407.

———. "'Who Has Written This Book?': Visionary Autobiography in Langland's

C-Text." In *The Medieval Mystical Tradition in England*, ed. Marion Glasscoe, 101–16. Exeter Symposium, vol. 5. Cambridge: D. S. Brewer, 1992.

Kerby-Fulton, Kathryn and Denise Despres. *Iconography and the Professional Reader: The Politics of Book Production in the Douce Piers Plowman.* Minneapolis: University of Minnesota Press, forthcoming.

Kerby-Fulton, Kathryn and Steven Justice. "Langlandian Reading Circles and the Civil Service in London and Dublin, 1380–1427." *New Medieval Literature* 1 (1997).

———. "The Ilchester Manuscript of *Piers Plowman*." In *Essays in Honour of Derek Pearsall*, ed. Alastair Minnis, forthcoming.

King, John N. "Robert Crowley's Editions of *Piers Plowman*: A Tudor Apocalypse." *Modern Philology* 73 (1976): 342–52.

Kirk, Elizabeth D. "Langland's Plowman and the Recreation of Fourteenth-Century Religious Metaphor." *Yearbook of Langland Studies* 2 (1988): 1–21.

Knowles, David. *The Religious Orders in England*. 2 vols. Cambridge: Cambridge University Press, 1948–1955.

Kuhl, Ernest P. "Chaucer's Burgesses." *Transactions of the Wisconsin Academy of Sciences, Arts, and Letters* 18, 2 (1916): 652–76.

"The Kyng and the Hermyt [IMEV 1764]." In *Remains of the Early Popular Poetry of England*, ed. W. Carew Hazlitt, 11–34. London: Russell Smith, 1864.

Laberge, P. Damasus. "Fr. Petri Ioannis Olivi, O.F.M.: Tria scripta sui ipsius apologetica annorum 1283 et 1285." *Archivum Franciscanum Historicum* 28 (1935): 115–55, 374–407.

Lacey, Kay E. "Women and Work in Fourteenth- and Fifteenth-Century London." In *Women and Work in Pre-industrial England*, ed. Lindsey Charles and Lorna Duffin, 24–82. London: Croom Helm, 1985.

Lambert, Malcolm D. *Franciscan Poverty: The Doctrine of the Absolute Poverty of Christ and the Apostles in the Franciscan Order, 1210–1323*. London: SPCK, 1961.

Langholm, Odd. *Economics in the Medieval Schools*. Leiden: Brill, 1992.

Lawton, David A. "The Subject of *Piers Plowman*." *Yearbook of Langland Studies* 1 (1987): 1–30.

———. "The Unity of Middle English Alliterative Poetry." *Speculum* 58 (1983): 72–94.

Leclercq, Jean. *Chances de la spiritualité occidentale*. Paris: Cerf, 1966.

———. *L'eremitismo in occidente nei secoli XI e XII.* Vol. 4, *Miscellanea del centro di studi medioevali*. Milan: Vita e Pensiero, 1965.

Leff, Gordon. *Heresy in the Later Middle Ages: The Relation of Heterodoxy to Dissent c. 1250–c. 1450*. Manchester: Manchester University Press, 1967.

Le Goff, Jacques. "The Town as an Agent of Civilisation." In *The Fontana Economic History of Europe: The Middle Ages*, ed. Carlo M. Cipolla, 71–106. Glasgow: Collins/Fontana Books, 1972.

Lerner, Robert E. "Ecstatic Dissent." *Speculum* 67(1992): 33–57.

———. *The Powers of Prophecy: The Cedar of Lebanon Vision from the Mongol Onslaught to the Dawn of the Enlightenment*. Berkeley and Los Angeles: University of California Press, 1983.

Leyser, Henrietta. *Hermits and the New Monasticism: A Study of Religious Communities in Western Europe 1000–1150*. New York: St. Martin's, 1984.

Liber albus: The White Book of the City of London. Ed. Henry Thomas Riley. London: Richard Griffin, 1861.

Liber pontificalis Chr. Bainbridge, archiepiscopi Eboracensis. Publications of the Surtees Society 61. Durham: Andrews, 1865.

Liber pontificalis of Edmund Lacy, Bishop of Exeter. Ed. Ralph Baines. Exeter: Roberts, 1847.

Lipson, Ephraim. *The Economic History of England*. Vol. 1: *The Middle Ages*. London, 1959.

Little, Lester K. *Religious Poverty and the Profit Economy in Medieval Europe*. Ithaca, N.Y.: Cornell University Press, 1978.

Loewenstein, Joseph F. "The Script in the Marketplace." In *Representing the English Renaissance*, ed. Stephen Greenblatt, 265–76. Berkeley and Los Angeles: University of California Press, 1988. Originally published in *Representations* 12 (1985): 101–14.

Malory, Sir Thomas. *The Works*. Ed. Eugène Vinaver. Oxford: Clarendon Press, 1948.

Manly, John M. "The Lost Leaf of Piers the Plowman." *Modern Philology* 3 (1906): 359–66.

Mann, Jill. *Chaucer and Medieval Estates Satire: the Literature of Social Classes and the General Prologue to the Canterbury Tales*. Cambridge: Cambridge University Press, 1973.

———. "The Power of the Alphabet: A Reassessment of the Relation Between the A and B Versions of *Piers Plowman*." *Yearbook of Langland Studies* 8 (1994): 21–50.

———. "Satiric Subject and Satiric Object in Goliardic Literature." *Mittellateinisches Jahrbuch* 15 (1980): 63–86.

Marotti, Arthur. " 'Love Is Not Love': Elizabethan Sonnet Sequences and the Social Order." *ELH* 49 (1982): 396–427.

———. *John Donne: Coterie Poet*. Madison: University of Wisconsin Press, 1986.

———. *Manuscript, Print and the English Renaissance Lyric*. Ithaca, N.Y.: Cornell University Press, 1995.

Mathew, F. D., ed. *The English Works of Wycliffe Hitherto Unprinted*. EETS o.s. 74.

Mayr-Harting, H. "Functions of a Twelfth-Century Recluse." *History* 60 (1975): 337–52.

McCaffrey, Patrick. *The White Friars: An Outline of Carmelite History with Special Reference to the English Speaking Province*. Dublin: M. H. Gill, 1926.

McDonnell, Ernest W. *The Beguines and Beghards in Medieval Culture*. New York: Octagon, 1969.

McFarlane, Kenneth Bruce. *Lancastrian Kings and Lollard Knights*. Oxford: Oxford University Press, 1972.

McHardy, A. K. "Careers and Disappointments in the Late Medieval Church: Some English Evidence." *Studies in Church History* 26 (1989): 111–30.

———. *The Church in London 1375–1392*. London: London Historical Society, 1977.

———. "Ecclesiastics and Economics: Poor Priests, Prosperous Laymen and Proud

Prelates in the Reign of Richard II." *Studies in Church History* 24 (1987): 129–37.

McKisack, May. *The Fourteenth Century 1307–1399*. Oxford: Clarendon Press, 1959.

McLaughlin, Mary M. "Abelard as Autobiographer: The Motives and Meaning of His 'Story of Calamities.'" *Speculum* 42 (1967): 463–88.

Mencherini, P. Saturninus, OFM. "Constitutiones generales ordinis fratrum minorum a capitulo Perpiniani anno 1331 celebrato editae." *Archivum Franciscanum Historicum* 2 (1989): 269–92, 412–30, 575–99.

Methley, Richard. "Richard Methley: To Hew Heremyte a Pystyl of Solytary Lyfe Nowadayes." In *Boniface of Savoy: Cartusian and Archbishop of Canterbury*, ed. James Hogg, 91–119. Analecta Cartusiana 31. Salzburg: Institut für Englische Sprache und Literatur, 1977.

Middleton, Anne. "The Audience and Public of *Piers Plowman*." In *Middle English Alliterative Poetry*, ed. David Lawton, 101–23. Cambridge: D. S. Brewer, 1982.

———. "Langland's Lives: Reflections on Late-Medieval Religious and Literary Vocabulary." In *The Idea of Medieval Literature: New Essays on Chaucer and Medieval Culture in Honor of Donald R. Howard*, ed. James M. Dean and Christian K. Zacher, 227–42. Newark: University of Delaware Press, 1992.

———. "Life in the Margins, or, What's an Annotator to Do?" *Library Chronicle of the University of Texas at Austin* 20 (1990): 167–83.

———. "Making a Good End: John But as a Reader of *Piers Plowman*." In *Medieval English Studies Presented to George Kane*, ed. Edward Donald Kennedy, Ronald Waldron, and Joseph S. Wittig, 243–66. Woodbridge: D. S. Brewer, 1988.

———. "Narration and the Invention of Experience: Episodic Form in *Piers Plowman*." In *The Wisdom of Poetry: Essays in Early English Literature in Honor of Morton W. Bloomfield*, ed. Larry D. Benson and Siegfried Wenzel, 91–122. Kalamazoo, Mich.: Medieval Institute Publications, 1982.

———. "William Langland's 'Kynde Name': Authorial Signature and Social Identity in Late Fourteenth-Century England." In *Literary Practice and Social Change in Britain, 1380–1530*, ed. Lee Patterson, 15–82. Berkeley and Los Angeles: University of California Press, 1990.

Mills, David. "The Role of the Dreamer in *Piers Plowman*." In *Piers Plowman: Critical Approaches*, ed. S. S. Hussey, 180–212. London: Methuen, 1969.

Milton, John. *The Complete Prose Works of John Milton*. Vol. 4. New Haven, Conn.: Yale University Press, 1968.

Minnis, Alastair J. *Medieval Theory of Authorship: Scholastic Literary Attitudes in the Later Middle Ages*, 2d ed. Philadelphia: University of Pennsylvania Press, 1988.

Moore, Samuel. "Patrons of Letters in Norfolk and Suffolk, c. 1450." *PMLA* 28 (1913): 79–105.

Moorman, John. *A History of the Franciscan Order from Its Origins to the Year 1517*. Oxford: Clarendon Press, 1968.

Morin, G. "Rainaud l'ermite et Ives de Chartres: Un episode de la crise du cénobitisme au xie–xiie siècle." *Revue Bénédictine* 40 (1928): 99–115.

Munimenta Gildhalliae Londoniensis. Ed. Thomas Riley. Rolls Ser., vol. 1. London: Longman, Brown, 1859.

Mustanoja, Tauno F. "The Suggestive Use of Christian Names in Middle English

Poetry." In *Medieval Literature and Folklore Studies: Essays in Honor of Francis Lee Utley*, ed. Jerome Mandel and Bruce A. Rosenberg, 51–76. New Brunswick, N.J.: Rutgers University Press, 1970.

Myers, A. R. *London in the Age of Chaucer*. Norman: University of Oklahoma Press, 1972.

Newman, Barbara. "On the Ethics of Feminist Historiography." *Exemplaria* 2 (1990): 702–5.

Nichols, Stephen. "Voice and Writing in Augustine and in the Troubadour Lyric." In *Vox intexta: Orality and Textuality in the Middle Ages*, ed. A. N. Doane and Carol Braun Pasternak, 137–61. Madison: University of Wisconsin Press, 1991.

Noonan, J. T. *The Scholastic Analysis of Usury*. Cambridge, Mass.: Harvard University Press, 1957.

Nursia, Benedict of. *Regula*. Ed. H. Rochais and E. Manning. Rochefort: La Documentation Cistercienne, 1980.

Oliger, Livarius. "Regula reclusorum Angliae et Quaestiones tres de vita solitaria saec. XIII–XIV." *Antonianum* 9 (1934): 37–84, 243–68.

———. "Regulae tres reclusorum et eremitarum Angliae saec. XIII–XIV." *Antonianum* 3 (1928): 151–90, 299–320.

———, ed. *Expositio quatuor magistrorum super regulam fratrum minorum (1241–1242)*. Rome: Edizioni di Storia e Letteratura, 1950.

Olivi, Peter John. *Peter Olivi's Rule Commentary*. Ed. David Flood. Wiesbaden: Franz Stiner, 1972.

Olson, Linda. "William Langland's *Piers Plowman*: Spiritual Revisions in the Age of Wyclif." Unpublished manuscript.

———. "A Fifteenth-Century Reading of *Piers Plowman* and the Tradition of Monastic Autobiography." Unpublished manuscript.

Orme, Nicholas. "Langland and Education." *History of Education* 11 (1982): 251–66.

The Orcherd of Syon. Ed. Phyllis Hodgson and Gabriel M. Liegey, EETS o.s. 258. London: Oxford University Press, 1966.

Owl and the Nightingale. Ed. E. G. Stanley. London: Nelson, 1960.

Owst, G. R. *Literature and Pulpit in Medieval England*. Cambridge: Cambridge University Press, 1933.

Pace, George and Alfred David, eds. *The Minor Poems*. Vol. 5, *A Variorum Edition of the Works of Geoffrey Chaucer*. Norman: University of Oklahoma Press, 1982.

Parkes, M. B. *The Medieval Manuscripts of Keble College, Oxford: A Descriptive Catalogue*. London: Scolar, 1979.

———. "Patterns of Scribal Activity and Revisions of the Text in Early Copies of Works by John Gower." In *New Science Out of Old Books: Studies in Manuscripts and Early Printed Books in Honour of A. I. Doyle*, ed. Richard Beadle and A. J. Piper, 81–121. Aldershot (Hants): Scolar, 1995.

———. "The Production, Dissemination and Revision of the Earliest Manuscripts of the Works of John Gower." Presented at the Sixth York Manuscripts Conference, July 5–8, 1991.

Patterson, Annabel. *Censorship and Interpretation: The Conditions of Writing and Reading in Early Modern England*. Madison: University of Wisconsin Press, 1984.

Patterson, Lee. "Court Politics and the Invention of Literature." In *Culture and History, 1350–1600*, ed. David Aers, 7–41. London: Harvester Wheatsheaf, 1992.

———. *Negotiating the Past: The Historical Understanding of Medieval Literature.* Madison: University of Wisconsin Press, 1987.

———. "Writing Amorous Wrongs: Chaucer and the Order of Complaint." In *The Idea of Medieval Literature: New Essays on Chaucer and Medieval Culture in Honor of Donald R. Howard*, ed. James M. Dean and Christian K. Zacher, 55–71. Newark: University of Delaware Press, 1992.

Pearsall, Derek. *An Annotated Critical Bibliography of Langland.* Hemel Hempstead: Harvester Wheatsheaf, 1990.

———. "Hoccleve's *Regement of Princes*: The Poetics of Royal Self-representation." *Speculum* 69 (1994): 386–410.

———. "The 'Ilchester' Manuscript of *Piers Plowman.*" *Neuphilologische Mitteilungen* 82 (1981): 181–93.

———. *The Life of Geoffrey Chaucer.* Oxford: Blackwell, 1992.

———. "'Lunatyk Lollares' in *Piers Plowman.*" In *Religion in the Poetry and Drama of the Late Middle Ages in England*, ed. Piero Boitani and Anna Torti, 163–78. Cambridge: D. S. Brewer, 1988.

———, ed. *Piers Plowman, by William Langland: An Edition of the C-Text.* Berkeley and Los Angeles: University of California Press, 1978.

———. "Poverty and Poor People in *Piers Plowman.*" In *Medieval English Studies Presented to George Kane*, ed. Edward Donald Kennedy, Ronald Waldron, and Joseph S. Wittig, 167–86. Woodbridge: D. S. Brewer, 1988.

Pearsall, Derek and Kathleen Scott. *Piers Plowman: A Facsimile of Bodleian Library, Oxford, MS Douce 104.* Cambridge: D. S. Brewer, 1992.

Pecham, John. *Tractatus de paupertate.* Ed. C. L. Kingsford et al. Aberdeen: Aberdeen University Press, 1910.

Pecock, Reginald. *The donet.* Ed. Elsie Vaughan Hitchcock. EETS o.s. 156. London, 1921.

Penn, Simon A. C. and Christopher Dyer. "Wages and Earnings in Late Medieval England: Evidence from the Enforcement of the Labour Laws." *Economic History Review* 2d ser. 43 (1990): 356–76.

Petrarch, Francis. *Rerum familiarum libri.* Trans. Aldo S. Bernardo. 3 vols. Albany: State University of New York Press, 1975.

Petti, Anthony G. *English Literary Hands from Chaucer to Dryden.* Cambridge, Mass.: Harvard University Press, 1977.

Poos, L. R. "The Social Context of Statute of Labourers Enforcement." *Law and History Review* 1 (1983): 27–52.

Pottinger, David. *The French Book Trade in the Ancien Régime.* Cambridge, Mass.: Harvard University Press, 1958.

Power, Eileen and M. M. Postan, eds. *Studies in English Trade in the Fifteenth Century.* London: Routledge, 1933.

Putnam, Bertha Haven. *The Enforcement of the Statutes of Labourers During the First Decade After the Black Death, 1349–59.* (1908). Columbia Studies in the Social Sciences 85. New York: AMS Press, 1970.

———. "Maximum-Wage Laws for Priests After the Black Death, 1348–1381." *American Historical Review* 21 (1915): 12–32.

Quirk, Randolf. "Langland's Use of 'Kind Wit' and 'Inwit'." *Journal of English and Germanic Philology* 52 (1953): 182–88.

Reeves, Marjorie. *The Influence of Prophecy in the Later Middle Ages: A Study in Joachimism.* Oxford: Clarendon Press, 1969.

The Register of Edmund Lacy, Bishop of Exeter, 1420–1455. Part 3. Devon and Cornwell Record Society n.s. 13. Torquay: Devonshire Press, 1963.

The Register of Thomas Bekynton, Bishop of Bath and Wells, 1443–1465. Ed. Sir H. C. Maxwell-Lyte and M. C. B. Dawes. Somerset Record Society. London: Bucker and Tanner, 1934–35.

Registrum Thome Myllyng, episcopi Herefordensis. Ed. Arthur Thomas Bannister. Canterbury and York Ser. 26. London: Canterbury and York Society, 1920.

Ribton-Turner, C. J. *Vagrants and Vagrancy.* London, 1887.

Richardson, Malcolm. "The Earliest Known Owners of *Canterbury Tales* MSS and Chaucer's Secondary Audience." *Chaucer Review* 25 (1990): 17–21.

Rigg, A. G. *A Glastonbury Miscellany of the Fifteenth Century.* Oxford: Oxford University Press, 1968.

Rigg, A. G. and Charlotte Brewer, eds. *Piers Plowman: The Z Version.* Toronto: Pontifical Institute of Mediaeval Studies, 1983.

Riley, Henry Thomas, ed. *Memorials of London and London Life in the XIIIth, XIVth, and XVth centuries, 1276–1419.* London: Longmans, Green, 1885.

Robbins, Rossell Hope, ed. *Historical Poems of the XIVth and XVth Centuries.* New York: Columbia University Press, 1959.

Rolle, Richard. *An Edition of the Judica me Deus.* Ed. John Philip. Salzburg: Universität Salzburg, 1984.

———. *The Fire of Love: or, Melody of Love . . . .* Translated by Richard Misyn. EETS o.s. 106. London: Methuen, 1914.

———. *The Melos amoris of Richard Rolle of Hampole.* Edited by E. J. Arnould. Oxford: Blackwell, 1957.

Root, Robert K. "Publication before Printing." *PMLA* 8 (1913): 417–31.

Roth, Francis, OSA. *The English Austin Friars: 1249–1538.* 2 vols. New York: Augustinian Historical Institute, 1966.

Rotuli parliamentorum. London: HMSO, 1783.

Russell, George H. "As They Read It." *Leeds Studies in English* n.s. 20 (1989): 173–87.
———. "Some Early Responses to the C-Version of *Piers Plowman*." *Viator* 15 (1984): 275–303.

Saenger, Paul. "Silent Reading: Its Impact on Late Medieval Script and Society." *Viator* 13 (1982): 367–414.

Samuels, M. L. "Dialect and Grammar." In *A Companion to Piers Plowman*, ed. John A. Alford, 201–21. Berkeley and Los Angeles: University of California Press, 1988.

———. "Langland's Dialect." *Medium Ævum* 54 (1985): 232–47.

Sandler, Lucy Freeman. "*Omne bonum: Compilatio* and *ordinatio* in an English Illustrated Encyclopedia of the Fourteenth century." In *Medieval Book Production,*

Assessing the Evidence, ed. Linda L. Brownrigg. Los Altos, Calif.: Anderson-Lovelace, 1990.

Sargent, Michael G. "Contemporary Criticism of Richard Rolle." *Analecta Cartusiana* 55.1 (1981): 160–87.

Sayles, G. O., ed. *Select Cases in the Court of King's Bench.* Vols. 6, 7. Publications of the Selden Society 82, 88. London: Quaritch, 1965, 1971.

Scase, Wendy. *Piers Plowman and the New Anticlericalism.* Cambridge: Cambridge University Press, 1989.

———. "Two *Piers Plowman* C-Text Interpolations: Evidence for a Second Textual Tradition." *Notes and Queries* 232 (1987): 456–63.

Scattergood, V. J. "Literary Culture at the Court of Richard II." In *English Court Culture in the Later Middle Ages*, ed. V. J. Scattergood and J. W. Sherborne, 29–43. London: Duckworth, 1983.

Schmidt, A. V. C. "A Note on Langland's Conception of 'Anima' and 'Inwit.'" *Notes and Queries* n.s. 15 (1968): 363–64.

———, ed. *The Vision of Piers Plowman: A Critical Edition of the B-Text.* London: J. M. Dent, 1978.

Scott, Kathleen. "The Illustrations of *Piers Plowman* in Bodleian Library Douce 104." *Yearbook of Langland Studies* 4 (1990): 1–86.

Seville, Isidore of. *Etymologiae.* Ed. W. M. Lindsay. Oxford: Clarendon Press, 1911.

Seymour, M. C. "MS Portraits of Chaucer and Hoccleve." *Burlington Magazine* 124 (1982): 618–23.

Sharpe, Reginald R., ed. *Calendar of Letter-books, preserved among the archives of the Corporation of the City of London: Letter-book H, circa A.D. 1375–1399.* London: John Edward Francis, 1907.

Shirley, W. W., ed. *Fasciculi zizaniorum magistri Johannis Wyclif cum tritico*, by Thomas Netter. Rolls 5th Ser. London, 1858.

Siebert, Frederick Seaton. *Freedom of the Press.* Urbana: University of Illinois Press, 1952.

Simpson, James. "'After Craftes Conseil Clotheth Yow and Fede': Langland and London City Politics." In *England in the Fourteenth Century: Proceedings of the 1991 Harlaxton Symposium*, ed. Nicholas Rogers, 109–27. Stamford, Eng.: Paul Watkins, 1993.

———. "The Constraints of Satire in 'Piers Plowman' and 'Mum and the Sothsegger.'" In *Langland, the Mystics and the Medieval English Religious Tradition: Essays in Honour of S. S. Hussey*, ed. Helen Phillips, 11–30. Cambridge: D. S. Brewer, 1990.

———. "Spiritual and Earthly Nobility in *Piers Plowman.*" *Neuphilologische Mitteilungen* 86 (1985): 467–81.

———. "Spirituality and Economics in Passus 1–7 of the B Text." *Yearbook of Langland Studies* 1 (1987): 83–103.

Skeat, Walter W., ed. *Langland's Vision of Piers Plowman: The Vernon Text; or Text A.* EETS o.s. 28. London, 1867.

———, ed. *The Vision of William Concerning Piers the Plowman, in Three Parallel Texts.* 2 vols. London: Oxford University Press, 1886.

Smith, Jeremy J. "Linguistic Features of Some Early Fifteenth-Century Middle English Manuscripts." In *Manuscripts and Readers in Fifteenth-Century England: The Literary Implications of Manuscript Study*, ed. Derek Pearsall, 104–12. Cambridge: D. S. Brewer, 1983.

Smith, Toulmin and Lucy Toulmin Smith, eds. *English Gilds*. EETS, o.s. 40, 1870.

Southern, R. W. "The Letters of Abelard and Heloise." In *Medieval Humanism and Other Studies*, 86–104. New York: Harper and Row, 1970.

Spiegel, Gabrielle M. "History, Historicism and the Social Logic of the Text." *Speculum* 65 (1990): 59–86.

Spenser, Edmund. *The Works of Edmund Spenser*. Ed. Edwin Greenlaw et al. Baltimore: Johns Hopkins University Press, 1932–1957.

Spitzer, Leo. "Note on the Poetic and the Empirical 'I' in Medieval Authors." *Traditio* 4 (1946): 414–22.

Statutes of the Realm. 11 vols. London: HMSO, 1810.

Storey, R. L. "Liveries and Commissions of the Peace, 1388–90." In *The Reign of Richard II: Essays in Honour of May McKisack*, ed. F. R. H. DuBoulay and Caroline M. Barron, 131–52. London: Athlone Press, 1971.

Strohm, Paul. *Hochon's Arrow: The Social Imagination of Fourteenth-Century Texts*. Princeton, N.J.: Princeton University Press, 1992.

———. "Politics and Poetics: Usk and Chaucer in the 1380s." In *Literary Practice and Social Change in Britain, 1380–1530*, ed. Lee Patterson, 83–112. Berkeley and Los Angeles: University of California Press, 1990.

———. *Social Chaucer*. Cambridge, Mass.: Harvard University Press, 1988.

———. "The Textual Environment of Chaucer's 'Lak of Stedfastness,'" in *Hochon's Arrow: The Social Imagination of Fourteenth-Century Texts*, 54–74. Princeton, N.J.: Princeton University Press, 1992.

Swanson, R. N. "Chaucer's Parson and Other Priests." *Studies in the Age of Chaucer* 13 (1991):

Szittya, Penn R. *The Antifraternal Tradition in Medieval Literature*. Princeton, N.J.: Princeton University Press, 1986.

Tanner, Norman. *The Church in Late Medieval Norwich, 1370–1532*. Studies and Texts 66. Toronto: Pontifical Institute of Mediaeval Studies, 1984.

Tawney, R. H. *Religion and the Rise of Capitalism*. Harmondsworth: Penguin, 1928.

Testamenta eboracensia: A Selection of Wills from the Registry at York. Surtees Society 45. Durham: The Society, 1836.

Thomas, A. H., ed. *Calendar of Plea and Memoranda Rolls, Preserved among the Archives of the Corporation of the City of London at the Guildhall, A.D. 1381–1412*. Cambridge: Cambridge University Press, 1983.

Tierney, Brian. "The Decretists and the Deserving Poor." *Comparative Studies in Society and History* 1 (1959): 360–73.

———. *Medieval Poor Law: A Sketch of Canonical Theory and Its Application in England*. Berkeley and Los Angeles: University of California Press, 1959.

Tolkien, J. R. R., ed. *Ancrene Wisse*. EETS o.s. 249.

Tout, T. F. *Chapters in the Administrative History of Mediaeval England: The Wardrobe, the Chamber, and the Small Seals*. Vol. 3. Manchester: Manchester University Press, 1928.

Trevisa, John, trans. *Defensio curatorum*. EETS o.s. 167.

Trigg, Stephanie, ed. *Wynnere and Wastoure*. EETS 297.

Tuck, J. A. "The Cambridge Parliament, 1388." *English Historical Review* 84 (1969): 225–43.

Turley, Thomas. "John XXII and the Franciscans: A Reappraisal." In *Popes, Teachers and Canon Law in the Middle Ages*, ed. James A. Sweeney and Stanley Chodorow, 74–88. Ithaca, N.Y.: Cornell University Press, 1989.

Turville-Petre, Thorlac, ed. *Alliterative Poetry of the Later Middle Ages: An Anthology*. London: Routledge, 1989.

———. *The Alliterative Revival*. Cambridge: Cambridge University Press, 1977.

———. "The Prologue of *Wynnere and Wastoure*." *Leeds Studies in English* n.s. 18 (1987): 19–29.

Uhart, Marie-Claire. "The Early Reception of *Piers Plowman*." Ph.D. diss., University of Leicester, 1988.

Vale, Juliet. *Edward III and Chivalry*. Woodbridge: Boydell and Brewer, 1982.

Van Engen, John H. *Rupert of Deutz*. Berkeley and Los Angeles: University of California Press, 1983.

Vicaire, M.-H., O.P. *L'imitation des apôtres: moines, chanoines, mendiants (IVe–XIIIe siècles)*. Paris: Éditions du Cerf, 1963.

von Nolcken, Christina. "*Piers Plowman*, the Wycliffites, and *Pierce the Plowman's Creed*." *Yearbook of Langland Studies* 2 (1988): 71–102.

Wallace, David. "Chaucer and the Absent City." In *Chaucer's England: Literature in Historical Context*, ed. Barbara A. Hanawalt, 59–90. Minneapolis: University of Minnesota Press, 1992.

Walsh, Katherine. *The "De vita evangelica" of Geoffrey Hardeby, O.E.S.A. (c. 1320– c. 1382): A Study in the Mendicant Controversies of the Fourteenth Century*. Rome: Augustinian Historical Institute, 1972.

———. *A Fourteenth-Century Scholar and Primate: Richard FitzRalph in Oxford, Avignon, and Armagh*. Oxford: Clarendon Press, 1981.

Watenpuhl, Heinrich and Heinrich Krefeld, eds. *Die Gedichte des Archpoeta*. Heidelberg, 1958.

Watson, Nicholas. "Censorship and Cultural Change in Late-Medieval England: Vernacular Theology, the Oxford Translation Debate, and Arundel's Constitutions of 1409." *Speculum* 70 (1995): 822–64.

———. "The Composition of Julian of Norwich's *Revelation of Love*." *Speculum* 68 (1993): 637–83.

———. *Richard Rolle and the Invention of Authority*. Cambridge: Cambridge University Press, 1991.

Weber, Edouard-Henri. *Dialogue et dissension entre St. Bonaventure et St. Thomas d'Aquin . . . Paris (1252–1273)*. Paris: Vrin, 1974.

Wilkins, David, ed. *Concilia Magnae Brittaniae et Hiberniae*. London, 1737.

Williams, Arnold. "*Protectorium pauperis*, A Defense of the Begging Friars by Richard of Maidstone, O. Carm." *Carmelius* 5 (1958): 132–80.

Williams, Gwyn A. *Medieval London: From Commune to Capital*. University of London Historical Series 11. London: Athlone Press, 1963.

Williams, S. J. "An Author's Role in Fourteenth-Century Book Production." *Romania* 90 (1969): 433–54.

Wimbledon, Thomas. *Wimbledon's Sermon Redde rationem villicationis tue: A Middle English Sermon of the Fourteenth Century*. Ed. Ione Kemp. Pittsburgh: Duquesne University Press, 1967.

Wimsatt, W. K. and Monroe K. Beardsley. "The Intentional Fallacy." In *The Verbal Icon: Studies in the Meaning of Poetry*, 3–18. Lexington: University Press of Kentucky, 1954.

Wittig, Joseph S. "*Piers Plowman* B IX–XII: Elements in the Design of the Inward Journey." *Traditio* 28 (1972): 211–80.

Wood, Robert A. "A Fourteenth Century London Owner of *Piers Plowman.*" *Medium Ævum* 53 (1984): 83–89.

Wood-Leigh, K. L. *Perpetual Chantries in Britain*. Cambridge: Cambridge University Press, 1965.

Wright, Sylvia. "The Author Portraits in the Bedford Psalter-Hours: Gower, Chaucer, and Hoccleve." *British Library Journal* 18 (1992): 190–201.

Wright, Thomas, ed. *Political Poems and Songs*. Rolls Series 14. London: Longmans, 1859.

Wyclif and His Followers: An Exhibition to Mark the 600th Anniversary of the Death of John Wyclif: December 1984 to April 1985. Oxford: Bodleian Library, 1984.

Wylie, James Hamilton. *History of England Under Henry the Fourth*. 4 vols. London: Longmans, 1884–1898.

Yunck, John A. *The Lineage of Lady Meed: The Development of Mediaeval Venality Satire*. Publications in Mediaeval Studies 17. South Bend, Ind.: University of Notre Dame Press, 1963.

Contributors

Lawrence Clopper, Professor of English at Indiana University, edited the Chester volume of the Records of Early English Drama. His study of Langland, *Songes of Rechelesnesse: Langland and the Friars* is forthcoming in 1997.

Ralph Hanna III is Professor of English at the University of California, Riverside. Some of his many essays on literary, textual, and codicological matters have been collected in *Pursuing History: Middle English Manuscripts and Their Texts* (1996).

Steven Justice teaches at the University of California, Berkeley, and is the author of *Writing and Rebellion: England in 1381* (1994).

Kathryn Kerby-Fulton, Associate Professor of English at the University of Victoria, is author of *Reformist Apocalypticism and* Piers Plowman (1990), and (with Denise Despres) *Iconography and the Professional Reader: The Politics of Book Production in the Douce* Piers Plowman, forthcoming.

Anne Middleton is Professor of English at the University of California, Berkeley, and author of such influential essays as "The Idea of Public Poetry in the Reign of Richard II," "The Audience and Public of *Piers Plowman*," and "William Langland's 'Kynde Name': Social Identity and Authorial Signature in Late-Medieval England."

Derek Pearsall is Gurney Professor of English at Harvard University. *The Life of Geoffrey Chaucer* (1992) is the most recent of his many books.

Index

There are three idiosyncrasies in the following index. 1) The work of modern scholars is not indexed. 2) Langland's personifications are listed under their own names; concepts with the same names can be distinguished by the use of lower case (e.g., "clergy" and "Clergie"). 3) Langland manuscripts are listed in two places: those discussed merely as textual sources are listed by sigil in the General Index under *"Piers Plowman"*; those discussed codicologically are listed by shelf mark in the Index of Manuscripts.